LIBRARY OF NEW TESTAMENT STUDIES

603

Formerly Journal of the Study of the New Testament Supplement Series

Editor
Chris Keith

FAILURE AND PROSPECT

Lazarus and the Rich Man (Luke 16:19-31) in the Context of Luke-Acts

Reuben Bredenhof

Bloomsbury T&T Clark
An imprint of Bloomsbury Publishing Plc

B L O O M S B U R Y
LONDON · OXFORD · NEW YORK · NEW DELHI · SYDNEY

Bloomsbury T&T Clark

An imprint of Bloomsbury Publishing Plc

Imprint previously known as T&T Clark

50 Bedford Square	1385 Broadway
London	New York
WC1B 3DP	NY 10018
UK	USA

www.bloomsbury.com

BLOOMSBURY, T&T CLARK and the Diana logo are trademarks of Bloomsbury Publishing Plc

First published in Great Britain 2019

© Reuben Bredenhof, 2019

Reuben Bredenhof has asserted his right under the Copyright, Designs and Patents Act, 1988, to be identified as Author of this work.

Cover design: Terry Woodley

A catalogue record for this book is available from the British Library.

A catalogue record for this book is available from the Library of Congress

ISBN:	HB:	978-0-5676-8174-4
	ePDF:	978-0-5676-8175-1
	ebook:	978-0-5676-8178-2

Series: Library of New Testament Studies, ISSN 2513-8790, volume 603

Typeset by Forthcoming Publications (www.forthpub.com)
Printed and bound in Great Britain

To find out more about our authors and books visit www.bloomsbury.com and sign up for our newsletters.

CONTENTS

ACKNOWLEDGMENTS

This is a revised version of the PhD thesis that in 2016 I submitted to St Mary's University, Twickenham. The genesis of this project was my curiosity over the puzzling parable in Luke 16:19-31 about the beggar with a name and the rich man who is consigned to the fiery side of a great chasm. But curiosity and random reading do not a thesis (or monograph) make, so I am deeply grateful to those individuals who have provided me with so much invaluable guidance, stimulation, and assistance in this project.

First and foremost, it was a privilege to be under the expert supervision of Professor Steve Walton. I began with him at the London School of Theology, then followed him a couple of years later to St Mary's University, Twickenham. Steve always offered a fine blend of encouragement, challenge and recommendation in the many hours that we spent in supervision sessions, both electronically and in person. His impact on this project has been immeasurable, and I thank him heartily for it. In the time at LST my secondary supervisor was Dr Stephen Motyer – I thank him for the interaction that we could have. After transferring to St Mary's I was grateful to receive secondary supervision from Dr Chris Skinner (now at Loyola University, Chicago), who provided rigorous proof-reading and incisive feedback on my work. The moderator of my studies at St Mary's was Professor Richard Burridge (King's College, London), and I thank him for advising on and overseeing the various aspects of this project.

Though I was doing research for this book at a considerable distance from the university (first residing in Canada, then in Australia), I was blessed with the opportunity to attend the British New Testament Conference numerous times, where I also participated in the Synoptic Gospels seminar group. My thanks goes to Dr Andy Angel and Dr Elizabeth Shively, co-chairs of the group, who gave the opportunity to present some of the findings of my research. Whenever in the UK, I was able to make use of the outstanding research facilities at Tyndale House in Cambridge and to enjoy its collegial atmosphere. I have also benefited from the collections at a variety of university libraries, including those associated with the University of Western Ontario, McMaster University, the University of Toronto, and the Canadian Reformed Theological Seminary, as well as the libraries of Murdoch University and Trinity Theological College in Perth, Western Australia.

This project was started while I was the pastor of the Pilgrim Canadian Reformed Church in London, Ontario, Canada. I appreciated the congregation's genuine interest and encouragement as I studied, and I am thankful for how they provided some time away from my regular duties in the pulpit so that I could write "the next chapter." Likewise supportive was my next pastoral charge, the Free Reformed Church of Mount Nasura in Western Australia, who willingly allowed me time for travel, research and writing.

I am also grateful to my family members for their unstinting enthusiasm for this project – even if they sometimes wondered aloud just how much could be written about one parable! I was blessed by the interest and encouragement of my wife's parents, Ed and Ellen Hekert. I am also thankful for how my parents, Jake and Lee Bredenhof, offered their support and generously provided financial help for overseas travel and tuition.

Finally, I realize that I have inflicted a not insignificant burden on my wife and four daughters as I pursued a PhD. The girls tolerated their dad being overseas every year for a couple of weeks, and then being preoccupied and busy in his office for many other weeks while yet another chapter was being written. I thank Abigail, Kyra, Sasha and Tori for their patience, and for cheerfully keeping things in perspective for me when the work seemed to stall. My wife Rebecca gladly accepted that my education was *still* not done, and patiently listened to my convoluted explanations of arcane details from the world of parable research and Luke-Acts. While I was consumed with this project over the last five years, she provided willing support for me in many ways – to her I express my loving thanks. With gratitude to God, this book is dedicated to her.

Chapter 1

THE CONTINUING STUDY OF LUKE 16:19–31

1. *Introduction*

Luke 16:19–31 is part of Luke's Gospel – most readers of the Bible will consider such a remark to be a case of needlessly stating the obvious. Others will be aware that Luke wrote a companion volume to his Gospel, the book of Acts, and that it is within this double literary context that the story of Lazarus and the Rich Man is set.[1] This aspect is often overlooked despite the potential of its pronounced impact on interpretation, and it gives rise to the basic purpose and approach of this study. We are investigating the function of this parable in relation to Luke's two-volume work.[2] Having listened to his account so far, how does Luke's audience hear the story of Lazarus, the rich man, and Abraham? What responses are elicited

---

1. The author of the Third Gospel and Acts has traditionally been identified as Luke, the companion of Paul (Phlm 24; 2 Tim 4:11) and the 'beloved physician' (Col 4:14). This identification is based to a large degree on the ascription of the third Gospel to Luke in the oldest manuscript of the Gospel ($\mathfrak{P}^{75}$) and in the Muratorian canon, dated by some scholars to the second century. The identification of this Luke as the author of Luke-Acts is said to be congruous with the 'we-passages' in Acts (16:10–17; 20:5–21:18; 27:1–28:16) in which the narrator is portrayed as a companion of Paul during certain episodes of his itinerant ministry; see, e.g., C. Hemer, *The Book of Acts in the Setting of Hellenistic History*, ed. C. Gempf, WUNT 1/49 (Tübingen: Mohr, 1989), 315–21. However reliable the external and internal evidence of Luke's authorship may be judged, throughout this work the anonymous author of the Gospel and Acts will be referred to as 'Luke', with little else being presupposed about the writer's identity beyond his gender; see L. C. A. Alexander, *The Preface to Luke's Gospel: Literary Convention and Social Context in Luke 1.1–4 and Acts 1.1*, SNTSMS 78 (Cambridge: Cambridge University Press, 1993), 2 n. 2.

2. While terming it a parable, we acknowledge that Luke 16:19–31 is not desig‍nated a παραβολή by the author. For convenience, we will refer to this passage as a 'parable', considering the question more closely in Chapter 3, §3.1.3.

by the description of the rich man's affluence, the poor man's misery, their respective post-mortem reversals, and Abraham's commentary on their destinies? Through the previous Gospel narratives what evaluation of these three characters is the audience led to form, and what reactions are provoked? Furthermore, as the Lukan audience continues to listen to his account, how do the later narratives of the Third Gospel and Acts shape the reception of the parable and its message? Specifically, how does an awareness of Jesus's death and resurrection and a familiarity with the activities of the early Christian community in Acts transform how the parable is heard and re-heard? In this study we will advance a narrative, rhetorical and intertextual understanding of Luke 16:19–31 by reading it within this Luke-Acts context. To orient ourselves in this chapter we will consider past scholarship on the parable's unity, origin, and themes. Then we will review three methods that have been applied to the study of this parable. Finally, we will outline our own approach for this investigation.

2. *A Wealth of Scholarship*

If Lazarus lying at the rich man's gate was neglected, the same cannot be said of the story found in Luke 16:19–31. With its memorable characters of Lazarus, the rich man, his five brothers, and Abraham, with its evocative landscape of urban life and afterlife, and with its dramatic reversal of earthly positions, this parable has suffered no neglect at the hands of biblical interpreters. There has been no fewer than five PhD theses written on Luke 16:19–31 in the last ten years,[3] as well as a recent volume dedicated largely to methodological, textual, and theological issues pertaining to this passage.[4] Yet for all of the scholarly interest there

---

3. Some of these theses have been published in revised form; see O. Lehtipuu, *The Afterlife Imagery in Luke's Story of the Rich Man and Lazarus*, NovTSup 123 (Leiden: Brill, 2007); S. Perry, *Resurrecting Interpretation: Technology, Hermeneutics, and the Parable of the Rich Man and Lazarus* (Eugene, OR: Pickwick, 2012); J. A. Szukalski, *Tormented in Hades: The Rich Man and Lazarus (Luke 16:19–31) and Other Lucan Parables for Persuading the Rich to Repentance* (Eugene, OR: Pickwick, 2013); J. J. Stigall, 'Reading the Parable of the Rich Man and Lazarus (Luke 16:19–31) as the Authorial Audience' (PhD diss., Baylor University, 2012); M. R. Hauge, *The Biblical Tour of Hell*, LNTS 485 (London: T&T Clark, 2013). An earlier full-length treatment is the thesis of J. Hintzen, *Verkündigung und wahrnehmung: Über das Verhältnis von Evangelium und Leser am Beispiel Luke 16, 19–31 im Rahmen des lukanischen Doppelwerkes* (Frankfurt: Hain, 1991).

4. S. E. Porter and M. J. Boda, eds., *Translating the New Testament: Text, Translation, Theology* (Grand Rapids: Eerdmans, 2009).

are ongoing debates and discussions about this parable. Some of these questions concern the parable in a general sense: What does the story mean? What is its principal message? Alternately, discussion centres on particular aspects of the parable's content. For instance, why is the beggar named? Why is the rich man punished? What is the background of the parable's afterlife topography? The questions multiply, and while some may be considered to have been answered satisfactorily, other questions persist and invite further investigation. Restricting our attention to the history of interpretation since the end of the nineteenth century when there was a burgeoning of parable research, we observe that scholars have investigated numerous elements related to Luke 16:19–31.[5]

3. *The Parable's Unity*

3.1. *A Two-Part Parable?*

Prompted by an interest in identifying possible sources and reconstructing the history of redaction that lies behind the biblical text, some scholars focus on this parable's unity and origin.[6] As is the case with so many parable studies we must begin with consideration of Jülicher's seminal work *Die Gleichnisreden Jesu*.[7] He posits that vv. 19–26 comprise the original story of Jesus, albeit one that has origins in popular notions of the afterlife. Verses 27–31 are a secondary, pre-Lukan Christian addition.[8]

---

5. For a compilation of patristic commentary on the parable, see A. A. Just, ed., *Luke*, ACCS 3 (Downers Grove, IL: IVP, 2003). S. L. Wailes, in *Medieval Allegories of Jesus' Parables* (Berkeley, CA: University of California Press, 1987), 255–60, provides an overview of the parable's interpretation in the medieval period. Cf. R. C. Trench, *Notes on the Parables of Our Lord*, 11th ed. (New York: D. Appleton, 1861), 366–90; S. I. Wright, *The Voice of Jesus: Studies in the Interpretation of Six Gospel Parables*, Paternoster Biblical Monographs (Carlisle: Paternoster, 2000), 90–95; F. Bovon, *Luke 2: A Commentary on the Gospel of Luke 9:51–19:27*, trans. D. S. Deer, ed. H. Koester (Minneapolis: Fortress, 2013), 485–88. John of Chrysostom preached seven sermons on this parable; see C. P. Roth, trans. *St. John Chrysostom: On Wealth and Poverty* (Crestwood, NY: St. Vladimir's Seminary Press, 1984).

6. Hintzen, *Verkündigung*, 271–347, uses redactional analysis to suggest the parable's previous literary strata.

7. A. Jülicher, *Die Gleichnisreden Jesu* (Darmstadt: Wissenschaftliche Buchgesell-schaft, 1963). He also designates as a *Beispielerzählung* the Good Samaritan (10:25–37), the Rich Fool (12:16–21), and the Pharisee and the Tax Collector (18:10–14). Such 'example stories' are said to lack a figurative element, and instead offer models of behaviour.

8. Jülicher, *Gleichnisreden*, 634–40.

Both sections of the parable are considered to have discrete meanings, with vv. 19–26 about poverty and possessions being the more significant section. In bifurcating the parable, an important consideration for Jülicher is the perceived problem in v. 31 of the five brothers (understood to be representative of the Jewish people) not believing in the resurrection of 'one from the dead', who is understood to be emblematic of Jesus. The parable's notion of resurrection is deemed by Jülicher to be unoriginal, and a later concern for the author of the Third Gospel.[9]

The story's bifurcation has been taken for granted in much of subsequent scholarship.[10] For instance, after accepting the two-part structure and acknowledging the interpretive assumption that a parable can only have one point, Bultmann considers that the two parts of the parable actually stand in contrast with each other.[11] Among more recent scholars, Crossan's treatment is representative, for he does not consider the parable in its literary context in Luke 16 and he only accepts vv. 19–26 as original.[12]

3.2. A Cohesive Parable?

Not all are convinced that the parable needs to be read as an intrinsically uneven two-part story. Despite the conventional bifurcation, there are sound reasons to conclude that the parable in its final form constitutes a unity and should be studied as such. In the first place, the proposed division of vv. 19–26 and 27–31 is implausible because it separates the parable in mid-conversation, as the rich man and Abraham dialogue together.[13]

9. Jülicher, *Gleichnisreden*, 638.

10. See, e.g., J. M. Creed, *The Gospel according to St. Luke* (London: Macmillan, 1960), 208; E. Ellis, *The Gospel of Luke*, NCB (London: Nelson, 1966), 205; H. J. Degenhardt, *Lukas, Evangelist der Armen: Besitz und Besitzverzicht in den lukanischen Schriften* (Stuttgart: Katholisches Bibelwerk, 1965), 133–34; B. B. Scott, *Hear then the Parable: A Commentary on the Parables of Jesus* (Minneapolis: Fortress, 1989), 145–46; C. F. Evans, *Saint Luke* (London: SCM, 1990), 615; Hintzen, *Verkündigung*, 347–51.

11. R. Bultmann, *History of the Synoptic Tradition*, trans. J. Marsh, 2nd ed. (New York: Harper & Row, 1968), 178, 203–6.

12. J. D. Crossan, *In Parables: The Challenge of the Historical Jesus* (New York: Harper & Row, 1973), 67–68, argues that vv. 27–31 were contributed by the early church, pointing to several similarities in language with the Luke 24 resurrection account.

13. R. F. Hock, 'Lazarus and Micyllus: Greco-Roman Backgrounds to Luke 16:19–31', *JBL* 106 (1987): 447–63, citing 454. A recent discourse analysis of the parable is likewise suggestive of its internal unity, for which see S. E. Porter and

Schnider and Stenger propose a structuralist argument in support of the unity of the parable, positing a tripartite structure of 'before' (vv. 19–21), 'after' (vv. 22–23), and a dialogue (vv. 24–31).[14] Snodgrass addresses the matter of the parable's unity and its conventional division, and concludes that the two halves do not conflict but are congruent; indeed, the second portion brings the whole narrative to completion in that the irreversibility and avoidability of the rich man's torment are made overt through Abraham's responses.[15] Likewise, Snodgrass cautions against overemphasizing the traditional rule of 'end stress' in interpreting the parables,[16] and suggests that the themes of the use of wealth and the sufficiency of Scripture are equally important to the parable's message.[17] In this study we will consider that vv. 19–31 are a unified illustration of the Lukan perspectives on wealth and poverty, as well as on authoritative revelation. We will also observe that the question of the parable's internal cohesiveness has interpretive consequences.[18]

4. *The Parable's Origin*

Luke 16:19–31 is patently unique among the other Synoptic parables. While every other parable is set within the socio-economic setting typical of the first-century Palestinian world, Luke 16:19–31 largely takes place in another realm, with the rich man suffering in Hades and Lazarus resting

M. Brook O'Donnell, 'Comparative Discourse Analysis as a Tool in Assessing Translations, Using Luke 16:19–31 as a Test Case', in Porter and Boda, eds., *Translating*, 185–99, who suggest discourse breaks at vv. 21, 24, 28, and 29.

14. F. Schnider and W. Stenger, 'Die offene Tür und die unüberschreitbare Kluft: strukturanalytische Überlegungen zum Gleichnis vom reichen Mann und armen Lazarus', *NTS* 25 (1979): 273–83; cf. the story's division into three temporal periods by W. Vogels, 'Having or Longing: A Semiotic Analysis of Luke 16:19–31', *EgT* 20 (1989): 27–46. For a discussion of unity, see I. H. Marshall, *The Gospel of Luke: A Commentary on the Greek Text*, NIGTC (Exeter: Paternoster, 1978), 633–34.

15. K. Snodgrass, *Stories with Intent: A Comprehensive Guide to the Parables of Jesus* (Grand Rapids: Eerdmans, 2008), 427–28.

16. See an application of this rule in the study of Luke 16:19–31 in J. Jeremias, *The Parables of Jesus*, rev. ed. (London: SCM, 1963), 186.

17. Snodgrass, *Stories*, 428–29.

18. M. A. Tolbert, *Perspectives on the Parables* (Philadelphia: Fortress, 1979), 71, contends that the interpretation of parables is methodologically valid when the integrity of the story's structure is preserved; an interpretation 'must deal with the entire configuration of the story and not just one part of it'.

in the bosom of Abraham.[19] As a consequence there has been copious scholarly attention to these exceptional elements and their provenance. We will see that suggestions for the origin or background of this narrative about the respective post-mortem destinies of a poor man and a rich man have ranged from an original setting in Jesus's ministry, to the stories of Egyptian mythology, to the legends of the Greek heroes, Jewish folk tales, and Cynic literature.

4.1. *A Teaching of Jesus?*

Some assume that Jesus spoke this parable in its entirety during his ministry.[20] Luke, having considered the testimony of the 'eyewitnesses' (αὐτόπται, 1:2) and having 'investigated everything from the source' (παρηκολουθηκότι ἄνωθεν πᾶσιν, 1:3), accurately recorded the parable for posterity with little – if any – editorial modification.[21] Bock observes that the parable's unique character prompts the question of whether the account stems from Jesus, yet in favour of its originality he notes that 'Jesus' critique of wealth for its own sake exists in many levels of the tradition'.[22] Others take a different view of the parable's provenance. Accepting the two-fold division of the text, they contend that at minimum the first part is the preservation of an actual teaching of Jesus, while the remainder owes its origin to later theologizing about Jesus's resurrection in the Christian community.[23] Hendrickx, while noting extensive Lukan redaction in the parable, suggests a context in Jesus's ministry in which this parable may have been told: 'Originally the words

19. See the discussion of its unusual features in N. A. Huffman, 'Atypical Features in the Parables of Jesus', *JBL* 97 (1978): 207–20.

20. Jeremias famously asserted that 'the parables are a fragment of the original rock of tradition' (*Parables*, 11). The assumption of authenticity is often evident in that questions of the parable's origin are not addressed. See, e.g., F. W. Danker, *Jesus and the New Age: A Commentary on St. Luke's Gospel* (Philadelphia: Fortress, 1988), 669; W. R. Herzog, *Parables as Subversive Speech* (Louisville, KY: Westminster John Knox, 1994), 116; J. A. Fitzmyer, *The Gospel according to Luke X–XXIV*, AB 28a (Garden City, NY: Doubleday, 1985), 1127; L. Morris, *Luke: An Introduction and Commentary*, TNTC, rev. ed. (Leicester: Inter-Varsity, 1988), 275.

21. For a discussion of the stability of the history of traditions, see C. L. Blomberg, *The Historical Reliability of the Gospels*, 2nd ed. (Downers Grove, IL: IVP Academic, 2007), 53–62.

22. D. L. Bock, *Luke*, 2 vols., BECNT (Grand Rapids: Baker Books, 1994), 2:1361.

23. See, e.g., Crossan, *In Parables*, 68; cf. Scott, *Hear Then*, 142–46.

about rising from the dead may have referred to Jesus' ministry, during which the Pharisees had "sought from him a sign from heaven" (Lk 11:16), and had rejected him, notwithstanding the fact that, according to Luke's account, Jesus raised several people from the dead (Lk 7:14-15, 22; 8:53-55)'.[24] Regardless of this context, and apart from the endeavour of reconstructing an 'original' version of the parable, the Lukan stamp on the parable – whether perceived in its 'Christian resurrection language' or its 'wealth ethics' or another thematic element – requires our investigation and analysis.

4.2. *A Borrowed Tale?*

Returning to Jülicher's study of the parable, we note his suggestion that its afterlife imagery was based on popular notions of the afterlife that were current in Jesus's time.[25] While he does not detail what precise notions he is referring to, later scholarship embraced his proposal. Scholars provide a variety of suggestions for the basis of the parable's narrative about the disparate post-mortem fates of two persons. The first to do so is Gressmann, who observes the existence of an Egyptian folktale that concerns the reversals that were experienced by two men after death.[26] He posits that the folktale had its origin in an earlier Egyptian story, no longer extant; he suggests that this Egyptian folktale was also known in Palestine,[27] evident in the variations of the story found in rabbinic writings.[28] Since Jülicher and Gressmann, the suggestion has gained wide acceptance that Luke and his contemporaries were familiar with these stories, and that the Lukan audience would have understood the parable against this background.[29]

24. H. Hendrickx, *The Parables of Jesus* (San Francisco: Harper & Row, 1986), 208; after suggesting a consideration of this original context, he concludes that 'it seems probable that Luke writes this final clause having in mind the resurrection of Jesus'.

25. Jülicher, *Gleichnisreden*, 623.

26. H. Gressmann, *Vom reichen Mann und armen Lazarus: eine literargeschichtliche Studie*, Abhandlungen der Königlich preussichen Akademie der Wissenschaften: Philosophisch-historische Klasse, 1918 no. 7 (Berlin: Verlag der Königlich Akademie der Wissenschaft, 1918).

27. Gressmann, *Vom reichen Mann*, 31–32.

28. The rabbinic versions are in Gressmann, *Vom reichen Mann*, 70–86.

29. See, e.g., Grundmann, *Lukas*, 325. Somewhat unusual among scholars, E. Pax, 'Der Reiche und der arme Lazarus: Eine Milieustudie', *SBFLA* 25 (1975): 254–68, denies any formal parallels with other folk tales.

The question of the parable's principal influences is far from resolved, however. Already Bultmann noted that the intentions of the Egyptian and rabbinic stories are different from that of Luke 16:19–31.[30] For this reason he preferred to speak of the parable's origin as stemming from a Jewish legend. More recently, Bauckham discounts the theory of an Egyptian source.[31] He provides a sobering analysis of the alleged parallels with both the Egyptian and Jewish folktales, adducing notable ways in which both the proposed Egyptian and Jewish stories are dissimilar from the parable. He points out that the folk tales begin with a contrast in the manner of burial for a rich man and a poor man, while the Lukan parable gives little attention to the burial and more consideration to the economic status of the two characters. He also notes that in two of the folk tales a character learns of the fate of the principal characters; in the parable, the living brothers are expressly refused knowledge of the afterlife by Abraham. A final difference is that the folk tales explain the respective destinies of the rich man and the poor man on the basis of their goodness or wickedness, while the parable leaves such a basis implied. Having outlined the numerous differences, Bauckham contends that the parable is informed by a common folkloric motif, in which messengers from the realm of the dead visit the living in order to warn, comfort, reveal, or take vengeance.[32]

Hock also criticizes the scholarly consensus that an Egyptian folktale lies behind the parable.[33] Like Bauckham, he remarks on the dozens of stories in various cultures around the Mediterranean that purport to be an account of trips to the realm of the dead. He argues that none of these tales recommend themselves for direct comparison with the Lukan parable. While such stories of 'descents' were widely known in the first century,[34] a cursory comparison reveals that this parable is markedly different, especially in that it does not describe an afterlife tour nor an explicit

---

30. Bultmann, *Synoptic Tradition*, 196–97.

31. R. Bauckham, 'The Rich Man and Lazarus: The Parable and the Parallels', *NTS* 37 (1991): 225–46.

32. See also R. Bauckham, *The Fate of the Dead: Studies on the Jewish and Christian Apocalypses*, NovTSup 93 (Leiden: Brill, 1998), 95–96, referring to the account in *y. Ḥag.* 77d; and his 'Visiting the Places of the Dead in the Extra-Canonical Apocalypses', *PIBA* 18 (1995): 78–93, citing 92–93.

33. Hock, 'Lazarus and Micyllus'.

34. See, e.g., M. Himmelfarb, *Ascent to Heaven in Jewish and Christian Apocalypses* (New York: Oxford University Press, 1993); and her *Tours of Hell: An Apocalyptic Form in Jewish and Christian Literature* (Philadelphia: University of Pennsylvania Press, 1983).

rationale for the rich man's reversal of fortunes.[35] Instead, Hock suggests that the parable has more specifically Graeco-Roman origins, and finds an intriguing parallel in the works of Lucian, the early second-century Cynic. In the *Gallus* and *Cataplus*, Lucian writes about the reversals experienced by two hedonistic rich men and their impoverished neighbour Micyllus. Hock suggests that these narratives have a variety of correspondences with Luke 16:19–31 and as such provide the parable's 'missing' criterion for judgment.[36]

4.3. *Reframing the Question*

The quest for sources has more recently been reframed to take into account the narrative's intertextual nature. Instead of endeavouring to find a relationship of direct dependence on one or more source texts through the identification of fixed parallels, it is possible that this parable is better understood as informed by an allusive interaction with its wider cultural milieu. Lehtipuu focuses particularly on the story's representation of the afterlife in an attempt to determine both its significance for the parable's interpretation, as well as its consonance with the Lukan eschatological perspective.[37] While Lehtipuu acknowledges that the main point of the parable is not a revelation of the afterlife, she maintains that this imagery has a real function in the parable, serving as 'a serious threat for those who stay unrepentant'.[38] To make this point Lehtipuu surveys how the parable's imagery reflects popular belief, noting descriptions of the afterlife in Graeco-Roman sources, such as the Homeric epics, Cicero, and Plutarch. She then traces the notion of differentiated fates in the Jewish sources, such as the Hebrew Bible and apocalyptic literature. She contends that the picture of the afterworld in the Lukan parable fits well into the contemporary milieu.[39] Observing both dissimilarities and

35. Hock, 'Lazarus and Micyllus', 452–54.
36. T. Brookins, 'Dispute with Stoicism in the Parable of the Rich Man and Lazarus', *JGRChJ* 8 (2011): 34–50, builds on Hock's suggestion, and argues that the parable demonstrates resistance to Stoic ideas; for example, instead of being 'indifferent', disease and poverty are unfortunate and inherently bad (49).
37. Lehtipuu, *Afterlife Imagery*; see also her article, 'The Imagery of the Lukan Afterworld in the Light of Some Roman and Greek Parallels', in *Zwischen den Reichen: Neues Testament und Römische Herrschaft, Texte und Arbeiten zum neutestamentliche Zeitalter*, ed. M. Labahn (Tübingen: Francke, 2002), 133–46. See J. G. Griffiths, 'Cross-cultural Eschatology with Dives and Lazarus', *ExpTim* 105 (1993): 7–12; E. F. Bishop, 'A Yawning Chasm', *EvQ* 45 (1973): 3–5.
38. Lehtipuu, *Afterlife Imagery*, 6.
39. Ibid., 155.

correspondences between the parable's imagery and those found in the Hellenistic matrix, Lehtipuu is reluctant to say that the similarities mean there is direct dependence of Luke on any particular source. However, she argues that this intertextual reframing of the question of origins contributes a more nuanced view of the parable's correspondences and echoes. The perspective of intertextuality holds promise; therefore we will return to the intertextual qualities of Luke 16:19–31.

5. *The Parable's Principal Themes*

The focus of more recent scholarship on this parable, while not disregarding questions of unity and origin, has been at the textual level. Such study concentrates not only on these thirteen verses of Luke 16, but on the parable's contiguous material. We have already asserted that investigating not just the context of a given section but Luke-Acts as a whole is integral to a responsible interpretation of the parable. An optimal way to achieve this contextual consideration is by surveying the Third Gospel's characteristic themes.[40]

There is an element of subjectivity in declaring what themes are present in a literary work. Any suggestion must be evaluated on the basis of textual evidence, whether the terminology and concepts that are indicative of a particular theme appear within the unit. In this chapter we will introduce two principal Lukan themes: first, that of material possessions and the required response to poverty; and secondly, the revelation through 'Moses and the prophets'.[41] Three secondary themes will be addressed in a subsequent chapter: namely, the patriarch Abraham, the possibility of repentance, and the place of resurrection.[42] We will examine these primary and secondary themes in our study of the parable within its Luke-Acts context. Besides the five mentioned, scholars recognize that there are other characteristically Lukan themes present in the parable. These motifs

---

40. For general discussions of thematic aspects of Lukan theology, see I. H. Marshall, *Luke: Historian and Theologian* (Exeter: Paternoster, 1970); D. Bock, *A Theology of Luke and Acts: Biblical Theology of the New Testament* (Grand Rapids: Zondervan, 2012); J. Fitzmyer, *Luke the Theologian: Aspects of his Teaching* (London: Geoffrey Chapman, 1989); J. B. Green, *The Theology of the Gospel of Luke*, New Testament Theology (Cambridge: Cambridge University Press, 1995); R. Maddox, *The Purpose of Luke-Acts*, Studies of the New Testament and its World (Edinburgh: T. & T. Clark, 1982).

41. See further discussion in Chapter 4, §2.

42. See further discussion in Chapter 5, §3.

and themes include God's promised salvation,[43] the symbolic character of meal scenes,[44] status reversal,[45] and eschatology.[46]

5.1. *Poor and Possessions*

A principal thematic emphasis in the parable and Luke-Acts is the proper treatment of the poor through the right use of one's material possessions. A focus on this theme is evident from the adjoining parable of the Dishonest Steward (vv. 1–9) and the subsequent teachings on wealth (vv. 10–13), the characterization of the Pharisees as 'lovers of money' (v. 14), as well the parable's sharply contrasting portraits of poverty and wealth (vv. 19–21).[47] Already from an early juncture in Luke's Gospel, attention is

43. J. B. Green, 'Acts of the Apostles', in *Dictionary of the Later New Testament and Its Developments*, ed. R. Martin and P. Davids (Downers Grove, IL: InterVarsity, 1997), 7–24, citing 14; Marshall, *Historian and Theologian*, 116; Hintzen, *Verkündigung*, 378–79.

44. J. P. Heil, *The Meal Scenes in Luke-Acts: An Audience-oriented Approach*, SBLMS 52 (Atlanta: Society of Biblical Literature, 1999), concludes that all the meals in Luke-Acts anticipate the ultimate meal fellowship to be enjoyed at the eschatological banquet in the kingdom of God (312); see the discussion of the parable on 131–45. D. E. Smith, 'Table Fellowship as a Literary Motif in the Gospel of Luke', *JBL* 106 (1987): 613–38, also examines the motif of table fellowship in Luke; cf. W. Braun, *Feasting and Social Rhetoric in Luke 14*, SNTSMS 85 (Cambridge: Cambridge University Press, 1995).

45. J. York, *The Last Shall be First: The Rhetoric of Reversal in Luke*, JSNTSup 46 (Sheffield: JSOT, 1991). Identifying several occurrences of 'bi-polar reversal' in Luke where a two-part statement or event is first presented and then negated, York says 'the repetition of bi-polar reversal, once established in the mind of the reader, becomes the vehicle that shapes the reader's expectations' (166). For his commentary on Luke 16:19–31, see 62–71.

46. See, e.g., the studies of Lukan eschatology in H. Conzelmann, *The Theology of St Luke* (London: Faber & Faber, 1960); J. Dupont, 'L'après-mort dans l'œuvre de Luc', *RTL* 3 (1972): 3–21; A. L. Moore, *The Parousia in the New Testament*, NovTSup 13 (Leiden: Brill, 1966); M. Hengel, *Acts and the History of Earliest Christianity* (London: SCM, 1979), 59–60; J. Osei-Bonsu, 'The Intermediate State in Luke-Acts', *IBS* 9 (1987): 115–30; A. J. Mattill Jr., *Luke and the Last Things: A Perspective for the Understanding of Lukan Thought* (Dillsboro, NC: Western North Carolina, 1979); Maddox, *Purpose*, 100–57; S. G. Wilson, 'Lukan Eschatology', *NTS* 16 (1969–70): 330–47; J. T. Carroll, *Response to the End of History: Eschatology and Situation in Luke-Acts*, SBLDS 92 (Atlanta: Scholars Press, 1988); E. Ellis, *Eschatology in Luke* (Philadelphia: Fortress, 1972).

47. See also J. L. Story, 'Twin Parables of Stewardship in Luke 16', *ATI* 2 (2009): 105–20.

given to the promised help for poor persons (οἱ πτωχοί) and other marginalized individuals,[48] while there is a concomitant emphasis on the proper
stewardship of one's wealth.[49] In subsequent chapters the Third Gospel's
accent on this theme is amply evidenced, perhaps more so than in any
other New Testament book.[50] Consequently, there is no paucity of studies
on the place and function of the poor and possessions in Luke-Acts.[51]
While most agree on the centrality of this theme in Luke-Acts, perspectives differ on the work's precise conception of poverty and wealth. Some
suggest that Luke is opposed to any accumulation and retention of wealth.
Others judge that he is opposed to wealth insofar as those with abundant
material goods fail to use their wealth to alleviate the suffering of their
poor and marginalized neighbours.

48. See, e.g., the Song of Mary in 1:46–55.

49. See, e.g., the preaching of John the Baptist in 3:7–14.

50. Bock, *Theology*, 328; cf. Bock's summary of the Lukan theology of wealth on
328–30 and 352–57. For a similar characterization of Luke, see Fitzmyer, *Theologian*,
137; P. F. Esler, *Community and Gospel in Luke-Acts: The Social and Political
Motivations of Lucan Theology*, SNTSMS 57 (Cambridge: Cambridge University
Press, 1987), 169.

51. For a survey of the literature, see T. E. Phillips, 'Reading Recent Readings
of Issues of Wealth and Poverty in Luke and Acts', *CurBR* 1 (2003): 231–69; cf.
the earlier work of J. R. Donahue, 'Two Decades of Research on the Rich and Poor
in Luke-Acts', in *Justice and the Holy: Essays in Honour of Walter Harrelson*, ed.
W. J. Harrelson, D. A. Knight, and P. J. Paris (Atlanta: Scholars Press, 1989), 129–44.
Representative studies include Degenhardt, *Evangelist der Armen*; D. P. Seccombe,
Possessions and the Poor in Luke-Acts (Linz: Fuchs, 1982); L. T. Johnson, *The
Literary Function of Possessions in Luke-Acts*, SBLDS 39 (Missoula, MT: SBL Press,
1977); J. B. Green, 'Good News to Whom? Jesus and the "Poor" in the Gospel of
Luke', in *Jesus of Nazareth: Lord and Christ*, ed. J. B. Green and M. Turner (Grand
Rapids: Eerdmans, 1994), 59–74; C. M. Hays, *Luke's Wealth Ethics: A Study in Their
Coherence and Character*, WUNT 2/275 (Tübingen: Mohr Siebeck, 2010); R. J.
Karris, 'Poor and Rich: The Lukan *Sitz im Leben*', in *Perspectives on Luke-Acts*, ed.
C. H. Talbert (Danville, VA: Association of Baptist Professors of Religion; Edinburgh:
T. & T. Clark, 1978), 112–25; W. E. Pilgrim, *Good News to the Poor: Wealth and
Poverty in Luke-Acts* (Minneapolis: Augsburg, 1981); R. J. Cassidy, *Jesus, Politics,
and Society: A Study of Luke's Gospel* (Maryknoll, NY: Orbis Books, 1978); Esler,
Community and Gospel; J. Gillman, *Possessions and the Life of Faith: A Reading
of Luke-Acts* (Collegeville, MN: Liturgical, 1991); H. Moxnes, *The Economy of the
Kingdom: Social Conflict and Economic Relations in Luke's Gospel* (Philadelphia:
Fortress, 1988); D. Kraybill and D. M. Sweetland, 'Possessions in Luke-Acts: A
Sociological Perspective', *PRSt* 10 (1983): 215–39.

The view that Luke presents a generally anti-wealth message is manifest when interpreters comment on the rationale for the parable's reversal of earthly positions. As mentioned, Luke 16:19–31 presents two potential outcomes for life – the rich man enters torment, and poor Lazarus is carried to Abraham's bosom – though neither personal piety nor immorality is attributed to either man. Consequently, the reason for the rich man's degradation is said to be the inherent wrongness of possessing earthly wealth.[52] As for Lazarus, 'he is blessed in the next life just because he was poor in this life'.[53] This interpretation is in some cases a consequence of viewing the text as consisting of two parts: the pre-Lukan vv. 19–26, and the later Lukan interpretation in vv. 27–31.[54] Since 'repentance' is not mentioned until v. 30 (and is therefore unoriginal) Abraham's words to the rich man are not directed against specific misconduct needing amendment, but are a categorical condemnation of wealth. Metzger contends that the rich man is punished not for failing to give alms nor for acquiring his wealth unjustly, but for being wealthy, which in Jesus's teaching is impermissible under any circumstances.[55]

While the rich man is neither condemned for a specific wrongdoing, nor is Lazarus explicitly commended for piety, some consider that Luke 16:19–31 does not present a negative conception of wealth. Rather, consistent with the perspective evidenced throughout Luke-Acts, there is a strong implication of warning against wealth's abuse.[56] For instance, Hays suggests that the parable functions as more than a simple critique of luxury;[57] rather, it argues for a proper use of God-given riches.[58] In this

52. See, e.g., L. Schottroff and W. Stegemann, *Jesus and the Hope of the Poor*, trans. M. J. O'Connell (Maryknoll, NY: Orbis, 1986), 25; cf. D. L. Mealand, *Poverty and Expectation in the Gospels* (London: SPCK, 1980), 'The man's wealth seems to be the main reason for his translation to Hades' (32).

53. Bauckham, 'Rich Man and Lazarus', 232–33; cf. Schottroff and Stegemann, *Hope of the Poor*, 26.

54. See, e.g., Schottroff and Stegemann, *Hope of the Poor*, 25.

55. J. A. Metzger, *Consumption and Wealth in Luke's Travel Narrative*, BibInt 88 (Leiden: Brill, 2007), 146–47; for a critique, see C. M. Hays, 'Beyond Mint and Rue: The Implications of Luke's Interpretive Controversies for Modern Consumerism', *Political Theology* 11 (2010): 383–98, citing 389, 392.

56. See D. Warden, 'The Rich Man and Lazarus: Poverty, Wealth and Human Worth', *SCJ* 6 (2003): 81–93.

57. Hays, *Wealth Ethics*, 154.

58. Hays, 'Mint and Rue', 391; Hays concludes about Luke's wealth ethics in general that he 'calls his readers to a complete commitment of their goods to the service of the Kingdom' (*Wealth Ethics*, 261).

view, the rich man is not condemned for his wealth, but for his failure to obey the call of 'Moses and the prophets' to be merciful to a poor neighbour.[59] In his seminal study of possessions in Luke-Acts, Johnson argues that the use of wealth frequently stands as indicative of the state of a person's heart before God.[60]

Unsurprisingly, between these positions there is a spectrum of different perspectives on the Lukan view of poverty and possessions. The foregoing survey is indicative of the difficulty in crafting a succinct and coherent summary of the theme that accounts for every discrete text.[61] However, an important aspect of the Lukan viewpoint on poverty and possessions inviting further investigation is how this theme in Luke 16:19–31 relates not only to the Third Gospel, but to Acts. It has often been observed that the terms 'poor' or 'rich' do not appear in Acts, which is especially striking when the frequency of the terms πλούσιος (12×) and πτωχός (10×) in the Gospel is considered.[62] Nevertheless, Luke includes in Acts several accounts of individual and community responses to the poor.[63] Esler

59. See, e.g., J. Dupont, *Les Béatitudes*, vol. 3 (Paris: Gabalda, 1973), 181–82; J. Nolland, 'The Role of Money and Possessions in the Parable of the Prodigal Son (Luke 15:11–32)', in *Reading Luke: Interpretation, Reflection, Formation*, ed. C. G. Bartholomew, J. B. Green, and A. C. Thiselton (Grand Rapids: Paternoster, 2005), 178–209, citing 190; Marshall, *Luke*, 635; J. Ernst, *Das Evangelium nach Lukas*, RNT 3 (Regensburg: Pstet, 1977), 473; Fitzmyer, *Luke X–XXIV*, 2:1128.

60. See, e.g., *Literary Function*, 158–59. Johnson's conclusion is echoed by others; see, e.g., Hays, 'Mint and Rue', 387, who observes that in Luke's Gospel, mercy is a 'necessary corollary' of faith in Jesus; S. I. Wright, 'Parables on Poverty and Riches', in *The Challenge of Jesus' Parables*, ed. R. Longenecker (Grand Rapids: Eerdmans, 2000), 217–39, citing 233.

61. The diversity of the references has led R. Nadella, *Dialogue Not Dogma: Many Voices in the Gospel of Luke*, LNTS 431 (New York: T&T Clark, 2011), 88–110, to posit a Lukan polyphony on this topic in the Third Gospel. He contends that 'a fragmentary and centrifugal, rather than a unitary and centripetal, view of wealth' is evident (88). Rather than supply an internally consistent series of directives about wealth, Luke has set varying and sometimes contradictory voices in dialogue with each other.

62. E.g. L. E. Keck, 'The Poor Among the Saints in the New Testament', *ZNW* 56 (1965): 100–29, citing 103.

63. For a summary of the presentation of rich and poor in Acts, see R. F. O'Toole, *The Unity of Luke's Theology* (Wilmington, DE: Glazier, 1984), 129–35; Kraybill and Sweetland, 'Possessions', 215–39, observe that the Gospel and Acts represent different stages in the movement, a change from the rudimentary and enthusiastic phase, to a secondary stage of institutionalization. They argue that one aspect of this shift is seen in how the Gospel's teaching to abandon one's possessions is modified to a promotion of the communal ownership of goods (234).

remarks that as Luke's narrative continues in Acts, there is a demon-stration of how Jesus's instructions to the rich are put into practice,[64] while Kim notes a thematic continuity in the practice of almsgiving between the Gospel and Acts.[65] Commenting on Acts, Tannehill points out 'that Jesus' call has the power to create a community that cares for the poor so that there are no longer needy persons among them'.[66]

While these comments are generally suggestive of this theme's links within Luke's two volumes, there has not been a comprehensive study of how Luke 16:19–31 relates to the rest of Luke-Acts in this respect. The degree to which an awareness of charity in the early church was intended to influence the audience of Luke's Gospel and this parable, or conversely, how Luke utilizes the parable to anticipate and prepare for his second volume, is a potentially fruitful avenue for our investigation.

5.2. *Moses and the Prophets*

A second principal theme in Luke-Acts and this parable is the testimony of 'Moses and the prophets'. As with poverty and possessions, the motif of Scripture is present in the parable's immediate context; in 16:16 Jesus announces the end of the era of law and prophecy in the person of John the Baptist. The statement is clarified in v. 17 with a pronouncement about the law's enduring authority, which Jesus then illustrates in v. 18 with his saying on divorce.[67] The theme of authoritative revelation is reprised by Abraham in the parable, for the rich man's request for Lazarus to be sent from his post-mortem state in order to warn his brothers (v. 28) is answered by the patriarch's repeated insistence on the sufficiency of 'Moses and the prophets' (vv. 29, 31). Outside of the parable, the Jewish Scriptures are referred to with regularity in the Third Gospel,[68] a pattern sustained in Acts, where believers are portrayed as living in accordance with the law,[69] and where the Scriptures have a regular place in keryg-matic activity.[70]

---

64. Esler, *Community and Gospel*, 195; cf. Karris, 'Poor and Rich', 117.

65. Kyoung-Jin Kim, *Stewardship and Almsgiving in Luke's Theology*, JSNTSup 155 (Sheffield: Sheffield Academic, 1998), 233–34; Gillman, *Possessions*, 107, high-lights how both the proper use of money in charity and its abuse in greed or gluttony are represented in Acts in terms similar to those of the Third Gospel.

66. R. C. Tannehill, *The Narrative Unity of Luke-Acts: A Literary Interpretation* (Philadelphia: Fortress, 1986), 1:132.

67. See the further discussion of the Luke 16 context in Chapter 3, §3.2.

68. See, e.g., Luke 1:6; 4:21; 5:14; 10:26; 18:31; 21:22; 24:27, 44.

69. See, e.g., Acts 2:46; 3:1.

70. See, e.g., Acts 13:27; 26:22–23; 28:23.

Several studies examine the function of Scripture in Luke-Acts.[71] In general, the Scriptures have both an ethical role in directing proper conduct,[72] as well as a prophetic role in anticipating the work of Jesus.[73] Green contends that in Luke-Acts the narrated events are grounded in 'God's purpose, evident in Israel's Scriptures and the history of God's people'.[74] Particularly in Acts, Scripture's principal import is 'ecclesiological and hermeneutical', for the community uses the Scriptures to define their identity and declare allegiance to Christ, often against those who read the Scriptures but do not believe in him.[75]

As with the Lukan perspective on poverty and possessions, the function of 'Moses and the prophets' within the parable and in relation to Luke-Acts is worthy of further consideration. For instance, a question that lingers from the parable's conclusion is whether some will continue to misread 'Moses and the prophets' and fail to see the importance of the events of Jesus's life, death and resurrection.[76] In this vein Anderson

---

71. See C. A. Evans and J. A. Sanders, *Luke and Scripture: The Function of Sacred Tradition in Luke-Acts* (Minneapolis: Fortress, 1993); C. K. Barrett, 'Luke/Acts', in *It Is Written: Scripture Citing Scripture. Essays in Honour of Barnabas Lindars, SSF*, ed. D. A. Carson and H. G. M. Williamson (Cambridge: Cambridge University Press, 1988), 231–22; C. A. Kimball, *Jesus' Exposition of the Old Testament in Luke's Gospel*, JSNTSup 94 (Sheffield: Sheffield Academic, 1994); J. Fitzmyer, 'The Use of the Old Testament in Luke-Acts', in *Society of Biblical Literature 1992 Seminar Papers*, SBLSP 31 (Missoula, MT: Scholars Press, 1986), 524–38; H. Ringgren, 'Luke's Use of the Old Testament', *HTR* 79 (1986): 227–35.

72. C. L. Blomberg, 'The Law in Luke-Acts', *JSNT* 22 (1984): 53–80; J. Jervell, *Luke and the People of God: A New Look at Luke-Acts* (Minneapolis: Augsburg, 1972), 136–37, discusses the uniquely Lukan terminology for the law. In connection with the Scriptures' ethical function in Luke-Acts, there is contention over Luke's view of the law; Jervell characterizes Luke's view of the law as 'fundamentally Mosaic'; he has been critiqued by S. G. Wilson, *Luke and the Law*, SNTSMS 50 (Cambridge: Cambridge University Press, 1983), 103–17.

73. D. Bock, *Proclamation from Prophecy and Pattern: Lucan Old Testament Christology*, JSNTSup 12 (Sheffield: Sheffield Academic, 1987); C. H. Talbert, 'Promise and Fulfillment in Lucan Theology', in *Luke-Acts: New Perspectives from the Society of Biblical Literature Seminar*, ed. C. H. Talbert (New York: Crossroad, 1984), 91–103; W. S. Kurz, 'Promise and Fulfillment in Hellenistic Jewish Narratives and in Luke and Acts', in *Jesus and the Heritage of Israel: Luke's Narrative Claim Upon Israel's Legacy*, ed. D. P. Moessner (Harrisburg, PA: Trinity, 1999), 147–70; D. L. Tiede, *Prophecy and History in Luke-Acts* (Philadelphia: Fortress, 1980).

74. Green, *Theology*, 30.

75. Green, 'Acts', 18.

76. Green, *Theology*, 72.

makes the suggestive comment that after the risen Jesus in 24:27 reads the Scriptures with reference to himself on the way to Emmaus, 'The words of Abraham in Luke 16:31 gain renewed force'.[77] Such renewed force will be evident only through a close examination of this theme within the whole of Luke-Acts.

6. *Methodology Review*

So far we have surveyed questions of the parable's unity and origin, as well as its two principal themes. The literature can be considered from a third angle, the methodological, which will bring into focus fruitful areas for additional study of the parable. Scholars have employed each of the methods outlined below to the study of Luke 16:19–31, but in every case the work has the potential to be advanced. Thus we turn to the methods of narrative criticism and rhetorical criticism, and the interpretive perspective of intertextuality.

6.1. *Narrative Criticism*

With its place in the New Testament discipline well established, narrative criticism needs little introduction. Narrative criticism attends to an author's artistry in the arranging of narrative features, and evaluates how these are marshalled in order to communicate through story.[78] Despite potential weaknesses and misapplications of narrative criticism,[79] as one

---

77. K. L. Anderson, *'But God Raised Him from the Dead': The Theology of Jesus' Resurrection in Luke-Acts* (Bletchley, Milton Keynes: Paternoster, 2006), 179.

78. On the application of this method in New Testament studies, see D. Marguerat and Y. Bourquoin, *How to Read Bible Stories: An Introduction to Narrative Criticism*, trans. J. Bowden (London: SCM, 1999); Marguerat and Bourquoin, 'Narrative Criticism', in *Hearing the New Testament: Strategies for Interpretation*, ed. J. B. Green, 2nd ed. (Grand Rapids: Eerdmans, 2010), 240–58; M. A. Powell, *What Is Narrative Criticism?* (Minneapolis: Fortress, 1990); R. A. Culpepper, 'Story and History in the Gospels', *RevExp* 81 (1984): 467–78; F. J. Moloney, 'Narrative Criticism of the Gospels', *Pacifica* 4 (1991): 181–201; J. B. Green, 'Narrative Criticism', in *Methods for Luke*, ed. J. B. Green (Cambridge: Cambridge University Press, 2010), 74–112; J. L. Resseguie, *Narrative Criticism of the New Testament: An Introduction* (Grand Rapids: Baker Academic, 2005); Resseguie, 'Reader-Response Criticism and the Synoptic Gospels', *JAAR* 52 (1984): 307–24.

79. Green, 'Narrative Criticism', 98, notes the vast number of literary devices which can be identified in a narrative, and emphasizes the need to develop literary sensibilities. S. D. Moore, 'Are the Gospels Unified Narratives?', *Society of Biblical Literature 1987 Seminar Papers*, SBLSP 26 (Atlanta: Scholars Press, 1987), 443–58,

exegetical method inter alia it offers a profitable means of studying New Testament texts.[80]

Several studies have employed narrative criticism in connection with Luke-Acts, or provided theoretical reflection on how to do so.[81] Johnson investigates the literary function of possessions in Luke-Acts utilizing this method.[82] Tannehill's pioneering study employs this method by providing narrative commentary on the work as a whole.[83] In numerous works Kurz considers narrative elements in the Lukan literature, noting the use of gaps, ambiguity and reticence; such features, he contends, invite a filling-in process by the audience.[84] Roth analyses narrative character-types in Luke-Acts, and concludes that the presentation of the impoverished and underprivileged serves to elicit the sympathy of Luke's audience.[85] Darr's

argues that while narrative criticism has often been employed to establish the Gospels' textual unity, its practitioners have not adequately reflected on the method's basis in literary theory, which regards notions of 'textual unity' as unreliable; cf. his *Literary Criticism and the Gospels: The Theoretical Challenge* (New Haven, CT: Yale University Press, 1989).

80. Powell, 'Narrative Criticism', 253–54. On the continued viability of narrative criticism in New Testament studies, see P. Merenlahti, *Poetics for the Gospels? Rethinking Narrative Criticism*, SNTW (London: T&T Clark, 2002), 115–30; D. Rhoads, 'Narrative Criticism: Practices and Prospects', in *Characterization in the Gospels: Reconceiving Narrative Criticism*, ed. D. Rhoads and K. Syreeni, JSNTSup 184 (Sheffield: Sheffield Academic, 1999), 264–85; J. B. Green, 'Narrative and New Testament Interpretation: Reflections on the State of the Art', *LTQ* 39 (2004): 153–66; M. A. Powell, 'Narrative Criticism: The Emergence of a Prominent Reading Strategy', in *Mark as Story: Retrospect and Prospect*, ed. K. R. Iverson and C. W. Skinner, SBLRBS 65 (Leiden: Brill, 2011), 19–43.

81. For narrative-critical works on Luke-Acts specifically, see W. S. Kurz, *Reading Luke-Acts: Dynamics of Biblical Narrative* (Louisville, KY: Westminster, 1993); Kurz, 'Narrative Approaches to Luke-Acts', *Bib* 68 (1987): 195–220; J. N. Aletti, *L'Art de Raconteur Jésus Christ: L'écriture narrative de l'évangile de Luc* (Paris: Seuil, 1989); K. Syreeni, 'The Gospel in Paradigms: A Study in the Hermeneutical Space of Luke-Acts', in *Luke-Acts: Scandinavian Perspectives*, ed. P. Luomanen, Publications of the Finnish Exegetical Society 54 (Göttingen: Vandenhoeck & Ruprecht/Helsinki: Finnish Exegetical Society, 1991), 36–57.

82. Johnson, *Literary Function*.

83. Tannehill, *Narrative Unity*, vols. 1–2.

84. See, e.g., 'Narrative Approaches'; *Reading Luke-Acts*; 'The Open-Ended Nature of Luke and Acts as Inviting Canonical Actualisation', *Neot* 31 (1997): 289–308.

85. S. J. Roth, *The Blind, the Lame and the Poor: Character Types in Luke-Acts*, JSNTSup 144 (Sheffield: Sheffield Academic, 1997), 192–93.

studies focus on methods and effects of characterization in Luke, as do the works of Gowler and Dicken.[86]

The appropriateness of applying narrative criticism to parables such as Luke 16:19–31 is patent, as these are 'stories within a story', miniature narratives set within the broader narrative of Jesus's ministry.[87] Lehtipuu details the way in which the three main personages are characterized, and how Luke uses these characterizations to guide his reader to a proper response.[88] Szukalski studies this parable, as well as other Lukan parables, from a socio-narratological perspective.[89] Reviewing past narrative-critical study of Luke-Acts and this parable in particular, it is evident that further investigation may provide insight into such elements as the characterization of Lazarus, the rich man and his five brothers, and Abraham; the interrelationships of the characters; the narrative setting and events; and also into the way in which these features engage the audience of Luke-Acts. We will consider such narrative elements in Chapter 2.

6.2. *Rhetorical Criticism*

A second method applied to this parable's study is rhetorical criticism, an approach that studies the features of an author's persuasive strategies as apparent in a given text. Undergirding the rhetorical-critical approach to a New Testament text is the Graeco-Roman tradition of rhetoric,[90] where

86. J. A. Darr, *On Character Building: The Reader and the Rhetoric of Characterization in Luke-Acts* (Louisville, KY: Westminster John Knox, 1992), 27–28; Darr, *Herod the Fox: Audience Criticism and Lukan Characterization*, JSNTSup 163 (Sheffield: Sheffield Academic, 1998); D. B. Gowler, 'Characterization in Luke: A Socio-Narratological Approach', *BTB* 19 (1989): 54–62; F. Dicken, *Herod as a Composite Character in Luke-Acts*, WUNT 2/375 (Tübingen: Mohr Siebeck, 2014).

87. See, e.g., P. Borgman's narrative study of Luke-Acts, *The Way according to Luke: Hearing the Whole Story of Luke-Acts* (Grand Rapids: Eerdmans, 2006), 156–70, in which he treats Luke 16:19–31 in conjunction with the accounts in Luke 12:13–34; cf. D. B. Gowler, '"At his Gate Lay a Poor Man": A Dialogic Reading of Luke 16:19–31', *PRSt* 32 (2005): 249–65; Green, 'Narrative Criticism', 98–112, who uses this parable as his case study. Narrative readings of the parable can also be found in Tannehill, *Narrative Unity*, 1:131–32, 185–86; cf. his *Luke*, ANTC (Nashville, TN: Abingdon, 1996), 251–54; Metzger, *Consumption and Wealth*, 132–57; Vogels, 'Having or Longing', 29–36; L. T. Johnson, 'Narrative Perspectives on Luke 16:19–31', in Porter and Boda, *Translating*, 207–11.

88. O. Lehtipuu, 'Characterization and Persuasion: The Rich Man and the Poor Man in Luke 16:19–31', in Roads and Syreeni, eds., *Characterization*, 73–105.

89. Szukalski, *Tormented in Hades*.

90. C. Gempf, 'Public Speaking and Published Accounts', in *The Book of Acts in its Ancient Literary Setting*, ed. B. W. Winter and A. D. Clarke, BAFCS 1 (Grand

rhetoric is understood as 'that quality in discourse by which a speaker or writer seeks to accomplish his purposes'.[91] Elements from the study of Graeco-Roman discourse have been brought to bear on New Testament literature in numerous studies.[92] There is some reluctance to apply the method of rhetorical criticism to this literature,[93] and practitioners must be cautioned against imposing rhetorical schemes onto texts,[94] or reducing texts to agglomerations of assorted stylistic devices.[95] Nevertheless, it remains likely that Luke had rhetorical training,[96] and that his audience

Rapids: Eerdmans, 1993), 259–303. Already in the fourth century BCE, Aristotle taught rhetoric as a necessary skill for the courts or public assemblies, articulating the basic rhetorical components in his *Ars Rhetorica*. While instruction in the methods and styles of rhetoric became more sophisticated in secondary levels of Greek education, rhetoric had a pervasive place in Graeco-Roman culture.

91. G. A. Kennedy, *New Testament Interpretation through Rhetorical Criticism* (Chapel Hill: University of North Carolina Press, 1984), 3. K. Berger, 'Hellenistiche Gattungen im Neuen Testament', in *ANRW* 25.2, ed. W. Haase (Berlin: de Gruyter, 1984), 1031–432, offers a broad analysis of the rhetorical forms in the New Testament.

92. A review of New Testament rhetorical criticism should commence with a visit to the works of G. A. Kennedy; see his *Rhetorical Criticism*, and *Classical Rhetoric and Its Christian and Secular Tradition from Ancient to Modern Times* (London: Croom Helm, 1980); for Kennedy's legacy, see C. C. Black, 'Kennedy and the Gospels', in *Words Well Spoken: George Kennedy's Rhetoric of the New Testament*, ed. C. C. Black and D. F. Watson (Waco, TX: Baylor University Press, 2008), 63–80. See also W. Wuellner, 'Where Is Rhetorical Criticism Taking Us?' *CBQ* 49 (1987): 448–63; S. Walton, 'Rhetorical Criticism: An Introduction', *Them* 21 (1996): 4–9; J. Weima, 'What Does Aristotle Have to Do with Paul? An Evaluation of Rhetorical Criticism', *CTJ* 32 (1997): 458–68; B. Witherington III, *New Testament Rhetoric* (Eugene, OR: Cascade, 2009); C. C. Black, 'Rhetorical Criticism', in Green, ed., *Hearing the New Testament*, 166–88; R. A. Burridge, 'The Gospels and Acts', in *Handbook of Classical Rhetoric in the Hellenistic Period (330 B.C.–A.D. 400)*, ed. S. E. Porter (Leiden: Brill, 1997), 507–32; B. L. Mack, *Rhetoric and the New Testament* (Minneapolis: Fortress, 1990); C. J. Classen, *Rhetorical Criticism of the New Testament* (Boston: Brill, 2002).

93. Weima, 'Aristotle', 458, points out that the tools of rhetoric were employed in crafting and delivering speeches, while most New Testament material is in the form of narratives or letters.

94. C. C. Black, *The Rhetoric of the Gospel: Theological Artistry in the Gospels and Acts* (St. Louis, MO: Chalice, 2001), 21.

95. Weima, 'Aristotle', 464–65.

96. As Burridge, 'Gospels and Acts', 530, points out with respect to Luke: 'Given his command of several different Greek styles and his composition of speeches, it is not unreasonable that he might have had some rhetorical training which emerges in his writing'.

was familiar with the traditions of speech – including comparative discourse – from the Hebrew Scriptures and other Jewish literature.[97]

Jülicher considered the parables as rhetorical tools in relation to the מְשָׁלִים of the Hebrew Scriptures and the similitudes and parables of Aristotle's rhetoric.[98] Scholars have continued to investigate Luke's rhetoric, differing on whether the model is to be found within the scope of Graeco-Roman rhetorical conventions or among the traditions of Jewish speech. There have been attempts to study the parables in comparison to the Aristotelian tradition in which a παραβολή or a similar figure of speech is employed in order to confirm a principle, or to persuade an audience of a particular truth or activity.[99] Reich analyses the Third Gospel for rhetorical figures, and discovers that Luke makes frequent and adept use of the constructions and figures that are typically found in the Graeco-Roman rhetorical treatises.[100] He suggests that the effects of the rhetorical figures in Luke's Gospel provide an emphasis of instruction, offer persuasion, and promote audience participation in the Gospel narrative.[101] Some contend that Luke was trained in the *progymnasmata*, the elementary rhetorical handbooks, and they seek parallels for the basic literary units of the Gospel in these exercises.[102] Graeco-Roman pedagogy in Luke's day placed a high value on writing creatively in a mimetic spirit, and such patterns of 'imitation and reconfiguration' are said to be evident in Luke-Acts.[103]

---

97. See, e.g., C. A. Evans, 'Parables in Early Judaism', in Longenecker, ed., *Challenge*, 51–75; D. Flusser, *Die rabbinische Gleichnisse und der Gleichniserzahler Jesus*, JudChr 4 (Bern: Lang, 1981); B. Gerhardsson, 'The Narrative Meshalim in the Synoptic Gospels', *NTS* 34 (1988): 339–63; C. Blomberg, *Interpreting the Parables*, 2nd ed. (Downers Grove, IL: IVP Academic, 2012), 68–81.

98. Jülicher, *Gleichnisreden*, 32–42.

99. See, e.g., M. A. Beavis, 'Parable and Fable', *CBQ* 52 (1990): 473–98; R. Zimmermann, 'Jesus' Parables and Ancient Rhetoric: The Contributions of Aristotle and Quintilian to the Form Criticism of the Parables', in *Hermeneutik der Gleichnisse Jesu: Methodische Neuansätze zum Verstehen urchristlicher Parabeltexte*, ed. R. Zimmerman, WUNT 2/231 (Tübingen: Mohr Siebeck, 2008), 238–58.

100. K. A. Reich, *Figuring Jesus: The Power of Rhetorical Figures of Speech in the Gospel of Luke*, BibInt 107 (Leiden: Brill, 2011).

101. Reich, *Figuring Jesus*, 137, 143–44.

102. M. Parsons, 'Luke and the *Progymnasmata*: A Preliminary Investigation into the Preliminary Exercises', in *Contextualizing Acts: Lukan Narrative and Greco-Roman Discourse*, ed. T. Penner and C. Vander Stichele, SBLSymS 20 (Atlanta: SBL Press, 2003), 43–63; cf. Burridge, 'Gospels and Acts', 510.

103. T. Penner, 'Reconfiguring the Rhetorical Study of Acts: Reflections on the Method in and Learning of a Progymnastic Poetics', *PRSt* 30 (2003): 425–39, citing 434.

Hughes offers one of the few examinations of the Graeco-Roman rhetoric of Luke 16:19–31, and suggests an explanation for the oft-cited parallels between this parable and various Egyptian, Jewish, and Greek stories.[104] He argues that the parable may be a rhetorical declamation written in the style of *imitatio*,[105] and posits that if the writer of Luke-Acts had once been assigned to make a progymnasmatic declamation in the genre of Rich Man *versus* Poor Man, it would not have been difficult for him when later composing the parable.[106] Hauge also examines *imitatio* in Luke 16:19–31,[107] and asserts that the distinctive features of this story are the result of an imitation and transformation of the descent of Odysseus into Hades in Homer's *Odyssey*.

While some concentrate on the parable's possible models in Graeco-Roman rhetoric, the alternative claim is that the Synoptic parables especially owe their form to the rhetorical traditions of the מָשָׁל as it occurs in the Hebrew Scriptures and rabbinic literature.[108] For instance, Evans analyses what he terms the 'proto-rabbinic' mould of Jesus's rhetoric.[109] He focuses on Jesus's style of argument and prophetic criticism in the parables that are directed against the leading religious and political figures

104. F. Hughes, 'The Parable of the Rich Man and Lazarus (Luke 16.19–31) and Greco-Roman Rhetoric', in *Rhetoric and the New Testament: Essays from the 1992 Heidelberg Conference*, ed. S. E. Porter and T. H. Olbricht, JSNTSup 90 (Sheffield: JSOT, 1993), 29–41.

105. Hughes, 'Rich Man', 32, defines imitation as the repetition and transforemation of older texts into new texts.

106. Hughes, 'Rich Man', 38, concludes that Luke intended the rich man of the parable to be an *exemplum* of the Jewish refusal of God's purposes, a rejection culminating in the rejection of the risen Jesus in Acts.

107. Hauge, *Tour of Hell*; cf. the prior study of M. J. Gilmour, 'Hints of Homer in Luke 16:19–31', *Did* 10 (1999), 23–33.

108. See Evans, 'Parables', 51–75; Flusser, *Die rabbinische Gleichnisse*; Gerhardsson, 'Narrative Meshalim', 339–63; Blomberg, *Parables*, 68–81; see Str-B 2:222–34. W. O. E. Oesterley, *The Gospel Parables in the Light of their Jewish Background* (London: SPCK, 1936), 203–11, comments on the parable's potential background in rabbinical writings; cf. J. Lightfoot in *A Commentary on the New Testament from the Talmud and Hebraica, Matthew – I Corinthians* (Peabody, MA: Hendrickson, 1989), 165–77; H. K. McArthur and R. M. Johnston, *They Also Taught in Parables* (Grand Rapids: Academie, 1990), 195.

109. C. A. Evans, 'Jesus' Rhetoric of Criticism: The Parables Against His Friends and Critics', in *Rhetorical Criticism and the Bible*, ed. S. E. Porter and D. L. Stamps, JSNTSup 195 (Sheffield: Sheffield Academic Press, 2002), 256–79; cf. D. Flusser, *Jewish Sources in Early Christianity* (Tel-Aviv: MOD Books, 1989).

in Palestine. Evans suggests that Luke 16:19–31 is spoken with reference to the evils of the Herodian dynasty.[110]

In sum, we have seen that a study of this parable utilizing the method of rhetorical criticism has potential. In Chapter 3 we will examine Luke's persuasive strategy in Luke 16:19–31 in relation to the Graeco-Roman *progymnasmata* and the rhetorical conventions of the παραβολή, as well as in relation to the Jewish traditions of the מָשָׁל, cognizant that these traditions may well intersect in the Lukan parables.[111] An examination of the parable's form will serve as a useful adjunct to considering its rhetorical function within Luke-Acts as a whole.

6.3. *Intertextuality*

A third method to survey in previous studies concerns aspects of intertextuality, a perspective which studies 'patterns of literary borrowing among literary texts proper and textual relationships between specific literary corpora'.[112] What is read in the New Testament is the result of a process of interpretation and commentary on earlier texts,[113] and an intertextual approach aims to illustrate how texts interact in a variety of ways.[114] An accumulation of approaches under the elastic term 'intertextuality' can make the method too unwieldy to be helpful,[115] or can engender the

110. Evans, 'Rhetoric of Criticism', 277–78.

111. Ibid., 259; cf. Beavis, 'Parable and Fable', 494; Burridge, 'Gospels and Acts', 521.

112. G. R. O'Day, 'Intertextuality', in *Dictionary of Biblical Interpretation*, ed. J. H. Hayes (Nashville, TN: Abingdon, 1999), 1:546–48, citing 547; P. Koptak, 'Intertextuality', in *Dictionary for Theological Interpretation of the Bible*, ed. K. Vanhoozer, C. Bartholomew, D. Treier, and N. T. Wright (Grand Rapids: Baker Academic, 2005), 332–34, citing 334.

113. On the use of the Hebrew Scriptures in the New Testament, see R. B. Hays and J. B. Green, 'The Use of the Old Testament by New Testament Writers', in Green, ed., *Hearing the New Testament*, 222–38. Noting the traditional focus of New Testament scholars on explicit quotations, K. D. Litwak in 'The Use of the Old Testament in Luke-Acts: Luke's Scriptural Story of the "Things Accomplished Among Us"', in *Issues in Luke-Acts: Selected Essays*, ed. S. A. Adams and M. Pahl, Gorgias Handbooks 26 (Piscataway, NJ: Gorgias, 2012), 147–70, appeals for more attention to the diversity of ways in which a successor text reads the intertext.

114. H. F. Plett, 'Intertextualities', *Intertextuality*, ed. H. F. Plett, Research in Text Theory 15 (Berlin: de Gruyter, 1991), 3–29, provides an orientation to some key aspects of intertextuality.

115. S. Moyise, 'Intertextuality and Biblical Studies: A Review', *Verbum et Ecclesia* 23 (2002): 418–31, identifies five types of intertextuality: echo, narrative, exegetical, dialogical, and postmodern.

proposition of tenuous connections between one text and another.[116] While this potential weakness is real, it demonstrates that intertextuality must be clearly defined. Our approach will be based on the notion of 'dialogical intertextuality' or the study of the web of interactions between texts together with their contexts.[117] Dialogic intertextuality is well-suited for our investigation because while the parable lacks any quotation formulae or explicit exegesis of a prior text, there is a range of literature that can be regarded as part of the parable's cultural context. Such a context potentially shapes the audience's reception of the text.

Past studies have investigated general Lukan patterns of intertextuality.[118] Brawley notes that Luke-Acts appropriates Scripture through a variety of techniques, resulting in the transformation of the new text by the original, particularly when the original text is considered in its broader context.[119] Litwak posits the central place of scriptural resources in Luke's shaping of the expectations of his readers.[120] When Luke takes up the Jewish Scriptures, he causes 'the voices of Scripture to sound out in a new way and in a new context', which provide interpretive clues about the narrative and its direction.[121]

116. Here the caution proffered by S. Sandmel in 'Parallelomania', *JBL* 81 (1962): 1–13, is still needed, warning against extravagance in finding literary connections between various passages and drawing unwarranted conclusions about their source, derivation, and significance; see also the caveats of T. R. Hatina, 'Intertextuality and Historical Criticism in New Testament Studies', *BibInt* 7 (1999): 28–43. Similarly, P. Foster, 'Echoes without Resonance: Critiquing Certain Aspects of Recent Scholarly Trends in the Study of the Jewish Scriptures in the New Testament', *JSNT* 38 (2015): 96–111, opines that speculation and subjectivity can plague intertextual studies of Scripture.

117. See S. Moyise, 'Intertextuality and the Study of the Old Testament in the New', in *The Old Testament in the New Testament*, ed. S. Moyise, JSNTSup 189 (Sheffield: Sheffield Academic, 2000), 14–41.

118. An example of this methodology applied to a Lukan parable is M. Rindge, *Jesus' Parable of the Rich Fool: Luke 12:13–34 Among Ancient Conversations on Death and Possessions*, SBLECL 6 (Atlanta: SBL, 2011). Rindge outlines a spectrum of Jewish and Graeco-Roman texts in which themes of death and possessions intersect, and he notes how the parable of Luke 12:13–34 participates in this conversation.

119. R. L. Brawley, *Text to Text Pours Forth Speech: Voices of Scripture in Luke-Acts* (Bloomington, IN: Indiana University Press, 1995).

120. K. D. Litwak, *Echoes of Scripture in Luke-Acts: Telling the History of God's People Intertextually*, JSNTSup 282 (London: T&T Clark, 2005); cf. his 'Use of the Old Testament', 147–70.

121. Litwak, *Echoes*, 53.

With respect to Luke 16:19–31 in particular, attention has been paid to its possible allusions to and echoes of the Jewish Scriptures.[122] Brodie identifies it as 'distinctively dependent' on the Septuagint (hereafter LXX), but does not elaborate on the ways in which the parable is thus reliant.[123] Regalado likewise remarks on numerous allusions to Jewish writings in the parable, and observes ways in which this cultural and religious background informs its setting, dialogue, and events.[124] However, he does not explain how it affirms and reconfigures these materials. It has also been claimed that portions of 1 Enoch have influenced the parable's afterlife imagery, as well as shaping the parable's message about wealth and poverty.[125] Similarly, it is supposed that Deuteronomy's legislation and exhortation with respect to the material relief of the needy have informed the Third Gospel and this parable.[126]

The foregoing indicates the desirability of further intertextual investigation of this parable. In the first place, we can re-examine Abraham's assumption that the rich man and his brothers will know the injunctions of 'Moses and the prophets' regarding the treatment of the poor and needy. Similarly, the parable's notion of soliciting a messenger from the afterlife

---

122. See, e.g., D. W. Pao and E. Schnabel, 'Luke', in *Commentary on the New Testament Use of the Old Testament*, ed. G. K. Beale and D. A. Carson (Grand Rapids: Baker, 2007), 252–414.

123. T. Brodie, 'The Unity of Proto-Luke', in *The Unity of Luke-Acts*, ed. J. Verheyden, BETL 142 (Leuven: Leuven University Press, 1999), 627–38, citing 627.

124. F. O. Regalado, 'The Jewish Background of the Parable of the Rich Man and Lazarus', *AsJT* 16 (2002): 341–48.

125. Portions of 1 Enoch relating to poverty, wealth, and the afterlife have invited comparisons with Luke 16:19–31. See, e.g., L. W. Grensted, 'The Use of Enoch in St. Luke xvi. 19–31', *ExpTim* 26 (1914): 333–34; S. Aalen, 'St. Luke's Gospel and the Last Chapters of I Enoch', *NTS* 13 (1966–67): 1–13; L. Kreitzer, 'Luke 16:19–31 and 1 Enoch 22', *ExpTim* 103 (1992): 139–42; G. W. Nickelsburg: 'The Apocalyptic Message of *1 Enoch* 92–105', *CBQ* 39 (1977): 309–28; Nickelsburg, 'Revisiting the Rich and the Poor in 1 Enoch 92–105 and the Gospel According to Luke', in *George W. E. Nickelsburg in Perspective*, ed. J. Neusner, JSJSup 80 (Leiden: Brill, 2003), 2:547–71; Nickelsburg, 'Riches, the Rich and God's Judgment in 1 Enoch 92–105 and the Gospel According to Luke', *NTS* 25 (1978–79): 324–44.

126. See, e.g., C. F. Evans, 'The Central Section of St. Luke's Gospel', in *Studies in the Gospels: Essays in Memory of R. H. Lightfoot*, ed. D. E. Nineham (Oxford: Blackwell, 1955), 37–53; D. P. Moessner, 'Luke 9:1–50: Luke's Preview of the Journey of the Prophet Like Moses of Deuteronomy', *JBL* 102 (1983): 575–605; D. Rusam, 'Deuteronomy in Luke-Acts', in *Deuteronomy in the New Testament: The New Testament and the Scriptures of Israel*, ed. M. J. J. Menken and S. Moyise, LNTS 358 (London: T&T Clark, 2007), 63–81.

can be considered as the subject of an intertextual conversation involving both Graeco-Roman cultural participants and voices from the Jewish Scriptures. We will turn to an intertextual conversation surrounding Luke 16:19–31 in Chapter 4.

7. *The Parable in Relation to Luke-Acts*

A final facet of past scholarship pertains to the function of Luke 16:19–31 within its Luke-Acts context. There is general agreement that the Gospel of Luke and the Acts of the Apostles are essentially two parts of a unified work.[127] The unity and continuity of Luke-Acts are evidenced in several ways: structural similarities between the narratives of the two books,[128] characters who appear to be presented in deliberate parallel,[129] various theological and thematic associations,[130] and schematic patterns such as prophecy/promise and fulfilment bridging the narratives.[131] This literary unity is signalled in the opening words of the two volumes.[132] In Luke 1:1 he refers to 'the things that have been fulfilled among us' (τῶν πεπληροφορημένων ἐν ἡμῖν πραγμάτων).[133] In Acts 1:1 the author describes this first work as his πρῶτον λόγον, a narrative about 'that which Jesus began to do and teach' (ὧν ἤρξατο ὁ Ἰησοῦς ποιεῖν τε καὶ διδάσκειν).[134]

127. H. J. Cadbury, *The Making of Luke-Acts*, 2nd ed. (London: SPCK, 1958), has been influential in this regard, with his agenda-setting contention, 'They are not merely two independent writings from the same pen; they are a single continuous work' (8–9). For an observation of the general consensus, see J. Verheyden, 'The Unity of Luke-Acts: What Are We Up To?', in Verheyden, ed., *Unity of Luke-Acts*, 3–56, citing 3.

128. I. H. Marshall, 'Acts and the "Former Treatise"', in Winter and Clarke, *BAFCS* 1:163–82, citing 180–82.

129. S. M. Praeder, 'Jesus–Paul, Peter–Paul, and Jesus–Peter Parallelisms in Luke-Acts: A History of Reader Response', in *Society of Biblical Literature 1984 Seminar Papers*, SBLSP 23 (Chico, CA: Scholars Press, 1984), 23–39; see also C. K. Barrett, 'The Third Gospel as a Preface to Acts? Some Reflections', in *The Four Gospels 1992: Festschrift Frans Neirynck*, ed. F. Van Segbroeck, C. M. Tuckett, G. Van Belle, and J. Verheyden, 3 vols., BETL 100 (Leuven: Leuven University Press, 1992), 2:1451–66.

130. See, e.g., Tannehill, *Narrative Unity*, vols. 1–2.

131. Kurz, 'Promise and Fulfillment', 147–70.

132. Marshall, 'Former Treatise', 172–74.

133. See the discussion of Luke 1:1 in Alexander, *Preface*, 106–11; cf. D. Bock, 'Understanding Luke's Task: Carefully Building on Precedent', *CTR* 5 (1991): 183–202.

134. See the discussion of Acts 1:1 in Alexander, *Preface*, 142–46.

Consequently, it may be understood that in his second volume Luke is providing an account of how Jesus's 'doing and teaching' was perpetuated by the apostles and the community of believers.[135] An investigation of Acts' concluding chapters (27–28) in relation to the Gospel's prologue bears out this internal unity.[136] The author of Luke-Acts aims to shape his collection of diverse stories into a coherent narrative.[137]

Some contend, however, that there is not sufficient proof of the compositional unity of Luke and Acts.[138] There are tensions and inconsistencies in the two books' literary devices, generic conventions, and theological interests,[139] and their unity needs to be construed in a way that is less authorially deliberate.[140] While rightly reminding scholars of the need to demonstrate unity rather than assume it, these arguments fail to bear up under the weight of the evidence adduced in support of an integral unity between Luke-Acts.[141] It will therefore be our assumption that

135. The verb ἤρξατο in Acts 1:1 should be understood as more than an unnecessary auxiliary verb (equivalent to the Aramaic שרי) but having its own meaning, signifying the commencement of the ongoing work of Jesus in Acts; see, e.g., C. K. Barrett, *The Acts of the Apostles*, 2 vols., ICC (Edinburgh: T. & T. Clark, 1994), 1:66–67; W. Van Unnik, 'The "Book of Acts" and the Confirmation of the Gospel', *NovT* 4 (1960): 26–59, citing 58: Acts is a 'confirmation of what God did in Christ as told in the first book'.

136. L. C. A. Alexander, 'Reading Luke-Acts from Back to Front', in Verheyden, *Unity of Luke-Acts*, 419–46.

137. L. T. Johnson, 'Luke-Acts, Book of', in *Anchor Bible Dictionary*, ed. D. N. Freedman (New York: Doubleday, 1992), 4:403–20 (405).

138. For a survey of the debate, see M. Bird, 'The Unity of Luke-Acts in Recent Discussion', *JSNT* 29 (2007): 425–48; cf. Verheyden, 'Unity', 3–56.

139. M. C. Parsons and R. I. Pervo, *Rethinking the Unity of Luke and Acts* (Minneapolis: Fortress, 1993), 126 (emphasis original).

140. P. Walters, *The Assumed Authorial Unity of Luke and Acts: A Reassessment of the Evidence*, SNTSMS 145 (Cambridge: Cambridge University Press, 2009), compares the two books' 'seams and summaries' and identifies numerous stylistic differences between them, concluding that Luke and Acts cannot be attributed to a common author. C. K. Rowe, in 'History, Hermeneutics and the Unity of Luke-Acts', *JSNT* 28 (2005): 131–57; and in 'Literary Unity and Reception History: Reading Luke-Acts as Luke and Acts', *JSNT* 29 (2007): 449–57; as well as A. Gregory, 'The Reception of Luke and Acts and the Unity of Luke-Acts', *JSNT* 29 (2007): 459–72, contend that reception history does not support the modern practice of reading the two works together.

141. For an evaluation of and response to the reassessment of the literary unity of Luke-Acts provided by Walters, Rowe, and Gregory, see J. Green, 'Luke-Acts, or Luke and Acts? A Reaffirmation of Narrative Unity', in *Reading Acts Today: Essays in Honour of Loveday C. A. Alexander*, ed. S. Walton, T. E. Phillips, L. K. Pietersen,

Luke planned and wrote Acts as a companion volume and sequel to his Gospel, and that together these fifty-two chapters comprise essentially one complete narrative account.

An important corollary of this literary unity is that Luke 16:19–31 can be read in correlation to the larger corpus, as the parable's themes are echoed and its implications developed in Acts. Situating it within the framework of Luke-Acts, connective elements are developed through such strategies as narrative anticipation,[142] incompletion and gap-filling,[143] prophecy or prediction,[144] and the resolution of thematic tensions or discordances.[145] Reading with attention to these patterns links the parable not only to the immediate context of Jesus's ministry but also to what will ensue in the story of the community in Acts.[146]

While many affirm this unity, the parable's literary connections to what is recounted elsewhere in Luke's two volumes – and especially to what is narrated in Acts – have usually merited little more than a passing mention, and have not been considered for their potential effect on his audience.[147] Because reading the parable within the Luke-Acts context has

---

and F. S. Spencer, LNTS 427 (New York: T&T Clark, 2011), 101–19. P. E. Spencer, 'The Unity of Luke-Acts: A Four-Bolted Hermeneutical Hinge', *CurBR* 5 (2007): 341–66, argues the unity of Luke-Acts is secure, with considerations of genre, narrative, theology, and reception history.

142. Kurz, *Reading Luke-Acts*, 17–36.

143. M. C. Parsons, 'Narrative Closure and Openness in the Plot of the Third Gospel: The Sense of an Ending in Luke 24:50–53', in *Society of Biblical Literature 1986 Seminar Papers*, SBLSP 25 (Missoula, MT: Scholars Press, 1986), 201–23.

144. C. K. Rothschild, *Luke-Acts and the Rhetoric of History: An Investigation of Early Christian Historiography*, WUNT 2/175 (Tübingen: Mohr Siebeck, 2004), 142–84.

145. D. Marguerat, 'The Unity of Luke-Acts: The Task of Reading', in *The First Christian Historian: Writing the 'Acts of the Apostles'*, trans. K. McKinney, G. J. Laughery, and R. Bauckham, SNTSMS 121 (Cambridge: Cambridge University Press, 2002), 43–64; cf. his 'Luc-Actes: Une Unité à Construire', in Verheyden, *Unity of Luke-Acts*, 57–81.

146. A further explanation of these patterns of literary association is provided in Chapter 5.

147. For such passing comments, see, e.g., Tannehill, *Narrative Unity*, 1:186 (on 'bearing witness'); Johnson, *Literary Function*, 110 (on the success of apostolic preaching in Acts); Johnson, 'Narrative Perspectives', 211; Tannehill, *Narrative Unity*, 1:132 (on wealth); Evans, *Luke*, 252 (on repentance); Anderson, *God Raised*, 179 (on the testimony of 'Moses and the prophets'). Hintzen, *Verkündigung*, 368–74, is one of the few to develop the parable's anticipations of later events, focusing on Jesus's resurrection and ascension.

been neglected, Chapter 5 will examine the ways in which this text closely coheres with the Third Gospel and how it anticipates and prepares for Acts. Such a reading can enhance an understanding of authorial purpose, and assist to articulate the possible effects of this parable on the Lukan audience.

8. *Towards a Multi-dimensional Methodology*

While the parable of Lazarus and the Rich Man has suffered no neglect in past studies, our survey has identified several areas for further investigation. In various respects Jülicher set an agenda for the study of this narrative that dominated the discussion for the next one hundred years. His bifurcation of the parable into vv. 19–26 and vv. 17–31 was accepted by many, with a resultant neglect of either the first section as too incomplete to be meaningful, or the second section as too manipulated by later Christian theology to be a reliable Gospel tradition. Similarly, Jülicher's suggestion that the narrative has a background in popular notions of the afterlife prompted a wide-ranging search for cultural parallels and influences. While these investigations are interesting, other germane issues for understanding the parable require attention, and one particularly promising area is the parable's meaning and function within the framework of Luke-Acts.

A parable can be investigated from a variety of methodological perspectives.[148] In order to investigate this parable's meaning and function within Luke-Acts, we will study it with the application of three methods as developed in New Testament studies: the literary perspectives of narrative criticism (Chapter 2), rhetorical criticism (Chapter 3), and intertextuality (Chapter 4). This multi-dimensional approach is a departure from past studies, which have focused on the parable's narrative elements alone, or on matters related to its rhetoric in the Graeco-Roman or Jewish traditions, or on aspects of its intertextuality in relation to the parable's afterlife imagery. It is our contention that no single perspective can offer a definitive reading of the text. Accordingly, we are interested to see whether a plurality of methodological perspectives can be joined to provide a fulsome interpretation of Luke 16:19–31 that offers new

148. T. Penner, 'Madness in the Method? The Acts of the Apostles in Current Study', *CurBR* 2 (2004): 223–93, offers a review of methodological concerns with reference to Acts, though much of what he says also applies to the study of Luke's Gospel; cf. F. S. Spencer, 'Acts and Modern Literary Approaches', in Winter and Clarke, eds., *The Book of Acts in its Ancient Literary Setting*, 381–414.

insights.[149] We will then employ the findings of the various perspectives to concentrate on a significant question that has as yet been unexamined in detail, namely, the relation of the parable to both of Luke's volumes (Chapter 5). We will see that this parable illustrates, anticipates, and advances key aspects of the author's theological interests in Luke-Acts. Finally, we will surmise Luke's purpose in accenting and developing these themes.

149. See Tannehill, *Narrative Unity*, 2:4, 'Methodological pluralism is to be encouraged, for each method will have blind spots that can only be overcome through another approach'; cf. Merenlahti, *Poetics*, 118.

Chapter 2

LUKE 16:19–31 AS NARRATIVE

1. *Hearing Luke's Story*

In the Gospel's preface (1:1–4) Luke speaks of his work as a narrative (διήγησις) which he has recounted with care (ἀκριβῶς καθεξῆς). This attention to crafting an orderly account encourages the audience to read closely the subsequent stories, including the parable of Lazarus and the Rich Man. A cursory glance reveals features that typically constitute a narrative,[1] such as different settings (an urban home with a gate to the outside street, the afterlife), characters (Lazarus, the rich man, Abraham, and the rich man's brothers), and narrative events (dying, being tormented, and dialoguing). What can we discover about Luke's literary artistry and its effect through an examination of this parable with the aid of the tools of narrative criticism?[2]

2. *The Speaker and the Hearers*

2.1. *The Parable's Narrator*

A question that is separate from actual authorship concerns who is relating these words to the audience, and whether this perspective presented to the reader as reliable.[3] While a narrator is most often 'invisible' and does

---

1. See, e.g., R. Alter, *The Art of Biblical Narrative* (London: Allen & Unwin, 1981), and Powell's appendix, 'Using Narrative Criticism in Exegesis', in *Narrative Criticism*, 103–5.

2. See the brief introduction to narrative criticism in Chapter 1, §6.1.

3. Powell, *Narrative Criticism*, 24, explains that if the narrator's perspective is presented as reliable, then accepting the narrator's point of view – norms, values, and general worldview – is essential for understanding the story, as it provides the standards of judgment by which the implied reader evaluates the elements of the narrative. By contrast, J. L. Staley, *The Print's First Kiss: A Rhetorical Investigation of the Implied Reader in the Fourth Gospel*, SBLDS 82 (Atlanta: Scholars Press, 1988), contends that a narrator – in his study, the narrator of John's Gospel – can be unreliable, victimizing the audience by providing unreliable information.

not participate in the events of the story, the narrator remains an essential character, shaping the audience's responses.[4] For Luke-Acts it may be presumed that it has 'a single, omniscient, (usually) third-person, reliable narrator'.[5] The narrator presents this parable as being told by Jesus, a component of his continued teaching of the disciples (16:1), and simultaneously a response to the scoffing Pharisees (16:14).

2.2. *The Parable's Reader*

Exist in the mind of author

Related to the concept of the passage's implied author is its implied reader, for while recounting a narrative the author assumes that the audience will know certain truths or have values that assist in making meaning.[6] The implied reader holds to certain social and cultural norms and possesses a literary proficiency, such that the reader can respond to the text in a meaningful way.[7] Contours of what the Lukan audience was expected to know are discerned through a consideration of Luke-Acts as a whole, drawing inferences from the text and his cultural context.[8] Tyson and others have sketched helpful profiles of the implied reader.[9] For our purposes, we highlight that the audience was likely Greek-speaking; was generally well-educated; had a knowledge of existing social structures; was probably knowledgeable about the practices and institutions of Jewish religion; was familiar with the Hebrew Scriptures in their Greek translation (LXX), and considered them authoritative in terms of what

Not real!

4. J. A. Darr, 'Narrator as Character: Mapping a Reader-Oriented Approach to Narration in Luke-Acts', *Semeia* 63 (1993): 43–60, citing 44.

5. Darr, *Herod the Fox*, 61. Against the view that the Lukan narrator is reliable, J. M. Dawsey, *The Lukan Voice: Confusion and Irony in the Gospel of Luke* (Macon, GA: Mercer University Press, 1986), argues that the narrator's view of Jesus is at odds with Jesus's own conception of his ministry; see the response to Dawsey by Tannehill, *Narrative Unity*, 1:7; Darr, 'Narrator'; S. D. Moore, *Literary Criticism*, 30–34.

6. W. Iser, *The Act of Reading: A Theory of Aesthetic Response* (London: Routledge & Kegan Paul, 1974), 27–38. For a relation of the theory of Iser (among others) to the Synoptic Gospels, see Resseguie, 'Reader-Response', 307–24.

7. Resseguie, 'Reader-Response', 308.

8. Darr, *Character Building*, 27; Luke's reader is 'a culturally literate member of the late first-century Mediterranean world... [one who] is well aware of, indeed lives by, the cultural scripts and norms of that world'.

9. J. B. Tyson, *Images of Judaism in Luke-Acts* (Columbia, SC: University of South Carolina Press, 1992), 35–36; Esler, *Community and Gospel*, 33–45; Downing, 'First Reading', 92–96; cf. Darr, *Character Building*, 26–29; and his *Herod the Fox*, 61–63.

Assumption!

they affirmed, prophesied, and commanded.[10] To clarify the latter characteristic about the knowledge of the Hebrew Scriptures, the implied reader of Luke-Acts is probably not to be understood as Jewish, but as one of the 'God-fearers', or devout Gentiles who were attracted to the Jewish religion.[11]

Adopting Iser's terminology, we have been speaking about the parable's 'readers'. However, we are mindful of the oral character of the culture in which Luke wrote. It is likely that his Gospel's first audience will have heard this narrative in a public reading, not read it in a private setting.[12] This context for the initial dissemination of Luke's work seems to have impacted its design, for it has structural and literary qualities that facilitate listening and remembering.[13] Nevertheless, because the narrative comes in a textual or written form we will alternately speak of the audience as readers and as hearers, those who were expected to respond to the parable in ways consistent with the expectations ascribed to the implied author.[14]

3. *The Lukan Narrative Context*

3.1. *Context of the Gospel*

While Luke 16:19–31 needs to be studied as a unit, it should not be read in isolation from its Luke-Acts context. Luke's claim to have written a carefully ordered narrative necessitates that the Gospel and Acts be

---

10. While Darr agrees with Tyson that the implied reader was familiar with the LXX, he adds that the implied reader is also 'at home in popular Greco-Roman literature' (*Character Building*, 27).

why Palestine ...?

11. Tyson, *Images*, 36.

12. Burridge, 'Gospels and Acts', 529–30. On rates of literacy in first-century Palestine, see C. Keith, *Jesus' Literacy: Scribal Culture and the Teacher from Galilee*, LNTS 413 (New York: T&T Clark, 2011).

13. Rhoads, 'Narrative Criticism', 276. We will return to the oral/aural qualities of Luke-Acts in Chapter 3, where the rhetorical qualities of the parable are examined.

14. The question of Luke's implied audience is to be distinguished from discussions on the identity of Luke's actual audience; see Esler, *Community and Gospel*, 24–33, for the view that Luke-Acts was written for a Christian audience composed largely of Gentile converts; cf. the essays in response to Esler in R. Bauckham, ed., *The Gospels for all Christians: Rethinking the Gospel Audiences* (Grand Rapids: Eerdmans, 1998); and E. W. Klink III, ed., *The Audience of the Gospels: The Origin and Function of the Gospels in Early Christianity*, LNTS 353 (London: T&T Clark, 2010).

read sequentially, completely, and repeatedly in order to understand its component parts.[15] Luke's audience already knows the basic outline and central outcomes of the narrative being recounted (1:1), for these things are described as 'the events that were fulfilled among us' (τῶν πεπληροφορημένων ἐν ἡμῖν πραγμάτων).[16] Luke assists his audience in interpreting these events through the selection, ordering, and emphases of the narrative. A sequential reading reveals that this parable is not the first time that particular themes and motifs are encountered, including poverty and possessions, authoritative Scripture, the patriarch Abraham, repentance, and resurrection. Pre-formed perspectives on these tropes are part of the dynamic involved in listening and responding to this story.

To appreciate the story world of which Luke 16:19–31 is a part, we will rehearse briefly the plotline of the Lukan narrative. Chapters 1 and 2 recount the births of John the Baptist and Jesus, two principal characters for Luke's story. After John's heralding ministry, Jesus's ministry commences with his oration in the Nazareth synagogue in 4:16–21, in which he quotes Isa 61 with reference to himself in 'announcing good news to the poor'. The activities of his Galilean ministry are described in Luke 4–8, until a watershed moment is reached in Luke 9. Having been confessed by Peter as the Christ of God (9:20), Jesus predicts his suffering and death at the hands of the elders, chief priests, and teachers of the law (9:22), and informs his disciples that three days after his death he will be raised to life. Following the appearance of Jesus with Moses and Elijah on a mountain (9:28–36), Luke says in v. 51 that Jesus 'set his face toward Jerusalem', the beginning of a long journey (9:51–19:44).[17] During this

---

15. Powell, 'Narrative Criticism', 244; cf. Johnson, 'Narrative Perspectives', 208. On reading a second, third, or fourth time, see Tannehill, *Narrative Unity*, 1:6; Moloney, 'Narrative Criticism', 191–92, contends that the implied reader is 'able to look back over what has already been told'.

16. Kurz, 'Narrative Approaches', 208–9.

17. A key study of the travel narrative is that of C. F. Evans, 'The Central Section'; see also D. P. Moessner, *Lord of the Banquet: The Literary and Theological Significance of the Lukan Travel Narrative* (Minneapolis: Fortress, 1989). On the structure of this collection, see M. C. Parsons, 'Landmarks Along the Way: The Function of the "L" Parables in the Lukan Travel Narrative', *SwJT* 40 (1997): 33–47; C. L. Blomberg, 'Midrash, Chiasmus, and the Outline of Luke's Central Section', in *Gospel Perspectives III: Studies in Midrash and Historiography*, ed. R. T. France and D. Wenham (Sheffield: JSOT, 1983), 217–62. Johnson, *Literary Function*, contends that in Luke-Acts Jesus is being presented as God's prophet in the model of Moses, a prophet who is rejected and then vindicated; cf. Moessner, 'Luke 9:1–50', 575–605; and his *Lord of the Banquet*. For a critique of this view, see Blomberg, 'Midrash',

journey the majority of the uniquely Lukan parables are told,[18] as Jesus addresses three distinct groups: the anonymous crowd, his disciples, and the religious leaders, whose animosity intensifies as he nears Jerusalem.[19] This context of crisis and escalating opposition heightens the urgency of hearing Jesus's message.[20] Luke's audience is confronted with the challenge of Jesus's words about his identity about being his disciples.[21]

217–62. For a literary outline of the travel narrative, see K. E. Bailey, *Poet and Peasant: A Literary Cultural Approach to the Parables in Luke* (Grand Rapids: Eerdmans, 1976), 79–85.

18. There are eleven illustrative narratives distinctively Lukan, which may be referred to as the 'L' parables: the Two Debtors (7:41–43); the Good Samaritan (10:25–37); the Friend at Midnight (11:5–8); the Rich Fool (12:16–21); the Barren Fig Tree (13:6–9); the Prodigal Son (15:11–32); the Dishonest Steward (16:1–8); Lazarus and the Rich Man (16:19–31); the Dutiful Servant (17:7–10); the Unrighteous Judge (18:2–8); the Pharisee and Tax Collector (18:10–14). When the 'L' parables are viewed as an aggregate, a variety of characteristics typify this collection: many of the parable plots feature characters in crisis, characters in contrast with other characters, a sense of moral ambiguity or subtlety, dialogue, and the theme of reversal. On the characteristics of the Lukan collection of parables, see G. P. Anderson, 'Seeking and Saving What Might Have Been Lost: Luke's Restoration of an Enigmatic Parable Tradition', *CBQ* 70 (2008): 729–49; K. Paffenroth, *The Story of Jesus According to L*, JSNTSup 147 (Sheffield: Sheffield Academic, 1997), 96–104; J. Drury, *The Parables in the Gospels: History and Allegory* (London: SPCK, 1985), 111–25; D. M. Parrott, 'The Dishonest Steward (Luke 16.1–8a) and Luke's Special Parable Collection', *NTS* 37 (1991): 499–515.

19. Johnson, 'Narrative Perspectives', 209.

20. Johnson, *Literary Function*, 152; on this theme of conflict, see F. J. Matera, 'Jesus' Journey to Jerusalem (Luke 9.51–19.46): A Conflict with Israel', *JSNT* 51 (1993): 57–77.

21. A consistent component of Jesus's teaching in the travel narrative is the misuse of possessions. This theme appears just prior to Luke 16, where the parable of the Prodigal Son (15:11–32) presents a portrait of the 'misuse of wealth', according to J. J. Kilgallen in *Twenty Parables of Jesus in the Gospel of Luke* (Rome: Editrice Pontificio Istituto Biblico, 2008), 123; and in 'Luke 15 and 16: A Connection', *Bib* 78 (1997): 367–74. By contrast, Nolland, 'Money and Possessions', argues that while the parable of Lazarus and the Rich Man 'does seem to be about wealth' (189), the parable of the Prodigal Son is *not* about 'attitudes to and the use of money and possessions' (205). Hendrickx observes several textual and structural features linking Chapter 15 to Chapter 16 (*Parables*, 170). On the relationship between the parables of the Prodigal Son and of Lazarus and the Rich Man in Lukan theology, see also H. Roose, 'Umkehr und Ausgleich bei Lukas: die Gleichnisse vom verlorenen Sohn (Lk 15.11–32) und vom reichen Mann und armen Lazarus (Lk 16.19–31) als Schwestergeschichten', *NTS* 56 (2010): 1–21.

As Jesus concludes his journey, the predictions of his rejection and demise are fulfilled in the passion accounts of Luke 22–23. The final narrative events in Luke 24 take place after Jesus's death, when he is resurrected on the third day, commissions his disciples, and ascends into heaven.

3.2. *Context of Luke 16*

In general, Lukan parables are framed within a specific setting in Jesus's ministry, in close association with the surrounding events and teachings.[22] This is true also for the parable of Lazarus and the Rich Man. While its beginning is signalled in 16:19 with a conventional Lukan phrase (ἄνθρωπος δέ τις ἦν), this is the continuation of a section that commenced with Jesus's instruction of his disciples in v. 1 (ἔλεγεν δὲ καὶ πρὸς τοὺς μαθητάς). The parable of the Dishonest Steward in vv. 1–9 includes a patent thematic connection of wealth and possessions to vv. 19–31.[23] The steward has been wasting his master's possessions and will be removed from his position (vv. 1–2). However, before giving a final accounting, he reduces the amounts owed to his master by debtors, with the design of securing their favour when the steward is unemployed (vv. 3–7). Learning of his behaviour (v. 8), the master commends him for acting shrewdly (φρονίμως). This commendation is echoed by Jesus's words in v. 9 about using worldly wealth to gain friends on earth, with the result of being received in eternal dwellings (δέξωνται ὑμᾶς εἰς τὰς αἰωνίους σκηνάς). The audience will see in vv. 19–31 that this was exactly the rich man's failure: irresponsible and uncharitable conduct with one's possessions.

Following the parable of the Dishonest Steward, vv. 10–12 speak of the handling of 'unrighteous mammon' (ἀδίκῳ μαμωνᾷ) as an essential indicator of one's ability to handle true riches. Johnson summarizes, 'The way a man handles possessions, the attitude he assumes towards possessions, is not irrelevant to his inner response to God but expresses in the

---

22. S. Curkpatrick, 'Parable Metonymy and Luke's Kerygmatic Framing', *JSNT* 25 (2003): 289–307, argues that the Lukan parables would be ineffectually ambiguous without the narrative framing provided by Luke.

23. J. D. Derrett, *Law in the New Testament* (London: Darton, Longman & Todd, 1970), 80, 85–86. Story, 'Parables of Stewardship', argues that the two parables in Luke 16 should be understood together with their call to responsible stewardship in the present with a view to the future; this call is illustrated positively by the manager (vv. 1–8) and negatively by the rich man (vv. 19–31); cf. M. Ball, 'The Parables of the Unjust Steward and the Rich Man and Lazarus', *ExpTim* 106 (1995): 329–30; and A. Feuillet, 'La parable du Mauvais Riche et du Pauvre Lazare', *NRT* 101 (1979): 212–23, for the correlation between the two parables.

most vivid and concrete manner the quality of that response'.[24] Jesus's
declaration in v. 13 that one cannot serve God and mammon anticipates
the rich man's need for repentance because of his slavish devotion to
worldly wealth.[25]

The subject matter of the context continues to cohere well in vv. 14–
18, when an interlude is initiated by the Pharisees' response to Jesus's
words.[26] Scholars puzzle over the function of these intervening verses.[27] It
is asserted that they are unrelated to what follows,[28] and that they evince
an uncharacteristic lack of literary skill on Luke's part.[29] Because there is
no narrative partition but rather a link provided by the Pharisee's response
to Jesus and his rejoinder, we conclude that vv. 14–18 belong to the same
unit of thematic material and prepare for the narrative of vv. 19–31.[30]
Jesus derides the Pharisees for self-justifying hypocrisy (v. 15), a charge
that could simultaneously be leveled against the rich man for valuing
highly what is detestable (βδέλυγμα) to God. Jesus then announces the
end of the epoch of law and prophecy in the person of John the Baptist
(v. 16).[31] The point of the law's abrogation is partially modified in vv. 17–
18, where its abiding validity is proclaimed.[32] The theme of law is reprised
by Abraham in the parable where there is an implied reference to the
Scriptures' directives to support the poor.[33]

Another important factor of the Luke 16 context is the parable's
addressees. Jesus addresses his disciples in 16:1; the implication is that
they continue listening after v. 14, where we learn of the presence of
the Pharisees.[34] They hear Jesus's words about faithfulness in handling

24. Johnson, *Literary Function*, 158.
25. Karris, 'Poor and Rich', 122.
26. See the discussion in Chapter 5, §4.3.2.
27. See, e.g., Dupont, *Les Béatitudes*, 3:164–67.
28. J. T. Sanders, *The Jews in Luke-Acts* (London: SCM, 1987), 202–3.
29. W. R. Farmer, 'Notes on a Literary and Form-Critical Analysis of Some of the Synoptic Material Peculiar to Luke', *NTS* 8 (1962): 301–16, citing 309–10.
30. Hendrickx, *Parables*, argues that the parable is not without an introduction, but it comes in 16:14, about 'lovers of money' (172); cf. Kilgallen, *Twenty Parables*, 124; and R. A. Piper, 'Social Background and Thematic Structure in Luke 16', in Van Segbroeck et al., *Four Gospels 1992*, 2:1637–62.
31. On the question of the law in Luke-Acts, see O'Toole, *Unity*, 24–6; Jervell, *People of God*, 136–37; Wilson, *Luke and the Law*; and Blomberg, 'Law in Luke-Acts'.
32. D. E. Garland, *Luke* (Grand Rapids: Zondervan, 2012), 674.
33. Johnson, 'Narrative Perspectives', 210.
34. Wright, 'Poverty and Riches', 220; he argues further that the narrative does not give reason to assume that the tax collectors and sinners (15:1) had departed.

possessions, and respond by ridiculing him (ἐξεμυκτήριζον αὐτόν).[35] If it was not so pejorative, the narrator's comment that the Pharisees are 'lovers of money' (φιλάργυροι ὑπάρχοντες) could almost be termed parenthetical.[36] However, this characterization is consistent with their portrayal in the preceding narrative.[37] After appearing in an early series of disputes (5:17–6:11), they are described as rejecting God's purpose for themselves (7:30), and are rebuked for greed and covetousness (11:39–40). In desire for honour they have exalted themselves (11:43; cf. 14:7), and rejected those who were considered public sinners (15:1–2). Because of their love of wealth and honour, their banquets are not for the poor (14:7–14),[38] in the same way that the rich man dines sumptuously without thought for Lazarus. As such, the parable amplifies the themes of 16:14–15, 'that wealth is not necessarily a sign of righteousness'.[39] Coming as it does after a series of confrontations with the Pharisees, the parable is ostensibly told for their sake.[40] But within Luke's implied audience, any wealthy person neglectful of the poor is targeted by the narrative's message.[41]

Following the parable we are not told of a response from Jesus's listeners, whether by the Pharisees or the disciples. In 17:1 Luke signals a change of audience, as Jesus addresses specifically the disciples.

35. Green, 'Narrative Criticism', 99; cf. Tannehill, *Narrative Unity*, 1:181. That the Pharisees are noted as being within the immediate audience can be compared with the Luke 15 parables, described as being told in response to their grumbling that Jesus eats with tax collectors and sinners (15:1–3). Cf. Anderson, 'Seeking and Saving', 737, who notes the Lukan use of narrative audience in 16:14 as giving interpretive direction to the parable's reader.

36. There is some difficulty in understanding the sense in which the Pharisees were lovers of money, since historically, they were not associated with the possession of wealth. Green, 'Narrative Criticism', 102, notes that this should be understood as 'a slur…to label others as concerned with self-aggrandizement'.

37. See D. B. Gowler, *Host, Guest, Enemy, and Friend: Portraits of the Pharisees in Luke and Acts* (New York: Lang, 1991); cf. his 'A Dialogic Reading', 252–55; Green, *Theology*, 70–75; S. Mason, 'Chief Priests, Sadducees, Pharisees and Sanhedrin in Acts', in *The Book of Acts in Its Palestinian Setting*, ed. R. Bauckham, BAFCS 4 (Grand Rapids: Eerdmans, 1995), 115–77.

38. See L. Schottroff, *The Parables of Jesus*, trans. L. M. Maloney (Minneapolis: Fortress, 2006), 164.

39. C. H. Talbert, *Reading Luke: A Literary and Theological Commentary* (New York: Crossroad, 1982), 156.

40. P. Minear, 'Jesus' Audiences, according to Luke', *NovT* 16 (1974): 81–109, observes that Luke brings together 'four units of tradition' in 16:14–31 that find different audiences in the other Gospels and addresses these units to the Pharisees.

41. Tyson, *Images*, 73.

Who are
you disagreeing
with?

Who are your interlocutors?

This is accompanied by a shift from the theme of possessions, as Jesus teaches about forgiveness and faith (17:1–10). For the moment, there is a suspension in the developing conflict between the Pharisees and Jesus.

3.3. *Context of Luke-Acts*

This parable is heard not only within Luke's account of Jesus's ministry, but his broader work relating the events after Jesus's resurrection and ascension. We have argued that Luke-Acts is literarily and thematically unified,[42] and that the audience listens in order to better comprehend the import of Jesus's life.[43] Thus when Acts begins, Luke is pressing forward the theological agenda that has dominated his narrative since Luke 1. Within the context of this two-volume narrative, we may expect to see forms of connection from the parable to the story of the early believers. Because of the detailed nature of such a study, we will investigate this wider Lukan context in a subsequent chapter.[44]

4. *The Parable's Narrative Setting*

Luke 16:19–31 has narrative setting in terms of space, time, and social location. The parable is marked by two principal scenes: the first scene, described in vv. 19–21, contrasts the rich man and Lazarus in their earthly positions by juxtaposing the former's great wealth with the latter's acute physical need; the second scene, described in vv. 22–31, continues the contrast by depicting them in their respective eternal habitations of torment and beatitude.

4.1. *Setting: Separated by a Gate*

The parable's first scene features contrasting details of luxury and penury in the physical circumstances of the rich man and Lazarus. Already their spatial setting reveals differing social statuses. Lazarus is stationed at the rich man's house, a position indicative of his expectation of receiving

---

42. See the discussion of Luke-Acts unity in Chapter 1, §7.

43. See J. B. Green, 'Internal Repetition in Luke-Acts: Contemporary Narratology and Lucan Historiography', in *History, Literature and Society in the Book of Acts*, ed. B. Witherington III (Cambridge: Cambridge University Press, 1996), 283–99, citing 287–88. Green builds on the work of G. W. Trompf, *The Idea of Historical Recurrence in Western Thought: From Antiquity to the Reformation* (Berkeley, CA: University of California Press, 1979), especially 116–79; Trompf situates Luke's internal repetitions within the context of Hellenistic historiography.

44. See the discussion in Chapter 5.

relief from someone with the physical means to help. He is at the gate
(ὁ πυλών) or the opening in the wall that likely enclosed the rich man's
house (v. 20).[45] Here Lazarus has been 'thrown down', which is also
suggestive of physical disability.[46] Unknown individuals have placed him
there, and it is unclear whether he is able to move independently.[47] While
the gate prevents Lazarus from entering to receive the scraps of food from
the rich man's table (v. 21), the rich man would be anticipated to emerge
here regularly from his house, at which time Lazarus might entreat him for
assistance.[48] Meanwhile, the rich man enjoys the physical benefits of his
position, such as relishing his daily fare (v. 19). As a physical obstruction
the gate also prevents the rich man from seeing Lazarus, and thereby
from being confronted with the need to respond.[49] The spatial separation
established by the gate serves as a symbol of the division between the two
men; the rich man is 'inside', Lazarus is 'outside'.[50] While the division
is unmistakable and has real consequence for Lazarus, the audience will
recognize that the barrier is not insurmountable.

4.2. *Setting: Separated by a Chasm*

The parable's second narrative scene, after the deaths of Lazarus and
the rich man, continues the depiction of starkly differentiated settings.
The setting is no longer an urban residence and street, but the afterlife
with its own geographical features.[51] It is notable that within Luke-Acts,
the dominant setting of narrative events is on earth. Even the arrival
or departure of angels (Luke 1:11, 26) or the ascension of Jesus into

45. For the architecture of such gates, see BDAG, 897, s.v. πυλών; cf. A. Plummer,
A Critical and Exegetical Commentary on the Gospel According to S. Luke, ICC, 5th
ed. (Edinburgh: T. & T. Clark, 1901), 391.

46. J. B. Green, *The Gospel of Luke*, NICNT (Grand Rapids: Eerdmans, 1997),
606.

47. According to Metzger, *Consumption and Wealth*, 139 n. 113, the pluperfect
passive ἐβέβλητο suggests that Lazarus is not laid at the gate each morning, but
having been laid there once long ago, 'this is now his permanent home'.

48. Tannehill, *Narrative Unity*, 1:131.

49. See an analysis of the gate's significance in Schnider and Stenger, 'Die offene
Tür', 273–83.

50. Scott, *Hear Then*, 150–51. By contrast, V. Tanghe, 'Abraham, son fils et son
envoyé (Luc 16:19–31)', *RB* 91 (1984): 557–77, sees the division between Lazarus
and the rich man symbolized not by existence on two sides of a gate, but by the
contrast between the gate and table (565–67).

51. Pax, 'Milieustudie', 254–68, highlights this change in scenery from earth to
Hades.

heaven (Luke 24:51; Acts 1:9) are viewed from an earthly perspective.[52] Contrasted with this earth-bound viewpoint, the parable is unique with its account of the locales and circumstances of an afterlife.[53] The setting of urban life was recognizable to Luke's audience,[54] but while aspects of the afterlife setting may have accorded with the audience's conceptions from Second Temple Judaism,[55] this memorable staging will likely have had a dramatic effect on the parable's hearers.

Augmenting this effect is how the contrast in social settings depicted in the first scene is radically reversed in the second.[56] In v. 22 Lazarus is described as being in 'the bosom of Abraham' (τὸν κόλπον Ἀβραάμ), an image suggestive of individual protection and provision.[57] As for the rich man, he is in Hades (ὁ ἅδης, v. 23) where there are flames (φλογός, v. 24).[58] The two locales are separated by a great distance (v. 23), for the rich man sees Abraham 'from afar'. During their conversation, Abraham in v. 26 points out to the rich man that between them is fixed a 'great chasm' (χάσμα μέγα) which cannot be crossed, though the rich man will request it. His destiny is truly unalterable.[59] Johnson notes the narrative importance suggested by the spatial detail of the abyss: 'In every respect… there is the great divide between the rewarded and the punished'.[60]

52. An exception may be Stephen's glimpse of Jesus standing at the right hand of God (Acts 7:56), but this too is described from a terrestrial vantage point.

53. J. D. Kingsbury, *Conflict in Luke: Jesus, Authorities, Disciples* (Minneapolis: Fortress, 1991), 2; cf. Huffman, 'Atypical Features', 215.

54. See Tyson, *Images*, 24–26, for evidence of audience familiarity with the towns of Judea, particularly Jerusalem.

55. See Bauckham, *Fate of the Dead*; in particular, 'Descents to the Underworld', 9–48; 'Early Jewish Visions of Hell', 49–80; and 'Visiting the Places of the Dead in the Extra-Canonical Apocalypses', 81–96. Cf. also Lehtipuu, *Afterlife Imagery*, 119–54, 197–230; Lehtipuu, 'Lukan Afterworld', 133–46; Griffiths, 'Cross-cultural Eschatology', 7–12; Bishop, 'Yawning Chasm', 3–5.

56. York, *Reversal*, 67–68.

57. R. C. Tannehill, *Luke* (Nashville, TN: Abingdon, 1996), 252. Such a characterization is based on the description of Abraham's bosom in *T. Abr.* 20:14, where 'there is no toil, no grief, no mourning, but peace, exultation and endless life'; cf. *4 Macc.* 13:17. Abraham's generous hospitality is noted in Gen 18:1–15 and celebrated in later Jewish literature.

58. While views of Hades were fluid in Second Temple Judaism, in the parable Hades is the place where the rich man is 'experiencing torments' (ὑπάρχων ἐν βασάνοις). Besides 16:23, see the occurrence of ἅδης in Luke 10:15 and Acts 2:27, 31.

59. Schottroff and Stegemann, *Hope of the Poor*, 25.

60. L. T. Johnson, *The Gospel of Luke*, SP 3 (Collegeville, MN: Liturgical, 1991), 253.

In sum, the afterlife staging demonstrates the significance of the issues at stake.[61] Already before the reasons for the rich man's condemnation and Lazarus's reward are intimated (v. 25), this setting helps the listener to evaluate the relative worth of their ways of life. The audience knows there is a weighty consequence to a reception of the parable's message, and the narrative setting heightens interest in the events that are unfolding.[62]

5. *The Parable's Discourse*

Paralleling the change in settings from the present life to the afterlife, and from an urban landscape to an otherworldly landscape, is a change in discourse.[63] The first part (vv. 19–23) is narrated discourse, where the positions, appearances, events and outcomes of Lazarus and the rich man are described. The second part (vv. 24–31) is marked by direct discourse between the two men.[64] This shift reduces the parable's narrative distance, as the listener is brought close to the action instead of observing the characters in their respective positions. This signals the importance of what is said between the rich man and Abraham.[65]

Attendant with the shift in narrative discourse is a change in the narrative subject, or focalizer.[66] The principal subject of the first part is Lazarus and the details of his suffering (vv. 20–21). But for the entirety of the dialogue between the rich man and Abraham, Lazarus is mute. The subject of the second part is the rich man, as the audience hears of his despair in the flames of Hades, and the tenacity with which he requests a messenger.[67] As with the reduction of narrative distance, this change fosters the parable's dramatic effect and underscores its message for the 'money-loving' Pharisees in Jesus's immediate vicinity, and those in the Lukan audience.

---

61. Maddox, *Purpose*, 103, comments that the parable '[dramatizes] pictorially the seriousness of each individual's responsibility for his conduct during his lifetime'.

62. See Lehtipuu, *Afterlife Imagery*, 264, who contends that Luke's eschatology is always subservient to his paraenesis. This conclusion is similar to that reached by I. H. Marshall, 'How Did the Early Christians Know Anything about Future States?', *JEBS* 9 (2009): 7–23, citing 12.

63. See the division represented in Roth, *Character Types*, 188–89.

64. Schnider and Stenger, 'Die offene Tür', 275–83, speak of the narrated world of vv. 19–23 and the dialogical world of vv. 24–31.

65. Tolbert, *Perspectives*, 75.

66. See Marguerat and Bourquoin, *Bible Stories*, 74.

67. Roth, *Character Types*, 190, argues that the entire parable concentrates on the rich man, with attention given to his reversal, post-mortem agony, and dialogue with Abraham.

6. The Parable's Characters and Characterization

6.1. The Construction of Character

Essential to the interpretation of a narrative is a readerly reflection on the characters. A character is a construct of the implied author, an image created to fulfill a particular role in the story.[68] In general, characters correspond to reality, while also having a unique existence as a product of their literary environment.[69] The author tells about a character and guides the audience response through commenting on a character's moral qualities. Absent overt characterization, the audience makes inferences and evaluations based on more indirect elements,[70] such as the character's words, deeds, and thoughts.[71] In order for the listener to interpret characters, it is necessary to take into account a number of factors,[72] including narrative sequence and inter-character relationships.[73] Sequence is an important

68. S. Chatman, *Story and Discourse: Narrative Structure in Fiction and Film* (Ithaca, NY: Cornell University Press, 1980), 137; cf. also F. Kermode, *The Genesis of Secrecy: On the Interpretation of Narrative* (Cambridge, MA: Harvard University Press, 1979), 77, who observes that character generates narrative, just as narrative generates character.

69. Chatman, *Story and Discourse*, 119; cf. C. Bennema, 'A Theory of Character in the Fourth Gospel with Reference to Ancient and Modern Literature', *BibInt* 17 (2009): 375–421; and C. Skinner, *John and Thomas – Gospels in Conflict? Johannine Characterization and the Thomas Question*, Princeton Theological Monograph Series 115 (Eugene, OR: Wipf & Stock, 2009), 24–27, on a mimetic or realist versus functional or purist understanding of character. For a recent revaluation of characterization, see S. D. Moore, 'Why There Are No Humans or Animals in the Gospel of Mark', in *Mark as Story: Retrospect and Prospect*, ed. K. R. Iverson and C. W. Skinner, SBLRBS 65 (Leiden: Brill, 2011), 71–93.

70. M. Sternberg, *The Poetics of Biblical Narrative: Ideological Literature and the Drama of Reading* (Bloomington, IN: Indiana University Press, 1985), 322.

71. Alter, *Biblical Narrative*, 116–17, notes several factors, both direct and indirect, that can reveal character. Sternberg, *Poetics*, 475–81, describes how the Bible shapes a response to character and event through a rhetorical repertoire (e.g. evaluation of an agent or action, a single epithet, loaded language, explicit judgment, dramatization, inside view of characters, play of perspectives); cf. Darr, *Character Building*, 43; Merenlahti, *Poetics*, 77–97.

72. Darr, *Herod the Fox*, 65, says an approach to characterization must be holistic and contextual, sequential and cumulative, rhetorical, and sensitive to extratextual factors; cf. his *Character Building*, 37–50.

73. In addition to these factors, Gowler, 'Characterization', 54, argues for a socio-narratological approach to characterization, averring that characters in ancient literature are incomprehensible without understanding the cultural processes and codes which influence the text (54).

factor because character is cumulative; the audience must be conscious of the degree to which a character has been constructed up to that stage of the story. Relationships are also essential to understanding a narrative, for it is through interaction that 'characters serve "to reveal other characters"'.[74] To these dynamics we will return below.

In the parable are three principal personages: the rich man, Lazarus, and Abraham. To this list of characters we add the rich man's five brothers; though absent and not having an active role in the plot, they are referred to by both the rich man and Abraham and thus have a narrative function.[75] What then does the audience learn from this parable's characters? We begin with a consideration of Lazarus.[76]

6.1.1. *The Characters: Lazarus*

6.1.1.1. *Physical Description of the Poor Man*. From the parable's first words, the audience is invited to place in parallel the rich man in v. 19 (ἄνθρωπος δέ τις ἦν πλούσιος) and Lazarus in v. 20 (πτωχὸς δέ τις).[77] Lazarus is described as a poor man or a beggar, and his physical description confirms this soubriquet. As mentioned, he has been 'thrown down' (ἐβέβλητο) at the rich man's gate.[78] As for his external appearance, he is covered in sores (εἱλκωμένος). It is questionable if this was leprosy, as he is still allowed to beg in public.[79] However, such a skin condition would likely cause him physical pain, and his unappealing appearance would also contribute to social marginalization. Sitting at the gate, v. 21 tells us that he is unable to fend off the feral dogs, who lick his sores.[80] Rather than giving relief, such attention will not have been welcome,

74. Darr, *Herod the Fox*, 72.

75. F. W. Burnett, 'Characterization and Reader Construction of Characters in the Gospels', *Semeia* 63 (1993): 3–28, citing 4, asserts that in the reading process, 'even secondary characters may momentarily achieve "individuality"'.

76. Sternberg's observation about characterization in the Bible is particularly apt for this parable, 'The Bible is a reticent text...but even a single tale of about 400 words brings to bear a range of persuasion that few literary works could emulate' (*Poetics*, 481).

77. To the name Λάζαρος we will return below; see §6.1.1.3 and this chapter's Excursus.

78. The action (passive of βάλλω) is often descriptive of those sick persons who are confined to bed (e.g. Matt 8:6, 14; Mark 7:30); see BDAG, 163, s.v.

79. See Lev 13:45–46.

80. The unlikely suggestion has been made that instead of being feral, the dogs belonged to the rich man and that they enjoyed the morsels that Lazarus cannot receive (Derrett, *Law*, 89); cf. the discussion in Hock, 'Lazarus and Micyllus', 458 n. 41.

as dogs were considered unclean animals.[81] The overall aspect of his character makes clear that within the social setting of the ancient world he is classed among the 'expendables'.[82]

While Lazarus is an obvious object of charity, his hunger is not being relieved. In v. 21 his longing to have even a small share in the rich man's food is dramatically described: to eat even 'the crumbs from the table' (τῶν πιπτόντων ἀπὸ τῆς τραπέζης).[83] As Derrett describes, 'Lazarus wishes to enter the Rich Man's house in the meanest possible capacity, as a scavenger'.[84] Perhaps he can hear the celebrations taking place within, or smell the food that is being served; certainly he can picture scraps of food falling from the rich man's table as he dines. Yet Lazarus is prevented from collecting this potential sustenance by at least two obstacles, his physical condition and the gate of separation, with a possible third: the rich man's apparent unwillingness to allow the beggar to satisfy his hunger.

6.1.1.2. *Audience Response to the Poor Man.* How is the implied reader to evaluate the character of the poor man? In itself the epithet πτωχός does not convey a moral judgment; Lazarus has no personality, whether base or honourable.[85] He merely exists, first in his poverty, then at Abraham's side; he does not speak, and does not act. Even when the rich man, later tormented in the fire of Hades, attempts to prompt Lazarus to bring refreshment, he does so through Abraham. Because of Lazarus's passivity in the parable, no personal or ideological point of view can be attributed to him.[86] The reason for being rewarded as described by Abraham in v. 25 does not have an explicit religious-ethical basis, nor is there an intimation that the narrator is exhorting the audience to be like Lazarus. The lurid description of his poverty might even elicit readerly aversion, as destitution could be interpreted as a sign of God's curse on the wicked.[87]

81. See Lev 11:27; cf. F. Bovon, *Das Evangelium nach Lukas*, vol. 3, EKKNT (Zurich: Benziger, 2001), 108.

82. Green, *Luke*, 605; cf. G. E. Lenski, *Power and Privilege: A Theory of Social Stratification*, 2nd ed. (Chapel Hill: University of North Carolina Press, 1984), 281–84.

83. Such knowledge of a character's innermost thoughts is indicative of an omniscient narrator (Gowler, 'Characterization', 55).

84. Derrett, *Law*, 89.

85. Roth, *Character Types*, 190.

86. Ibid.

87. See, e.g., Deut 28:15, 18, 38, 48; Prov 6:10–11; 10:4; cf. the discussion in Chapter 4, §§4.1.2 and 4.3.1. D. H. Reinstorf, 'The Rich, the Poor, and the Law', *HTS* 60 (2004): 329–48, makes the startling inference that since poverty was God's punishment of the disobedient, the people were excused from supporting poor neighbours (345).

Which one?

How does πτωχός mean that?

An essential aid in reconstructing a readerly response to the parable's
πτωχός is the narrative context. While Lazarus has not appeared previously in the Third Gospel, the sequential and cumulative characterization
of the poor by Luke makes this word πτωχός suggestive. From an early
juncture in the Third Gospel attention is given to the poor, who are
promised favour from God.[88] Luke's use of the term πτωχός conveys
the understanding that God's grace is given to not just the economically disadvantaged, but to the sick, the blind, the demon-possessed,
and the prisoners.[89] In particular, Jesus's prior words about the reversal
of status and position for the rich and poor would resonate.[90] Sitting
outside the rich man's gate Lazarus has been described as longing to
be filled (χορτασθῆναι) with food; this is a narrative echo of what the
poor and hungry are promised by Jesus in 6:21, 'You shall be filled'
(χορτασθήσεσθε). As the opening scene is portrayed (vv. 19–21) and
before the afterlife outcomes are detailed (vv. 22–23), the audience
might question the veracity of what Luke has told them to expect, for
the rich man is supplied with everything while the poor man seems to
go without. But while satisfaction does not come in this life, upon dying
in v. 25 Lazarus receives his comfort (παρακαλεῖται). The audience is
being persuaded to see the truth of Jesus's declarations, and to respond
appropriately. Portrayed in his condition of helplessness, suffering, and
marginalization, Lazarus is a credible character type of the poor. Within
the Lukan narrative he may be understood as representative of the needy
who are objects of God's special care.

6.1.1.3. *The Name 'Lazarus'.* We return to a final aspect of the poor
man's characterization: his name. He is introduced as πτωχὸς δέ τις
ὀνόματι Λάζαρος. It has frequently been noted that Lazarus is the only
character in the Lukan parables – or any of the parables in the Synoptic
Gospels – who is not nameless. Tucker points out that this observation
is not entirely accurate, for the same parable includes a character named
'Abraham', one of the patriarchs of Israel.[91] However, Abraham appears
repeatedly in Luke's Gospel, where he has a central theological function as
the recipient of God's covenant promises.[92] Consequently, the assignation
of the name Lazarus must still be considered exceptional. As mentioned

88. See, e.g., the Song of Mary in 1:46–55.

89. See 4:16–19; 6:20–26; 7:22–23; see the discussion in Seccombe, *Possessions*,
27–38; cf. Green, 'Narrative Criticism', 105.

90. See, e.g., Luke 1:51–53; 6:20–26; cf. York, *Reversal*, 70.

91. J. T. Tucker, *Example Stories: Perspectives on Four Parables in the Gospel
of Luke*, JSNTSup 162 (Sheffield: Sheffield Academic, 1998), 249.

92. See the discussion in §6.1.3 of this chapter.

above, the name has attracted many suggestions as to its meaning.[93] We will examine one favoured explanation, before reading the name from a narrative-critical perspective.

An ancient and still prevalent approach is to explain Λάζαρος by means of its etymology.[94] The name is a Grecized and abbreviated form of the Hebrew or Aramaic אֶלְעָזָר,[95] which means 'God helps/has helped'.[96] Snodgrass captures the import of this reading of Λάζαρος: 'It signifies God's identification with the poor and does not permit the hearer to think Lazarus is cursed because of his condition. He is poor and miserable, but God is still on his side.'[97] As observed earlier, there is no explicit mention of Lazarus's faith, piety, or any other grounds for his afterlife reward. The reading of his name as 'God helps' is sometimes understood to imply the righteousness of Lazarus,[98] or to be an appropriate designation for a person who is rewarded for his poverty.[99]

While the etymologically based explanation appears to resolve the disputed matter of why Lazarus is rewarded in the afterlife, it falters on the question of whether Luke's audience will have understood the Hebrew or Aramaic background of Λάζαρος.[100] First, returning to the portrait of

---

93. See the discussion in this chapter's Excursus. Snodgrass, *Stories*, 729 n. 196, notes that characters are typically unnamed in Graeco-Roman or Jewish parables, but occasionally feature a named character. He cites Plato's *Phaedrus* 2.5, and *Gen. Rab.* 65.11; in the rabbinic tale, however, the name is given an explicit narrative function: a woman names her dwarf son 'Tallswift'.

94. This interpretation has been advocated from an early period, e.g., by Jerome in his homilies 'On Lazarus and Dives' (as noted in Just, *Luke*, 260–64). In more recent scholarship, see, e.g., Grundmann, *Lukas*, 327; Jeremias, *Parables*, 183–85; York, *Reversal*, 67; Bock, *Luke*, 2:1365–66; Garland, *Luke*, 669; Blomberg, *Parables*, 259; Ernst, *Lukas*, 474; Johnson, *Luke*, 252; Schnider and Stenger, 'Die offene Tür', 277; S. I. Wright, *Jesus the Storyteller* (London: SPCK, 2014), 130.

95. R. Bauckham, *Jesus and the Eyewitnesses: The Gospels as Eyewitness Testimony* (Grand Rapids: Eerdmans, 2006), 85, notes that Lazarus/Eleazar was the third most common male name among Palestinian Jews from 330 BCE to 200 CE; he cites T. Ilan and T. Ziem, *Lexicon of Jewish Names in Late Antiquity*, Part 1, TSAJ 91 (Tübingen: Mohr Siebeck, 2002), a collection of the recorded names in the period of 330 BCE–200 CE. For the list of popular names, see *Lexicon*, 56.

96. J. Nolland, *Luke*, vol. 2, WBC 35b (Dallas: Word, 1993), 828; cf. Str-B, 2:223.

97. Snodgrass, *Stories*, 429.

98. G. W. Forbes, *The God of Old: The Role of the Lukan Parables in the Purpose of Luke's Gospel*, JSNTSup 198 (Sheffield: Sheffield Academic, 2000), 193.

99. Hays, *Wealth Ethics*, 155.

100. M. D. Goulder, *Luke: A New Paradigm*, vol. 2, JSNTSup 20 (Sheffield: JSOT, 1989), 638.

Luke's implied audience, we observe that a knowledge of Aramaic or Hebrew does not seem to be assumed.[101] For instance, in some passages in Acts the author provides the meaning of Aramaic and Hebrew names,[102] presumably when they are deemed important for the reader to understand.[103] Such names are not translated in other Lukan passages.[104] From this evidence we can surmise that the name Λάζαρος in its Hebrew or Aramaic equivalent would not have significance to the audience, or its etymology would have been explained.[105] Secondly, this particular name would be just as appropriate in being applied to other hapless characters in the Lukan parables.[106] These two factors argue against the name's etymology being determinative for its interpretation. The etymological explanation of Λάζαρος is therefore not satisfactory.

Good

A different approach to Λάζαρος is to evaluate it from the perspective of narrative criticism.[107] In general, a proper name is vital to characterization in fiction. It is often the first attribute of a character, distinguishing him or her from their environment; a name is also an attribute that remains unchanged, unlike other characteristics or qualities.[108] If clan or family

101. Tyson, *Images*, 29.

102. See Acts 1:19 (Akeldama); 4:36 (Barnabas); 9:36 (Dorcas); 13:8 (Elymas). This is a pattern that Parsons and Pervo identify as a differentiation in the style between Luke and Acts, where 'the narrator of Acts translates the names of characters as a means of identifying them' unlike in Luke (*Rethinking*, 69).

103. Lehtipuu, *Afterlife Imagery*, 164.

104. E.g. Acts 1:23; 15:22.

105. Lehtipuu, 'Characterization', 90; cf. J. P. Meier, *A Marginal Jew*, vol. 2, ABRL (New York: Doubleday, 1994), 825; Hock, 'Lazarus and Micyllus', 454.

106. See, e.g., the man attacked by robbers in the Good Samaritan (10:25–37), or the humble tax collector in the Pharisee and the Tax Collector (18:10–14); cf. Meier, *Marginal Jew*, 2:825.

107. Lehtipuu examines the parable from this perspective in 'Characterization'. With respect to the use of the name Λάζαρος, she concludes it is a vital handle for the dialogue between Abraham and the rich man, and personalizes the poor man, helping the reader to sympathize with him, in contrast to the rich man (89–90).

108. T. Docherty, *Reading (Absent) Character: Towards a Theory of Characterization in Fiction* (Oxford: Clarendon, 1983), 43–45; cf. Burnett, 'Reader Construction', 17. Working with Docherty's perspective into naming and anonymity, D. R. Beck, 'The Narrative Function of Anonymity in Fourth Gospel Characterization', *Semeia* 63 (1993): 143–58, notes the significant textual treatment that is given to several anonymous characters in the Gospel of John, and how these characters draw the reader into subjective participation in the narrative; cf. Skinner, *John and Thomas*, 34–35, on how anonymous characters in the Gospel of John function differently than in the Synoptics.

names indicate a variety of things, such as origins, place in class structure and ritual order, personal names are only marginally less saturated with meaning.[109] In this connection, the Hebrew Bible's assignation of proper names to persons who would otherwise be peripheral or insignificant to a narrative is a unique phenomenon; many characters in the literatures of the ancient world remain anonymous.[110] In Sternberg's words, 'To remain nameless is to remain faceless, with hardly a life of one's own. Accordingly, a character's emergence from anonymity may correlate with a rise in importance'.[111] Even when a name's etymology is provided, such etymology is not everything that can be said about a character, since aspects of character are revealed by other means.[112]

If the Hebrew Bible is exceptional in affording proper names to insignificant characters in narrative, the example of Lazarus is still more exceptional. Even in the biblical tradition it is unusual to have an entirely passive and silent individual who is identified with a name, as Lazarus is. Though the reader might wonder what would be different if the poor man was not named, apparently innocuous references to a character – including a character's name – raise specific expectations and invite a filling-in process.[113] As characters in biblical narratives are evaluated, any textual silence is an encouragement to fill the gaps.[114] In the case of Lazarus, of whom so little is attributed, the audience must read his name within the parameters suggested by Luke's Gospel.[115]

With what, then, is the character 'Lazarus' to be filled? While Lazarus's physical circumstances are bleak, and while his personality is devoid of features either base or noble, the naming honours him in a way that is consistent with the rest of Luke's Gospel. Unexpectedly – even undeservedly – honoured with a name, Lazarus is understood as representative of the needy who are the objects of God's special care through Jesus. A name has conferred being and status on this poor man.[116] The carefully constructed contrast between the poor man and the rich man

109. B. Hochman, *Character in Literature* (Ithaca, NY: Cornell University Press, 1985), 37.
110. Sternberg, *Poetics*, 329–30.
111. Ibid., 330.
112. Ibid., 331.
113. Darr, *Character Building*, 44; cf. Docherty, *Reading Character*, 47.
114. Merenlahti, *Poetics*, 80.
115. Sternberg, *Poetics*, 188–89, insists that any 'gap-filling' carried out by a reader in constructing the world of a literary work must not be arbitrary, but legitimated by the text through its language and perceptual set.
116. Sternberg, *Poetics*, 330.

in vv. 19–22 thus anticipates the eschatological reversal toward which
the parable is building: Lazarus is known, while the rich man is not.[117]
Within the parable's story world, it is expected that the townspeople will
know the rich man's name but be ignorant of the beggar's, yet the dignity
afforded to Lazarus is not extended to him. While naming has bestowed
status on the beggar, anonymity parallels the rich man's loss of position,
for in the end he is left with nothing.[118] Metzger aptly describes the digni-
fying of Lazarus in distinction from the rich man: 'The town's somebody
is forgotten; its nobody is remembered'.[119]

6.1.2. *The Characters: The Rich Man*
6.1.2.1. *Physical Description of the Rich Man.* If the physical portrayal
of Lazarus's poverty is shocking in its bleakness, the depiction of the rich
man's wealth is remarkable for its magnificence. In v. 19 he is shielded
by the gate of his estate in the fine trappings of his earthly position. He is
clothed in purple and fine linen (καὶ ἐνεδιδύσκετο πορφύραν καὶ βύσσον).[120]
In first-century Palestine wearing purple garments was associated with
elite status.[121] Likewise, linen garments implied wealth and luxury.[122]
Besides the opulence of his dress is the manner of his life; the rich
man is occupied with extravagant feasting (εὐφραινόμενος καθ᾽ ἡμέραν
λαμπρῶς).[123] The term for dining (εὐφραίνω) in v. 19 is used of the feasting
at special occasions,[124] while λαμπρῶς connotes this feasting's brilliance
and grandeur – such was the rich man's activity every day.

While the Lukan audience has not been prepared by prior parables to
expect any of their characters to possess names, the poor man's naming

117. Green, *Luke*, 606: 'The poor man's only claim to status is that he is named
in the story; this alone raises the hope that there is more to his story than that of being
subhuman'.

118. Resseguie, *Narrative Criticism*, 128–29.

119. Metzger, *Consumption and Wealth*, 138.

120. Resseguie, *Narrative Criticism*, 108, observes that in narrative contexts,
clothing can reveal the social or spiritual state of a person.

121. BDAG, 855, πορφύρα; the word is rare in the New Testament (see Mark
15:17, 20 and Rev 18:12). Fitzmyer, *Luke X–XXIV*, 1130, observes the narrator's
insinuation that the rich man 'lived like a king'.

122. BDAG, 185, βύσσος; the word occurs only here in the New Testament; cf.
Bovon, *Lukas*, 3:106.

123. Pax, 'Milieustudie', 257, curiously denies that the rich man's clothing
suggests inordinate luxury.

124. BDAG, 414–15, s.v.; cf. Luke 12:19, where it is central to the rich fool's
desire to enjoy his prosperity; and 15:23–32, describing the feast for the returned
prodigal.

in v. 20 serves to attract attention to this aspect of the rich man's person, his namelessness.[125] Despite his high station, he is introduced as merely 'a certain rich man' (ἄνθρωπος δέ τις ἦν πλούσιος). The dignity afforded to Lazarus is not extended to him, though his earthly status might suggest he was highly regarded. This disjunction between being named and unnamed presages the degradation that the anonymous rich man is soon to undergo, and it strengthens the eschatological-reversal motif of the parable.[126]

While the physical descriptions of Lazarus and the rich man are paralleled in intensity,[127] their narrative activity stands in contrast. Unlike hapless Lazarus who is deposited at the gate to wait passively for relief, the rich man is active, engaged in the enjoyment of his material prosperity. Even when he dies he remains at the centre of the parable's action, heard in dialogue with Abraham in an effort to mitigate his ruinous circumstances. He is someone with favourable earthly opportunities and who wants to plays an active role in his self-determination.[128] The audience will note, however, that these same characteristics are critical factors in his demise.

---

125. An early textual tradition assigns a name to the rich man, surely prompted by the fact that his counterpart in the parable is named. Customarily the rich man has been referred to as 'Dives', from the Latin adjective for 'wealthy'. However, Luke's Gospel in Papyrus Bodmer XIV/XV (𝔓⁷⁵) includes a reference to Νεύης as the name of the rich man. See the discussions in P. Comfort, 'Two Illustrations of Scribal Gap Filling in Luke 16:19', in Porter and Boda, eds., *Translating*, 111–13; Bruce M. Metzger, 'Names for the Nameless in the New Testament: A Study in the Growth of Christian Tradition', in *Kyriakon: Festschrift Johannes Quasten*, vol. 1, ed. P. Granfield and J. A. Jungmann (Münster: Aschendorff, 1970), 79–99 (88–89); H. J. Cadbury, 'A Proper Name for Dives', *JBL* 81 (1962): 399–402; and Cadbury, 'The Name for Dives', *JBL* 84 (1965): 73. K. Grobel, '"…Whose Name Was Neves"', *NTS* 10 (1964): 381–82, suggests that this is a shortened form of the name 'Nineveh' found in an early Sahidic manuscript; cf. L. Th. Lefort, 'Le nom du mauvais riche (Lc 16,19) et la tradition copte', *ZNW* 37 (1938): 65–72.

126. R. W. Paschal Jr., 'Lazarus', in *Dictionary of Jesus and the Gospels*, ed. J. B. Green, S. McKnight and I. H. Marshall (Downers Grove, IL: InterVarsity, 1992), 461–63, citing 463.

127. Gowler, 'Characterization', 57, notes how characterization may be strengthened by comparing or contrasting one character with another.

128. G. B. Caird, *The Gospel of St Luke* (Harmondsworth: Penguin, 1963), 191, interestingly characterizes the rich man as a Sadducee, not only because of his social standing but because it was evident he had no belief in the afterlife. This suggestion does not seem to account for the parable's immediate narrative context, where Jesus is responding to the Pharisees as φιλάργυροι (16:14).

6.1.2.2. *Audience Response to the Rich Man*. As with the epithet πτωχός, the adjective πλούσιος does not convey a moral evaluation of the rich man. Neither is there any other overt judgment passed on the rich man's character as the basis for his affliction. In v. 25 Abraham simply explains that the rich man received good things in his life (τὰ ἀγαθά) while Lazarus received bad (τὰ κακά). It may then be questioned what evaluation of the rich man's character the narrator encourages. A cursory characterization might be positive simply because he is wealthy, for Luke's implied audience will have been familiar with the religious and cultural association of wealth with divine blessing.[129] This, combined with Abraham's value-free rationale for the rich man's reversal, has led to a questioning of the basis on which he is consigned to torment, with some insisting that it cannot have been for neglect of Lazarus.[130]

An analysis of the Lukan context is again instructive. The rich are routinely portrayed in a negative light (e.g. the rich fool in 12:16–21), and judgment has been pronounced on them (e.g. in Mary's song in 1:51–53). The audience knows from 6:24–25 that the rich man has already received his comfort (παράκλησις) and will now 'mourn and weep'. With this narrative preparation the audience is not surprised to see the rich man brought low, and the reason is discernible. While he received good things, he did not employ them as directed by 'Moses and the prophets'. This scriptural direction is underlined in the Lukan context by John the Baptist (3:10–14) and Jesus (6:30; 12:21). Though the rich man has not committed an outrightly wicked deed, he has neglected to perform an obviously righteous deed.[131] The sight of the poor and hungry man did not move him, nor did Scripture direct him. The rich man stands condemned for his blatant callousness toward the poor, and his resultant suffering is emphasized.[132] The 'gate' that could have been crossed on earth was not, and now the separation has been fixed.[133]

---

129. See Gen 26:12–14; Lev 26:3–5; Deut 6:1–3; cf. the discussion in Chapter 4, §4.1.2.

130. See, e.g., Grundmann, *Lukas*, 327; Crossan, *In Parables*, 67; Hock, 'Lazarus and Micyllus', 453–54; Schottroff and Stegemann, *Hope of the Poor*, 26–27; Nickelsburg, 'Riches', 338; Mealand, *Poverty*, 32; K. H. Rengstorf, *Das Evangelium nach Lukas* (Göttingen: Vandenhoeck & Ruprecht, 1974), 193.

131. Gowler, 'Characterization', 56, notes that acts both of commission and omission can be of great import for characterization.

132. See the repetition of both βάσανος (vv. 23, 28) and ὀδυνάω (vv. 24, 25).

133. Green, *Luke*, 608.

The negative appellation of the Pharisees (φιλάργυροι, v. 14) strengthens ~~Which?~~
in rhetorical impact with the rich man's introduction in v. 19. The audience ~~audience?~~
is incited to identify the rich man with the Pharisees.[134] According to Jesus
they show disdain for the law they purport to uphold. Prior to this parable,
he explains in v. 15 how the love of money inhibits whole-hearted service
of God, and how what is exalted among people (τὸ ἐν ἀνθρώποις ὑψηλόν) is
an abomination (βδέλυγμα) to God. This dictum anticipates the rich man's
reversal; he might have been honoured for his wealth, spoken of respect-
fully and afforded places of honour, but he failed to do right before God.
He later acknowledges this failing, albeit indirectly; with reference to his
five brothers, he asks for Lazarus to bring a warning so they will avoid
punishment (v. 28). Implicit is the admission that he is being tormented
because of his wicked inaction.[135]

The parable's audience will also recall Jesus's exhortation in Luke
14:12–14 to invite to one's dinner not friends, family, or the wealthy, but
the poor, lame, and blind. Though such guests will be unable to repay this
kindness, Jesus promises in v. 14: 'It will be repaid to you at the resurrection of the righteous' (ἀνταποδοθήσεται γάρ σοι ἐν τῇ ἀναστάσει τῶν
δικαίων). This promise is the positive counterpart to the parable's warning:
the rich man is now being 'repaid' with punishment for his lack of generosity to the poor.[136]

6.1.3. *The Characters: Abraham*

The parable's third character receives no formal introduction. Where
he appears in other Lukan passages, Abraham is identified with the title
'father' (πάτηρ),[137] or is introduced together with 'Isaac and Jacob',[138]
which makes clear his identity as one of Israel's patriarchs. Not until
the rich man commences addressing him in v. 24 does the reader
learn that this is Πάτερ Ἀβραάμ. Unlike that of the rich man and
Lazarus, the physical appearance of Abraham is not described, besides
having a κόλπος. As mentioned, this is not the first time Abraham

---

134. Roth, *Character Types*, 192.
135. Blomberg, *Parables*, 257, notes how the rich man was late in four respects:
'He pays attention to Lazarus too late, he sees the unbridgeable chasm too late, he
worries about his brothers too late, and he heeds the Law and the prophets too late'.
Cf. O. Glombitza, 'Der reiche Mann und der arme Lazarus: Luk xvi 19–31, Zur Frage
nach der Botschaft des Textes', *NovT* 12 (1970): 166–80.
136. Tannehill, *Narrative Unity*, 1:183; cf. Snodgrass, *Stories*, 424.
137. As in Luke 1:73 and 3:8.
138. As in Luke 3:34; 13:28; 20:37.

appears in the Third Gospel.[139] According to Hebrew Scripture[140] –
and confirmed in Luke 1:55 – he is the first recipient of God's covenant
promises. And yet, while the Jews considered Abraham their father in a
physical and spiritual sense, John the Baptist has said in 3:8 that the reality
of whether one truly aligns with Abraham is demonstrated by repentance,
not by physical descent.

6.1.3.1. *Audience Response to Abraham.* The patriarch is integral to
this narrative. It is to his bosom that Lazarus is taken, and to him that the
rich man appeals three times. In view of what Luke has told his audience
about Abraham, what is the significance of now seeing and hearing him?
Mindful that the employment of terms of address aids in characterization,
the rich man's reference to Abraham as 'father' confirms that he functions
in the parable as the father of his people.[141] Not Lazarus but Abraham
is mentioned as the one whom the rich man first sees 'from afar' in
v. 23; clearly, the attention is on the father of the nation. He is Lazarus's
heavenly host and the rich man's post-mortem interlocutor, but more
than this, Abraham mediates God's judgment as the story's authoritative
voice.[142] In v. 25 he explains the outcomes of the lives of the two men,[143]
which the audience would consider a reliable perspective and normative
judgment.[144] Abraham legitimates what the audience has heard about the
true nature of Abraham's children being manifest by repentance (3:8),
about God's blessing upon the poor (6:20–21), and the hazards of wealth
(6:24–26). His words simultaneously invite reflection on the audience's
own response to Jesus's message. In v. 29 Abraham gives a recommendation to the living about how to be with him after death: listen to 'Moses

---

139. See 1:55, 73; 3:8, 34; 13:16; see also Acts 3:13; 7:2–8; 13:26. This Lukan
pattern has also been investigated in past scholarship; e.g. N. A. Dahl, 'The Story
of Abraham in Luke-Acts', in *Studies in Luke-Acts: Essays Presented in Honor of
Paul Schubert*, ed. L. E. Keck and J. L. Martyn (Nashville, TN: Abingdon, 1966),
139–58; R. Brawley, 'For Blessing All Families of the Earth: Covenant Traditions in
Luke-Acts', *CurTM* 22 (1995): 18–26; Brawley, 'Abrahamic Covenant Traditions and
the Characterization of God in Luke-Acts', in Verheyden, *Unity*, 109–32; J. S. Siker,
Disinheriting the Jews: Abraham in Early Christian Controversy (Louisville, KY:
Westminster John Knox, 1991); H. M. Kim, 'From Israel to the Nations: A Critical
Study of the Abraham Motif in Luke-Acts' (PhD diss., Trinity Evangelical Divinity
School, 2007).

140. See, e.g., Gen 12:1–3; 15:1–21; Exod 3:6.

141. On the importance of terms of address in characterization, see Gowler,
'Characterization', 56.

142. Lehtipuu, 'Characterization', 97–98.

143. Grundmann, *Lukas*, 329.

144. Herzog, *Subversive Speech*, 130.

and the prophets'.[145] As a corollary, Abraham predicts in v. 31 that those who do not listen to the Scriptures will not be persuaded by 'one risen from the dead'. This closing prediction serves to anticipate the accounts in the latter portions of Luke and Acts, because 'from a retrospective point of view outside the narrative, what the rich man requests has already come in Jesus'.[146] The audience knows about one who has risen, and that the response to him has been indeterminate. To this question of the response to Jesus we will return.[147]

6.1.4. *The Characters: The Five Brothers*

A final character, functioning collectively, is the rich man's five brothers. Theirs is not a prominent narrative role, but they are referenced by their late brother as possible recipients of a warning (v. 31). This proposed 'warning seems to imply that people would certainly do or not do something if they knew all the dangerous consequences'.[148] Though not stated, the reader might justifiably assume that the five brothers are wealthy like their brother.[149] It is probable that they also passed by Lazarus regularly, implying their culpability.[150]

Some seek particular significance in the number five.[151] Rather than attach a significance to their quantity, the brothers' role in the narrative

145. Brawley, 'Abrahamic Covenant', 122.

146. Ibid., 123.

147. See the discussion in Chapter 5.

148. Vogels, 'Having or Longing', 34.

149. Tannehill, *Luke*, 253.

150. E. Matthews, 'The Rich Man and Lazarus: Almsgiving and Repentance in Early Syriac Tradition', *Diakonia* 22 (1988–89): 89–104, suggests that the rich man's servants and guests passed by Lazarus each day, 'yet not a single one of them ever stopped to give him the least bit of food and drink' (93).

151. Jülicher, *Gleichnisreden*, 639, posits that the five brothers, plus the deceased rich man, makes six, and as such this is a representation of the nation of Israel's unbelieving half. However, it may be observed that five is a characteristically Lukan number for objects occurring in Jesus's teachings; see Goulder, *New Paradigm*, 2:636, who dubs the five brothers 'a Lucan handful'. The number five occurs several times, in 9:31 (loaves); 12:6 (sparrows), 12:52 (household members), 14:19 (yoke of oxen), 19:18 (minas), 19:19 (cities). This may reflect a Jewish rhetorical preference; as observed by R. Jewett, 'The Rhetorical Function of Numerical Sequences in Romans', in *Persuasive Artistry: Studies in New Testament Rhetoric in Honor of George A. Kennedy*, ed. D. F. Watson, JSNTSup 50 (Sheffield: JSOT, 1991), 227–45, 'Series of fives appear to have emerged as more distinctively Jewish because of the association with the five books of the Torah and the later collection of the five "megillot"' (citing 231).

should receive attention. In the first place, the rich man's reference to his brothers occasions his own indictment. As noted, part of the listener's immediate recall is Jesus's words in 14:12–14, when he urges that kindness be extended not to friends, relations, and the wealthy – those in a position to repay – but to the disadvantaged. Yet the rich man demonstrates precisely the opposite approach, valuing those with whom there is a reciprocal relationship while overlooking the needy. Instead of being commended for his brotherly concern, the rich man is implicitly censured.

What then of the brothers? In the second place, it is argued that Abraham's words in v. 31 imply the certainty of their failure. The first part of the verse (Εἰ Μωϋσέως καὶ τῶν προφητῶν οὐκ ἀκούουσιν) is a first-class condition which assumes for the sake of argument the reality of what is said: 'If they do not listen to Moses and the prophets – and they do not…'[152] Like their brother, 'they are equally locked into their rejection of the Law and Prophets, for they live as heedlessly as he had'.[153] Even if Lazarus is sent to them, they will not be convinced of what they have not yet seen for themselves. Nevertheless, this verse's first-class condition should not be over-translated as implying their definite lack of faith.[154] An element of open-endedness marks the five brothers, as their response falls beyond the limits of the story.[155] If Abraham addressed the rich man as 'son' even in his torment, certainly his living brothers would be addressed similarly. They may yet prove to be true children of the patriarch. This possibility is consistent with the immediate Lukan context, particularly the three parables in 15:1–31, which concern how the lost can be found. Especially in the parable of the Prodigal Son (15:11–32), the response of the older brother is an indeterminate question that parallels the uncertainty surrounding the rich man's five brothers: Will he be instructed by the positive outcome of his younger brother's life, or will he close his eyes to it?[156] As Wright

152. Bock, *Luke*, 2:1376.

153. Johnson, *Luke*, 256; cf. his *Possessions*, 143, 'Luke pictures his situation and that of his brothers as hopeless'.

154. See the discussion of first-class conditions in D. B. Wallace, *Greek Grammar Beyond the Basics: An Exegetical Syntax of the New Testament* (Grand Rapids: Zondervan, 1996), 679–712.

155. K. R. Maxwell, *Hearing Between the Lines: The Audience as Fellow-worker in Luke-Acts and its Literary Milieu*, LNTS 425 (London: T&T Clark, 2010), 134; cf. Green, 'Narrative Criticism', 112.

156. Roose, 'Umkehr und Ausgleich', develops how this parable helps to interpret what repentance as depicted in Luke 15:11–31 is intended to involve; cf. D. S. Morlan, *Conversion in Luke and Paul: An Exegetical and Theological Exploration*, LNTS 464 (London: Bloomsbury T&T Clark, 2013), 52–79, who considers 15:11–32 to 'the most explicit depiction of repentance in Luke' (53).

observes, 'The five brothers at home correspond quite closely to the older brother in the prodigal son. "Resurrection" is happening, but they cannot see it.'[157] Within the parable they are not afforded the revelation of a resurrected messenger, since the call to repentance is clear in 'Moses and the prophets'.[158] Nevertheless, the five brothers' destiny remains indefinite after v. 31, an ambiguity that draws the audience into the story.[159]

This uncertainty of response is maintained in Luke's second volume. As the story of the believers unfolds in Acts it is an open question whether the Jews, as the physical descendants of Abraham, will see the truth of 'Moses and the prophets' as explained by the apostles. More than that, there is ambiguity whether the Jewish people will receive the message about 'one risen from the dead', the one to whom Moses and the prophets testified.[160] Abraham's pessimistic prediction notwithstanding, the audience is intrigued whether 'the five brothers' will respond to the testimony given.[161]

6.2. *Interrelationships of Character*

The parable's characters reveal key Lukan emphases, particularly when the characters are studied in association with one another. It is in 'the crucible of relationships' that a narrative's characters are formed and evaluated.[162] As with other Lukan parables,[163] the relational structure of Luke 16:19–31 can be schematized as a triangle, comprised of three characters:

157. N. T. Wright, *Jesus and the Victory of God*, Christian Origins and the Question of God 2 (Minneapolis: Fortress, 1996), 256.

158. Wright, *Victory*, 256; cf. Seccombe, *Possessions*, 178.

159. Metzger, *Consumption and Wealth*, 154; cf. K. M. Hatcher, 'In Gold We Trust: The Parable of the Rich Man and Lazarus', *RevExp* 109 (2012): 277–83, citing 281.

160. Darr, *Character Building*, 55–56, observes the rhetoric of recognition through Luke-Acts, and the frequent use of verbs of seeing/hearing, even into the final episode in Acts.

161. Jeremias, *Parables*, 187, identifies this as one of four 'double-edged parables', where the stress of meaning is intended to fall on the second part. The consequence of this emphasis is that Jesus is not commenting in this parable on the possessions nor on the afterlife, but rather is warning those people who resemble the rich man's five brothers of impending danger: 'He who will not submit to the Word of God, will not be converted by a miracle'.

162. Darr, 'Narrator as Character', 51.

163. Parables of this kind are the Two Debtors (7:41–43), the Faithful and Unfaithful Servants (12:42–48), the Lost Sheep and the Lost Coin (15:4–10), the Prodigal Son (15:11–32).

an authority figure (often a king, father, or master) and two contrasting
subordinates.[164] In these so-called monarchic parables, the authoritative principal functions as a determiner, with the other two representing
divergent responses.[165] Also common is a change in the subordinates'
respective values, and a reversal in their characterization.[166] The respective interactions of Lazarus and the rich man with Abraham are revealing
of the parable's lessons.

6.2.1. *Relationship: Lazarus and the Rich Man*

Though separated in life by barriers both physical and social, Lazarus
and the rich man are in relationship as fellow members of the nation
Israel.[167] The Mosaic law placed on them an obligation of mutual love
(Lev 19:18). As one materially well-endowed, the rich man is expected to
show mercy to the beggar at his gate, for 'Moses and the prophets' legislated and exhorted proper treatment of the needy.[168] As observed earlier,
the proximity of Lazarus and the rich man makes their contrast starker.[169]
This physical closeness also engenders dramatic tension, whether the rich
man will act to alleviate the suffering of Lazarus. What Lazarus desires is
simple for the rich man to accommodate, yet he takes no action to effect
relief.

When the scene shifts to the afterlife, the personal name that afforded
the poor man a measure of dignity is now seen to have a corollary that is
reflective of the rich man's failure. By his reference to the beggar in v. 24,

164. See R. W. Funk, *Parables and Presence: Forms of the New Testament Tradition*
(Philadelphia: Fortress, 1982), 19–54; cf. G. Sellin, 'Lukas als Gleichniserzähler: die
Erzählung vom barmherzigen Samariter (Lk 10,25–37)', *ZNW* 65 (1974): 166–89;
Blomberg, *Parables*, 197–98.

165. Funk, *Parables and Presence*, 37; see his representation of the parable of
Lazarus and the Rich Man on p. 41. Similar to Sellin, Funk identifies parables having
three principal characters and comparable plot structures, though he does not include
the parable of Lazarus and the Rich Man (19).

166. Sellin, 'Lukas als Gleichniserzähler', 183.

167. Seccombe, *Possessions*, 176. By contrast, Pax, 'Milieustudie', 258, claims
that the rich man ignores Lazarus because he does not regard Lazarus as a member
of his clan; such a view on the rich man's part would be indefensible in the context
of Jewish society.

168. See, e.g., Deut 14:28–29; 26:12–14; Isa 5:7–8; 32:6–7; Jer 5:26–28; Ezek
18:12–18; Mic 2:1–2; 6:8; Mal 3:5; cf. the discussion in Chapter 4, §4.1.3.

169. Tanghe, 'Abraham, son fils', 565–67. Cadbury, *Making of Luke-Acts*,
234, notes the Lukan characteristic of contrasting and paralleling personages in the
parables.

it is clear that the rich man knew about Lazarus at his gate, even being familiar with his name. To him Lazarus was more than anonymous, but he had a position within the rich man's life.[170] He knew him, yet did not 'see' him.[171] His failure to share his wealth with a needy person in close proximity is obvious, and according to the tenets established earlier in Luke's Gospel makes him deserving of torment.[172]

The immediacy of the relationship of Lazarus and the rich man is supplanted by a separation in the afterlife, in the form of the gulf.[173] Able to communicate across the chasm, the rich man does not address Lazarus but Abraham. In itself this address is unsurprising, as Abraham is clearly the figure of authority. However, the rich man's questions directly involve the unspeaking Lazarus, for he is first requested to be sent to Hades in order to bring relief to the rich man (v. 24). The second request is that Lazarus be sent to earth in order to warn the five brothers (vv. 27–28). These two requests lead some to posit that the rich man has not changed his view of Lazarus, but still considers him socially subordinate and available for his personal advantage.[174] In this view, Lazarus is little more than a lowly servant, conveying waters of refreshment; or an envoy, relaying a heavenly message. Though it is true that the rich man disregarded Lazarus in life, the parable provides no grounds for extending that conclusion to his post-mortem requests. In itself, it cannot be termed a dishonour to be sent temporarily from Abraham's presence on an errand of mercy. On the contrary, in the Lukan context the activities of providing relief to the suffering or giving warning to the disobedient are always positively evaluated.[175] More revealing is that the requests are denied because the rich man already had an opportunity to respond to Moses and the prophets. His failure to do so is writ large in his relationship with Lazarus.

Eh

Probably has more to do w/ mythology

---

170. Seccombe, *Possessions*, 175; D. L. Bock, 'The Parable of the Rich Man and Lazarus and the Ethics of Jesus', *SwJT* 40 (1997): 63–72, citing 64.

171. S. I. Wright, *Tales Jesus Told: An Introduction to the Narrative Parables of Jesus* (Carlisle: Paternoster, 2003), 78.

172. See, e.g., 6:24–26; Tannehill, *Narrative Unity*, 1:131.

173. Schnider and Stenger, 'Die offene Tür', 281–82.

174. Gowler, 'Characterization', 56. This interpretation is found also in, e.g., Bock, 'Ethics of Jesus', 67; Heil, *Meal Scenes*, 138; Herzog, *Subversive Speech*, 123; Wright, *Tales*, 78–79.

175. For provision of physical relief, see Luke 3:11; 6:9; 10:25–37; for warning, see 6:42; 17:3.

6.2.2. Relationship: Lazarus and Abraham. The single textual detail speaking to the nature of the relationship between Lazarus and Abraham is that the former is taken (ἀπενεχθῆναι) to the latter's bosom.[176] After a life of misery the poor man receives his reward. This is consistent with Luke's consistent portrayal of blessing on the poor[177] and the promised reversal of their lowly position on earth.[178] As a child of Abraham, Lazarus is entitled to the benefits of salvation, including being granted a place with the patriarchs at the messianic banquet (13:28–30).

6.2.3. Relationship: Abraham and Rich Man

Though standing at a great distance the rich man is able to recognize Abraham from across the chasm.[179] In view of the rich man's abject failure, it may be questioned why Abraham engages with him. The patriarch does not deny their bond, and their conversation connotes closeness, as Abraham is called πάτερ and the rich man τέκνον. These terms are suggestive of the rich man's respect for the patriarch, and Abraham's concern for the rich man.[180]

Despite their ethnic bond the rich man has not shown himself a true son of Abraham.[181] He does not protest his judgment as unfair,[182] but attempts to move Abraham with his bargaining, submitting two requests (vv. 24,

---

176. See P. W. Van Der Horst, 'Abraham's Bosom, the Place Where he Belonged: A Short Note on ἀπενεχθῆναι in Luke 16.22', *NTS* 52 (2006): 142–44; he argues that in compound verbs beginning with ἀπο-, the preposition often has the sense of 'back to where it belongs', or a notion of 'deservedness'. Thus Luke might be conveying the idea of Lazarus's entitlement to a place of rest in Abraham's bosom (144). Such a notion is consistent with the Lukan beatitude of 6:20, while the term is also used in Acts 19:12.

177. The portrait of the comfort Lazarus receives from Abraham is paralleled when the healed woman of 13:10–16 is described 'a daughter of Abraham' (θυγατέρα Ἀβραάμ, v. 16).

178. See, e.g., Luke 1:52–53; 4:16–20; 6:20–21.

179. This unprompted recognition may be compared with how Peter, John, and James are able to recognize the personages of Moses and Elijah when Jesus is transfigured (Luke 9:30–31).

180. Τέκνον is also used by the prodigal's father to address his elder son in encouraging him to repent of his hardheartedness (15:31); this similarity leads Heil to conclude that Abraham is still urging the rich man to repent (*Meal Scenes*, 138–39). However, this claim does not accord with what Abraham says about the unalterable nature of the rich man's situation (16:26).

181. Cf. the words of John the Baptist in 3:8.

182. Bovon, *Lukas*, 3:110. Siker, *Disinheriting*, 105, asserts that the rich man's 'appealing to Abraham is a shorthand way for claiming God's salvation'.

27), then challenging the patriarch's refusal to send Lazarus to his father's house (v. 30). The respect afforded to Abraham by the rich man's filial address appears to wear thin as his suggestions are successively turned down. Abraham's speaking betrays a distinction between him and Lazarus (ἡμῶν, v. 26), and the rich man and those with him (ὑμῶν, v. 26). Abraham is patient, but there is no mistaking the berating tone in his responses.[183] While the audience has recently heard Jesus's statement about 'fathers' being willing to give good gifts to their children (11:13), Father Abraham refuses to help the rich man with even simple relief – the time for giving good gifts is over. The physical and irreversible separation from the patriarch speaks of the rich man's disinheritance of Abrahamic blessings.[184] Within Luke's narrative he is one of those who see 'Abraham, Isaac, and Jacob and all the prophets in the kingdom of God' (13:28), while they themselves are thrown out of the banquet (ἐκβαλλομένους ἔξω). The parable's proximity–partition dynamic has a powerful effect: the rich man is close to Abraham, yet distant. The obvious disjunction of this relationship serves as a warning to Luke's audience.

7. *The Sequence of Narrative Events*

The first true 'event' in this parable does not occur until the deaths of Lazarus and the rich man. Until then, the audience is left to consider both the misery and beatitude of the two characters, as well as the narrative tension that grows when there is no constructive interface between them. A resolution is demanded, and it is provided as the setting shifts and events of consequence transpire.

7.1. *Event: Death*

Following the physical description of the rich man and Lazarus, their deaths are recounted in the reverse order. Little is said beside the simple narration in v. 22 of what happened to Lazarus (ἐγένετο δὲ ἀποθανεῖν) and to the rich man (ἀπέθανεν). The shaming of Lazarus and honouring of the rich man initially seems perpetuated in death, for of the latter alone it is observed in v. 23 that he is buried (ἐτάφη); Lazarus might have suffered

---

183. Metzger, *Consumption and Wealth*, 143, questions whether the tone of Abraham's words to the rich man is berating, or a gracious explanation. F. Capron, '"Son" in the Parable of the Rich Man and Lazarus', *ExpTim* 13 (1901–1902): 523, observes that after referring to the rich man as 'son' once, Abraham 'drops the appellation', while the rich man persistently clings to the term 'Father'.

184. Kim, 'From Israel to the Nations', 312.

the final humiliation of being left unburied.[185] Though it is not mentioned that people removed his body, Lazarus in v. 22 is taken by angels[186] to the bosom of Abraham.[187]

7.2. Event: Entrance into Afterlife

The change in Lazarus's status intimated in being 'taken by angels' is confirmed by his position at the patriarch's side. As mentioned, the Lukan context connotes that this is the heavenly feast with the patriarchs (13:28–30). Lazarus is in an idyllic state, while the rich man experiences fiery torments and is desirous of the most basic form of relief. In the afterlife both characters have been dramatically stripped. The rich man has lost his well-stocked table, purple linen, comfortable estate, and apparent happiness. Lazarus has been freed of his diseased body, hunger, and obvious misery. These post-mortem destinies, while shocking, are understandable in light of the Gospel's standards for evaluating rich and poor[188] and its repeated motif of bi-polar reversal.[189] Between them is an impassable gulf, accentuating the significance of the rich man's choices in life.

7.3. Event: A Final Conversation

If the parable ended with Lazarus and the rich man in their respective abodes, the story would be one about 'a dramatic reversal of fortunes'.[190] But there is a complication of the narrative through the rich man's appeals. This intensifies the tragedy of the rich man's tardiness to listen to Scripture, for he has become the beggar; as Lazarus once craved crumbs, now the rich man craves a drop of water.

Abraham denies the rich man's three requests. Beginning with a call for the rich man to remember (μνήσθητι), he provides a recapitulation of the circumstances of his and Lazarus's life and how these have been reversed (v. 25). Next, Abraham emphasizes the unalterable nature of

185. Green, *Luke*, 607; not being buried was emblematic of God's curse (Deut 28:25–26; Jer 16:1–4).

186. Angels appear with frequency in Lukan narratives; see, e.g., Luke 1:11–13, 26–38; 2:9–12; 15:10; 22:43; 24:4–7; Acts 5:19–20; 8:26; 12:7, 23; 27:23. See the discussion of angels in Green, *Theology*, 40–41.

187. On the imagery of angels conducting the dead into the afterlife, see Lehtipuu, *Afterlife Imagery*, 198–205.

188. See 6:20–25.

189. York, *Reversal*, 68; see, e.g., 13:30.

190. Johnson, *Luke*, 256.

afterlife destinies (v. 26), insisting that no one can cross from one region of the afterlife to another. Finally, Abraham maintains the sufficiency of 'Moses and the prophets' to provide a warning, eliminating the necessity of Lazarus being sent to the five brothers (vv. 29, 31). Though there was a Graeco-Roman tradition of the dead returning to visit the living in order to warn about coming fates, in this narrative the possibility is ruled out emphatically.[191] Lazarus is not required to convey such communication, because Scripture has already done it.[192] Abraham's concluding words assert that those who do not listen to 'Moses and the prophets' will also not be persuaded 'if one rises from the dead' (v. 31).[193] The story's focus is thereby shifted back to the world of the living.[194] For the audience familiar with the events 'fulfilled among us' (1:1), this assertion fosters interest in the responses to the preaching about the risen Jesus from the Scriptures in Acts.[195]

8. *Understanding Luke's Story*

The narrative texture of Luke 16:19–31 is rich with interconnected characters: Lazarus, the rich man and his brothers, and Abraham. By vivid settings in life and after-life as well as by vibrant characterizations and the dynamics of interrelationships, the parable illustrates the helplessness and the hope of the poor, the corruption of the wealthy, and the consequences of failing to listen to 'Moses and the prophets'. The narrative thus engages and stimulates its audience to consider this warning.

The beggar Lazarus is categorically wretched: he is ulcerated, unsheltered, malnourished, and even harassed by dogs. Depicted in his condition of hapless suffering, he is paradigmatic of the needy in the Gospel who are promised God's favour and provision (1:52–53). Luke's use of πτωχός in the parable accords with this Gospel's signature message that God's mercy is shown not just to the economically disadvantaged, but to the sick, the blind, and the outcast (4:18–19). This truth is borne out by the beggar's surprising name, 'Lazarus', which is a subtle act of honouring

191. See the discussion of this tradition and its negation in Chapter 4, §§5.2–3.

192. Tannehill, *Luke*, 253; cf. Bock, 'Ethics of Jesus', 69: 'What Abraham refused to permit for the rich man's brothers, the parable does literarily for the parable's readers'.

193. The latter part of v. 31 is a third-class condition, indicating a possibility without comment on its likelihood.

194. Wright, *Storyteller*, 132.

195. See further discussion in Chapter 5.

him despite the shame of his condition. It is expected that the rich man's name is known while the beggar is anonymous, yet Lazarus is dignified with a name and the rich man is not – a contrast consistent with the Lukan motif of reversal (13:30). Though separated by barriers both physical and social, Lazarus and the rich man are in relationship as members of God's covenant people, making flagrant the rich man's failure to share with the needy person at his gate.

While anonymous, the rich man in the parable is familiar to Luke's audience. They have heard Jesus regularly describe wealthy people in a warning and condemnatory way on account of their self-satisfaction (6:24–25), greed (12:16–21), and devotion to mammon (16:13). With this narrative preparation the audience is not surprised to see the rich man debased after death. For though the rich man received good things, he did not employ them in acts of charity as 'Moses and the prophets' instructed. The parable does not describe an outrightly wicked deed on his part, but he neglected to respond to Lazarus's plight. This makes coherent the torment that he suffers. From his position in Hades he assumes the privilege of calling Abraham 'father', but the audience understands that the rich man is no child of Abraham. Because he failed to share his clothing or food with one who lacked, the rich man is not entitled to such an honorific.

In Luke 16:19–31 the patriarch Abraham plays the role of heavenly host for Lazarus and post-mortem interlocutor for the rich man. Jesus announced in 13:28–29 that many will eat at the messianic banquet with 'Abraham, Isaac, and Jacob and all the prophets'. While Lazarus enjoys this patriarchal fellowship in Abraham's bosom, the rich man is one of those who see the festivity from a wretched position outside. Even so, he can converse with Abraham across the chasm. Abraham is the authoritative voice who reliably mediates God's judgment and legitimates what has been heard about the true nature of Abraham's children (3:8–9), the announcement of salvation for the poor (4:18–19), and the hazards of earthly wealth (12:16–21). Finally, the audience will hear Abraham's closing declaration about the sufficiency of 'Moses and the prophets' in relation to one risen from the dead substantiated later in the Acts narratives.

While their role in the narrative is 'off-stage', the rich man's five brothers are referenced as possible beneficiaries of a warning given by a resurrected Lazarus. The rich man is concerned that they will come to share in his torturous fate, presumably because they are likewise dismissive of their responsibility to the needy. Abraham's prediction of their response has a doubtful tone, but whether the brothers are ever persuaded by 'Moses and the prophets' is not recounted. This omitted ending invites the audience to fill the narrative gap by reflecting on possible responses to the Scriptures' testimony. Being engaged in this contemplation poses the question of their own response to 'Moses and the prophets' in relation to someone who is risen from the dead.

9. *Excursus: Naming Lazarus*

Being the only character in the Synoptic parables spared from anonymity – apart from the patriarch Abraham in the same narrative – few interpreters can resist making a suggestion about the meaning of Lazarus's name.[196] That there is an enduringly enigmatic quality to this 'Lazarus' is palpable from the wide range of explanations. In this chapter we already observed two suggestions: the ancient, still prevalent, yet unsatisfactory approach of explaining Λάζαρος by means of its Hebrew or Aramaic etymology, 'God helps'; and the more plausible narrative-critical view of the name as subtly bestowing dignity in the midst of the poor man's suffering.[197] We now review several other suggested interpretations of this name, with some brief critical remarks.

9.1. *Of No Significance*

While granting that the naming of Lazarus is unique, some commentators regard it as insignificant, largely because of the character's minor role. Lazarus does not speak or act, but is passive: he has been 'thrown down' at the gate, merely 'desires' food scraps, and at death is 'carried away'. Even in the afterlife, he is not addressed directly by the rich man, but is the subject of his conversation with Abraham. Consequently, Jeremias asserts that Lazarus is a secondary character, and suggests calling the parable 'the story of the Six Brothers'.[198] Others note that Lazarus does not have any particular importance,[199] that he is merely a figure of contrast next to the rich man, and illustrative of the latter's 'unfulfilled possibility on earth'.[200] In the final analysis Lazarus represents nothing more than a lost opportunity.[201] While the poor man does have an inconspicuous

---

196. Meier, *Marginal Jew*, 2:825, puts it with some force: 'What is absolutely unparalleled and demands an explanation is the occurrence of a proper name in a parable'.

197. See the discussion above, in §6.1.1.3.

198. Jeremias, *Parables*, 186.

199. Johnson, *Literary Function*, 142.

200. H. Kvalbein, 'Jesus and the Poor: Two Texts and a Tentative Conclusion', *Them* 12 (1987): 80–87, citing 84.

201. Tannehill, *Luke*, 252.

position in the narrative – and while it is true that 'Lazarus' was the third most common male name at that time[202] – the singular quality of his being named invites more attention than some have afforded it.

9.2. A Real Person

The assignation of a name to the beggar is one of the principal reasons for the conclusion that this story is based on real events involving known persons, and is not a fictional account. This explanation has a time-honoured place in the history of interpretation.[203] The notion that Luke 16:19–31 depicts actual events is said to be supported by the absence of its categorization as a παραβολή, unlike some other Lukan stories.[204] However, it must be pointed out that several stories conventionally dubbed 'parables' also lack the designation παραβολή.[205] Furthermore, textual features indicate that it was told as an illustrative narrative akin to other Lukan stories, such as its indefinite introductory formula in v. 19 (ἄνθρωπος δέ τις ἦν), and its typical parabolic structure. While not impossible that 16:19–31 has its origins in real events, its broad similarity with other parables suggests that the name is fictional and has another significance.

9.3. Typical Lukan Detail

The name Λάζαρος is typical of the colour of Lukan narratives. More frequently than the other evangelists, Luke names individuals who might otherwise have been left anonymous.[206] Three of his parables 'depict named characters or individual characters designated by the name of the group to which they belong', namely, the priest, Levite, and Samaritan (10:25–37); the Pharisee and Tax Collector (18:10–14); and Lazarus and Abraham (16:19–31).[207] In fact, eight of the pericopae that are unique to Luke's Gospel – not only parables – contain personal names.[208] This pattern of including individual characters' names might substantiate Luke's claim in 1:3 to have written his narrative carefully (ἀκριβῶς) and

202. Bauckham, *Eyewitnesses*, 85, with reference to naming patterns among Palestinian Jews from 330 BCE to 200 CE.

203. Tertullian, *An.* 7; Irenaeus, *Haer.* 4.3.2.

204. See, e.g., 12:16 and 19:11.

205. See, e.g., 10:25–37; 14:15–25; 15:11–32; 16:1–9.

206. Cadbury, *Making of Luke-Acts*, 53; e.g. Zacchaeus, Cornelius, Roman officials and some magicians.

207. Tucker, *Example Stories*, 253.

208. Paffenroth, *Story*, 119; see 4:25–27 (Elijah, Elisha, Naaman); 7:36–50 (Simon); 10:39–42 (Mary, Martha); 13:1–5 (Pilate), 10–17 (Abraham), 31–32 (Herod); 16:19–31 (Lazarus, Abraham); 19:2–10 (Zacchaeus).

with due investigation (παρηκολουθηκότι). However, this meticulousness is not an explanation of the name's significance as such.

9.4. *Typical of 'Descents'*

Scholars suggest a background of Luke 16:19–31 in various mythologies or folk tales, including Jewish, Graeco-Roman and Egyptian.[209] Popular folk tales roughly contemporaneous with Luke include the genre of 'descents', which depict journeys to and from the netherworld. This is a genre to which Luke 16:19–31 bears broad resemblance.[210] In this connection, Bauckham notes that in 'descents', the individual making the journey is almost always named; consequently, 'the name Lazarus would assist the impression that the parable belongs to the category of such stories'.[211] While this similarity of named characters navigating the netherworld is intriguing, there are several other significant narrative features that distinguish Luke 16:19–31 from the 'descents' genre.[212] Consequently, the occurrence of the name Lazarus would likely not be sufficient to suggest to the audience that the parable should be read according to the conventions of this particular genre.

9.5. *A Needed Preclusion*

The specificity inherent in the poor man's name has been understood as a needed preclusion. While not commending this particular explanation, Nolland notes the view that 'this specification prevents the reversal pattern of the parable from being automatically applicable to every poor person'.[213] That is to say, because there is only one 'Lazarus', not every destitute individual can expect a similar experience in life and afterlife. However, this approach fails to take into account the prevalence of the bi-polar reversal motif in Luke's Gospel.[214] The motif appears with such consistency that it is doubtful whether Luke wants his audience to hear 16:19–31 with any sense of being precluded from the realities portrayed. Instead, the parable depicts in personalized form what Jesus repeatedly says in the Gospel about the reversal of the lowly and humbling of the exalted.[215]

---

209. See the discussion in Chapter 1, §4.2.
210. See the discussion in Chapter 4, §5.3.1.
211. Bauckham, 'Rich Man and Lazarus', 244.
212. Hock, 'Lazarus and Micyllus', 452; cf. Chapter 1, §4.2.
213. Nolland, *Luke*, 2:828.
214. See, e.g., 1:52–53; 3:11; 6:20–25; 13:30; 14:11.
215. York, *Reversal*, 92.

9.6. *A Name Written in Heaven*

In Luke 10:20 Jesus says that the names of his disciples are 'written in heaven' (ἐγγέγραπται ἐν τοῖς οὐρανοῖς). It has been suggested that this motif of one's name being known or written by God would inform the audience's understanding of the character Λάζαρος.[216] Hendrickx characterizes this interpretation of the name Lazarus: 'The use of the proper name indicates that the poor man is not just "anyone": God knows him and is aware of his need'.[217] While this is an observation that is consistent with the Lukan portrayal of the salvation of the poor, the notion in 10:20 of names being written (ἐγγέγραπται) likely connotes the ancient practice of physically inscribing names in a record of citizens, which became a metaphor of belonging in God's book of life.[218] The assignation of a name to the poor man is conceptually dissimilar.

9.7. *To Facilitate Dialogue*

The reason that Lazarus is named has received a pragmatic explanation. Danker opines that the name was included 'in order to expedite the succeeding dialogue'.[219] Having a convenient moniker for the poor man allowed the subsequent conversation between the rich man and Abraham to proceed without repeated cumbersome references to an anonymous beggar.[220] While the name may indeed have had the effect of facilitating conversation, other Lukan parables include dialogue but ensue without the use of proper names.[221] The reason that this particular parable requires the convenience of a proper name is not clear.

9.8. *Abraham's Servant*

As mentioned above, the Greek name Λάζαρος is based on the Hebrew or Aramaic אֶלְעָזָר, rendered in English as Eleazar or Eliezer. Consequently, some suggest identifying the character in Luke 16 with the patriarch Abraham's chief servant or steward Eliezer. As Abraham sent Eliezer on assignments as his personal representative, so Lazarus of Luke 16 is sent by Abraham to see how some of his children (namely, the rich man) are dealing with their inheritance. This explains his return to

---

216. This interpretation is proposed by Augustine, *Serm.* 33A.4.

217. Hendrickx, *Parables*, 200.

218. See, e.g., Marshall, *Luke*, 430.

219. Danker, *New Age*, 283; cf. Bauckham, 'Rich Man and Lazarus', 244; Cadbury, 'Proper Name', 399.

220. Bauckham, 'Rich Man and Lazarus', 244.

221. See, e.g., 11:5–8; 15:11–32; cf. Snodgrass, *Stories*, 429.

Abraham's bosom when his mission is completed.[222] Interestingly, there is a midrashic tradition surrounding Eliezer, Abraham's servant, where he is 'the prototype of the perfect servant, supremely loyal and utterly devoted to the interests of his master'.[223] According to a Jewish legend, Eliezer is one of nine individuals who entered the Garden of Eden during their lifetime.[224] This tradition is seen as reinforcing the link from the Eliezer of Genesis to the Lazarus of Luke 16, and elucidating the name's occurrence in the parable. While ingenious, this explanation stretches credulity, for Lazarus of the parable is not 'sent' anywhere, but he dies and is not heard reporting to the patriarch.

9.9. *Known to the Rich Man*

It is proposed that naming the poor man makes him 'more than a "faceless" beggar; it gives him a place within the rich man's life'.[225] It is clear that the rich man knew about Lazarus at his gate, even to the point of being familiar with his name. To refer to the poor man by name is to personalize him; within the narrative, it means that he and the rich man knew each other and even interacted while existing in close proximity.[226] As noted earlier in this chapter, this familiarity with someone in need is a factor in the rich man's culpability.[227] He displays audacity in requesting Abraham to send the beggar whose name he knew but never helped.[228] However, the rich man is guilty of neglect whether or not he knew Lazarus's name, so this explanation provides no new insight into the name's significance.

9.10. *An Allusion to Isaiah 61*

In Jesus' sermon in the Nazareth synagogue (Luke 4:16–21), Isa 61 and its message of relief for the poor and liberation for the captives figure prominently. To Goulder this programmatic passage suggests an explanation

---

222. Derrett, *Law*, 86–87. This theory has received elaboration by Tanghe, 'Abraham, son fils', 557–77; cf. C. H. Cave, 'Lazarus and the Lukan Deuteronomy', *NTS* 15 (1969): 319–25.
223. *Gen. Rab.* 59.12; see the discussion in L. I. Rabinowitz, 'Study of a Midrash', *JQR* 58 (1967): 143–61, citing 148; I. Abrahams, *Studies in Pharisaism and the Gospels* (New York: Ktav, 1967), 203, on the tradition of 'Eleazar-Lazarus' as a type of humble but zealous man who is privileged to serve Abraham in Paradise as he had served him on earth.
224. Rabinowitz, 'Midrash', 161.
225. Seccombe, *Possessions*, 174–75.
226. Tannehill, *Narrative Unity*, 1:131.
227. See the discussion in §6.2.1 of this chapter.
228. Green, *Luke*, 608.

for 'Lazarus', for in the same Isaiah chapter the poor are promised, 'You shall be priests for the Lord' (61:6). Goulder observes that the first of Israel's priests was called אֶלְעָזָר, a name Graecized to Λάζαρος.[229] The name Lazarus in the parable is therefore an allusion to the eschatological elevation of all Israel to the priesthood, consistent with the Isaianic message of good news for the destitute and suffering. Commending this explanation is its contextual support from Isaiah, whose theology is significant in shaping the Lukan narrative.[230] However, the parable contains nothing else that suggests a priestly motif, so the association of the poor man with sacerdotal duties must be judged tenuous.

9.11. *A Connection to the Lazarus of John 11*

The name 'Lazarus' has prompted interpreters to posit an association with the Lazarus raised from the dead by Jesus in John 11, a proposal with a long pedigree.[231] It is certainly remarkable that Lazarus is the only named character in any Synoptic parable, and that Lazarus is the only named recipient of a miracle in John's Gospel.[232] Besides proper names, similarities of content include the death of both characters, the possibility – and in John 11, the reality – of their return to life, and also a wider context of antagonism toward Jesus in both narratives.[233] However, the relationship between the Lukan and the Johannine pericopae remains impossible to delineate, and even the direction of influence has been debated. Some posit that the story of Lazarus's resurrection was contrived by John, developed out of the already-extant parable of Lazarus and the Rich Man.[234]

---

229. Goulder, *New Paradigm*, 2:638. To be more precise, Aaron was the first of Israel's ordained priests (8:1–36), and Eleazar his son was appointed as chief over the principal Levites (Num 3:32) after the death of Nadab and Abihu (Lev 10:1–2).

230. See, e.g., P. Mallen, *The Reading and Transformation of Isaiah in Luke-Acts*, LNTS 367 (London: T&T Clark, 2008).

231. Origen, *Fr. Jo.* 77.

232. See Meier, *Marginal Jew*, 2:822–32. D. J. Bretherton, 'Lazarus of Bethany: Resurrection or Resuscitation?', *ExpTim* 104 (1993): 169–73, identifies the two Lazaruses, and makes the peculiar contention that Lazarus in John 11 was not actually dead, but in a state of suspended animation. Upon resuscitation, he recounted his near-death experiences to Jesus, which became the basis for this parable.

233. R. Dunkerley, 'Lazarus', *NTS* 5 (1959): 321–27, citing 322.

234. K. Pearce, 'The Lucan Origins of the Raising of Lazarus', *ExpTim* 96 (1984–85): 359–61; cf. U. Busse, 'Johannes und Lukas: Die Lazarusperikope, Frucht eines Kommunikationsprozesses', in *John and the Synoptics*, ed. A. Denaux, BETL 101 (Leuven: Leuven University Press, 1992), 281–306, who argues that John's audience was intended to read his story with the Lukan parable in mind.

An alternate suggestion is that Jesus tells the Luke 16 parable shortly after raising his friend Lazarus from the dead[235] when there was intensified opposition from the Jewish leadership (John 11:45–54; 12:9–10).[236] Attractive as a connection between this Lukan parable and the Johannine miracle story may be, any proposal is hampered by a lack of evidence and must remain hypothetical.[237]

Good excurses

9.12. *A Christ Figure*

A final interpretation of Λάζαρος builds on one previously mentioned, that the audience is intended to know its etymology as 'God helps'. In this interpretation, Lazarus is regarded as a Christ figure, for he is 'the one in whom God's help is made available'.[238] Furthermore, in v. 31 Abraham intimates that a message from this Lazarus might not be effective in persuading the brothers, a prediction borne out by the ensuring rejection.[239] We already discounted the etymological explanation of 'Lazarus', and by implication we can discard this proposed interpretation as well. Nevertheless, Abraham's reference to one rising from the dead (v. 31) can be heard as a narrative anticipation of the subsequent preaching about the resurrected Jesus in Acts.[240] To this proleptic reference we will return.[241]

235. J. Van Bruggen, *Christ on Earth: The Gospel Narratives as History*, trans. Nancy Forest-Flier (Grand Rapids: Baker, 1998), 199–200, posits a geographical connection between the raising of Lazarus in John 11 and the parable's telling, near Bethany; cf. Dunkerley, 'Lazarus', 323–26.

236. As an alternative to this theory, J. Kremer, 'Der arme Lazarus: Lazarus, der Freund Jesu: Beobachtungen zur Beziehung zwischen Lk 16:19–31 und Joh 11:1–46', in *À cause de l'Évangile: Études sur les Synoptiques et les Actes offertes au P. Jacques Dupont*, ed. F. Refoulé (Paris: Cerf, 1985), 571–84, suggests that the original parable lacked a proper name for the poor man, but it was later supplied by the Johannine tradition from an early version of the miracle story. W. E. North, *The Lazarus Story within the Johannine Tradition*, JSNTSup 212 (Sheffield: Sheffield Academic, 2011), 120–21, discounts this suggestion because John makes nothing of the name itself, and introduces the name in a way that intimates it was not known to his readers.

237. Fitzmyer, *Luke X–XXIV*, 1129; cf. the conclusion of R. Schnackenburg, *The Gospel According to St John* (New York: Crossroad, 1982), 2:341; and C. H. Dodd, *Historical Tradition in the Fourth Gospel* (Cambridge: Cambridge University Press, 1963), 229.

238. As summarized in Snodgrass, *Stories*, 729 n. 199; see, e.g., Tanghe, 'Abraham, son fils', 577.

239. Glombitza, 'Der reiche Mann', 178–80.

240. R. F. Capon, *The Parables of Grace* (Grand Rapids: Eerdmans, 1988), 159: 'Lazarus is the Christ-figure in this parable. Like Jesus, he lives out of death.'

241. See the discussion in Chapter 5, §§5.5.2–4.

Chapter 3

RHETORIC IN LUKE 16:19–31

1. *Why a Parable?*

The question is worthy of reflection: When Jesus wanted to teach a lesson or give a rebuke, why did he choose a parable as the vehicle for this activity? He could have assigned his disciples a list of tasks, or warned his detractors with an admonition. Instead, Jesus speaks often in parables to audiences both amicable and antagonistic. What difference does this choice of form make for the communication of the message? Such an inquiry lies at the heart of this chapter's rhetorical-critical investigation of Luke 16:19–31, our second perspective into the parable as revealing key aspects of the theology of Luke-Acts.[1]

Rhetoric can be described as 'that quality in discourse by which a speaker or writer seeks to accomplish his purposes'.[2] Already in his preface (1:1–4) Luke speaks of the care he has taken in crafting his account. He has done this, he informs Theophilus in v. 4, in order that he might know the truth and reliability of the things he was taught (ἵνα ἐπιγνῷς περὶ ὧν κατηχήθης λόγων τὴν ἀσφάλειαν).[3] Luke's message is grounded in historical events,[4] and with his presentation of these events he wants to persuade Theophilus to appreciate their certainty.[5] This authorial claim to having been purposeful in composition is an incipient encouragement to the audience to listen to the subsequent work for its persuasive effect. It may be surmised that if he was to communicate effectively, Luke needed to utilize the rhetorical conventions available, and his audience would likewise have expected such a use of rhetoric.[6]

---

1. See the brief introduction to the method of rhetorical criticism in Chapter 1, §6.2.
2. Kennedy, *Rhetorical Criticism*, 3.
3. See the discussion in Alexander, *Preface*, 136–42.
4. Cf. use of ἀσφαλής in Acts 21:34 and 22:30.
5. Green, *Luke*, 45.
6. Walton, 'Rhetorical Criticism', 6. For the application of rhetorical criticism to Luke-Acts specifically, see B. Witherington III, *The Acts of the Apostles: A*

In this chapter we will first consider Luke's general rhetorical abilities. Secondly, we will investigate the forms and conventions that might inform Luke 16:19–31, whether the Greek rhetorical use of παραβολή (and related terms) or the use of מָשָׁל (and other parabolic material) in the Jewish wisdom tradition, or perhaps a combination thereof. Finally, we will identify this parable's rhetorical purposes and functions within the context of Luke-Acts.

2. *Hearing Luke's Rhetoric*

An investigation of the rhetorical qualities of Luke 16:19–31 begins with the question of whether it is reasonable to expect to identify rhetorical forms and patterns in this Gospel.[7] As intimated, it is our assumption that Luke wrote with purpose, which he employed the conventions of language in order to achieve. The words and their arrangements in his Gospel will have been shaped by the prevalence of rhetoric imbuing daily modes of discourse at that time.[8]

Socio-Rhetorical Commentary (Grand Rapids: Eerdmans, 1998); K. Bass, 'The Narrative and Rhetorical Use of Divine Necessity in Luke-Acts', *Journal of Biblical and Pneumatological Research* 1 (2009): 48–68. A recent study of the rhetoric of the Lukan parables is Lauri Thurén, *Parables Unplugged: Reading the Lukan Parables in Their Rhetorical Context* (Minneapolis: Fortress, 2014). Two relatively recent rhetorical studies of this parable are Evans, 'Rhetoric of Criticism', and Hughes, 'Rich Man'.

7. Because the primary method of publication in the Graeco-Roman world was public reading, authors generally wrote with a sensitivity to how their words sounded when read aloud. The aural character of written works supports the claim that New Testament authors such as Luke were aware of their words' rhetorical potential, and would have employed rhetorical tools to that effect. See, e.g., F. G. Downing, 'Theophilus' First Reading of Luke-Acts', in *Luke's Literary Achievement: Collected Essays*, ed. C. M. Tuckett, JSNTSup 116 (Sheffield: Sheffield Academic, 1995), 91–109; M. E. Dean, 'The Grammar of Sound in Greek Texts: Toward a Method for Mapping the Echoes of Speech in Writing', *Australian Biblical Review* 44 (1996): 53–70. A synopsis of the study of New Testament orality is provided by K. R. Iverson, 'Orality in the Gospels: A Survey of Recent Research', *CurBR* 8 (2009): 71–106. See also E. Eve, *Behind the Gospels: Understanding the Oral Tradition* (Minneapolis: Fortress, 2014); and his 'Memory, Orality and the Synoptic Problem', *Early Christianity* 6 (2015): 311–33; R. Rodríguez, *Oral Tradition and the New Testament: A Guide for the Perplexed* (London: Bloomsbury T&T Clark, 2014); and his 'Reading and Hearing in Ancient Contexts', *JSNT* 32 (2009): 151–78.

8. Witherington, *Rhetoric*, 23; cf. Black, 'Rhetorical Criticism', 167–68.

What can be surmised about Luke's rhetorical skill as a Greek-speaking author? In evaluating his ability, Burridge considers to what degree the components of classical rhetoric are present in Luke's Gospel. With respect to arrangement, Luke follows similar patterns to those present in the ancient *bioi*, or character portraits.[9] For instance, Luke's use of invention (or the discovery of the subject matter) revolves to a large extent around the deeds and words of Jesus, the main protagonist of his narrative.[10] An evaluation of the aspect of style reveals Luke's facility with a variety of composition styles for different segments of his narrative.[11] With public reading as the primary means of publication in the Graeco-Roman world, it is also necessary to consider the audible impression of a written work,[12] and Luke's Gospel has characteristics that are conducive to aural reception and retention.[13] From this evidence scholars conclude that Luke 'shows at least some level of skill in the tradition of Hellenistic rhetoric',[14] and demonstrates a competence that is, at minimum, comparable with the standards of that time.[15] While we cannot speculate on his education, it is probable that Luke received some rhetorical training that informs his writing.[16]

9. Burridge, 'Gospels and Acts', 514–21, cites as evidence Luke's prologue, careful geographic arrangement, use of literary units, and epilogue; cf. his conclusions about the genre of the Gospels in *What Are the Gospels? A Comparison with Graeco-Roman Biography* (Cambridge: Cambridge University Press, 1992), 191–219.

10. Burridge, 'Gospels and Acts', 521–25.

11. Ibid., 526; cf. Kennedy's appraisal of Luke's rhetorical ability (*Rhetorical Criticism*, 107–8). Witherington, *Rhetoric*, 33–43, suggests that the rhetoric of Luke-Acts should be termed the 'rhetoric of history' (34), because it is in the form of a reliable continuation of the salvation history recounted in the Hebrew Scriptures (or LXX); cf. W. S. Kurz, 'Luke-Acts and Historiography in the Greek Bible', in *Society of Biblical Literature 1980 Seminar Papers*, SBLSP 19 (Missoula, MT: Scholars Press, 1980), 283–300.

12. Downing, 'First Reading', proposes an intriguing reconstruction of the audience's character, composition and setting for an early public recitation of Luke-Acts.

13. Burridge, 'Gospels and Acts', 529–30.

14. Maxwell, *Between the Lines*, 124; cf. Kennedy, *Rhetorical Criticism*, 107–8. More sweeping is the claim of Witherington, *Rhetoric*, 33, that Luke is a 'rhetorically informed and skilled Hellenistic historian'.

15. For a favourable comparison of Luke's rhetorical technique with Quintilian's handbook of rhetoric, see R. Morgenthaler, *Lukas und Quintilian: Rhetorik als Erzählkunst* (Zurich: Gotthelf, 1993). Rhetorical ability could, of course, be gained in ways other than following a formal education: an intentional use of rhetorical theory, a deliberate imitation of the practice of others, an unconscious borrowing from others, or a natural gift for effective speaking (Walton, 'Rhetorical Criticism', 7).

16. Burridge, 'Gospels and Acts', 530.

A second and correlated question to Luke's rhetorical facility is whether its exercise registered with any significance on his audience.[17] Considering again how rhetorical traditions pervaded Graeco-Roman discourse, Luke's audience will have been prepared to respond to the persuasive language and structures present in his Gospel. It need not be insisted that they had received rhetorical training, nor is it likely.[18] Nevertheless, as competent listeners they heard the Gospel in the context of the rhetorical traditions with which they were broadly familiar, whether these were consistent with Graeco-Roman or Jewish genres.[19] When they listened to Luke's rhetoric on the broader soundstage of that culture, the audience was primed to listen to a discourse that – at the most superficial level – offered an element of interest or diversion. Yet this discourse was also able to affirm the convictions that they already held, and perhaps to effect change in their quotidian thinking or doing.[20]

Having established that Luke generally demonstrates a rhetorical ability in his Gospel,[21] and that his audience likely had a receptivity toward such a demonstration, we are prepared to investigate Luke 16:19–31 with attention for its rhetorical qualities and their desired effect. We will consider this passage first in terms of its form and then in terms of its function.

3. *A Question of Form:*
Looking for Rhetorical Models for the Parables

Beginning with an analysis of the form of Luke 16:19–31 will assist us in articulating the function of its rhetoric. We do not intend to take a strictly formalistic or stylistic approach to the text, nor reduce this study to a perfunctory listing of the figures of speech that might be identified.[22]

---

17. See the discussion of Luke's implied audience in Chapter 2, §2.2.

18. Mack, *Rhetoric*, 31.

19. Downing, 'First Reading', 97.

20. Ibid., 102.

21. As for Acts in particular, its rhetorical qualities have been studied in connection with its speeches; see, e.g., D. Watson, 'Paul's Speech to the Ephesian Elders (Acts 20.17–38): Epideictic Rhetoric of Farewell', in Watson, ed., *Persuasive Artistry*, 184–208; and for its general patterns, see A. C. Clark, *Parallel Lives: The Relation of Paul to the Apostles in the Lucan Perspective* (Carlisle: Paternoster, 2001); Kennedy, *New Testament Interpretation*, 114–40.

22. See the lament of Wuellner, 'Rhetorical Criticism', 451–52, in appraising recent works on the rhetoric of biblical texts; cf. Penner, 'Reconfiguring', 425–39.

Not really rhetorical...

However, through exploring possible rhetorical forms, the parable's communicative purpose can be better understood. The recognition that a work corresponds at least partially to an identifiable rhetorical form conditions an audience to respond appropriately. Even if hearers remain unaware of the precise mechanics of the discourse, it is by its careful styling and structuring that an author's argument obtains influence.[23]

No

According to some scholars the search for a formal pattern for the Gospel parables is bound to be fruitless.[24] The parables of Jesus are considered *sui generis*, inimitable among the contemporary literature. Jeremias describes the parables as revealing 'a unique clarity and simplicity, a matchless mastery of construction'.[25] Likewise, in his examination of rhetoric in the early church, Wilder lauds the novelty of the Gospels' rhetoric, asserting that Jesus's ministry was 'the occasion for a new utterance and new forms of utterance'.[26]

While it can probably be agreed that the Gospel parables have a marked rhetorical freshness, their formal exceptionality should not be exaggerated.[27] Indeed, there is the competing claim that the parables owe their form to the cultural traditions of which Jesus and the Gospel writers were part. Those who evaluate the Gospel parables against the background of this milieu differ on whether the rhetorical model is to be found in the sphere of the Hellenistic use of the παραβολή or that of the Hebrew מָשָׁל. For instance, in their study of rabbinic parables McArthur and Johnston cite favourably many מְשָׁלִים in comparison with the parables of Jesus, and they see Jesus as continuing in the narrative

23. C. C. Black, 'Rhetorical Criticism and Biblical Interpretation', *ExpTim* 100 (1988–89): 252–58: 'Meaning in discourse is communicated most profoundly by the marriage of a message and its means of conveyance' (257).

24. Kennedy, though a proponent of the classically based rhetorical study of the New Testament literature, nevertheless asserts that 'the gospels are unique works which do not exactly fit any classical literary genre and which have a subtle internal rhetoric of their own' (*Classical Rhetoric*, 138).

25. Jeremias, *Parables*, 12; cf. J. Breech, *Jesus and Postmodernism* (Minneapolis: Fortress, 1989), who surveys many of the narratives of late Western antiquity and concludes that 'Jesus' parables were dissimilar from all extant contemporary stories' (24–25).

26. A. Wilder, *Early Christian Rhetoric: The Language of the Gospel* (Cambridge, MA: Harvard University Press, 1971), 18; while acknowledging some similitude with the rabbinic parables, Wilder highlights the uniqueness of certain features of the Gospel parables, such as sober style, dramatic immediacy, realistic authenticity and use of common idiom (71–77).

27. Kennedy, *Classical Rhetoric*, 128.

traditions of the rabbis.[28] However, on the same question Mack concludes that the Synoptic parables are best understood in the context of Graeco-Roman rhetoric.[29]

It is possible, of course, that an awareness of both Graeco-Roman rhetorical conventions and the traditions of Jewish speech will be helpful for our inquiry.[30] Thus we turn to an examination of each form, beginning with the use of παραβολή (and related terms) in the *progymnasmata* and other Graeco-Roman rhetorical writings, then considering the מָשָׁל and similar forms in the Hebrew Scriptures and subsequent literature. For both traditions we will note important differences from and similarities to Luke 16:19–31, and then appraise their effect on understanding the parable's meaning and function.

3.1 *Graeco-Roman Rhetorical Forms*

3.1.1. *Consulting the Progymnasmata*
In the search for identifiable rhetorical forms within the Gospels, scholars have consulted the *progymnasmata*.[31] The *progymnasmata* were part of the latter stages of grammatical training in Graeco-Roman culture, and a component of early rhetorical study. These were elementary writing exercises in a variety of types of rhetoric by which students could hone their skills.[32] The earliest extant progymnasmatic textbook, one approximately contemporaneous with Luke, is the treatise *Progymnasmata* by

28. McArthur and Johnston, *Parables*, 98; on the question of dating the rabbinic material, see the discussion in §3.2.3.1, below.

29. B. L. Mack, 'Teaching in Parables: Elaboration within a Chreia', in *Patterns of Persuasion in the Gospels*, ed. B. L. Mack and V. K. Robbins (Sonoma, CA: Polebridge, 1989), 143–60, citing 146–47.

30. See the observation of Burridge, 'Gospels and Acts', 521, about the Gospels generally: 'It is better to see them within the broad genre of *bios*, showing both Graeco-Roman rhetorical influence and also the patterns and methods of Jewish story telling within their syncretistic culture'; cf. Evans, 'Rhetoric of Criticism', 259.

31. See, e.g., Parsons, 'Luke and the *Progymnasmata*'; V. K. Robbins, 'Progymnastic Rhetorical Composition and Pre-Gospel Tradition', in *The Synoptic Gospels: Source Criticism and the New Literary Criticism*, ed. C. Focant; BETL 110 (Leuven: Leuven University Press, 1993), 111–47.

32. Parsons, 'Luke and the *Progymnasmata*', 44; R. O. P. Taylor drew attention to these handbooks in *The Groundwork of the Gospels* (Oxford: Basil Blackwell, 1946), averring with confidence, 'It is perfectly easy to classify the contents of the Gospels by these…terms, Chreia, Recollection, Narrative and Parable' (81). G. A. Kennedy has compiled and translated such exercises in *Progymnasmata: Greek Textbooks of Prose Composition and Rhetoric* (Leiden: Brill, 2003).

Aelius Theon of Alexandria.[33] Like other teachers of rhetoric, Theon aimed to have students develop persuasive ability through composing such forms as the *chreia*, fable, and narrative.[34] Much of this writing was done in a mimetic spirit, where familiar cultural stories were freely recast for new rhetorical purposes.[35] As an enduring by-product of this elementary training, 'if students subsequently undertook serious literary work, they tended to utilize progymnasmatic forms in the development of their thought'.[36]

Of most relevance for our investigation is the progymnasmatic activity of composing or paraphrasing fables and narratives.[37] Theon describes a fable (μῦθός) as 'a fictitious story giving an image of truth'.[38] As for a narrative (διήγημα), he says that it features 'language descriptive of things that have happened or as though they had happened'.[39] Employing narrative anecdotes was essential for strengthening a spoken or written work's persuasive value.[40] The notable point of connection that invites comparison is from the progymnasmatic fable to the Gospel parables, for

33. Parsons, 'Luke and the *Progymnasmata*', 46. A recent critical edition is M. Patillon, *Aelius Theon Progymnasmata: Texte etabli et traduit* (Paris: Société d'édition Les Belles Lettres, 1997); see the English translation of Theon's treatise in Kennedy, *Progymnasmata*, 3–72.

34. Parsons, 'Luke and the *Progymnasmata*', 47. On the Lukan practice of attaching a parable to a *chreia*, see Farmer, 'Literary and Form-Critical Analysis', 301–16, who cites Luke 16:14–15 and 19–31 as an example of less than the typical care Luke shows in structuring his work.

35. See the comprehensive study of mimesis in Hauge, *Tour of Hell*, 35–59. Cf. T. Brodie, 'Greco-Roman Imitation of Texts as a Partial Guide to Luke's Use of Sources', in *Luke-Acts: New Perspectives from the Society of Biblical Literature*, ed. C. H. Talbert (New York: Crossroad, 1984), 17–46; and Robbins, 'Writing as a Rhetorical Act in Plutarch and the Gospels', in Watson, ed., *Persuasive Artistry*, 142–68; Hughes, 'Rich Man'.

36. Kennedy, *New Testament Interpretation*, 22. Penner, 'Reconfiguring', 436, notes that students who received progymnasmatic training may have later mixed different genres and styles of discourse.

37. On this tradition, see Beavis, 'Parable and Fable', 476–78; cf. V. K. Robbins, 'Narrative in Ancient Rhetoric and Rhetoric in Ancient Narrative', in *Society of Biblical Literature 1996 Seminar Papers*, SBLSP 35 (Atlanta: Scholars Press, 1996), 368–84, especially 373–76.

38. *Aelius Theon* 72.28 (Kennedy, *Progymnasmata*, 23). Theon's definition of μῦθός is echoed by Aphthonius and Nicolaus (Kennedy, *Progymnasmata*, 96, 133).

39. *Aelius Theon* 78.16–17 (Kennedy, *Progymnasmata*, 28).

40. Robbins, 'Ancient Rhetoric', 371.

the latter can also be characterized as 'fictitious stories imaging truth'.[41] While parables were typically short comparisons based on common experience and should be distinguished from fables which sometimes included fantastic elements from the world of flora and fauna, the disparity of these two forms should not be exaggerated.[42]

3.1.2. *Luke 16:19–31 and the Progymnasmata*

Evaluating the features of Luke 16:19–31 according to the preliminary writing exercises, three recommended features of a μῦθός are manifest.[43] In the first place, Theon encourages 'a mixture of constructions' in a student's manipulation of fables. An instance of this mixture is the movement from indirect discourse to direct discourse.[44] Such variety is pleasing to the reader and strengthens the fable's appeal, if not rhetorically, then aesthetically. This combination of constructions is evident in the move from a description of the outward circumstances of Lazarus and the rich man (vv. 19–23) to an extended dialogue between the rich man and Abraham (vv. 24–31). This shift heightens audience attention and it prompts consideration of the words of the patriarch as having a broad application.[45]

A second suggestion for progymnasmatic composition is the incorporation of the μῦθός into a narrative.[46] Stigall summarizes this technique: 'The fable does not have to be an entirely discrete composition, but can be part of a broader work'.[47] Besides its position within the Gospel narrative, the parable is linked tightly with the immediate context as a companion

41. Parsons, 'Luke and the *Progymnasmata*', 50.

42. Witherington, *Rhetoric*, 39–40. On the Graeco-Roman tradition of parables, see M. H. McCall, *Ancient Rhetorical Theories of Simile and Comparison* (Cambridge, MA: Harvard University Press, 1969), who notes that 'parable' is current as a technical term of comparison before Aristotle.

43. While observing how Luke honours the progymnasmatic ideal of economizing words, Robbins notes also that 'the Lukan text contains quite long, well-crafted fable-parables like the Rich Man and Lazarus' ('Ancient Rhetoric', 374). An analysis of the parable of the Rich Fool (Luke 12:16–21) according to progymnasmatic rubrics is provided by J. J. Stigall, 'The Progymnasmata and Characterization in Luke's Parables: The Parable of the Rich Fool as a Test Case', *PRSt* 39 (2012): 349–60.

44. *Aelius Theon* 74.33–75.5 (Kennedy, *Progymnasmata*, 25).

45. Schnider and Stenger, 'Die offene Tür', 280–83.

46. *Aelius Theon* 75.6–10 (Kennedy, *Progymnasmata*, 25); cf. Demetrius, *Eloc.* 157–58.

47. Stigall, 'Progymnasmata', 351.

piece to the parable of the Dishonest Steward (16:1–9), and is ostensibly told in response to the money-loving Pharisees who sneered at Jesus for his unambiguous views on the corrupting power of μαμωνᾶς (16:14–15). Luke has clearly represented the narrative occasion for the parable's telling.

Theon also suggests that a μῦθός be concluded with a gnomic statement.[48] After being engaged by the telling of a fable, the audience should be supplied with a concise statement of the main points for remembrance and reflection. It may be argued that such a moral forms the parable's conclusion in v. 31, Abraham's sobering words to the rich man: Εἰ Μωϋσέως καὶ τῶν προφητῶν οὐκ ἀκούουσιν, οὐδ᾽ ἐάν τις ἐκ νεκρῶν ἀναστῇ πεισθήσονται.[49] This general statement about the importance of heeding the Scriptures not only encapsulates the subject of their conversation, it also states a truth that applies more broadly.[50] After having been enticed by the appeal of the discourse, the hearers have a lesson to ponder about the sufficiency of Scripture's testimony.

While three general features of an ideal progymnasmatic fable can be found in Luke 16:19–31, we also note a point of divergence. In his handbook Theon promotes the employment of a simple and natural style for a μῦθός.[51] Such a style presumably aids the audience in retaining the material. This unadorned mode is not evident. Instead, there is a fulsome description of the rich man's feasting in v. 19, the application of a proper name to the voiceless beggar in v. 20, the colourful detailing of both Lazarus's longing for crumbs in v. 21, and the rich man's request in v. 24 for a drop of water on his tongue. Such literary embellishments, while pleasing to an audience and likely conducive to their engagement with the narrative, are a departure from the suggested unadorned style for a progymnasmatic μῦθός.

---

48. *Aelius Theon* 75.12–15 (Kennedy, *Progymnasmata*, 26–27).

49. See Hauge, *Tour of Hell*, 117, on Abraham's summative declaration. According to Theon, a fable can also have multiple conclusions or morals (*Aelius Theon* 75.28–31; see Kennedy, *Progymnasmata*, 26). Parsons, 'Luke and the *Progymnasmata*', 50, suggests that Luke may have realized this was a legitimate way to end a parable, in view of how the parable of the Dishonest Steward (16:1–9) appears to have a variety of applications in subsequent verses (vv. 9–13). The apparent 'double ending' or controverted 'main lesson/s' of Luke 16:19–31 may be of similar origin.

50. Bovon, *Lukas*, 3:112–13; cf. Brookins, 'Dispute', 45–46, on the gnomic statements or *sententiae* that conclude the parable (vv. 25–26, 29, 31).

51. *Aelius Theon* 74.6 (Kennedy, *Progymnasmata*, 24).

Considered overall, the rhetorical ability that Luke demonstrates in this parable suggests the possibility that he received elementary instruction in the *progymnasmata*.[52] However, it remains an open question how much significance should be afforded to the *progymnasmata* in the formation of Luke's rhetorical skill. The cited instances may be more general stylistic resemblances than products of specific training. While the *progymnasmata* in general do suggest parallels for many textual units in the Gospel,[53] it must be considered possible, though not certain, that Luke had been tutored in these exercises. Our exploration of the rhetorical models informing Luke 16:19–31 will now venture into another area of Graeco-Roman tradition, the use of the παραβολή.

3.1.3. *Is Luke 16:19–31 a* Παραβολή?

It must be acknowledged that the story of Lazarus and the Rich Man is not designated a παραβολή.[54] This is unlike other formally similar Lukan illustrative narratives that do receive this nomenclature, such as the parable of the Rich Fool (12:16–21) or the parable of the Unrighteous Judge (18:2–8).[55] Partly because of its lack of designation as a παραβολή, this text has been described not as a parable but as an 'example story'.[56] At the same time, we note that the term παραβολή is used in Luke's Gospel to designate a wide range of materials.[57] Named according to their

---

52. Parsons, 'Luke and the *Progymnasmata*', 44; cf. Kennedy, *Progymnasmata*, ix, who suggests that the writings of the early Christians 'were molded by the habits of thinking and writing learned in schools'.

53. Burridge, 'Gospels and Acts', 517.

54. As a textual variant, Codex Bezae explicitly identifies this narrative as a parable: Ειπεν δε και ετεραν παραβολην; cf. C. Ray, 'The Rich Man and Lazarus', *TTE* 56 (1997): 77–84, citing 78; and Comfort, 'Two Illustrations', 112.

55. See also 15:3–7; 18:9–14; 19:11–27; 20:9–16.

56. See Jülicher, *Gleichnisreden*, 114, 630. He classifies Luke 16:19–31 as one of four 'example stories' (*Beispielerzählung*) among the other parables (*Parablen*) and similitudes (*Gleichnisse*). Jülicher is perhaps best known for championing a non-allegorical reading of the Synoptic parables in general, and for insisting that each parable has only one principal point. The classification as an 'example story' means that it requires no transfer from one sphere to the spiritual realm in order to be interpreted; it is to be considered a genuinely literal story – without symbolic or figurative elements – and as a result, its meaning is directly applicable to its hearers. Jülicher's classification of this text has endured in scholarship; see, e.g., A. Loisy, *L'évangile Selon Luc* (Frankfurt: Minerva, 1971), 414; W. Grundmann, *Das Evangelium nach Lukas*, THNT 3 (Berlin: Evangelische Verlagsanstalt, 1961), 324.

57. On the question of classifying parables in the Synoptic Gospels, see Snodgrass, *Stories*, 9–15; cf. C. H. Peisker, 'Parable, Allegory, Proverb', *NIDNTT* 2:746–60;

content, such textual units can alternately be called proverbs (4:23; 6:39), metaphorical sayings (5:36–39), enigmatic sayings (8:10), general rules (14:7–11), narratives depicting common occurrences (8:4–8; 12:41–48; 13:6–9; 15:3–6; 21:29–30), narratives depicting a singular occurrence (18:2–8; 19:11–27; 20:9–16), and illustrative narratives (12:16–21; 18:9–14). Despite the fluidity of παραβολή, the designation of 16:19–31 as an 'example story' and not as a 'parable' is suspect.[58] That Luke 16:19–31 is akin to other narrative παραβολαί so designated is evidenced by the parabolic introductory formula in v. 19 (ἄνθρωπος δέ τις ἦν). This formula is typical of other Lukan parables or comparative stories.[59] The passage also evinces a conventional parabolic structure[60] and is formally consistent with other Lukan parables.[61] These factors invite its comparison with other rhetorical units of similar characteristics.[62] We will continue to refer to this text as a parable, or an illustrative and fictional narrative told for purposes of instruction. This description is broad enough to allow its examination in relation to the Graeco-Roman forms and usages of παραβολή.

Tucker, *Example Stories*, 206, observes that while 'the Greek word παραβολή itself does not authorize a definitive model of a singular comparative mechanism operative in all narratives called by that name…[understanding] παραβολή as juxtaposition encourages readers or hearers to consider what is being set side by side, by what means and for what reasons'.

58. See Tucker, *Example Stories*, 264–74. He concludes that Luke 16:19–31 and the other 'example stories' do not exhibit any singular or peculiar features that distinguish them from the other narrative parables in the Synoptic Gospels,

59. The introductory phrase is uniquely Lukan, occurring in seven instances of what are conventionally described as parables (Luke 10:30; 12:16; 14:16; 15:11; 16:1, 19; 19:12), though only in 12:16 and 19:11 is the story termed a παραβολή by Luke. The phrase occurs in a *chreia* (Luke 14:2), and in a healing story (Acts 9:33). Hintzen, *Verkündigung*, 121, observes that this phrase is characteristic of fiction.

60. See Funk, *Parables and Presence*, 19–54; cf. Sellin, 'Lukas als Gleichniserzähler', 166–89; Blomberg, *Parables*, 166–67.

61. G. W. Knight, 'Luke 16:19–31: The Rich Man and Lazarus', *RevExp* 94 (1997): 277–83, citing 277; Blomberg, *Historical Reliability*, 52, notes, 'The objection that Luke does not specifically call this passage a "parable" is most decisively countered by form criticism; approximately half the stories in the gospels that are commonly called parables are not specifically labelled as such, but they are recognized by the common form and structure they share with passages specifically termed parables'.

62. Other Lukan narratives conventionally called parables but not described as a παραβολή include the parables of the Good Samaritan (10:25–37), the Prodigal Son (15:11–32), and the Dishonest Steward (16:1–9).

3.1.4. *The* Παραβολή *in Graeco-Roman Usage*

The previously mentioned conclusion that the Lukan parables have an entirely original character within their milieu is questionable. At minimum it should be acknowledged that the term παραβολή, familiar to readers of Luke's Gospel, was in common use already centuries before its composition.[63] In Graeco-Roman literature the παραβολή, akin to the μυθός,[64] was a comparison or illustration employed with a rhetorical purpose. It allowed persuasion to take place in an argumentative way: 'Parables were used to clinch a rhetorical argument and persuade someone to do or think something'.[65] In delineating varieties of comparison for use as proof in rhetorical discourse, Aristotle contrasted those illustrations drawn from ordinary life (παράδειγμα) and those based on historical examples (πράγματα).[66] While πράγματα were derived from the real stories of the nations and could be viewed as more plausible, fables (λογόι) or parables (παραβολαί) could more easily be manufactured by the speaker for a specific purpose.[67] The value of a παράδειγμα is its ability to elucidate or exhibit a component of the topic being explained. As an artificial inductive proof it can prove or buttress the speaker's point.[68] The strength of such a proof is that 'the agreement of the listener is more easily obtained on the level of comparison'.[69] This is a strategy that Aristotle described as the 'concealment of the final sentence' (κρύψις συμπεράσματος).[70] Plato in several of his discourses employs illustrations and allegories and uses

63. J. D. Crossan, 'Parable', in *The Anchor Bible Dictionary*, ed. D. N. Freedman (New York: Doubleday, 1992), 5:146–52, briefly outlines the Graeco-Roman parabolic tradition (146); cf. Berger, 'Hellenistiche Gattungen', 1074–75 and 1110–48 on παραβολή. For now we bypass the use of παραβολή in the LXX as a translation of the Hebrew noun מָשָׁל, where it has a broad meaning, signifying a range of speech units (see Peisker, 'Parable, Allegory, Proverb', 743–46). To the use of the מָשָׁל in the Hebrew Scriptures we return below.

64. Beavis, 'Parable and Fable', 478, notes that in literary-historical terms, parable and fable are closely related.

65. Witherington, *Rhetoric*, 31.

66. Aristotle, *Rhet.* 2.20.1393a (28–31); cf. Quintilian, *Inst.* 5.11.22–30, who argues that parables are most functional when they have apparent and immediate referents. Zimmermann, 'Ancient Rhetoric', 238–58, summarizes the place of parables and similitudes in Aristotle's and Quintilian's discussions of ancient rhetoric.

67. Aristotle, *Rhet.* 2.20.1393a (24–25).

68. Witherington, *Rhetoric*, 39–40; cf. Aristotle, *Rhet.* 2.20.1394a.

69. Zimmerman, 'Jesus' Parables', 246.

70. Aristotle, *Top.* VIII 1,155b 23.

figures of speech that he designates παραβολαί.[71] Stoic and Cynic writers also make use of illustrations that can be generally termed parables.[72] To the features of Luke 16:19–31 that are paralleled in this tradition we now turn.

3.1.5. *The* Παραβολή *of Luke 16:19–31*

If it can be granted that Luke wrote for an audience with some rhetorical awareness, his audience likely heard this parable with a consciousness of the genre's usage in Graeco-Roman rhetoric.[73] To what degree, then, does Luke 16:19–31 conform to or diverge from the Graeco-Roman forms and usages of the παραβολή? The methodological difficulty we face is that ancient rhetoricians said little about the formal characteristics for such a unit,[74] or they addressed different issues and categories in their discussions of the παραβολή.[75] This makes illegitimate a simple transfer of Graeco-Roman rhetorical classifications to a text such as this parable.[76] That being so, it is intuitive that the content, and not the form, is determinative for the effectiveness of the παραβολή as an inductive proof.

Beavis has helpfully adduced the general features of the content of the Graeco-Roman tradition of παραβολαί. She notes that they are 'brief, invented narratives about incidents which shed light on certain aspects of human experience and behavior'.[77] Further, they feature religious or

---

71. See, e.g., Plato, *Gorg.* 493d–94a; *Resp.* 6.487e–89a; 7.532a-d; *Phaed.* 246a–57a; 274–75c; and the well-known 'Allegory of the Cave' in *Resp.* 7.514–17; cf. the examples in F. Hauck, 'παραβολή', *TDNT* 5:746 (n. 7). The widespread use in the literature belies Quintilian's derogatory view that in rhetoric, fables were 'specially attractive to rude and uneducated minds, which are less suspicious than others in their reception of fictions, and when pleased, readily agree with the arguments from which their pleasure is derived' (*Inst.* 11.19); see the analysis of Quintilian's theory of comparison in McCall, *Simile and Comparison*, 178–236.

72. See, e.g., Epictetus, *Diatr.* I.24.19; II.14.21; III.25.6–10; cf. the examples in Hauck, *TDNT* 5:746 (n. 8).

73. Witherington, *Rhetoric*, 39.

74. McCall, *Simile and Comparison*, 27; cf. Mack, 'Teaching in Parables', 146, who notes: 'It is highly questionable whether genre-specific concerns are foremost in the designation of certain types of speech material as παραβολαί'.

75. McCall, *Simile and Comparison*, 27; cf. Tucker, *Example Stories*, 384–85, who cautions that the term παραβολή (as well as παράδειγμα, *similitude*, and *exemplum*) is not used in the rhetorical treatises with any consistency of reference.

76. Zimmerman, 'Jesus' Parables', 256, 258.

77. Beavis, 'Parable and Fable', 480; cf. Charles Hedrick, *Parables as Poetic Fictions* (Peabody, MA: Hendrickson, 1994), 32.

ethical themes such as the inevitability of divine retribution. She notes that despite being realistic in their descriptions, the fables contain elements of extravagance, such as in extreme behaviours or almost implausible circumstances.[78]

Three similarities with the Graeco-Roman tradition can be noted in the Luke 16:19–31 parable. First, it is a discourse that illuminates aspects of human experience or behaviour; it contrasts Lazarus's poverty and the rich man's wealth, and accentuates the latter's failure to respond to the beggar at his gate.[79] Secondly, it has religious and ethical themes. Such concerns are evident in the assignation of rest and torment to Lazarus and the rich man as the consequence of their earthly life, and in the patriarch Abraham's emphasis on listening to the Scriptures deemed sacred by the Jewish people. Thirdly, if parables in the Graeco-Roman tradition are characterized as being realistic yet having extravagant elements, Luke 16:19–31 can also be described in this way, with its conventional picture of a silent and hungry beggar at an urban gate juxtaposed with a rich man enjoying his wealth. This realism is joined with the extraordinary scene of the rich man crying out from the fiery torments of Hades.[80] In these three respects it conforms to Graeco-Roman patterns for παραβολαί.

While there are points of resemblance Luke 16:19–31 also seems to diverge from one broad pattern of Graeco-Roman usage. The Aristotelian tradition promoted the employment of a παραβολή (or similar figure of speech) in order to confirm a principle or to persuade an audience of a particular truth or activity. A general proposition in this parable is not stated. In contrast with other Lukan parables, it is told without introduction or subsequent explanation.[81] Nevertheless, as intimated in our discussion of the progymnasmatic ideal of weaving a fable into a wider narrative, Luke's integration of the parable into his larger literary

78. Beavis, 'Parable and Fable', 480.

79. Reich, *Figuring*, 121–22, observes the presence of the rhetorical figure of speech of *antithesis* in the comparison of Lazarus and the rich man in earthly life and afterlife.

80. Beavis, 'Parable and Fable', 481, observes that while Graeco-Roman parables regularly include supernatural involvement, only two of the Gospel parables do: the parable of the Rich Fool (12:16–21), where God addresses him directly for his greed; and this parable, which features a variety of supernatural elements (e.g. angels, Hades, 'Abraham's bosom').

81. Lukan parables with either introductory comments or concluding applications are 12:15–21; 16:1–9; 18:1–8; 18:9–14; 20:9–18.

composition suggests its persuasive function. Elements of prior discourse shape how the parable is heard and interpreted.[82]

Four significant statements preceding the parable give its rhetoric meaning and effect. First, we consider the conclusion of the parable of the Dishonest Steward (16:9), concerning the employment of unrighteous wealth to secure 'eternal dwellings' (αἰωνίους σκηνάς). The rich man is a negative example of someone who did not assure himself of eternal dwellings through the right use of wealth. A second important contextual factor is the dictum in 16:13 on the nature and danger of earthly riches: οὐ δύνασθε θεῷ δουλεύειν καὶ μαμωνᾷ. The rich man is a stark and memorable illustration of this danger. Thirdly, we hear Jesus's response to the derision of the 'money-loving' Pharisees in 16:15, asserting that what is favoured (ὑψηλόν) by people is judged an abomination (βδέλυγμα) by God. The rich man's fate depicts how God has a radically different valuation of material possessions than that held by humans. Fourthly, audience attention is shaped by Jesus's statement in v. 17 about the law's durability, that not even the smallest part of it will fall away (ἢ τοῦ νόμου μίαν κεραίαν πεσεῖν). Abraham's words portray the necessity of upholding both the law and prophets (v. 31). In view of these features, the parable's content is inextricably connected to the propositions previously submitted. Well in line with the Graeco-Roman rhetoricians' suggested use of the παραβολή, this parable seeks to persuade the audience of the truth and validity of these propositions.[83] In this respect, too, the function of Luke 16:19–31 is consistent with the general use of παραβολάι in the Graeco-Roman literature.[84]

Having observed general correspondences with the Graeco-Roman παραβολή, what does this contribute to our understanding of the text's rhetorical function? First, the currency of the literary genre of the παραβολή indicates the probability that Luke was employing this narrative in order to persuade his audience to adopt certain perspectives.[85] On matters of

---

82. Beavis, 'Parable and Fable', 496, says that because of their familiarity with the popular literary form of parables or fables, a first-century audience would have been inclined to seek a moral or application to sum up the meaning of the Gospel parables.

83. Zimmerman, 'Jesus' Parables', 257.

84. A. J. Hultgren, *The Parables of Jesus: A Commentary* (Grand Rapids: Eerdmans, 2000), 9 n. 43, commenting on the use of παραβολή and *parabola* in Greek and Latin writers, is overly dismissive: '*In no case* is their designated use comparable to that in the Gospels' (emphasis added).

85. M. Boucher, *The Mysterious Parable: A Literary Study* (Washington, DC: Catholic Biblical Association of America, 1977), 11, asserts with respect to the

rightly valuing earthly wealth, showing mercy to the poor and hearing the testimony of Scripture, Luke sought to effect change in those who listened. Secondly, because it is likely that Luke's audience was familiar with the rhetorical structures and figures of Graeco-Roman culture, they *Eh* would also be prepared to respond to the argument and persuasion present in the discourse. It is probable that as the parable engaged their attention both with its realism and extravagant detail, it affirmed some convictions and developed others. Besides the Graeco-Roman tradition, Luke and his audience would also be familiar with the traditions of speech from the Hebrew Scriptures and other Jewish literature. To these traditions we turn.

3.2. *Rhetorical Forms in the Jewish Tradition*

In an endeavour to make a sensible classification of the form of Luke 16:19–31, we give attention to the term מָשָׁל in Jewish literature. As with παραβολή in Graeco-Roman rhetoric, מָשָׁל occurs with some regularity in the Hebrew Scriptures, the writings of Second Temple Judaism, and later rabbinic literature.[86] We will briefly survey the use of the term παραβολή in the LXX as a regular translation of מָשָׁל. After summarizing these patterns of usage for the מָשָׁל and noting the general features of parabolic material found in the Hebrew Scriptures and subsequent Jewish writings, we will evaluate the rhetorical impact of this parable's literary form.

3.2.1. *The* מָשָׁל *in Hebrew Usage*
3.2.1.1. *The* מָשָׁל *in the Hebrew Scriptures and Other Jewish Writings.*
A survey of the Hebrew Scriptures reveals that the noun מָשָׁל has a wide breadth of utilization.[87] Considered according to its content, a מָשָׁל describes what can be characterized as a maxim or proverb (1 Sam 24:13 [24:14 MT]; Ezek 16:44), a byword or taunt (Deut 28:37; Ps 44:14 [44:15 MT]), a riddle (Ps 78:2 [77:2 MT]), an allegory (Ezek 17:2–10; 20:45–49 [21:1–5 MT]), a figurative discourse (Num 23:7–10; 24:3–9), and an

Graeco-Roman parabolic and fabulic tradition: 'When Jesus preached so strikingly in parables, he did not create a new literary genre. Rather, he made brilliant use of a genre which was familiar to all throughout the Mediterranean world.'

86. Flusser, *Die rabbinische Gleichnisse*, 141–60, contends that the Greek tradition of fables and illustrations may be the kernel from which the Hebrew מָשָׁל developed; cf. P. Dschulnigg, 'Rabbinische Gleichnisse und Gleichnisse Jesu', *Jud* 47 (1991): 185–97.

87. See Gerald Wilson, 'משׁל', *NIDOTTE* 2:1134–36; cf. Robert H. Stein, 'The Genre of the Parables', in Longenecker, ed., *Challenge*, 30–50, citing 40–41. See also Snodgrass, *Stories*, 567–74, for a useful summary of the occurrences of מָשָׁל in the Hebrew Scriptures (and παραβολή in the New Testament).

ode or a poem (Ps 49:4 [49:5 MT]). This diversity of reference makes it difficult to settle on a precise definition of the מָשָׁל.[88] Broadly, the מְשָׁלִים in the Hebrew Scriptures have three characteristics: they are short in length, portions of wider texts, and artistically designed.[89] In some of the מְשָׁלִים there is an element of comparison, but generally in the Hebrew Scriptures a מָשָׁל 'is any saying meant to stimulate thought and provide insight'.[90]

There are also passages in the Hebrew Scriptures that can loosely be called 'parables'. However, it should be noted that only a few of these stories (Ezek 17:2–10; 20:45–49 [21:1–5 MT]; 24:2–5) are actually termed מָשָׁל in the text.[91] The majority of these parabolic narratives are introduced without a generic classification. However, each is a fictional narrative making comparisons or drawing analogies between patently dissimilar realms of activity. These stories are told with the purpose of illustrating a lesson, warning against transgression, or eliciting judgment. Five to approximately one dozen examples are described as 'Old Testament parables', and are commonly suggested as counterparts to the Synoptic parables.[92] Such instances include the following:

1. Judg 9:8–15 – Parable of the Trees
2. 2 Sam 12:1–4 – Parable of the Ewe Lamb
3. 2 Sam 14:4–7 – Parable of the Two Brothers
4. 1 Kgs 20:38–43 – Parable of the Escaped Prisoner
5. 2 Kgs 14:8–10 – Parable of the Thistle and Cedar

88. Cf. K. J. Cathcart, 'The Trees, the Beasts and the Birds: Fables, Parables and Allegories in the Old Testament', in *Wisdom in Ancient Israel: Essays in Honour of J.A. Emerton*, ed. J. Day, R. P. Gordon and H. G. M. Williamson (Cambridge: Cambridge University Press, 1995), 212–21, notes that it 'seems futile to attempt to attach specific labels to every text of the parabolical and allegorical type' (214).

89. Gerhardsson, 'Narrative Meshalim', 340; he makes a helpful distinction between narrative *meshalim* and aphoristic *meshalim* in the Hebrew Scriptures, 'narrative' being taken in a broad sense of not only 'relating a course of events but also…describing a situation or phenomenon' (341–42). See his shorter version of this article, 'The Narrative Meshalim in the Old Testament Books and in the Synoptic Gospels', in *To Touch the Text: Biblical and Related Studies in Honor of Joseph A. Fitzmyer, S.J.*, ed. Maurya P. Horgan and P. J. Kobelski (New York: Crossroad, 1989), 289–304.

90. Snodgrass, *Stories*, 39.

91. D. Stern, *Parables in Midrash: Narrative and Exegesis in Rabbinic Literature* (Cambridge, MA: Harvard University Press, 1991), 9.

92. See, e.g., Gerhardsson, 'Narrative Meshalim', 343; and T. W. Manson, *The Teaching of Jesus: Studies of Its Form and Content* (Cambridge: Cambridge University Press, 1948), 59–66.

6. Isa 5:1–7 – Parable of the Vineyard
7. Ezek 15:2–5 – Parable of the Useless Vine
8. Ezek 17:2–10 – Parable of the Eagles, the Cedar, and the Vine
9. Ezek 19:1–9 – Parable of the Lioness
10. Ezek 19:10–14 – Parable of the Transplanted Vine
11. Ezek 21:1–5 [20:45–49 LXX] – Parable of the Forest Fire
12. Ezek 24:2–5 – Parable of the Seething Pot
13. Ezek 31:1–18 – Parable of the Great Tree

Besides these short narratives, other passages can be highlighted as extended metaphors or comparisons, such as the accounts of dreams and dream interpretations.[93] However, these typically lack identifiable narrative elements such as setting, characters, and plot, so they are excluded from consideration.[94]

Though generalizing can reduce uniquely featured texts into an amorphous mass, for our purpose we note how the parabolic material of the Hebrew Scriptures (as listed above) can be broadly characterized.[95] First, many of these narratives are deliberative, for the hearer is pressed by the speaker to pronounce a judgment on the hearer's own conduct or views (e.g. 2 Sam 12:1–4; 1 Kgs 20:38–43).[96] Even the parables that do not draw the listener into passing judgment outright have a juridical perspective.[97] Secondly, some of these narratives are framed as factual, told as if they are recounting real-life events (e.g. 2 Sam 14:4–7; Isa 5:1–7). In view of the deliberative tendency of these narratives, this feature may prevent the hearer from reaching a premature conclusion about the speaker's intended point. As Gerhardsson observes of these parables, 'Concrete and visual as they are, they catch the interest and engagement of the listeners and provoke them to react as the speaker wishes'.[98] Thirdly, some of this parabolic material is realistic, in that it describes material objects in an authentic way (e.g. Ezek 15:2–5), or plausibly recounts the attitudes and actions of persons (e.g. 2 Sam 14:4–7). Fourthly, these rhetorical units 'appear primarily in the mouth and writings of prophets' (e.g. 2 Sam

---

93. E.g. Gen 37:5–7, 9–10; 40:5–9; 41:1–7; Dan 4:1–27; 7:1–28; see Evans, 'Parables', 62.

94. C. Westermann, *The Parables of Jesus in the Light of the Old Testament*, trans. and ed. F. W. Golka and A. H. B. Logan (Minneapolis: Fortress, 1990), finds the Hebrew Scriptures replete with comparisons.

95. For some of these features, see Evans, 'Parables', 65–66.

96. Westermann, *Parables of Jesus*, 2.

97. Evans, 'Parables', 66.

98. Gerhardsson, 'Synoptic Gospels', 292.

12:1–4; 1 Kgs 20:38–43; Ezek 17:2–10; 31:1–18).[99] Fifthly, almost all of these parables are directed to kings or leaders of the people (e.g. 2 Sam 12:1–4; 1 Kgs 20:38–43; 2 Kgs 14:8–10; Ezek 19:1–9).[100] Sixthly, these narrative comparisons characteristically receive their meaning from the immediate context, which is usually dialogic in nature (e.g. Judg 9:8–15; 2 Kgs 14:8–10).[101] All of these narratives are contextually joined with explicit interpretations, which either precede or follow.[102]

The multiform use of מָשָׁל and translated equivalents continues to be in evidence in other early Jewish writings, in Hebrew, Aramaic, and Greek (and Latin translation) works that are dated as roughly contemporaneous with the Synoptic Gospels.[103] Instances can be seen in the apocalyptic 4 Ezra, where a παραβολή is a means of giving instruction about future events.[104] The use of παραβολή in 1 Enoch for describing eschatological visions is similar.[105] While the מָשָׁל is not found in the Qumran literature, the Genesis Apocryphon is an example of a parable in Abraham's dream of the Cedar and Date Palm.[106] Another parable from Qumran is the Fruitful Tree.[107] Parabolic material can be noted in LAB 37:3–8, 2 Bar. 22–23, 4 Bar. 7:26–27, and several short fables in the Story of Ahiqar. In general, however, material from the period after the time of the Hebrew Scriptures that can be deemed truly parabolic – short fictional narratives for the purpose of illustrating or warning – is scarce.[108]

99. Snodgrass, *Stories*, 40.

100. Evans, 'Parables', 66.

101. Westermann, *Parables of Jesus*, 153.

102. Snodgrass, *Stories*, 40.

103. Hauck, *TDNT* 5:747–50; cf. Wilson, *NIDOTTE* 2:1135–36; McArthur and Johnston, *Parables*, 105.

104. See, e.g., 4:13–21, 28–32, 38–43; 7:49–61; 8:1–3, 41–45; 9:30–37. P. Patten, 'The Form and Function of Parables in Select Apocalyptic Literature and Their Significance for Parables in Mark', *NTS* 29 (1983): 246–58, observes the use of מְשָׁלִים in 4 Ezra, as well as 1 Enoch, 2 Baruch, to convey divine secrets with an enigmatic quality and needing interpretation.

105. See, e.g., 1:2–3; and the later *Similitudes* in 37:5; 38:1; 45:1; 58:1.

106. 1QapGen 20.13–16; cf. the discussion in Evans, 'Parables', 63.

107. Identified as 4Q302a or 4Qpap Parable; cf. Evans, 'Parables', 63–64; Snodgrass, *Stories*, 42–43, cites a few instances of comparative material in the Qumran literature.

108. Stern, *Parables in Midrash*, 187, speculates that a reason for the scarcity of 'parables and fables' in 'early postbiblical literature' may be that they were considered popular literature, and thereby not worthy of being recorded for posterity by the scribes.

3.2.1.2. *The* מָשָׁל *in the Rabbinic Literature.* If the מָשָׁל as a short, illustrative fictional narrative occurs only infrequently in the Hebrew Scriptures, it is found comparatively often in rabbinic literature.[109] As Thoma defines them, 'Rabbinic parables are simple, secular, mono-episodic, fictional narrative units that serve to explain the rabbinic understanding of the Torah'.[110] These מְשָׁלִים are generally preserved not in narrative but exegetical contexts as part of Scripture interpretation. For מְשָׁלִים placed in a narrative context, it is their setting that provides the information necessary to understand their allusive meaning.[111] The מְשָׁלִים in the rabbinic literature have two parts: the *mashal* proper, and the *nimshal*, or explanation, which usually includes a verse from Scripture, functioning as the prooftext of the מָשָׁל. The rabbis used the מָשָׁל with rhetorical effect, not stating its message overtly but leaving the audience to deduce it for themselves.[112]

3.2.2. *The* Παραβολή *in the Septuagint*

As a subset of the use of מָשָׁל in Jewish literature, the LXX is a final corpus to survey. In the LXX the term παραβολή is found with some regularity, almost always as a translation of the Hebrew noun מָשָׁל.[113] The multiplicity of reference for מָשָׁל is paralleled in the LXX's use of παραβολή. There it denotes units of speech that can be variously charac-terized as proverbs (e.g. 1 Sam 24:13; 1 Kgs 4:32), parables (e.g. Ezek 17:2), riddles (e.g. Num 21:27), or sayings (e.g. 1 Sam 10:12).[114] This wide range of meanings for παραβολή in the LXX makes it difficult to arrive at any clear indication of genre when we review the term as employed by Luke.[115]

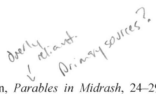

109. See Stern, *Parables in Midrash*, 24–29, for a series of rabbinic מְשָׁלִים in English translation; cf. R. Pautrel, 'Les canons du Mashal rabbinique', *RSR* 26 (1936): 6–45.

110. C. Thoma, 'Literary and Theological Aspects of the Rabbinic Parables', in *Parable and Story in Judaism and Christianity*, ed. C. Thoma and M. Wyschogrod, Studies in Judaism and Christianity (New York: Paulist, 1989), 26–40, citing 27.

111. Stern, *Parables in Midrash*, 16.

112. Ibid., 9.

113. Stein, 'Genre', 39; one exception is Eccl 1:17.

114. For a summary of the Septuagintal usage, see Evans, 'Parables', 52–54.

115. Tolbert, *Perspectives*, 17, notes that the diversity of reference for παραβολή is a natural result of its relationship to מָשָׁל; cf. Stein, 'Genre', 41.

3.2.3. *The* מָשָׁל *of Luke 16:19–31*

Having seen general contours of the usage of מָשָׁל and similar parabolic material in a variety of Jewish literature, we will now investigate Luke 16:19–31 more closely in comparison with this body of material.

3.2.3.1. Comparisons to Rabbinic Literature. Some have taken for granted that there are correlations between the מְשָׁלִים of the rabbis and the narratives found on the lips of Jesus in the Synoptic Gospels.[116] At one level it is natural to see the Jewish sages of the rabbinic literature in continuity with Jesus, insofar as they are alike in making use of the παραβολή or מָשָׁל form in their teaching. But it is essential to take into account the dating of the rabbinic material. Significantly, there is no rabbinic material in original form that dates from before the third century CE, well after the period during which (as is widely accepted) the New Testament Gospels were written.[117] Even assuming that the content of earlier rabbinic material has been faithfully preserved in the extant writings,[118] it is necessary to scrutinize the rabbinic attributions of a teaching and the period in which these rabbis lived.[119] Parables of suggested relevance to the Gospels should be shown to have an independence of and an antecedence to the document in which they occur, otherwise connections to the Gospel parables remain tendentious.[120]

This perspective suggests the need for a reappraisal of past assumptions on the relationship between the Gospel παραβολαί and the rabbinic מְשָׁלִים. For instance, Cadbury was sanguine that the Gospel parables evince Jewish technique as represented in the parables of the rabbis.[121] Others adduce points of resemblance in form, theme and function between the parables of Jesus and the rabbinic מְשָׁלִים.[122] McArthur and

---

116. See, e.g., Stern, *Parables in Midrash*, 20o.

117. D. Instone-Brewer, *Traditions of the Rabbis from the Era of the New Testament*. Vol. 1, *Prayer and Agriculture* (Grand Rapids: Eerdmans, 2004), 28.

118. G. Stemberger, 'Dating Rabbinic Traditions', in *The New Testament and Rabbinic Literature*, ed. R. Bieringer, JSJSup 136 (Leiden: Brill, 2010), 79–96, criticizes Instone-Brewer for too easily accepting the reliability of rabbinic tradition (93).

119. J. Neusner, *Rabbinic Literature and the New Testament: What We Cannot Show, We Do Not Know* (Valley Forge, PA: Trinity Press International, 1994), pleads that New Testament scholars make use of critical methods in examining the rabbinic literature (15).

120. Neusner, *Rabbinic Literature*, 13–15.

121. Cadbury, *Making of Luke-Acts*, 152.

122. C. A. Evans, *Jesus and His Contemporaries: Comparative Studies*, AGJU 25 (Leiden: Brill, 1995), 265–66, notes that while Jesus and the rabbis employed similar pedagogical forms and addressed similar themes, caution is required when comparing these two bodies of literature.

Johnston assert that the rabbinic מָשָׁל and the New Testament παραβολή largely cover the same semantic area.[123] This may be true at first glance, but is ultimately an anachronistic comparison.[124] The 325 known rabbinic parables that McArthur and Johnston cite are from the Tannaitic period, which is approximately from the beginning of the Christian era to 220 CE. This late dating obviously renders problematic any theory of dependence of the Lukan parables on the rabbinic מְשָׁלִים, whether that dependence is conceived of generally or with more specificity.[125] Nevertheless, Evans's observation remains valid, 'We should not suppose that Jesus was the originator of the popular parable, which was later taken up and developed in rabbinic circles. It is better to conclude that Jesus's habitual use of parables is itself evidence that parables were in use in his time.'[126] But absent any reliably datable material, it remains speculative to assert what precise features of the rabbinic parables are reflected in Luke 16:19–31. *Then why include this?*

3.2.3.2. *Comparisons to the Hebrew Scriptures and Other Jewish Writings.* We are on surer ground when juxtaposing Luke 16:19–31 with the parabolic materials from the Hebrew Scriptures and Second Temple Judaism.[127] Texts from these disparate traditions may be compared more readily if we consider their 'parables' to be illustrative and fictional narratives told for purposes of instruction or warning. Such comparisons

---

123. McArthur and Johnston, *Parables*, 98; cf. B. H. Young, *The Parables: Jewish Tradition and Christian Interpretation* (Peabody, MA: Hendrickson, 1998), 236. See Neusner's criticism of Young in *Rabbinic Literature*, 185–90.

124. McArthur and Johnston, *Parables*, 107–8, concede that only a few parables from the first-century rabbis are extant, and even then their authenticity is contested. This late dating does not dissuade them from suggesting 'parallels' between Luke 16:19–31 and an example story recounted in *Ruth Rab.* 3.3 and *Eccl. Rab.* 1.15.1 (195).

125. Snodgrass, *Stories*, 55.

126. Evans, *Contemporaries*, 266. Evans, 'Parables', 51–52, notes a statement in the Mishnah that supports this view. In *m. Sot.* 9:15 it is said, 'When Rabbi Meir [a fourth generation Tannaitic rabbi, who taught about 150 CE] died, makers of parables ceased'. Evans plausibly suggests that this statement implies that the rabbis who preceded Rabbi Meir were known for telling parables. Cf. Blomberg, *Parables*, 69: '[Jesus] most likely adopted a well-known method of instruction when he spoke in parables'.

127. Evans, 'Parables', 65; cf. Stephen Curkpatrick, 'Between *Mashal* and Parable: "Likeness" as a Metonymic Enigma', *HBT* 24 (2002): 58–71, citing 59–60. By contrast, Blomberg, *Parables*, 56–57, dismisses most of the material from the Hebrew Scriptures as being too formally dissimilar from the parables of Jesus.

may prove a profitable exercise in analysing the rhetorical effect of Luke 16:19–31. We will first review some differences between these two, followed by some important similarities.

3.2.3.3. *Differences from the Hebrew Parabolic Material*. Comparing the Lukan parables with the parabolic material of the Hebrew Scriptures and subsequent literature, two points of dissimilarity can be noted. First, some of the narrative מְשָׁלִים can be dubbed fables, in that they depict animals and plants engaged with human issues and conversing in a human manner.[128] By contrast, while some Lukan parables mention plants or animals, these are rarely of central interest to the narrative; instead, the emphasis is always on the world of humans and their interactions, as in Luke 16:19–31.[129]

A second difference is the way in which the parabolic material of the Hebrew Scriptures and the Third Gospel is textually framed. In the former, parables always serve to introduce or conclude additional discourse.[130] Relatedly, many of these parables are bound to their context, such that they would not readily function in another context. For instance, Nathan tells the parable of the Ewe Lamb (2 Sam 12:1–4) in response to a specific situation involving David, and he would not likely have occasion to repeat it. By contrast, Gospel parables rarely have 'a strong confinement to a specific situation or a specific speech'.[131] Though all the Lukan parables are textually framed to some extent, their content is rarely so situation-specific that they could not be placed elsewhere as an independent teaching.[132] Luke places these narratives into a particular situation in Jesus's ministry, but elements of this context remain ambiguous, unlike those in Hebrew parabolic tradition.

3.2.3.4. *Similarities with the Hebrew Parabolic Material*. There are also significant similarities with the Hebrew parabolic material, similarities that help us to discern the rhetorical gravity of Luke 16:19–31. First, as noted, many parables in the Hebrew Scriptures are deliberative

---

128. Gerhardsson, 'Narrative Meshalim', 345; he cites Judg 9:7–15; 2 Kgs 14:8–14; Isa 5:1–6; Ezek 17:3–10.

129. See, e.g., Luke 13:6–9.

130. See, e.g., Judg 9:7–15 (with explanation in vv. 16–20); 2 Sam 12:1–4 (vv. 7–9); 2 Kgs 14:9 (v. 10); Isa 5:1–6 (v. 7); Ezek 17:2–10 (vv. 11–24).

131. Gerhardsson, 'Narrative Meshalim', 350.

132. Ibid., 350; for Luke's narrative fittings and accessories, see Gerhardsson's 'Synoptic Gospels', 297–98, including editorial notices and statements of aim (e.g. Luke 14:7; 15:1–2; 18:1, 9; 19:11), as well as complementary statements (e.g. Luke 16:9–13) that facilitate audience understanding.

in nature.[133] In Luke's parable, too, judgment is elicited from the hearers, for through the careful portraiture of the rich man and Lazarus, followed by the palpable failure of the rich man to respond to his destitute neighbour's plight, the audience is pressed to pronounce a verdict. What 'Moses and the prophets' require of the rich man is clear.[134] Therefore the conclusion cannot be avoided, namely, that he deserves his torments. In passing this judgment, however, the parable's hearers are induced to reckon with their own response to the poor and whether it would be condemned or commended.

Secondly, the parabolic tradition in the Hebrew Scripture and subsequent literature often feature a presentation of events that is ostensibly factual, as if it is a narration of real-life events.[135] This element can impede the hearer from becoming guarded against the parable's point, and can draw the hearer into the concerns of the narrative.[136] In this way the judgment sought by the speaker can more readily be obtained. As Gerhardsson suggests in connection with the concrete and visual nature of the מָשָׁל, 'The mashal is a means to convince the listeners, a kind of argumentation, a metaphoric…*argumentum ad hominem*'.[137] An element which suggests that the parable was intended to be seen as having a basis in fact is the naming of the poor man (v. 20). As has been postulated by some,[138] this could indicate that the story is based on actual events involving a man named Λάζαρος.[139] The tenor of Luke 16:19–31 as ostensibly recounting actual events probably serves to disarm the audience, and renders them more disposed to accepting its lessons.[140]

---

133. See, e.g., Judg 9:8–15; 2 Kgs 14:8–10; Isa 5:1–7; Ezek 15:2–5.

134. See the discussion in Chapter 4, §§4.1.1–6.

135. See, e.g., 2 Sam 14:4–7; Isa 5:1–7.

136. The parable of the Ewe Lamb (2 Sam 12:1–4) can be cited as a prime example of such a disarming narrative. In recounting the unjust incident, Nathan causes King David to lower his defenses and to pass judgment on his own wrongdoing against Bathsheba and Uriah (Evans, 'Parables', 55).

137. Gerhardsson, 'Synoptic Gospels', 292.

138. See the discussion in the Excursus of Chapter 2, §9.2.

139. Oesterley, *Jewish Background*, 204, suggests conversely that a basis of the story in fact 'would have been sufficient reason for the non-mention of the name'.

140. Stein, 'Genre', 38, notes that the parables perform a persuasive function 'by disarming their hearers and by piercing through defenses and resistance. They can do this because the analogy in a parable is different from the sensitive reality with which it is dealing.'

Related to the preceding point is, in the third place, the authenticity
of the characters and events in some of the Jewish parabolic material.[141]
This rhetorical convention is maintained in Luke 16:19–31. Previously
we examined the characters' colourful outward portrayal.[142] Similarly
potent is the characterization of their inner life: impoverished Lazarus
in his longing for scraps of food (v. 21), and the tormented rich man in
his longing for a drop of water (v. 24) and his concern for the surviving
members of his family (vv. 27–28). These touches of detail promote the
hearer's engagement in the narrative and persuade the hearer to participate
in the narrative's lesson.

Fourthly, with few exceptions, the fictional narratives in the Hebrew
Scriptures are uttered by prophets.[143] This rhetorical form typically
conveyed a prophetic message from God to a particular audience. The
communication in Luke 16:19–31, too, has prophetic qualities. Jesus is
described as speaking (v. 15), and he is consistently portrayed in Luke's
Gospel as a prophet – or *the* prophet promised and sent by God.[144] His
parabolic expression in this text is consistent with his place within the
tradition of the prophets.

Jesus's prophetic role is underscored by the identification of the immediate audience for this parable. We noted how the parabolic material
of the Hebrew Scriptures and subsequent literature is almost uniformly
directed to kings or leaders.[145] Here, in the fifth place, a comparison to the
addressees of Luke 16:19–31 is instructive. Its audience can be termed
'mixed', in that Jesus is addressing his disciples (16:1), while the presence of the listening Pharisees is also noted by the narrator (16:14). Luke
has just characterized the Pharisees as φιλάργυροι (16:14), an appellation that finds an obvious concretization in the rich man. The story also
follows a series of escalating confrontations with the Pharisees.[146] Again
consistent with the rhetorical use of fictional narratives in the Hebrew
Scriptures, Jesus addresses this parable to persons who held a position
of authority among the people, as interpreters of the Hebrew Scriptures.[147]

141. See, e.g., 2 Sam 14:4–7; Ezek 15:2–5.

142. See Chapter 2, §§6.1.1–4, on the parable's characters and characterization.

143. See, e.g., 2 Sam 12:1–4; 1 Kgs 20:38–43; Ezek 19:1–9; 31:1–18.

144. For the portrayal of Jesus as prophet in Luke, see, e.g., 4:24; 7:16, 39; 9:7–9,
19; 13:33. Cf. the discussion of Jesus as prophet in Johnson, *Literary Function*,
70–78; Wright, *Victory*, 147–97; Moessner, 'Prophet Like Moses', 575–605.

145. See, e.g., 2 Sam 12:1–4; 1 Kgs 20:38–43; Ezek 31:1–18.

146. See, e.g., Luke 5:17–6:11; 7:30; 11:39–44; 14:7; 15:1–2.

147. Evans, 'Rhetoric of Criticism', 277–78, cites this parable as a possible
polemic against Herod through intentional allusions to Herod's opulent manner of

As such, the response of the Pharisees to Jesus's prophetic message is significant.[148]

Sixthly, the parables in the Jewish tradition are bound to their context, receiving an explanation in the surrounding verses.[149] Some Lukan parables are also elucidated in adjacent verses in order to aid the comprehension of the message and its application.[150] While Luke 16:19–31 includes no explicit explanation, the audience is given several cues for understanding from the immediate context.[151] This careful situating assists them in grasping its message. In this respect, too, it is akin to the Jewish parabolic material in that it is a fictional narrative told to stimulate thought and provide insight.[152] For Luke his parables function 'as illustrative, rhetorical catalysts for the Gospel narrative'.[153]

---

dress and his 'five brothers'. As he suggests: 'If the rich man does indeed allude to Herod Antipas, then we have here a bit of ironical and theological sedition' (278). More developed is the argument of M. Bates, 'Cryptic Codes and a Violent King: A New Proposal for Matthew 11:12 and Luke 16:16–18', *CBQ* 75 (2013): 74–93, who sees in Luke 16:16–18 (and in the subsequent parable of Lazarus and the Rich Man) a coded and denigrating reference to Herod Antipas.

148. It is debated whether Luke presents the Jews in general, or the Pharisees in particular, as being receptive to the message of Jesus in Luke-Acts. Some suggest that the response is wholly framed negatively (e.g. J. T. Sanders, 'The Salvation of the Jews in Luke-Acts', in Talbert, ed., *New Perspectives*, 104–28), in which even partial Jewish acceptance of Jesus is eclipsed by a collective rejection (cf. Tyson, 'Jewish Rejection', 137), while others say that Luke is careful to accentuate that individual Jews and Pharisees do accept Jesus as a true prophet, thereby encouraging others in Luke's audience to do likewise (e.g. J. A. Weatherly, 'The Jews in Luke-Acts', *TynBul* 40 [1989]: 107–17). Similarly, Mason, 'Pharisees', 158, notes that the Lukan presentation of the Pharisees is not static, for they are portrayed as sharing the Christian belief in the resurrection (153), while being a Pharisee is an aspect of Paul's credentials in Acts (155); cf. Gowler, *Pharisees*, 297–319.

149. See, e.g., Judg 9:8–15; 2 Sam 12:1–4; 14:6–7; 1 Kgs 20:39–40; 2 Kgs 14:8–10; Isa 5:1–6; Ezek 15:2–5; 17:2–10.

150. See, e.g., 7:41–42; 10:30–35; 11:5–7; 12:16–20.

151. See the discussion in §3.1.5; cf. Chapter 2, §3.2, on the parable's narrative context, and how the rhetorical units of ch. 16 cohere in theme.

152. A. W. Mosley, 'Jesus' Audiences in the Gospels of St Mark and St Luke', *NTS* 10 (1963–64): 139–49, citing 140, observes that 'among Jewish teachers the parable was a common and well-understood method of making teaching clear and giving it a cutting edge', a clarity that is also evidenced in audience response to the Lukan parables (e.g. 10:37). Relatedly, in Luke 8:15 Jesus maintains that his parables are accessible to 'those with a good and noble heart' (οἵτινες ἐν καρδίᾳ καλῇ καὶ ἀγαθῇ).

153. Curkpatrick, '*Mashal* and Parable', 67.

Having observed several points of correspondence between Luke 16:19–31 and the patterns associated with the מָשָׁל, what has been contributed to our understanding of the text's rhetoric? These similarities strongly suggest that this parable was rhetorically effective among those who were familiar with the Jewish Scriptures. As the prophet Jesus tells this authentically detailed and ostensibly factual account in response to the leaders of the people, the Lukan audience is prompted to make a judgment about their wrongdoings. At the same time the audience is invited to reflect on their own response to the parable's messages about valuing earthly wealth, showing mercy to the poor, and hearing the testimony of Scripture. That brings us to consider a final major point in this chapter: the purpose of the rhetoric of Luke 16:19–31.

4. *A Question of Function:*
What Is the Purpose of the Rhetoric in Luke 16:19–31?

While the preceding section focused on the form of Luke 16:19–31, this second section is concerned with its function. Having seen that the parable stands at an intersection of the conventions of Graeco-Roman rhetoric and the traditions of Jewish speech, what can be said about its persuasive intent? In this investigation we will follow the model of a five-stage rhetorical analysis developed by Kennedy.[154] The first step is the determination of the rhetorical unit, ascertaining what is the legitimate pericope to study. In the second step we define the rhetorical situation or exigence, which is the specific condition or situation inviting the utterance. Relatedly, attention is given to the genre of rhetoric that is best suited for this context, whether judicial, deliberative, or epideictic.[155] As a third stage, the discourse's arrangement is examined – how the speaker has chosen to structure the argument and to adduce certain kinds of arguments or proofs, those of *ethos, pathos,* and *logos.*[156] Fourthly, we analyse the unit's features of style and invention as the author employs techniques or devices in order to persuade. Finally, the unit's persuasive effectiveness as a whole is reviewed. Mindful that texts resist conformity to external

---

154. Kennedy, *New Testament Interpretation,* 33–38.

155. In judicial forms of argumentation, the speaker persuades the hearers to indict or acquit; in deliberative, the speaker moves people to act in particular way; in epideictic, the speaker seeks to confirm presupposed values or views through praise and censure (Kennedy, *New Testament Interpretation,* 19–20).

156. See Aristotle, *Rhet.* 1.2.3–6.

patterns,[157] this stepped analysis will be helpful in ascertaining Luke's purpose in 16:19–31.

4.1. *The Rhetorical Unit*

Up to this point it has been assumed that Luke 16:19–31 comprises a unified rhetorical unit. This assumption, however, requires validation. An elementary maxim is that a rhetorical unit must have 'a beginning, a middle, and an end'.[158] In terms of a beginning, the parable is marked in v. 19 by the signature Lukan phrase ἄνθρωπος τις.[159] This sets off the unit from the preceding sayings about the law (vv. 16–18), and signifies that a new message will be spoken. While the parable can be said to lack a conclusion,[160] that another new unit begins following v. 31 is clear from a reintroduction of Jesus's audience in 17:1, Εἶπεν δὲ πρὸς τοὺς μαθητὰς αὐτοῦ. The intervening verses thereby constitute a 'middle', the parable proper. We already noted that contextually, no explicit interpretation is provided. However, a lengthened interpretive context is supplied through viewing the Third Gospel in its entirety – together with Acts – as one rhetorical unit.[161]

4.2. *The Rhetorical Situation*

The parable is told within a particular rhetorical situation. A rhetorical situation comprises three elements: the exigence, a defect or obstacle marked by urgency, or something waiting to be done; the audience, those to be compelled by the address; and the constraints, those persons, events, objects and relationships with the ability to modify the exigence.[162]

The exigence of Luke 16:19–31 is closely associated with the setting of Jesus's ministry.[163] Luke is recounting his long journey to Jerusalem (9:51–19:44), which is primarily a journey of teaching, as Jesus speaks

---

157. Black, 'Biblical Interpretation', 257.

158. Aristotle, *Poet.* 1450b26; cf. Kennedy, *New Testament Interpretation*, 33.

159. See its use in Luke 10:30; 12:16; 14:16; 15:11; 16:1, 19; 19:12.

160. Maxwell, *Between the Lines*, 134.

161. On lengthening the narrative context, see Tolbert, *Perspectives*, 83: this 'gives the interpreter more material upon which to draw in understanding the total configuration of the parable'.

162. L. F. Bitzer, 'The Rhetorical Situation', in *Rhetoric: A Tradition in Transition*, ed. W. R. Fisher (East Lansing, MI: Michigan State University Press, 1974), 247–60, especially 252–54.

163. See the discussion of this narrative context in Chapter 2, §3.1.

to three groups accompanying him: the crowd, his disciples, and the religious leaders.[164] The escalating hostility with the Pharisees now comes into sharp relief. Jesus's words of instruction and warning in the parable are directed to them (vv. 14–15), if not also to the still-present disciples (v. 1). The specific question at issue, or the rhetorical problem,[165] is to correct an erroneous overvaluing of earthly possessions with an attendant neglect of one's poor neighbour.[166] Concurrently, Jesus wants to accentuate the sufficiency of the Scriptures (vv. 27–31).[167] At the level of Jesus's ministry this is the situation that has called for the parable's rhetoric, and as such it invites an appropriate response.[168] However, Luke notes no reaction on the part of Jesus's listeners. Instead, Luke's audience must monitor the various elements of the discourse in subsequent Third Gospel narratives and in the second volume. In a later chapter we will return to how Luke depicts the realization and expansion of the parable's key themes and motifs.[169]

4.3. *The Arrangement*

The arrangement of the discourse of Luke 16:19–31 and its internal architecture serve a persuasive purpose. Broadly, the parable can be divided in three:[170]

1. Situations in Life (vv. 19–21)
    a.   Rich Man (v. 19)
    b.   Lazarus (vv. 20–21)
2. Destinies in Death (vv. 22–23)
    a.   Lazarus with Abraham (v. 22)
    b.   Rich Man in Hades (vv. 22–23)

---

164. Johnson, 'Narrative Perspectives', 209.

165. Cf. Kennedy, *New Testament Interpretation*, 36.

166. Cf. Feuillet, 'Mauvais Riche', 212–23.

167. Tanghe, 'Abraham, son fils', 572–73, argues that Abraham's directive to listen to Moses and the prophets is not reflective of Luke's point of view, but is a Jewish perspective and contributes to an anti-Jewish rhetoric in Luke (cf. Hughes, 'Rich Man', 39–40). This means, implausibly, that the patriarch's injunction actually militates against the Lukan perspective.

168. Bitzer, 'Rhetorical Situation', 258: 'Every rhetorical situation in principle evolves to a propitious moment for the fitting rhetorical response'.

169. See Chapter 5.

170. Cf. Scott, *Hear Then*, 146–48; Bock, *Luke*, 2:1363–64.

3. Possibilities for the Dead and Living (vv. 24–31)
    a.   Plea for Water (vv. 24–26)
         i.   Request (v. 24)
         ii.   Reply (vv. 25–26)
    b.   Plea for Lazarus to be Sent (vv. 27–29)
         i.   Request (vv. 27–28)
         ii.   Reply (v. 29)
    c.   Plea for Message from Dead (vv. 30–31)
         i.   Request (v. 30)
         ii.   Reply (v. 31)

In the parable there is a movement from narrated discourse where the positions, appearances and outcomes of Lazarus and the rich man are described (vv. 19–23), to direct discourse where the dialogue between the rich man and Abraham is recounted (vv. 24–31). This shift signals the importance of what is said between the rich man and Abraham.[171] The dialogue is marked by a progression from concern for personal physical relief (v. 24), to an interest for the welfare of the living brothers (vv. 27–28), to an insistence on the necessity for a messenger from the dead (v. 30).[172] The structural concentration on the rich man underscores the parable's urgent message that the audience should avoid his errors of life and the consequences that he experienced in death.

4.4. *The Style and Invention*

We can highlight several features of the parable's style and invention. In Graeco-Roman rhetoric it was common to speak of the persuasive effect of *pathos* (the emotional reaction stimulated in the hearers), *ethos* (the credibility that the speaker is able to establish), and *logos* (the logical argument of the discourse). Such features are in evidence in Luke 16:19–31.

The realism of Lazarus's condition is depicted in vv. 20–21: he has been thrown down at the rich man's gate, he is covered in sores, unable to fend off the advances of dogs, and desirous to have even the remnants of the rich man's food. Such a description of his physical and emotional state, laden as it is with *pathos*, would be expected to engender

---

171. See the earlier discussion in §3.1.2 of this chapter; cf. Tolbert, *Perspectives*, 75.

172. Hock, 'Lazarus and Micyllus', 459.

pity.[173] Likewise, the failure of the rich man to assist the beggar makes Lazarus the more piteous.[174] On the other hand, the rich man's suffering in Hades (vv. 23–24) is framed in a way that brings his anguish close to the audience's notice.[175] He is in flames and torment, and requests even a drop of water to relieve his pain. The picture is rhetorically powerful, yet the ultimate reaction to the rich man is likely negative, due to the tenor of Abraham's words in response to his requests.[176] ✓

The figure of Abraham grounds the parable's message in a trustworthy and authoritative *ethos*.[177] Already before he speaks Abraham has an indisputable credibility as the father of his people.[178] What he says to the rich man concerning the sufficiency of the Scriptures has the ring of reliability for the listeners. ✓

It is also Abraham who demonstrates *logos* through his three negative responses to the rich man's requests. Abraham's conversation with him, while it might be characterized as paternal and sympathetic,[179] is also argumentative through the successive denials as Abraham seeks to prove various truths.[180] First, Abraham points out the legitimacy of the present reversal of τὰ ἀγαθά of the rich man and τὰ κακά of Lazarus (v. 25). Secondly, Abraham observes the sheer physical impassibility of the χάσμα μέγα as another reason that Lazarus cannot be sent on a relief mission (v. 26).[181] Thirdly, he insists on the adequacy of 'Moses and the prophets' to warn the living. The sufficiency of the Scriptures is underscored by its ability to convince equally as well as one risen from the dead. In the patriarch's closing words this is restated as an *enthymeme*, or a statement with

Too reliant on Aristotle.

---

173. Aristotle, *Rhet.* 2.8.1–16 includes in those conditions inciting pity such things as bodily injuries and afflictions, diseases, and lack of food, particularly among those not deserving of suffering; cf. the observation of Gilmour, 'Homer', 26.

174. Aristotle, *Rhet.* 2.8.10 notes that especially piteous is 'evil coming from a source from which good ought to have come'.

175. Aristotle, *Rhet.* 2.8.14–16 observes that the gestures, tones, and words of the sufferer will excite the listener's pity.

176. Gilmour, 'Homer', 26, suggests that an audience would be indignant because the rich man does not show himself worthy of prosperity (referring to Aristotle, *Rhet.* 2.8.9).

177. Aristotle, *Rhet.* 1.2.4–12 asserts that a person's character may almost be called the most effective means of persuasion that one possesses.

178. See the summary of Abraham in Luke-Acts in Chapter 2, §6.1.3.

179. Metzger, *Consumption and Wealth*, 143.

180. Aristotle, *Rhet.* 1.2.4.

181. One impossibility being ruled out by another impossibility is part of Aristotle's discussion of *logos* in *Rhet.* 2.19.15–16.

deductive proof.[182] If what is simpler to do has not been done (listening to Moses and the prophets), then the more difficult (sending a resurrected messenger) will certainly not elicit a different response.[183] The tight logic of Abraham's final response emphasizes the importance of listening to the Scriptures, and within Luke-Acts it underscores the importance of acknowledging the one to whom the Scriptures ultimately testify (24:27).[184]

4.5. *The Rhetorical Effectiveness of Luke 16:19–31*

So far this investigation has revealed a clear rhetorical strategy in the choice of a parabolic form in Luke 16:19–31. We now reflect on a final component of Kennedy's analysis, how the text advances Luke's overall rhetorical aim. What is its effectiveness in persuading the audience of given truths? Mindful that a rhetorical unit's effectiveness is impossible to judge according to objective parameters, we can adduce several aspects that suggest this parable had distinct value in persuading an appropriate response.

4.5.1. *Capturing Attention*

In general it can be observed that parables have a twofold nature: an informative dimension and an affective dimension. It is true that the inform-ative content of this parable can be interpreted with referential language, and putative meaning can be accurately expressed in non-metaphorical words.[185] When doing so, however, the affective dimension of the parable as a persuasive vehicle is lost. At the level of narrative, therefore, Luke 16:19–31 emotionally engages the hearers through the portrayal of Lazarus's pitiable condition in life and the rich man's anguish in Hades, and the text simultaneously begins to persuade the audience.[186] From its modest beginning to its gnomic conclusion, the narrative invites hearers to give attention to its message. As has been observed generally, 'A parable, being filled with imagery and action, and suggesting as it does that there is more meaning to be discovered here, has great power to catch and hold the attention of the hearer, and to be remembered long after it is heard'.[187]

---

182. Aristotle, *Rhet.* 1.28–22; 2.22–25; cf. Kennedy, *New Testament Interpretation*, 16.

183. Cf. Aristotle, *Rhet.* 2.19.1–7.

184. See the further discussion of this theme in Chapter 5, §§5.3, 5.5.

185. Stein, 'Genre', 48; as an example, he summarizes the meaning of the parable of the Prodigal Son in three declarative statements.

186. Maxwell, *Between the Lines*, 133.

187. Boucher, *Mysterious Parable*, 30; cf. S. McFague TeSelle, *Speaking in Parables: A Study in Metaphor and Theology* (Philadelphia: Fortress, 1975), 78.

If Luke was seeking to draw attention to one or more principal points of instruction, then framing it in this narrative was a judicious selection.

4.5.2. *Disarming with Realism*

A parable does not convey a message merely by being a narrative, but its success is dependent on its artistry and arrangement. Thus we again highlight the parable's realism as a quality intended to elicit a response.[188] By this realism – understood as being true to life, consistent with what can be observed in the world of human experience – the parable prompts listeners to lower their defenses. Credible details dissuade an audience from immediately responding critically,[189] and facilitate an empathetic consideration of the characters.[190] Contemplating things as mundane as daily food, physical health, and interaction with one's neighbour, the audience is led to realize that 'it is in the seemingly insignificant events... that the ultimate questions of life are decided'.[191]

4.5.3. *Surprising by Extravagance*

Though aspects of Luke 16:19–31 may be imagined readily, the characteristic of realism should not be overstated. In general the Synoptic parables evince what Ricoeur calls an 'extraordinary within the ordinary'.[192] Normal expectations are exceeded and accepted boundaries for behaviour are transgressed, as elements of extravagance are introduced.[193] In the

---

188. Wilder, *Early Christian Rhetoric*, 71; he notes further, 'The impact of the parables lay in their immediate realistic authenticity' (73).

189. W. G. Kirkwood, 'Storytelling and Self-Confrontation: Parables as Communication Strategies', *Quarterly Journal of Speech* 69 (1983): 58–74, citing 68.

190. N. Perrin, *Jesus and the Language of the Kingdom: Symbol and Metaphor in New Testament Interpretation* (Philadelphia: Fortress, 1976), 129.

191. TeSelle, *Speaking in Parables*, 77.

192. P. Ricoeur, 'Biblical Hermeneutics', *Semeia* 4 (1975): 29–149, citing 99–100. Huffman, 'Atypical Features', 207–20, observes this to be true of other Lukan parables, such as the unusual generosity of the father in the Prodigal Son (15:11–32), and the kindness of a Samaritan to a Jew in the Good Samaritan (10:25–37). Likewise, Tolbert, *Perspectives*, 90, cites as 'exaggerated details' in Lukan parables: *all* the guests refusing the invitation in the Wedding Feast (14:18), the father *running* to meet his son in the Prodigal Son (15:20), and the Unjust Judge fearing violence from the *widow* (18:5); cf. K. E. Bailey, *Jesus Through Middle Eastern Eyes: Cultural Studies in the Gospels* (Downers Grove, IL: IVP Academic, 2008), 181.

193. D. P. Seccombe, 'Incongruity in the Gospel Parables', *TynBul* 62 (2011): 161–72.

parables such surprising details are juxtaposed with features generally regarded as credible.[194]

This extravagance is evident Luke 16:19–31. The rich man's display of wealth in v. 19 is on a fantastic scale.[195] Consequently, the audience understands that any expression of material kindness to Lazarus would be an insignificant matter to him. Also foreign to the lived experience of the audience is the rich man's scorching afflictions in the afterlife (v. 24) and the intriguing topography of Hades (v. 26), a setting that demonstrates the narrative's uncomfortable seriousness. The rich man's impertinence in addressing someone as highly esteemed as the patriarch Abraham (vv. 24, 27, 30) would likely also be striking, for the Hebrew Scriptures and later writings emphasize the need to respect one's elders and defer to their wisdom.[196] His persistence again lays bare his failure to understand what it means to be a child of Abraham.[197]

Collectively, the parable's surprising features will have been powerful for an oral culture, in which oral delivery attracted attention to these features' strangeness and also impressed them on the memory.[198] Audience consternation in turn compels an inquiry about the parable's message. The parable's realism is modified by these exaggerated details, yet they do not destroy the story's internal unity.[199] The plot continues to unfold in believable ways, particularly when considered according to the values being advanced in Luke's Gospel: the poor are made rich, the high are brought low, and the true children of Abraham are those who live according to 'Moses and the prophets'.[200] Any element of surprise is tempered by these well-established Lukan tenets.

4.5.4. *Inviting Response*

Another rhetorical effect is the parable's implicit invitation for a response.[201] One desired response is the activity of making meaning, for all parables demand interpretation and compel the involvement of an

---

194. Tolbert, *Perspectives*, 89–90.

195. See the discussion of the various elements in v. 19 in Chapter 2, §6.1.2.

196. See, e.g., Lev 19:32; Deut 21:18–21; Job 32:7; *Ps.-Phoc.* 220–22.

197. See the description of Abraham's true children in Luke 3:8 (and 19:9).

198. Huffman, 'Atypical Features', 220.

199. Tolbert, *Perspectives*, 89.

200. Huffman, 'Atypical Features', 219, interprets these features as 'Jesus' usual way of revealing the unworldly character of the coming kingdom of God'.

201. Cf. the conclusions of Reich, *Figuring*, 137–44, on the effects of rhetorical figures of speech in Luke's Gospel as providing emphasis, offering persuasion, and inviting participation.

interpreter.[202] Interpretive factors are to be supplied by the listener, yet these factors must be congruent with the story.[203] Remembering what they have heard in Luke's Gospel – and upon subsequent re-listening – the audience is compelled to evaluate the parable's meaning accordingly. A second response closely follows: the effecting of change. As Kirkwood states: 'Parables are told to arouse both sympathetic and hostile listeners to recognize and overcome those thoughts, feelings, attitudes, and actions which impede their spiritual growth'.[204] Having met Lazarus and the rich man, and having seen their outcomes of life, the audience must reflect on what will now be different for their own thinking and doing with respect to possessions, poverty, and the Scriptures.

4.5.5. *Filling the Gap*

We have been evaluating the rhetoric of Luke 16:19–31 in terms of the words chosen and arranged, but there is also a rhetorical effect in what is *not* said. This is the rhetorical tool of omission.[205] Graeco-Roman rhetoricians were sensitive to the effect of leaving things unsaid, or suspending the narrative before a logical end has been reached.[206] Marguerat explains, 'Narrative suspension is a literary device whereby the author, by failing to bring certain narrative data to their resolution, hinders the closure of the narrative world for the reader'.[207] As a consequence, closure needs to be realized by the hearer who is compelled to conclude the story in a way consistent with its plot.[208] Maxwell investigates this phenomenon in Luke-Acts, where the audience is repeatedly left to fill narrative gaps and to imagine how a given story ends.[209] Luke 16:19–31 is one of several Lukan

---

202. Tolbert, *Perspectives*, 67; cf. T. Thatcher, *Jesus the Riddler: The Power of Ambiguity in the Gospels* (Louisville, KY: Westminster John Knox, 2006), 48, who identifies 'riddles' in the Synoptic Gospels, akin to the function of riddles and riddling sessions in the ancient world. He notes the power of ambiguity latent in many sayings in the Gospels, including Luke 16:19–31, which creates ambiguity in the mind of the audience, and leaves it to the hearer to resolve.

203. Tolbert, *Perspectives*, 49.

204. Kirkwood, 'Storytelling', 58. What Kirkwood observes in general about parables from a variety of cultures is true of the parables of Jesus in particular (62).

205. Kurz, *Reading Luke-Acts*, 17–36.

206. See, e.g., Quintilian, *Inst.* 2.13.12–13.

207. D. Marguerat, 'The End of Acts and the Rhetoric of Silence', in Porter and Olbricht, *Rhetoric and the New Testament*, 74–89, citing 81.

208. Marguerat, 'End of Acts', 81.

209. Maxwell, *Between the Lines*. In addition to individual passages, she suggests that this is true of Luke's Gospel as a whole, which in some respects can

parables with an omitted ending.[210] In response to the rich man's request to send Lazarus to warn the five brothers, Abraham says that those who do not listen to 'Moses and the prophets' will also not be persuaded by one who is resurrected. Though Abraham's words are not optimistic, whether the brothers will in fact listen to the Scriptures is left unsaid.[211] In this way the audience is invited to contemplate a range of potential responses to the Scriptures and to one who is resurrected within the Luke-Acts narrative.[212] Being engaged in such a contemplation concurrently poses the same question to the hearers, whether they will listen to 'Moses and the prophets' and be convinced by someone who rises from the dead.

5. *Conclusions on the Parable's Rhetoric*

Luke 16:19–31 is a well-crafted rhetorical unit whose features would likely have elicited a meaningful audience response. With respect to the elementary writing exercises of the *progymnasmata*, the mixture of constructions encouraged in the student's manipulation of fables is evident in the parable. This is first seen in the shift from a description of the outward circumstances of Lazarus and the rich man (vv. 19–21) to an extended dialogue between the rich man and Abraham (vv. 24–31); rhetorically, this change heightens attention. The *progymnasmata* also suggest the incorporation of a μυθός into a narrative, and Luke 16:19–31 is in fact linked tightly with the immediate context as a companion piece to the parable of the Dishonest Steward (16:1–9), and it is told in response to the greedy Pharisees who sneered at Jesus for his views on money. A third feature formally consistent with the progymnasmatic μυθός is its conclusion with a gnomic statement; such a moral forms the parable's conclusion in v. 31 about the significance of heeding the Scriptures. The currency of the literary genre of the παραβολή likewise indicates the

---

be said to remain open-ended, as the story of the resurrected Jesus's followers continues in Acts; in this way, the 'unfinished business finds its way into the lives of the audience' (148).

210. Maxwell, *Between the Lines*, 134–46. She comments on the open-endedness of the parable of the Two Debtors (7:41–43), the Good Samaritan (10:25–37), the Fig Tree (13:6–9), and the Prodigal Son (15:11–32). Additionally, she lists (134 n. 78) the parables of the Garments and Wineskins (5:36–39), Specks and Planks (6:41–42), A Man Building His House (6:46–49), and the Rich Man and Lazarus (16:19–31). Maxwell does not elaborate on how our parable lacks an ending.

211. Johnson, 'Narrative Perspectives', 211; see the discussion in Chapter 2, §6.1.4.

212. Metzger, *Consumption and Wealth*, 154.

probability that Luke was creatively employing this narrative in order to persuade his audience of his viewpoint on various subjects. Because it is likely that Luke's audience was also familiar with the rhetorical structures and figures of Graeco-Roman culture, they would be prepared to respond to his persuasion.

The parable's features are likewise paralleled in the various מְשָׁלִים of the Jewish Scriptures. Like many of the latter, it is juridical in nature, in that a judgment on personal misconduct is elicited from those who hear the parable. The parabolic tradition in the Jewish Scriptures presented narrated events as ostensibly factual, as does this parable. The fictional narratives in the Jewish Scriptures are uttered by prophets, as Jesus, the prophet *par excellence*, does in Luke 16:19–31. The Jewish parabolic material is uniformly directed to kings or leaders, and while the addressees of Luke 16:19–31 include Jesus's disciples (v. 1), the narrator observes that Jesus is also responding to the listening Pharisees (vv. 14–15) who hold a position of authority among the Jewish people. Parables in the Jewish tradition are explained by their literary context, and in the immediate context of Luke 16:19–31 are several cues for understanding. These similarities with the Jewish parabolic tradition suggest the likelihood that this parable was rhetorically effective among those in Luke's audience who were familiar with the Jewish Scriptures. As the prophet Jesus tells the authentically detailed and ostensibly factual account in response to certain of the elite, the audience is prompted to make a judgment about their misdemeanours. At the same time, the hearers are invited to contemplate the parable's message and their own response.

Considered rhetorically, Luke 16:19–31 is an apposite vehicle for Luke's persuasive purpose. Through its structural arrangement, and by its use of *ethos*, *pathos*, and *logos*, the parable conveys emphatic messages about handling wealth and responding to poverty, and listening to Scripture. With elements of realism the parable also prompts listeners to lower their defenses, for they can imagine themselves either in the position of Lazarus or the rich man. At the same time, the narrative demonstrates the 'extraordinary within the ordinary'. The excessive luxury and then the scorching afflictions of the rich man, the abject poverty and then the blissful state of Lazarus, were likely memorable in an oral culture and urged listener inquiry into causes and alternatives. The parable's rhetoric encourages reflection on how one's current responses to possessions, poverty, and the Scriptures may need to be altered. This rhetorical effect is intensified when the audience hears Luke 16:19–31 in the context of Acts, anticipating how its lessons will be concretized by Jesus's followers in the early church.

Chapter 4

INTERTEXTUALITY IN LUKE 16:19–31

1. *The Creation of Texts*

The parable of Lazarus and the Rich Man was not brought into existence *ex nihilo*. Almost invariably, authors make use of pre-existing material, echoing what has been written in the past, affirming long-established beliefs, and linking to contemporary themes and motifs. What is true of literature in general is true of the New Testament in particular; as Augustine's maxim puts it: *Novum testamentum in vetere latet, vetus in novo patet.*[1] This straightforward dictum belies the more complex reality that New Testament authors not only interacted with a range of materials besides the Old Testament, but carried out this process in a multiplicity of ways, overt and subtle.[2] What is read in Luke's Gospel is the result of a diverse process of interpretation and commentary on earlier texts.[3]

1.1. *Delimiting Intertextuality*

The concept of the interplay of diverse texts is called intertextuality.[4] Scholars point out the need for establishing objective parameters for conducting intertextual investigations, and it is an appropriate caveat.[5]

---

1. *Quaest. Hept.* 2.73; 'The New Testament is concealed in the Old, in the New the Old is revealed'.

2. For a helpful introduction to these issues, see Hays and Green, 'Use of the Old Testament', 222–38.

3. S. Moyise, 'Respect for Context Once More', *IBS* 27 (2006): 24–31: 'Whatever meanings and functions the text once had, the quoted material now takes its meaning from the contextual connections that the new author has established' (25).

4. See the brief introduction to the perspective of intertextuality in Chapter 1, §6.3.

5. Hatina, 'Intertextuality', 28–43, addresses the criteria for evaluating specific pre-texts; cf. the cautions of Foster, 'Echoes without Resonance', 96–111.

In this connection Hays has made a valuable contribution to the study of intertextuality. Acknowledging that the identification of textual resonances will involve a level of subjectivity, particularly when a reference or quotation is not explicitly signalled by the author, he proposes seven criteria for testing the claim that an echo of or an allusion to a prior text has been detected.[6] In this chapter we will employ his criteria to consider a range of materials that may be brought into conversation with this parable, and how this dialogue reveals key aspects of Lukan theology. We begin by reflecting on the legitimacy of conceiving a kind of 'discourse among texts' with this parable.

1.2. *Possibilities of Intertextuality in Luke 16:19–31*

Nothing in Luke 16:19–31 announces the presence of a direct quotation from previous Scriptures. Apart from the presence of explicit quotations, however, Litwak observes of this Gospel generally that Luke is 'taking up the Scriptures of Israel, causing the voices of Scripture to sound out in a new way and in a new context'.[7] This echoing occurs across a spectrum of passages and genres.[8] With respect to this parable, numerous allusions to and echoes of earlier Jewish traditions have been identified.[9] Abraham's answer in v. 29 to the rich man (Ἔχουσι Μωϋσέα καὶ τοὺς προφήτας· ἀκουσάτωσαν αὐτῶν) is itself an intertextually suggestive rejoinder. Within the parable's story, 'Moses and the prophets' is likely an overt recommendation that the rich man recall passages from Jewish Scripture which both

6. R. B. Hays, *Echoes of Scripture in the Letters of Paul* (New Haven, CT: Yale University Press, 1989), 29–32. His seven criteria are: availability, volume, recurrence, thematic coherence, historical plausibility, history of interpretation, and the test of satisfaction. Brawley, *Text to Text*, 13, suggests that only the first two are crucial, while the remaining criteria 'help to substantiate probable allusions on a subordinate level'. Hays has continued to make contributions to the discussion of New Testament intertextuality with *Reading Backwards: Figural Christology and the Fourfold Gospel Witness* (Waco, TX: Baylor University Press, 2014), and *Echoes of Scripture in the Gospels* (Waco, TX: Baylor University Press, 2016).

7. Litwak, *Echoes of Scripture*, 53.

8. There have been numerous studies of Luke's use of Scripture; see, e.g., Evans and Sanders, *Luke and Scripture*; Barrett, 'Luke/Acts'; Fitzmyer, 'Use of Old Testament'; Ringgren, 'Luke's Use'; Hays, *Gospels*, 191–280.

9. See summary of allusions in Pao and Schnabel, 'Luke', 345; e.g. they identify the rich man's clothing as reminiscent of Prov 31:22, the dogs that lick Lazarus's sores as an echo of passages in which dogs consume the dead (1 Kgs 14:11; 16:4; Jer 15:3), and the transfer of Lazarus by the angels as a possible allusion to the story of Enoch (Gen 5:24) and Elijah (2 Kgs 2:11).

legislate and exhort proper care for one's fellow human beings, particularly socially marginalized and underprivileged persons. Other allusions
to the Jewish Scriptures and later literature may also be present.[10]

Besides the regularly posited connections to Jewish literature, numerous
studies address the text's possible backgrounds in mythologies and
other cultural traditions.[11] The sheer variety of these possible origins
and influences suggests the need for restraint in the exercise of determining literary connections between Luke 16:19–31 and its antecedent or
contemporary traditions.[12] Nevertheless, an intertextual sensibility allows
us to bring a range of materials into conversation with this parable. A
variety of the parable's elements will benefit from being related to Luke's
broader literary milieu.

In this chapter we will first identify two key tropes on which to focus
our conversation with the cultural participants. Next, we will consider
ways in which both of these tropes can be the subject of an intertextual
dialogue that engages both Jewish Scripture and other Jewish literature,
as well as a variety of Graeco-Roman literature. Then we will investigate
how these traditions are affirmed and modified in the parable. Finally, we
will observe the continued echoes and developments of these themes in
Acts.

2. *Listening for the Principal Themes and Motifs of Luke 16:19–31*

What is the parable of Lazarus and the Rich Man about? This ostensibly
straightforward question can be answered in a diversity of ways, as there
is a variety of Lukan themes and motifs present.[13] Suggestions include the
theme of God's promised salvation (experienced by Lazarus in v. 22), the
proper use of money and possessions (intimated by Abraham in v. 25),
God's reversal of the rich and strong, and the poor and weak (vv. 22–23),
the patriarch Abraham as representative of God's salvific promises
(vv. 22–26), the symbolic character of the meal scene (suggested in

10. See review of past scholarship on this question in Chapter 1, §6.3.

11. See review of past scholarship on this question in Chapter 1, §4.2.

12. See the ever-relevant cautions in Sandmel, 'Parallelomania'.

13. For our purposes, we will use Alter's definitions of *theme* ('an idea which
is part of the value-system of the narrative—it may be moral, moral-psychological,
legal, political, historiosophical, theological—[and] is made evident in some recurring
pattern') and *motif* ('a concrete image, sensory quality, action, or object [that] recurs
through a particular narrative'); see *Biblical Narrative*, 95.

vv. 22–23), the close relation of the present life to the afterlife (portrayed in vv. 22–24, explained in v. 25), the resurrection from the dead (v. 31), the need for repentance (v. 30), and the reliable testimony of Scripture (vv. 29, 31).

In order to limit the subjects of the following dialogue, we will choose two principal Lukan themes: first, the use of possessions to alleviate poverty; and secondly, the possibility of receiving messengers from the realm of the afterlife. It must be insisted that such a selection does not indicate acceptance of the long-standing division of the parable into two parts, namely vv. 19–26 and 27–31, where the two sections have been characterized as having different or even conflicting thematic emphases: money and revelation, respectively.[14] We have argued that the parable is textually unified, and need not be bifurcated based on a conjectured history of redaction or alleged contradictions.[15] Additionally, the formerly almost-canonical view of a parable as having only one main point of comparison,[16] coupled with 'the rule of end stress' where the parable's conclusion is emphasized,[17] should not deflect attention from any component of the narrative. Thus it is legitimate to suggest that the parable has two principal themes: the requisite use of material possessions to alleviate poverty, and the impossibility and unnecessity of receiving messengers from the afterlife because of the sufficiency of 'Moses and the prophets'.[18]

The theme of possessions is suggested by the parable's immediate context. The parable of the Dishonest Steward in vv. 1–9 concerns using 'unrighteous mammon' for the right purposes: to gain a welcome into eternal habitations (v. 9), and to demonstrate faithfulness in handling

14. See Jülicher, *Gleichnisreden*, 634; see the discussion in Chapter 1, §3.1.

15. See the discussion of the parable's unity in Chapter 1, §3.2.

16. Jülicher, *Gleichnisreden*, 317, speaks of a straightforward, single-meaning comparison or simile (*Vergleichung*). For the interpretative tradition of finding singular didactic propositions in the parables, see the discussion in K. Snodgrass, 'From Allegorizing to Allegorizing: A History of the Interpretation of the Parables of Jesus', in *The Historical Jesus in Recent Research*, ed. J. D. G. Dunn and S. McKnight (Winona Lake, IN: Eisenbrauns, 2005), 248–68, citing 250–52. For a work that challenges the one-point perspective, see particularly Blomberg, *Parables*, 33–81.

17. Jeremias, *Parables*, 186, applies this rule to Luke 16:19–31.

18. Cf. Blomberg, *Parables*, 259; Hendrickx, *Parables*, 211, notes the complementarity of the two themes and sections: 'The second part completes the first by suggesting that if the rich man is lost, it is not only because he is rich, but because he did not convert in conformity with the message of the Scriptures'.

true riches (v. 10).[19] Subsequent to this parable Luke reports that the Pharisees heard Jesus's words about material wealth; their response in v. 14, as 'lovers of money' (φιλάργυροι), is to ridicule him. The following parable in vv. 19–31 is part of Jesus's response to his greedy detractors,[20] and is consistent with a thematic focus on the use of money. This focus is encapsulated in Abraham's comment to the rich man about receiving τὰ ἀγαθά and Lazarus receiving τὰ κακά (v. 25). Possessions are clearly a principal concern for Luke in this section, and by extension, in this parable.

The parable's thematic focus shifts in vv. 27–31 to the possibilities of receiving warning testimony about post-mortem destinations. This theme, too, is suggested by the immediate context. In v. 16 Jesus announces the end of the epoch of law and prophecy in the person of John the Baptist (ὁ νόμος καὶ οἱ προφῆται μέχρι Ἰωάννου). The statement is clarified in v. 17 with a pronouncement about its enduring status, which Jesus then demonstrates with his saying on divorce in v. 18. The theme of law is reprised by Abraham in the parable, for the rich man's request for Lazarus to be sent from his post-mortem state in order to warn his brothers (v. 28) is answered by the patriarch's twice-repeated reference to 'Moses and the prophets' (vv. 29, 31). The possibility of receiving a message from the realm of the dead is excluded by the sufficiency of the Scriptures,[21] a second principal focus of attention in this text.

3. *Choosing Dialogue Partners*

A final prefatory yet not insignificant matter for our investigation concerns those with whom we will bring this parable into dialogue as we examine the two selected themes.[22] It is here that some of Hays's previously mentioned criteria for intertextuality are most helpful. First is the criterion of availability, whether the suggested source of the intertextual

19. For the relationship between the two Luke 16 parables, see Ball, 'Unjust Steward', 329–30; Feuillet, 'Mauvais Riche', 212–23; Story, 'Twin Parables', 105–20; Piper, 'Social Background', 1637–62; C. J. A. Hickling, 'A Tract on Jesus and the Pharisees? Conjecture on the Redaction of Luke 15 and 16', *HeyJ* 16 (1975): 253–65.

20. Hintzen, *Verkündigung*, 366–68.

21. Snodgrass, *Stories*, 429.

22. The need to limit the 'conversation partners' in such a study is apparent. For example, Snodgrass identifies as 'helpful primary source material' for this parable no fewer than twelve early Jewish writings, four Graeco-Roman writings, and four later Jewish writings (*Stories*, 420–23).

echo was available to the author and original audience. Secondly, the volume of an echo must be tested by determining the extent of the repetition of words or patterns of syntax from the intertext. Thirdly, attention is given to recurrence, whether an author cites or alludes to the same passage elsewhere in the work. With these criteria, we will turn to two broad traditions of literature, Jewish and Graeco-Roman.

3.1. *The Jewish Tradition*

Abundant evidence in Luke's Gospel indicates authorial familiarity with the writings of the Hebrew Scriptures and the subsequent literature. His narrative is informed by various scriptural voices,[23] such as the Davidic Messiah of the Psalms,[24] the motif of 'a prophet like Moses',[25] the Abrahamic traditions,[26] and the prophecies of Isaiah.[27] There are also significant echoes of the literature of Second Temple Judaism.[28] We may therefore reasonably assume that Luke was familiar with a range of Jewish traditions that in turn shaped his narrative.

This assumption primes us to listen for other voices from this tradition. While certainly not excluding the possibility of hearing other texts from the Jewish Scriptures, in this chapter we have chosen to engage primarily with Deuteronomy.[29] The evidence of Luke-Acts commends this text as a

23. For Luke's use of Scripture as compared to first-century Jewish practice, see Kimball, *Jesus' Exposition*.

24. M. L. Strauss, *The Davidic Messiah in Luke-Acts: The Promise and Its Fulfillment in Lukan Christology*, JSNTSup 110 (Sheffield: Sheffield Academic, 1995); Peter Doble, 'The Psalms in Luke-Acts', in *The Psalms in the New Testament*, ed. M. J. J. Menken and S. Moyise, New Testament and the Scriptures of Israel (London: T&T Clark, 2004), 83–117.

25. Johnson, *Literary Function*, contends that in Luke-Acts Jesus is being presented as God's prophet in the model of Moses, a prophet who is rejected and then vindicated; cf. Moessner, *Lord of the Banquet*, and 'Prophet Like Moses'; cf. J. Robb, 'The Prophet Like Moses: Its Jewish Context and Use in the Early Christian Tradition' (PhD diss., King's College London, 2003).

26. See Dahl, 'Abraham in Luke-Acts'; Brawley, 'All Families', and 'Abrahamic Covenant'; Kim, 'From Israel to the Nations'.

27. See Mallen, *Reading and Transformation*.

28. See, e.g., the essays in C. R. Holladay, P. Gray, and G. R. O'Day, eds., *Scripture and Traditions: Essays on Early Judaism and Christianity in Honor of Carl R. Holladay* (Leiden: Brill, 2008); S. E. Porter and A. W. Pitts, eds., *Christian Origins and Hellenistic Judaism: Social and Literary Contexts for the New Testament* (Leiden: Brill, 2013).

29. Our study will be concerned with the text of Deuteronomy in its present form, which we will presume to be largely identical to the text that was familiar to Luke

viable dialogue partner for our selected tropes. Rusam provides a study of quotations from Deuteronomy in Luke-Acts, noting eight in total.[30] In most instances, Luke provides an almost exact repetition of the phraseology of the LXX version of Deuteronomy. To employ Hays's terminology: in Luke the Deuteronomic echoes have volume, indicating his predilection for this ancient text. In a few instances Luke quotes passages from the same chapters of Deuteronomy,[31] a recurring use that likewise strengthens the probability that he is echoing this book in other places. In addition to these quotations there are several allusions to Deuteronomy.[32] Beside the occurrence of extracts and allusions, some have argued for a close structural affinity between portions of Luke's Gospel, such as the travel narrative (9:51–19:44) and the book of Deuteronomy.[33] Indeed, Luke's portrayal of Jesus as a 'prophet like Moses' is a contextual factor that strengthens the plausibility that he constructed his narrative with deliberate reference to Deuteronomy.[34] Even apart from the question of this structural resemblance, by three of Hays's criteria (availability, recurrence, and volume) it may be assumed that Deuteronomy was accessible to Luke, he was familiar with it,[35] and he shaped its content to his own purposes.[36]

and his audience; questions of Deuteronomic tradition and redaction are not germane here. For the reception of Deuteronomy in the period leading up to the first century, as evidenced in the Qumran literature, phylacteries, and mezuzot, and its use by Philo and Josephus, see T. Lim, 'Deuteronomy in the Judaism of the Second Temple Period', in Menken and Moyise, eds., *Deuteronomy in the New Testament*, 6–26.

30. Rusam, 'Deuteronomy', 63; as quotations he cites Luke 4:4, 8, 12; 10:27; 18:20; 20:28; Acts 3:22; 7:37.

31. Rusam, 'Deuteronomy', 63; in Luke-Acts both Deut 6 and 18 are quoted on more than one occasion.

32. Rusam, 'Deuteronomy', 65.

33. C. F. Evans, 'Central Section', argues that Luke patterned this section after the LXX of Deut 1–26; cf. Moessner, *Lord of the Banquet*, and 'Luke 9:1–50', 575–605. See the critique in Blomberg, 'Midrash', 217–62, who observes that such a pattern is an unknown practice to ancient literature, some of the alleged parallels are vague and imprecise, and not all the content in Deuteronomy is paralleled. C. A. Evans, 'Luke 16:1–18 and the Deuteronomy Hypothesis', in Evans and Sanders, eds., *Luke and Scripture*, 121–39, counters this critique by proposing three criteria for evaluating the Deuteronomy hypothesis in particular Lukan passages: dictional coherence, thematic coherence, and overall exegetical coherence.

34. Evans, 'Deuteronomy Hypothesis', 127.

35. Cf. the discussion of parameters for determining an echo in Litwak, *Echoes of Scripture*, 61–63.

36. Green, 'Internal Repetition', 290; cf. C. A. Evans, 'Luke's Use of the Elijah/ Elisha Narratives and the Ethic of Election', *JBL* 106 (1987): 75–83, especially 77.

The assumption of Luke's intentionality in using Deuteronomy can be coupled with a second assumption about his audience's perceptive ability. We previously discussed Luke's implied audience,[37] and here we reiterate that they were probably familiar with the Jewish Scriptures in Greek translation,[38] and that they possessed a basic degree of insight into these texts.[39] It is important to emphasize that beside the quotations explicitly signalled, Luke presumes his audience will catch the more subtle allusions out of their cultural repertoire.[40] Litwak observes, 'Even if the original audience missed one or another of these echoes, they may well have heard enough of them to be led to see Luke's point'.[41]

3.2. *The Graeco-Roman Tradition*

That Luke was not writing in a literary vacuum is as true with reference to Graeco-Roman literature as it is with reference to the Jewish Scriptures and subsequent writings.[42] While this was a culturally complex milieu about which it is imprudent to generalize, many beliefs and values were broadly held – or were familiar to – people of diverse backgrounds. The parable can therefore be heard in dialogue with this wider cultural and literary context. As a discourse partner from the Jewish milieu we chose one principal spokesperson in Deuteronomy, but from the Graeco-Roman world we will listen to a variety of texts. Hays's criteria

37. See the discussion of the Lukan audience in Chapter 2, §2.2.

38. On Luke's use of LXX for quotations from the Jewish Scriptures in Luke-Acts, see Mallen, *Reading and Transformation*, 4; cf. W. K. L. Clarke, 'The Use of the Septuagint in Acts', in *The Beginnings of Christianity*, Part 1, vol. 2, ed. F. J. Foakes Jackson and Kirsopp Lake (London: Macmillan, 1922), 66–105.

39. Litwak, *Echoes of Scripture*, 60.

40. Brawley, *Text to Text*, 6.

41. Litwak, *Echoes of Scripture*, 61. On the issue of the competence of New Testament audiences to understand authorial quotations and allusions to Scripture, see C. D. Stanley, '"Pearls Before Swine": Did Paul's Audiences Understand His Biblical Quotations?', *NovT* 41 (1999): 124–44; and the response of B. J. Abasciano, 'Diamonds in the Rough: A Reply to Christopher Stanley Concerning the Reader Competency of Paul's Original Audiences', *NovT* 49 (2007): 153–83. While it is true, as Stanley avers, that the high cost of Scripture rolls and widespread illiteracy could impede familiarity with Scripture, Abasciano is right to point to the advantageous effects of community study, orality, the prioritization of Scripture in early Christianity, and the contextual nature of Paul's use of Scripture. Such factors apply equally to the Lukan use of Scripture.

42. For an introduction to these issues, see L. C. A. Alexander, 'The Relevance of Greco-Roman Literature and Culture to New Testament Study', in Green, ed., *Hearing the New Testament*, 85–101.

resist application in this instance, as it is more difficult to establish with certainty that Luke had access to specific texts, and allowed them to speak in his writing with volume and on a recurring basis. Nevertheless, the texts examined below will be considered reflective of the general milieu of the Graeco-Roman world. We again presume that Luke's implied audience was familiar with the general character and content of the secular literature in that time.[43]

4. *Voices on Poverty and Possessions*

We identified two primary themes in Luke 16:19–31, namely, the requisite use of material possessions in order to alleviate poverty, and the impossibility and unnecessity of receiving messages from the afterlife because of the sufficiency of 'Moses and the prophets'. We will now listen to an intertextual conversation on these topics, hearing the voices of Deuteronomy and Graeco-Roman literature, and being attentive to how these traditions are adopted and modified in Luke 16:19–31. We begin with a consideration of poverty and possessions.

4.1. *Deuteronomy on Possessions and Care for the Poor*

4.1.1. *An Assumed Connection*
Many take for granted that aspects of Luke 16:19–31 should be read in connection with Deuteronomy. In particular, the exhortations and regulations concerning charity are often mentioned as a background to the parable's implied teaching on benevolence for the poor.[44] After the rich man's failure to respond to the suppurating beggar, Abraham makes an overt reference to the testimony of Μωϋσέως (vv. 29, 31), which according to the Jewish understanding includes Deuteronomy.[45] As mentioned, the parable's context also prepares us to listen to Deuteronomy's teaching, for as recently as v. 17 Jesus proclaims the law's abiding validity. The rich man's failure to uphold the laws of benevolence is typically judged to be

What about actual readers?

43. To quote Darr again: Luke's implied reader is 'at home in popular Greco-Roman literature' (*Character Building*, 27).

44. See, e.g., Evans, *Luke*, 250; Bock, 'Ethics of Jesus', 68–69, and *Luke*, 1375; Marshall, *Luke*, 632; Scott, *Hear Then*, 158; Tannehill, *Luke*, 253; Herzog, *Subversive Speech*, 124–25; Johnson, *Luke*, 253; Schottroff, *Parables*, 164; Feuillet, 'Mauvais Riche', 221; Forbes, *God of Old*, 194; Hatcher, 'In Gold We Trust', 280–81; Metzger, *Consumption and Wealth*, 151; Hendrickx, *Parables*, 209; Talbert, *Reading Luke*, 157.

45. Josh 8:32; Sir 24:23; Mark 7:10; 10:3–5; 12:26; Luke 5:14.

blatant and blameworthy.[46] Possible allusions to Deuteronomy, however, have not been thoroughly investigated. What then does Deuteronomy say about the poor, the wealthy, and their treatment of the poor? And how is this voice heard in the parable?

4.1.2. *Perspectives on Rich and Poor*

Deuteronomy speaks repeatedly about poverty and possessions. While attention is given in contexts both juridical and parenetical to the poor and other disadvantaged individuals, we must first consider the author's view of the relative virtues of the poor and rich. That is to say, are Israel's needy strictly to blame for their plight on account of unfaithfulness to the law? Concomitantly, should the prosperous be understood categorically as enjoying the divine rewards for an obedient life? With respect to the latter, some passages speak of God's promise of material blessing on the righteous. Wealth is a marker of God's favour for covenant faithfulness; for instance, the faithful will receive abundant harvests and flourishing livestock.[47] This pattern has led some scholars to speak of something like an Israelite 'prosperity gospel'.[48] At the same time, poverty is never presented as a beneficial or desirable condition. Rather, destitution is one of God's threatened curses on disobedience in Deuteronomy; if the people fail to keep the law they will face economic difficulties such as failed crops, involuntary enslavement, and severe poverty.[49]

Promises of blessing and threats of curse are inadequate to explain all situations of plenty and need as represented in Deuteronomy. It is not necessarily the case that materially well-endowed people are reaping the rewards of their own righteousness. Rather, Deuteronomy insists that any prosperity must be viewed as an unmerited gift of God's kindness.[50] Likewise, it is not necessarily the case that someone who is impoverished is suffering divine punishment for offenses against the law. This conclusion is evidenced by three considerations.

46. See, e.g., Talbert, *Reading Luke*, 156: 'In the parable the rich man who was clothed in purple and fine linen and who feasted sumptuously every day is an example of the misuse of wealth. *He neglected the law relating to the poor*' (emphasis added).

47. That wealth is one of God's blessings on the righteous is seen in, e.g., Deut 6:1–3; 7:12–14; 8:6–9; 11:8–15; 28:4–5 (cf. Gen 26:12–14; Lev 26:3–5).

48. C. Levin, 'The Poor in the Old Testament: Some Observations', *R&T* 8 (2001): 253–73, citing 254; cf. Forbes, *God of Old*, 195.

49. Deut 28:15, 18, 38, 48.

50. In fact, Deut 8:10–18 gives a warning to the materially prosperous not to forget that their wealth has its source in God alone.

In the first place, the various causes of poverty in Israel – such as infertility of the soil, droughts, locust plagues, diseases, enemy invasions – typically affected the entire community, not just the unrighteous individuals.[51] Secondly, that poverty could afflict a diversity of members of the population, apart from their moral goodness or wickedness, is evident from four situations of need often described in Deuteronomy. Beneficent material provision is commanded in 26:12 to be extended לַלֵּוִי לַגֵּר לַיָּתוֹם וְלָאַלְמָנָה ('to the Levite, to foreigner, to the orphan, and to the widow'). The Levites are recipients of physical aid because, as those devoted to the work of ministry at the sanctuary, they did not receive an inheritance of land from which to earn an income.[52] As for foreigners or sojourners, such individuals could face precarious economic circumstances. Non-Israelites who found a permanent home in Israel but lacked the supporting presence of kin and the same opportunities of their neighbours could face hardship;[53] consequently, the author repeatedly mentions the sojourners as objects of the community's benevolence.[54] In a largely agrarian economy a woman or children suddenly deprived of the financial support of a working adult male would also find survival arduous.[55] Facing a predicament outside their control, orphans and widows could not be faulted for their condition; therefore the author exhorts the community to assist them.

A third factor to contemplate concerning poverty in Deuteronomy is that Israel is instructed to interpret the exodus from Egypt in terms of being hapless sojourners, divinely rescued.[56] God demonstrated mercy in granting liberation from Egyptian slavery and gifting them the land of Canaan. According to Deuteronomy, in the words of Baker, 'it follows that they too should be merciful to people in need, sharing the blessing they receive with others'.[57] Recalling their own previously oppressed

---

51. D. Gowan, 'Wealth and Poverty in the Old Testament', *Int* 41 (1987): 341–53, citing 348.

52. On their landlessness, see Num 26:62; for their inclusion on lists of those individuals requiring support, see Deut 14:28–29 and 26:12.

53. See A. H. Konkel, 'גור', *NIDOTTE* 1:836–39.

54. Deut 24:17–21; 26:12–13; 27:19.

55. See C. van Leeuwen, 'אלמנה', *NIDOTTE* 1:413–15.

56. Deut 5:15; 15:15; 16:12; 23:7; 24:18, 22; cf. Exod 22:21; 23:9; Lev 19:34; Ezek 16:3–5. See R. Garrison, *Redemptive Almsgiving in Early Christianity*, JSNTSup 77 (Sheffield: JSOT, 1993), 46.

57. D. L. Baker, *Tight Fists or Open Hands? Wealth and Poverty in Old Testament Law* (Grand Rapids: Eerdmans, 2009), 237.

condition should engender a sympathetic response to the poor.[58] The author enjoins such mercy apart from any question of whether the individual's misfortune is deserved for past offenses. Rather, Deut 10:18 says that it is an aspect of God's own identity to 'execute justice for the fatherless and widow' (עֹשֶׂה מִשְׁפַּט יָתוֹם וְאַלְמָנָה), and to 'love the foreigner and to give him food and clothing' (וְאֹהֵב גֵּר לָתֶת לוֹ לֶחֶם וְשִׂמְלָה). Israel's treatment of these underprivileged groups is to be no different than that demonstrated by Yahweh.[59]

4.1.3. *Response to the Poor*
Though they could not necessarily be blamed for their misfortune, to be poor in Israel as a 'widow, orphan, or foreigner' was to be subject to an array of daily hardships. Perhaps the most acute problem was the consequences of being powerless, the 'lack of status, lack of respect [that made] one an easy mark for the powerful and unscrupulous'.[60] The social status of the poor remained precarious for they were unable to maintain their rights and were prone to abuse or exploitation. Deuteronomy consequently denounces the unjust treatment of the poor, such as in 24:17, 'You shall not pervert the justice due to the sojourner or to the fatherless, or take a widow's garment in pledge'.[61] Despite the poor's powerlessness, they retain a basic dignity and are worthy of the same respect as other community members.[62]

More than simply refraining from exploiting the poor, the people are directed to assist them through a variety of benevolent means. Three regular provisions are legislated in Deuteronomy for helping the disadvantaged.[63] First, at harvest time grain must be left in the fields, olives on the trees, and grapes on the vines, to which the poor are allowed access (24:19–22).[64] Secondly, a triennial tithe is to be collected from all produce, out of which support is to be given to the poor as well as to the Levites (14:28–29).[65] Thirdly, permission is given to any Israelite to eat

58. See, e.g., Deut 15:12–15; 24:17–18.

59. See, e.g., Deut 10:19; 27:19.

60. Gowan, 'Wealth and Poverty', 344.

61. See also Deut 16:19; 24:10–13, 14–15; cf. Job 24:9; Ps 82:3; Isa 1:17.

62. See, e.g., the law that forbids taking a poor man's garment in pledge in Deut 24:10–13 (cf. a similar law for widows in 24:17); cf. Gowan, 'Wealth and Poverty', 351–52.

63. Baker, *Open Hands*; cf. C. S. Rodd, 'The Poor', in Rodd, *Glimpses of a Strange Land: Studies in Old Testament Ethics* (London: T&T Clark, 2001), 161–84, citing 169–70.

64. Cf. Lev 19:9–10; 23:22.

65. Cf. Deut 26:12–15.

what grows in proximate vineyards or fields in order to satisfy hunger (23:24–25). In addition to these benevolent means the Deuteronomic law of debt-remission stipulates that every seven years debts are to be forgiven (15:1–3). This law relieves the burden of those who have been unsuccessful in repaying debts.[66] Though there are no stipulations for the official enforcement of these laws, charity in Deuteronomy is to an extent institutionalized.[67]

4.1.4. *The Future of Poverty*

If Israel implemented the various means of benevolence commanded in Deuteronomy, could poverty have been eradicated? On this subject there is a range of perspectives. For instance, Gelin asserts that poverty was wholly 'a scandalous condition that never should have existed in Israel', because the Mosaic laws gave practical instruments for its elimination.[68] Rodd maintains that in Deuteronomy 'equality of wealth is not presented as an ideal', but there is an assumption that material differences will always be present.[69] Levin concurs, noting that despite legislation which attempted to remedy situations of need, it was understood that poverty in the land would endure.[70]

Central to these dissimilar perspectives is the text of Deuteronomy itself, which may be understood as relaying a mixed message on the future of poverty. On the one hand is the initial phrase of 15:4 (לֹא יִהְיֶה־בְּךָ אֶבְיוֹן). The Hebrew verb יִהְיֶה is a *Qal* imperfect, which can express a variety of aspects, moods, and tenses, depending on the context. For instance, in many English translations the opening phrase of Deut 15:4 is rendered in a future or predictive sense.[71] Already the LXX opted for a future or predictive meaning, οὐκ ἔσται ἐν σοὶ ἐνδεής, 'There will not be a needy person among you'.[72] This future tense is made more explicit and given a conditional sense in the Palestinian Targum of 15:4, 'If you will only be diligent in the precepts of the law, there will be no poor among you; for,

66. Baker, *Open Hands*, 279–80.

67. Gowan, 'Wealth and Poverty', 346.

68. A. Gelin, *The Poor of Yahweh*, trans. Kathryn Sullivan (Collegeville, MN: Liturgical, 1964), 15.

69. Rodd, *Glimpses*, 181.

70. Levin, 'Poor', 254.

71. See, e.g., ESV ('there will be no poor among you'); NRSV ('There will, however, be no one in need among you'); NASB ('However, there will be no poor among you').

72. As commented on by J. Dupont, 'The Poor and Poverty in the Gospels and Acts', in *Gospel Poverty: Essays in Biblical Theology*, trans. M. D. Guinan (Chicago: Franciscan Herald, 1977), 25–52, citing 33.

the Lord will bless you in the land which the Lord your God will give you for a possession to inherit'.[73] Nevertheless, the legislative or instructive genre of 15:4 argues in favour of reading the imperfect phrase not simply as a prediction, but as a strong recommendation, even an imperative.[74] Through charitable measures such as the triennial tithe (14:28–29) and the law of debt-remission (15:1–3), the community must ensure that nobody is poor.[75] Far from being complacent about the continued presence of impoverished persons, Deuteronomy assumes that there will be sufficient resources for everyone if the people obey the directives of God's law.[76]

Complicating this reading of a poverty-less state is the subsequent declaration in 15:11, כִּי לֹא־יֶחְדַּל אֶבְיוֹן מִקֶּרֶב הָאָרֶץ ('For the poor will never cease from the land'). The strong recommendation or imperative in 15:4 that the people should eliminate poverty is ostensibly nullified – or at the very least tempered – with the prediction in 15:11 that benevolent action will never be successful in abolishing indigence. The same verse that urges the eradication of poverty (15:4) includes the assurance of God's blessing if the people practise obedience to this commandment. Divine blessing will be concretized in the economic capacity to lend to other nations, and freedom from the need to borrow (15:6). Yet even this promise of communal material success is qualified by a note of realism in 15:7, which is an acknowledgment of the personal financial challenges faced by some: כִּי־יִהְיֶה בְךָ אֶבְיוֹן מֵאַחַד אַחֶיךָ בְּאַחַד שְׁעָרֶיךָ ('If there is a poor man among your brothers in any of your gates…').[77] This casuistic statement anticipates the v. 11 forecast that there will always be poor in the land. Indeed, v. 7 directs the community not to 'harden their hearts or to shut their hands' against the impoverished individuals still remaining in their midst: לֹא תְאַמֵּץ אֶת־לְבָבְךָ וְלֹא תִקְפֹּץ אֶת־יָדְךָ. Instead of displaying a lack of charity, v. 8 exhorts them to 'open their hands' in voluntary giving. While these charitable practices were likely not always honoured,[78]

---

73. Tg. Ps.-J. 15:4; cf. Dupont, 'Poor and Poverty', 33.

74. J. Dupont, 'La Communauté des biens aux premiers jours de l'leglise', in Dupont, *Études sur les Actes des Apôtres* (Paris: Cerf, 1967), 508.

75. Baker, *Open Hands*, 281; cf. translation of the NIV (1984), 'There should be no poor among you'.

76. P. C. Craigie, *The Book of Deuteronomy*, NICOT (Grand Rapids: Eerdmans, 1976), 237; cf. Gowan, 'Wealth and Poverty', 350–51, who observes that it is an eschatological hope in the later prophetic literature that 'there will be no hunger' (e.g. Ezek 36:29).

77. Gowan, 'Wealth and Poverty', 351.

78. The conditional interpretation of 15:4 is made explicit in Tg. Yer. I, 'If Israel would keep the precepts of the law, there would be no poor among them; but if they

nor ever wholly successful in eradicating poverty from the land, Deuteronomy consistently expresses God's desire to see people freed from the
burden of destitution through the benefaction of their brothers and sisters.

4.1.5. *The Jewish Tradition Outside of Deuteronomy*

Although our attention is on Deuteronomy's voice, the basic continuity in other Jewish literature on the topic of poverty amelioration is
instructive.[79] In the prophetic corpus of the Jewish Scriptures there is a
tradition of emphatic warnings against the unjust treatment of the poor.[80]
Common to the prophets are the themes that God desires genuine care
for the poor more than ritualized sacrifice and offering, and that God
denounces the affluent and powerful who abuse the needy.[81] The prophets
present the treatment of widows, orphans, and foreigners as emblematic
of a person's or community's righteousness or wickedness.[82] Outside of
these Scriptures,[83] there remains a consistent regard in Jewish literature
for the destitute.[84] Of note is Ben Sira, who affords a prominent place to

will forsake the precepts of the law, the poor shall not cease from the land'; see
also Gowan, 'Wealth and Poverty', 352. By contrast, Levin, 'Poor', 269, proposes a
resolution of the contradiction in Deut 15 which understands 'the poor' in the spiritual
sense of those who are in a close and dependent relationship with God. Thus, 'the
poor will never cease from the land' is a promise of future piety in Israel. However,
this reading of Deut 15 relies too heavily on the subsequent scriptural material cited
by Levin, such as Isa 1–3, Amos, and Pss 25:16; 40:17 (40:18 MT); 86:1; 88:15
(88:16 MT); 109:22.

79. See, e.g., J. Vanderploeg, 'Les pauvres d'Israël et leur piété', *OtSt* 7 (1950):
236–70; M. Schwantes, *Des Recht der Armen*, BBET 4 (Frankfurt: Lang, 1977);
Gelin, *Poor of Yahweh*, 17–19.

80. E.g. Amos 4:1; 5:11–15; Mic 2:1–2; Jer 5:26–29; Zech 7:9–10; Ezek 22:7;
Isa 1:10–17; 10:1–3.

81. Isa 3:13–15; 58:6–10; Ezek 22:29; Amos 2:6–7; 8:4–6; Mic 6:8.

82. E.g. Job 31:16–32; Ps 94:6; Prov 31:5, 9.

83. See R. Bauckham, 'The Relevance of Extracanonical Jewish Texts to New
Testament Study', in Green, ed., *Hearing the New Testament*, 65–84, who contends
that it is highly probable that New Testament authors read the extracanonical Jewish
literature.

84. E.g. Tob 1:3, 16–17; 4:7–11, 16; 7:32; 12:8–9; 1 En. 94:6–8; 96:4–8; 97:7–98:3,
9; 103:3, 5; 104:5; cf. B. W. Longenecker, *Remember the Poor: Paul, Poverty, and the
Greco-Roman World* (Grand Rapids: Eerdmans, 2010), 109–15. For the teaching on
wealth that is prominent in the Enochic literature, particularly the dangers of wealth
and God's threatened judgment on the rich, see Aalen, 'Last Chapters'; Kreitzer,
'Luke 16:19–31'; Nickelsburg, 'God's Judgment'; and 'Revisiting Poor and Rich';
B. Shellard, *New Light on Luke: Its Purpose, Sources and Literary Context*, JSNTSup
215 (Sheffield: Sheffield Academic, 2002), 190–95.

the poor and enjoins proper care for the disadvantaged.[85] Those who have
been wronged, as well as orphans, widows, and the sick, should receive
care; hospitality ought to be shown to one's neighbours;[86] and alms should
be given to the needy.[87] In what is likely a deliberate echo of Deut 15:8,
Ben Sira in 7:32 summons the community to 'to stretch out your hand
to the poor' in deeds of mercy.[88] Conversely, the rich are warned against
acquiring wealth dishonestly and being uncharitable.[89] This is a clear
continuation of the general pattern of Deuteronomy's regulations and
exhortations concerning the poor.

The Deuteronomic motif of prosperity as a divine reward is also paralleled in other Jewish writings. In narrative and prophetic texts there is
a prevalent notion that obedience to the commandments leads to God's
blessings in the present life.[90] At the same time, the possession of wealth is
sometimes associated with wickedness,[91] and rich people are warned not
to make faulty assumptions about their personal righteousness.[92] Finally,
in some Jewish texts there is a temporal shift of the promised rewards for
the righteous and punishments for the wicked from the present life to that
of an eschatological future.[93]

85. Sir 4:1–10; 29:8–9; for a summary of Ben Sira's perspective on possessions,
see Rindge, *Rich Fool*, 69–73.

86. Sir 4:9–10; 29:1–2.

87. Sir 3:20; 7:10; 12:3; 35:2.

88. On this intertextual echo, see Rindge, *Rich Fool*, 69; cf. B. G. Wright
III, 'The Discourse of Riches and Poverty in the Book of Ben Sira', in *Society of
Biblical Literature 1998 Seminar Papers*, SBLSP 37 (Atlanta: Scholars Press, 1998),
2:559–78. Unlike in Deuteronomy, which advocates means of benevolence that
are more naturally rooted in an agrarian economy (e.g. tithing of produce, leaving
harvest remnants), in Ben Sira the giving of alms is a particularly commendable use
of possessions in charity (Sir 3:14, 30; 7:10; 12:3; 16:14; 17:22, 29; 29:8, 12; 31:11;
35:2; 40:17, 24; cf. Garrison, *Redemptive Almsgiving*, 54–55).

89. Sir 5:8; 12:2–7.

90. See, e.g., Gen 26:12–14; Lev 26:3–5; Job 1:10; 42:10; Isa 3:10; Prov 10:22;
Tob 12:9; Sir 3:1, 6; 25:7–11; 35:13; 44:10–15; 51:27–30; Bar 4:1.

91. See, e.g., CD IV, 15–19; 1 QS XI, 1–2; Pss. Sol. 5:16.

92. See, e.g., 1 En. 96:4; 103:5–8; see the discussion of the Enochic (and Lukan)
perspective on riches and judgment in Nickelsburg, 'Riches', 324–44, and 'Revisiting
Poor and Rich', 547–71.

93. See, e.g., Dan 12:1–13; 2 Macc 7; 1 En. 92–105. For the projection of divine
blessing into an eschatological future in 1 En. 98 and 104 (and Luke 16:19–31), see
Aalen, 'Last Chapters', 5. On the various traditions in reward theology in the first
century, see J. G. Crossley, *Why Christianity Happened: A Sociohistorical Account of
Christian Origins (26–50 CE)* (Louisville, KY: Westminster John Knox, 2006), 63.

4.1.6. *Conclusions on Deuteronomy*

According to Deuteronomy, wealth is a covenant blessing on the obedient. While poverty is a curse on disobedience, it is not exclusively so, and Israel as a whole is directed to identify with the poor and sojourners. Accordingly, there is the expectation that those in disadvantaged positions will enjoy the community's care. Those gifted with abundant material resources are exhorted not to ignore the poor 'at their gate', but to emulate divine mercy by performing works of benevolence. Though God commands the elimination of poverty, this ideal will not easily be attained and the poor will invariably remain in the land. The instructions to demonstrate mercy to poor people and not mistreat them are also found in subsequent Jewish literature, which describes the activities of almsgiving and justice as befitting the righteous. We will return to the parable's dialogue with the Deuteronomic voice, after hearing Graeco-Roman texts on the same theme.

4.2. *Graeco-Roman Texts on Possessions and Care for the Poor*

4.2.1. *Broadening the Conversation*

Luke 16:19–31 can also be placed into dialogue with cultural voices outside the Jewish milieu. As noted, Luke's implied audience is familiar with the general content of the secular literature in that time.[94] We will listen to a selection of roughly contemporaneous Graeco-Roman texts, considering them broadly reflective of traditions in this milieu. What does this literature say about the poor, the wealthy, and their recommended treatment of the poor? And how does the parable echo and transform these voices?

4.2.2. *Indifferent to the Poor?*

It has often been asserted that societal norms in the Graeco-Roman world did not address the wealthy's obligation toward the needy.[95] For instance, Esler contends that the Third Gospel's accent on detachment from earthly wealth and attendant emphasis on charitable giving is an effort to rectify the Gentile audience's attitude toward the lower orders.[96] He argues, 'The Lukan gospel imposes on the rich an indispensable

---

94. See the discussion of implied audience in Chapter 2, §2.2.

95. As noted by D. L. Balch, 'Rich and Poor, Proud and Humble in Luke-Acts', in *The Social World of the First Christians*, ed. L. M. White and O. L. Yarbrough (Minneapolis: Fortress, 1995), 214–33, citing 214–15.

96. Jesus's characteristic teaching on wealth in Luke is seen in, e.g., 12:33 and 18:22.

requirement, *quite at odds* with the social values of their own society'.[97]
The historical evidence, however, does not support the notion that there
was an absence of charitable practice in the Graeco-Roman world. Rather,
it demonstrates currents of thought that poor people should be treated
fairly and even with acts of largesse.[98] Such munificence was the social
ideal encouraged by a variety of writers and philosophers.

4.2.3. *The Life of the Poor and Rich*

Providing forms of practical benevolence to the destitute was necessary
in societies that were often characterized by a pronounced gap between
the higher social orders and the rest of the population.[99] In Graeco-Roman
society the aristocracy enjoyed the material benefits of land-ownership,
such as accumulating the yields of harvests and collecting rents. This was
in addition to the social status and political power that came with being
members of the elite.[100] Meanwhile, the majority of society members were
subject to the daily vagaries of life without economic security.[101] While
merchants, traders, and artisans enjoyed a measure of financial stability,
the many unskilled workers, debt bondsmen, and slaves in Graeco-Roman
society were considered by the elite to be 'poor'.[102] These poor suffered
the plight of a subsistence employment, often lacking the material means
to meet their basic needs of food and shelter. They were 'ill-fed, housed
in slums or not at all, ravaged by sickness, precluded from all access to
social prestige and power over their own destinies'.[103]

Because of their naturally advantageous position in society and the
inevitable abuses perpetrated by some in their position, the wealthy are
occasionally characterized harshly in the Graeco-Roman literature. For
instance, as one who is typical of the Stoics, the Roman philosopher

---

97. Esler, *Community and Gospel*, 199 (emphasis added); cf. R. Rohrbaugh, 'The
Pre-Industrial City in Luke-Acts: Urban Social Relations', in *The Social World of
Luke-Acts: Models for Interpretation*, ed. J. H. Neyrey (Peabody, MA: Hendrickson,
1991), 125–49.

98. See the study of benevolent action in the classical world by A. R. Hands,
Charities and Social Aid in Greece and Rome (London: Thames & Hudson, 1968),
especially 63–88.

99. Esler, *Community and Gospel*, 172.

100. A. Fuks, 'Isokrates and the Social-Economic Situation in Greece', *Ancient
Society* 3 (1972): 17–44.

101. Esler, *Community and Gospel*, 173.

102. Philo, *Spec. Laws* 4.195–96; cf. B. Malina, 'Wealth and Poverty in the New
Testament and Its World', *Int* 41 (1987): 354–67, citing 359.

103. Esler, *Community and Gospel*, 179.

Seneca castigates the rich for taking great pride in their possessions and property.[104] He opines that having wealth often engenders laziness,[105] and that the desire for wealth is hazardous to one's mental equilibrium.[106] In his *De Cupiditate divitiarum*, Plutarch (46–120 CE) is similar in his negative depiction of the wealthy. He describes at length the rich hoarding and protecting their vast possessions (525A), being avaricious or profligate, then suffering the effects of decadence (525C). The affluent are typified as exercising a lack of scruples in exploiting others and amassing wealth that they cannot use (526B-C). Consistent with Plutarch's perspective in *De Cupiditate divitiarum*, ethical discourse about wealth in this milieu accents its inherent moral dangers and potential abuses.

Really T. Morgan need here.

4.2.4. *The Idealized Practice of Benevolence*

The negative portrayal of wealth by some Graeco-Roman authors is not to say that its possession is repudiated. Seneca asserts that riches should ideally be regarded as insignificant to personal contentment: that is, one can be wealthy, and still enjoy a happy life.[107] At the same time there is a recognition that wealth can be an instrument of virtue through giving to others.[108] Riches can be used to better those who are less privileged. A common notion among the Greek writers is that the physical necessities of life should be available to people of all classes or segments of society; it is unnecessary that any person be overlooked or ill-supplied.[109] The reality is that people may be in need because of drought, famine, war, or mismanagement.[110] It is for this reason that many writers recognize the abiding need for the practice of philanthropy by the rich in order to assist the needy.[111]

This tradition of benevolence is known in Graeco-Roman culture, in theory, if not in practice.[112] Being liberal with financial resources is

104. Seneca, *Ben.* 10.5–6; cf. T. E. Phillips, *Reading Issues of Wealth and Poverty in Luke-Acts*, Studies in the Bible and Early Christianity 48 (Lampeter: Mellen, 2001), 245–46.
105. Seneca, *De brevitate vitae* 12.6–8; *Ben.* 7.9–10.
106. Seneca, *Ben.* 7.2.4.
107. Seneca, *Vit. beat.* 20.3.
108. *Vit. beat.* 24.4.
109. Plutarch, *Cupid. divit.* 523F.
110. Malina, 'Wealth and Poverty', 363.
111. See, e.g., Dionysius, *Ant. rom.* 2.15.3.
112. A. Fuks, 'The Sharing of Property by the Rich with the Poor in Greek Theory and Practice', *Scripta Classica Israelica* 5 (1979): 46–63; cf. his 'Social-Economic Situation'; Hands, *Charities and Social Aid*, 77–88.

regarded as one of the virtues of an honourable man.[113] Plato maintains that a principal way to improve Greek society is through a supply of men who were willing to share their goods (ἀπορουμένοις κοινωεῖν) with those in situations of want.[114] He proposes that such charity be practised through remissions of debt (ἀφιέντας) and through distributions of land (νεμομένος) to the poor.[115] A recurring subtext is the notion that in the golden age of Greece's past the rich held a proper conception of their responsibility toward the poor, and members of society even practised a community of goods.[116] This attitude and approach toward the less fortunate needed to be recovered for the health of civilization.[117] Though the 'golden age' was no doubt a later idealization,[118] there are historical instances of the rich voluntarily sharing their property with the less fortunate.[119] Even while beggars were disdained for relying on the gifts of strangers,[120] there was a tradition of almsgiving in the Graeco-Roman world.[121] Aristotle, too, recommends that the poor be helped by the state through the collection of public revenues.[122] He suggests that honourable men might take personal responsibility for some of the poor in their city and provide them with the means of going to work.[123] In his *Politica*, Aristotle quotes with approval the proverb, 'Friends have goods in common' (κοινὰ τὰ τῶν φίλων), which can be construed as a promising maxim for poverty alleviation.[124] It should be noted that for Aristotle – as for other Graeco-Roman writers – this material communion takes place in the context of τῶν φίλων being a person's peers and social equals, namely,

113. Aristotle, *Eth. nic.* 4.1.6.

114. Plato, *Leg.* 736 D; cf. Fuks, 'Sharing', 47.

115. Plato, *Leg.* 736 D.

116. B. Capper, 'Reciprocity and the Ethic of Acts', in *Witness to the Gospel: The Theology of Acts*, ed. I. H. Marshall and D. Peterson (Grand Rapids: Eerdmans, 1998), 499–518, citing 504–8.

117. See Isokrates, *Aerop.* 20 and 31.

118. Fuks, 'Sharing', 51.

119. As recounted in Fuks, 'Sharing', 56–62; cf. the recorded instances of charitable initiatives by the Graeco-Roman elite in Longenecker, *Remember*, 80–85.

120. Menander, *Dysk.* 284–85; Plato, *Resp.* 552 D; Plautus, *Trin.* 339.

121. Longenecker, *Remember*, 74.

122. Aristotle, *Pol.* 1320B 2–3.

123. *Pol.* 1320B 7–9.

124. *Pol.* 1263A 21; B. Capper, 'The Palestinian Cultural Context of Earliest Christian Community of Goods', in *The Book of Acts in its Palestinian Setting*, ed. Richard Bauckham, BAFCS 4 (Grand Rapids: Eerdmans, 1995), 323–56, notes that this proverb was frequently quoted in Graeco-Roman literature (325).

other elite people.[125] Those who were not social counterparts and who lacked the means to reciprocate hospitality or other acts of kindness were excluded from such 'a communion of goods'. Despite the self-interest that could motivate charitable initiatives in the Graeco-Roman world, there is historical data which demonstrates a tradition of benevolence and sharing in Graeco-Roman society.[126]

4.2.5. *Conclusions on Wealth and Benevolence in Graeco-Roman Literature*

A key motif in the Graeco-Roman literature is that the possession of wealth has attendant dangers, such as engendering greed, decadence, and unkindness. It was also a commonplace that wealth is increased through exploiting those of a lower social status. At the same time, there is evidence of the view that the prosperous could demonstrate their honourable character through mitigating the suffering of the poor, whether on a personal or societal basis. This could be done through the forgiving of debts, distribution of property and food, or a general liberality with their goods. Underlying these recommendations is the assumption that there is a basic availability of material resources for the maintenance of every individual's life, and that a just society would validate this reality by caring for its disadvantaged members.

Writing for those broadly acquainted with these societal norms and ideals for benevolence, Luke's parable may be profitably contemplated as part of an intertextual dialogue involving this milieu.[127] As Karris states well about Lukan wealth ethics, 'Luke is concerned to make the Christian/Jewish teaching about the necessity of almsgiving and about fellowship intelligible to converts who come from a widely different cultural expectation'.[128] We now turn to this conversation, listening for how Luke 16:19–31 represents an affirmation and transformation of not only the ideals and paradigms of the wider Graeco-Roman tradition, but also that of Deuteronomy on the topic of poverty and possessions.

---

125. Capper, 'Reciprocity', 517; cf. S. Walton, 'Primitive Communism in Acts? Does Acts Present the Community of Goods (2:44–45; 4:32–35) as Mistaken?', *EvQ* 80 (2008): 99–111 (104); and B. Capper, 'Holy Community of Life and Property Amongst the Poor: A Response to Steve Walton', *EvQ* 80 (2008): 113–27.

126. Longenecker, *Remember*, 104–7; cf. Fuks, 'Sharing of Property', 63.

127. Degenhardt, *Evangelist der Armen*, 180–81, compares the Lukan teaching on almsgiving with the encouragement of charitable giving in the Hellenistic world.

128. Karris, 'Poor and Rich', 117.

4.3. *Conversing Together About Poverty and Possessions*

4.3.1. *The Reason for Wealth and Destitution*

The parable's portrayal of the rich man accentuates his extravagant conduct and lavish appearance, but it does not indicate how he acquired his prosperity.[129] For instance, it is not stated that his wealth was obtained through defrauding other people, such as can be inferred in the story of Zacchaeus the tax collector (Luke 19:8).[130] However, regarding the rich man through the lens of the stereotypically wealthy, some from Graeco-Roman culture – for example, Seneca or Plutarch – will suggest that he probably gained his wealth through the exploitation of the socially less-powerful, and maintained his wealth through avarice and tight-fistedness. Consequently, he is suffering post-mortem torments for his financial misconduct and neighbourly neglect. There is an intertextual dissonance on this question, however, for Deuteronomy's voice simultaneously reminds us that wealth is a divine blessing on those who obey Yahweh's commandments. It is consistent with this perspective to interpret the rich man's prosperity as God's blessing on his obedience.[131] His torments are an unexpected end for one who is assumed to be an observant Jew.

The listener's difficulty is that no explicit judgment is passed on the rich man for the manner in which he lived or for how his wealth was acquired. Consequently, though Abraham says that the rich man received τὰ ἀγαθά, or 'good things' (v. 25), this does not permit the conclusion that he was wealthy because he earned the material rewards promised

---

129. Contra Bailey, *Middle Eastern Eyes*, 302, who contends his feasting sumptuously 'every day' (v. 19) means that his servants were not given a day of rest, and 'thereby he publicly violated the Ten Commandments every week'. As will be seen, the implication is that the rich man is punished for a different offense against the law.

130. It is debated whether Luke portrays Zacchaeus as needing to repent from pursuing ill-gotten gains as a tax collector. The critical phrase is 19:8 (εἴ τινός τι ἐσυκοφάντησα) joined with his statements about giving to the poor and making four-fold restitution. Should Zacchaeus's words (δίδωμι and ἀποδίδωμι) be understood as futuristic in sense (Bock, *Luke*, 2:1519–20; Nolland, *Luke*, 2:906) or as a statement of his customary practice (Green, *Luke*, 671–72; Fitzmyer, *Luke X–XXIV*, 1220)? In favour of a repentant Zacchaeus referring to his actual past acts of defrauding, the εἴ is joined with the aorist ἐσυκοφάντησα, a first class conditional clause in which the subject views the condition as real for the sake of argument. Telling also is that the crowd complains to Jesus about Zacchaeus being a sinner (19:7), which is unlikely if he had been generous in the past (Bock, *Luke*, 2:1520).

131. Gillman, *Possessions*, 81; Hays, 'Mint and Rue', 389.

to the righteous.[132] Τὰ ἀγαθά is a value-free descriptor. Similarly, the parable does not taint the rich man's possessions with the hue of illicit activity.[133]

If the origin of the rich man's wealth is uncertain, the same must be said for the penurious condition of Lazarus. No direct indication is given as to the cause of his poverty. To be sure, he is covered with sores, a skin condition which could make it difficult to maintain employment. Furthermore, Lazarus is thrown (ἐβέβλητο) at the rich man's gate, perhaps indicative of his inability to walk.[134] Aside from these two physical factors in his destitution, there are passages in Deuteronomy which suggest that Lazarus's poverty could be interpreted as God's curse on unrepentant wickedness.[135] Furthermore, his affliction with sores (εἱλκωμένος) is consistent with one of the threatened punishments on disobedience in Deut 28:27 and 35, where Moses says that God will cause boils (בִּשְׁחִין, ἕλκει in LXX) on the people, the same ailment inflicted on the Egyptians during the plagues (Exod 9:10–11).[136] The covenant curses of Deut 28 also include a lack of burial among the consequences for continued disobedience; v. 26 describes the fate of Israel's carcasses being left as food for scavenging birds and animals.[137] Some conclude from Luke 16:22 that the corpse of Lazarus was in fact left unburied, for after the rich man's death it is reported that he is ἐτάφη, while this is not said of the beggar.[138] The silence of the text on Lazarus's burial could suggest this as another indicator of divine disfavour.[139] Thus when Lazarus is evaluated according to the Deuteronomic paradigm, the audience might plausibly conclude that he has been punished for his sin. Yet this evaluation, too, is discordant with the rest of the narrative. After his death Lazarus is comforted (v. 25). He is taken by angels up to Abraham, where he is rewarded with a place at his bosom (v. 22), a position that is probably symbolic of the messianic banquet described in 13:28–30.[140] Such post-mortem treatments imply

---

132. Metzger, *Consumption and Wealth*, 135; cf. Hays's response, 'Mint and Rue', 389 and 392.

133. Contra Derrett, *Law*, 90.

134. Green, *Luke*, 606.

135. Deut 28:15, 18, 38, 48; see also Prov 6:11; 10:4; 13:4, 18; 19:15; cf. Green, *Luke*, 605.

136. Crossley, *Christianity*, 65–66.

137. See also Jer 8:1–2; 16:1–4; Ezek 29:5; Tob 1:16–2:10.

138. See Chapter 3, §7.1.

139. Crossley, *Christianity*, 65.

140. See the discussion in Chapter 2, §4.2; cf. Heil, *Meal Scenes*, 136–40.

not Lazarus's disloyalty to God in life, but his faithfulness. In this way the parable again modifies the Deuteronomic perspective, and leaves an intertextual tension.[141]

4.3.2. *The Characterization of the Wealthy and the Destitute*

An intertextual conversation concerning the portrayal of the rich man leads to more unambiguously negative conclusions, for he embodies the spiritual dangers that threaten the wealthy. While Deuteronomy is largely positive concerning the prosperous in Israel,[142] some Graeco-Roman writers draw attention to the attendant dangers of possessing wealth. Riches can engender a spirit of greed, a lifestyle of decadence, and unkindness in conduct. Luke's vivid portrait of the rich man[143] – clothed in the purple and fine linen of the elite, occupied with extravagant feasting, without any demonstrable concern for hungry Lazarus – fully accords with such a picture and affirms the wider cultural voice.

As for Lazarus, his condition and activity in vv. 20–21 are unambiguous in their affect.[144] His position indicates an expectation of receiving relief from someone with the physical means to help. Lazarus longs for physical sustenance, even a share in the rich man's discarded food. Besides being hungry, he is unable to walk, afflicted with sores and harassed by dogs. While not belonging to Deuteronomy's conventional categories of the destitute – 'sojourner, orphan, and widow' – Lazarus is clearly an individual in need of receiving practical aid. His portrait is constructed to evoke a sympathetic response.[145] This is an affirmation of what Deuteronomy recurrently suggests, that the poor are those with whom God's people must identify and so act to mitigate their suffering.[146]

---

141. Blomberg's view that 'the parable overturns the common Jewish "wisdom" that saw the rich as blessed by God and the poor as punished for their wickedness' (*Parables*, 259–60) requires more nuance in light of the sympathetic presentation of the poor in Deuteronomy and elsewhere in the Jewish Scriptures.

142. But see the warning in Deut 8:10–18; the prophetic literature also cautions the rich against pride and exploitation of the poor (e.g. Isa 1:10–17; 3:13–15; 10:1–3; Jer 5:26–29; Ezek 22:29; Amos 2:6–7; 4:1; 5:11–15; 6:4; 8:4–6; Mic 2:1–2).

143. See the discussion of the various elements of the rich man's description in v. 19 in Chapter 2, §6.1.2.

144. See the discussion of the various elements of Lazarus's description in vv. 20–21 in Chapter 2, §6.1.1.

145. Resseguie, 'Reader-Response', 312.

146. Cf. Deut 10:19; 27:19.

4.3.3. *The Response of the Wealthy to the Destitute*

What do our conversation partners suggest that the rich man ought to have done for Lazarus? Deuteronomy is clear on the right use of possessions. According to Deut 15:7, there is an expectation that those gifted with material resources should ignore the poor brother or sister 'at your gate' (בְּאַחַד שְׁעָרֶיךָ), but to emulate divine mercy by performing works of benevolence. While 'the gate' in the parable is a physical barrier which prevents Lazarus from receiving food, it is also where Lazarus might entreat the rich man for assistance, and expect to receive it.

A compression of narrative time occurs in the parable, from the scene described in vv. 19–21 to when both Lazarus and the rich man die in v. 22. This narrative rapidity means that none of the rich man's conduct toward Lazarus is described. As mentioned, this has occasioned a questioning of the grounds on which the rich man is tormented, with some insisting that it cannot have been for a neglect of Lazarus but because of his riches; it is the Lukan censure of wealth and wealthy persons that demands a reversal of his position vis-à-vis Lazarus. The denunciations of the wealthy in 6:22–24 and the rebuke of the rich fool in 12:20 are said to indicate a general Lukan antipathy toward the affluent, now extended to the rich man because of his possessions and consumerist lifestyle.[147]

However, our intertextual conversation indicates possibilities for his material goods which the rich man left unemployed. The sight of the poor and hungry man 'at his gate' did not move him, nor did the precepts of the Scriptures direct him. He failed to employ any of the means suggested by Deuteronomy (and other Jewish literature) to express care for his impoverished neighbour, such as the sharing of one's material goods, the giving of alms or hospitality.[148] His unwillingness is rendered inexcusable if he considers himself a 'son of Abraham' (v. 24) living in adherence to the Jewish Scriptures.[149] Abraham's later insistence that the rich man's brothers listen to 'Moses and the prophets' implies that the rich man

---

147. See, e.g., Crossan, *In Parables*, 67; Hock, 'Lazarus and Micyllus', 453–54; Schottroff and Stegemann, *Hope of the Poor*, 26–27; Nickelsburg, 'Riches', 338; Mealand, *Poverty*, 32; Bauckham, 'Rich Man and Lazarus', 232; Roose, 'Umkehr und Ausgleich', 8–10; Metzger, *Consumption and Wealth*, 146.

148. Nolland, *Luke*, 2:831–32; Moxnes, *Economy*, 150; Seccombe, *Possessions*, 177; Forbes, *God of Old*, 192; Kim, *Stewardship and Almsgiving*, 189; Plummer, *Luke*, 395; Hays, *Gospels*, 205–6.

149. See John the Baptist's explanation of what characterizes a true child of Abraham, in Luke 3:8–11.

should himself have heeded this testimony.[150] The intertextual dissonance surrounding his prosperity as a possible indicator of divine favour is here resolved: he is not obedient and is therefore punished in the afterlife. The voluminous quantity of the exhortations in 'Moses and the prophets' to be generous makes more arresting the rich man's failure to open his hand toward the brother at his gate.

This failure is accentuated by hearing a second intertextual voice, for the rich man does not conform either to cultural mores of wider Graeco-Roman society regarding wealth and generosity. We saw evidence that the prosperous were expected to be willing to share material resources with the suffering poor, whether through the forgiving of debts, the distribution of property, or a general liberality. It was assumed that sufficient material resources were available for the maintenance of life, and that a just society would effect this reality in caring for its disadvantaged members. There are some analogies in this tradition with the view of possessions that is developed in Luke's Gospel.[151] Apart from the notion of reciprocal giving among friends in the Graeco-Roman tradition, the Lukan perspective was 'appropriate to the social and cultural context of the Graeco-Roman world', even as it transformed the familiar concepts of friendship.[152] Within such an intertextual conversation, the inexcusability of the rich man's failure to respond to the destitution of Lazarus is obvious – as is Luke's warning to his audience.

5. *Voices on Messengers from the Afterlife*

A second key motif in the parable concerns the possibility and necessity of contact between the realm of the dead and the living. This theme is evidenced in the rich man's request for the deceased Lazarus to be sent from Abraham's beatific presence in order to warn the five brothers. The suggestion is that such a remarkable visitation will be sufficient to prevent

---

150. Bovon, *Lukas*, 3:112–13; cf. Hays, *Wealth Ethics*, 157.

151. See, e.g., Luke 3:10–14; 12:33; 18:22.

152. Phillips, *Reading Issues*, 243; Balch, 'Rich and Poor', 218. Capper, 'Reciprocity', 517, examines the emphasis on meal-fellowship in the Gospel and concludes that it is consistent with Graeco-Roman writings on friendship, yet exceeds them, for Jesus insists in Luke 14:12–14 that there is no need for reciprocity in which the poor return the kindness of the rich. A. C. Mitchell, 'The Social Function of Friendship in Acts 2:44–47 and 4:32–37', *JBL* 111 (1992): 255–72, contends that unlike in the wider culture, the model of friendship in Luke 14:12–14 and Acts 20:35 can transcend status, as the poor are benefited by the rich.

the brothers from meeting a similar fate. We will hear the perspective of Deuteronomy on the possibility of Lazarus's return, and listen to Graeco-Roman voices on the same proposed event. Then, as with our first theme, we will bring these voices into an intertextual conversation and consider the outcomes.

5.1. *Deuteronomy and Necromancy* WHAT

5.1.1. *An Undervalued Connection*

Though many suggest a background in Deuteronomy's principles and practices of benevolence, on the parable's trope of post-mortem revelation scholars minimize or bypass the scriptural voice.[153] In so doing they do not give attention to the stringency with which soliciting messengers from the realm of the dead is prohibited in Deuteronomy. However, this motif should also be read in dialogue with the Deuteronomic perspective that is favoured in Luke's Gospel. What does Deuteronomy say about contact with the realm of the dead, and how should this shape our reading of the parable?

5.1.2. *A Clear Proscription* NO

The notion of seeking messages from the dead is infrequent in Deuteronomy, but the central text is perspicuous: communication with the dead, through consulting familiar spirits or performing necromancy, is forbidden. The proscription is found in 18:10–14, where among objectionable practices, such as child sacrifice, divination, sorcery, inter-pretation of omens, witchcraft, and casting spells, in v. 11 there is the interdiction of a consulter of familiar spirits (שֹׁאֵל אוֹב), a necromancer (יִדְּעֹנִי), and one who consults the dead (דֹּרֵשׁ אֶל־הַמֵּתִים).[154] All these activ-ities are characterized as typical of the surrounding nations and therefore not to be practised by God's people (v. 9).[155] This range of practices, with the common theme of attempting to gain divine knowledge or guidance,

---

153. Nolland, *Luke*, 2:831; Pao and Schnabel, 'Luke', 344, are exceptions, referring to the calling up of dead Samuel in 1 Sam 28:7–20.

154. Cf. the entries in D. J. A. Clines, *The Dictionary of Classical Hebrew* (Sheffield: Sheffield Academic/Sheffield Phoenix, 1993–2011); for שֹׁאֵל אוֹב, see 8:213–14; for יִדְּעֹנִי, see 4:113–14; for דֹּרֵשׁ אֶל־הַמֵּתִים, see 2:476. For a discussion of terms relating to necromantic practice, see B. B. Schmidt, *Israel's Beneficent Dead: Ancestor Cult and Necromancy in Ancient Israelite Religion and Tradition*, FAT 11 (Tübingen: Mohr Siebeck, 1994), 179–90.

155. See Deut 12:31 for a similar command to avoid the liturgical practices of the nations.

is indicative of the desire to receive a supernatural message.[156] Notable are two practices mentioned in v. 11: first, consulting familiar spirits, termed 'familiar' because some practitioners consulted only spirits that were known to the individual; and secondly, practising necromancy, communicating with the dead in order to predict or determine events.

There is a paucity of explicit references to the continuation of life after death in Deuteronomy or other Jewish Scriptures,[157] yet the dead were thought to have powers to know, revive, or harm.[158] The living sometimes tried to appease them through giving food, a practice that may be alluded to in Deut 26:14.[159] There are other indications that a cult of the dead was present in Israel,[160] and a desire to preserve community with the dead through communication.[161] Though it is forbidden in Deuteronomy,[162] the prohibition may have been necessitated by the continuing penchant to practise necromancy and that it existed as an illicit undercurrent in Israel's religion.[163]

In Deuteronomy necromantic and related activities are prohibited not merely because they were customs current among neighbouring nations,[164]

156. J. G. McConville, *Deuteronomy*, AOTC 6 (Downers Grove, IL: InterVarsity, 2002), 300.

157. R. E. Friedman and S. Dolansky Overton, 'Death and Afterlife: The Biblical Silence', in *Judaism in Late Antiquity: Part 4. Death, Life-after-Death, Resurrection and the World-to-Come in the Judaisms of Antiquity*, ed. A. J. Avery-Peck and J. Neusner, HdO 1: Der Nahe und Mittlere Osten 49 (Leiden: Brill, 2000), 35–59, citing 35.

158. K. Spronk, *Beatific Afterlife in Ancient Israel and in the Ancient Near East*, AOAT 219 (Neukirchen-Vluyn: Neukirchener, 1986), 251.

159. E. Bloch-Smith, *Judahite Burial Practices and Beliefs about the Dead*, JSOTSup 123 (Sheffield: Sheffield Academic, 1992), 146; cf. Friedman and Overton, 'Death and Afterlife', 40.

160. See, e.g., 1 Sam 28, discussed below; Friedman and Overton, 'Death and Afterlife', 36–37, note the archaeological evidence for such a cult; cf. Bloch-Smith, *Burial Practices*, 147–51.

161. Spronk, *Beatific Afterlife*, 252.

162. Schmidt, *Beneficent Dead*, 189, suggests that the prohibition in Deut 18 was a rhetorical strategy employed to polemicize against the contemporary cults competing with Yahwism. Deuteronomy 18, as a later work, is thus not deemed indicative of early Israelite belief (281); cf. A. E. Bernstein, *The Formation of Hell: Death and Retribution in the Ancient and Early Christian Worlds* (Ithaca, NY: Cornell University Press, 1993), 139, who suggests that the prohibition of necromancy was part of the centralizing efforts of the regime.

163. Bernstein, *Formation*, 138–39.

164. Compare this prohibition with Deut 17:14–15 and the laws of kingship, where a practice that was current among the nations was in fact permitted for Israel.

but because God rendered these activities unnecessary: Yahweh committed to making known to Israel the divine will. The dispensability of other forms of guidance is patent in Deut 18 following the proscriptions in vv. 10–14. The need for knowledge and direction is met in God's promised provision of a prophet (נָבִיא) for the people (v. 15). God will put divine words into the prophet's mouth, and the prophet will tell Israel everything that God commands (v. 18). The previous prohibitions should be interpreted in this context, for this is the chosen means by which Yahweh will speak.[165] Because God promised to communicate by chosen prophets, there is no need to solicit alternate messengers. *Jesus .. rose from the dead ..*

5.1.3. *Jewish Tradition Outside of Deuteronomy*

We may briefly highlight the continuity on this topic in the Jewish traditions outside of Deuteronomy. Similar proscriptions of necromancy and related practices occur in both legal and prophetic literature. Like Deut 18:10–14, Lev 19:31 prohibits the consultation of familiar spirits as well as necromancy (אֶל־הָאֹבֹת וְאֶל־הַיִּדְּעֹנִים אַל־תִּפְנוּ); this prohibition is repeated in 20:6, and characterized as a capital offense in 20:27.[166] The ban on consulting the spiritual realm outside of the approved channels is similarly emphasized by Isaiah in 8:19–20. Instead of conferring with necromancers and familiar spirits, which he describes as consulting 'the dead on behalf of the living', the people must go to the law and the testimony (לְתוֹרָה וְלִתְעוּדָה) for inquiring of God. The juxtaposition of the illicit and approved means of revelation from Yahweh is again significant. *DIVES IS DEAD – ITS DEAD-to-DEAD TALK*

The recurring prohibitions of necromancy and related practices did not entail a denial of its efficacy, however, as the example of Saul in 1 Sam 28 possibly indicates.[167] In this account, an anxious King Saul faces an imminent military encounter with the Philistines (28:1). Though previously guided by Samuel, the prophet has recently died. Earlier in Saul's reign – a time of more scrupulous obedience to the Mosaic law – the king had banished many of those who consulted spirits (28:3). But unable to receive any communication from God through dreams, the Urim, or prophets, Saul in v. 7 consults a woman at Endor who is known to have access to familiar spirits (בַּעֲלַת־אוֹב). In v. 8 he asks her to consult the ghost (בָּאוֹב) of Samuel, and she sees what she describes to Saul as a ghost

---

165. McConville, *Deuteronomy*, 302.

166. Comparable to the list of forbidden practices in Deut 18:10–13 is Exod 22:18, which commands that a sorceress be put to death, and Lev 19:26, which prohibits the practices of divination and sorcery.

167. See the discussion in Bernstein, *Formation*, 138–39; cf. Evans, *Luke*, 252.

or spiritual being (אֱלֹהִים) coming up from the earth (28:13).[168] Samuel then speaks to the king, reminding him of how his disobedience has led to his kingdom being forfeited and God's judgment being provoked – a judgment which Samuel says will culminate in the death of Saul and his sons by the Philistines (28:16–19).[169] Leaving aside the numerous interpretive questions concerning this passage, the events of 1 Sam 28 are indicative of a continuing, if clandestine, practice in Israel of consulting the dead in the absence of direction from the divinely approved prophets.[170]

In later Jewish literature the motif of contact with the dead through necromancy and related practices is no longer prevalent.[171] There is, however, a tradition of visionary journeys to the underworld or the place of the dead.[172] In these apocalypses, a visitor – often accompanied by angels – explores the various areas of the realm of the dead and returns to give an account to the living.[173] Such apocalyptic accounts attempt to impact the living through warning about the post-mortem consequences of a wicked life, or through encouraging righteous conduct with the promise of heavenly rewards. These cosmic tours, probably presupposing the ancient notions of journeys reflected in the *Odyssey* and the *Epic of Gilgamesh*, are prevalent in the Jewish apocalyptic tradition of 1 Enoch and 2 Enoch, as well as 3 Baruch, the Ascension of Isaiah, and the Apocalypse of Elijah. However, there is a critical disparity between

168. On the meaning of אֱלֹהִים, see Friedman and Overton, 'Death and Afterlife', 43–44.

169. See 1 Chr 10:13 for a postscript on Saul's reign, in which is mentioned his offense of consulting a medium for guidance.

170. Friedman and Overton, 'Death and Afterlife', 48; Bernstein, *Formation*, 138.

171. An exception is an account in the rabbinic and Talmudic literature, *m. Sanh.* 6:23c, 30–43, which describes the appearance of a deceased holy man to his friend. The holy man explains why he was not mourned when he died, and the tax collector Bar Mayan was: the tax collector's punishment comes in the afterlife, while the holy man is rewarded. For a translation of the legend, see M. E. Boring, K. Berger, and C. Colpe, *Hellenistic Commentary to the New Testament* (Nashville, TN: Abingdon, 1995), 228–29.

172. For a survey, see Bauckham, 'Visiting Places', 78–93; cf. his collection in *Fate of the Dead*. For related studies, see Himmelfarb, *Ascent to Heaven*, and *Tours of Hell*; cf. J. J. Collins, *The Apocalyptic Imagination: An Introduction to Jewish Apocalyptic Literature*, 2nd ed. (Grand Rapids: Eerdmans, 1998).

173. Collins, *Apocalyptic*, 4–5, defines an apocalypse as 'a genre of revelatory literature with a narrative framework, in which a revelation is mediated by an otherworldly being to a human recipient, disclosing a transcendent reality which is both temporal, insofar as it envisages eschatological salvation, and spatial insofar as it involves another supernatural world'.

the nature of an apocalyptic journey and the journey proposed by the rich man in the parable. In the former genre a *living* person visits the realm of the dead in order to report back, while in Luke 16:19–31 it is suggested that a *dead* person visit the realm of the living with his report. As such, the apocalypses are not directly pertinent. Not entirely.

5.1.4. *Conclusions on Deuteronomy*

Deuteronomy speaks clearly on the legitimacy of receiving messages from the dead: it is forbidden. This proscription was not to say that contact with the dead was considered strictly impossible or that it was not occasionally practised, but that it was not to be attempted by those desiring to be obedient to Yahweh. The immediate context of Deut 18:11, the account of Saul and the necromancer in 1 Sam 28, as well as the prophetic injunction of Isa 8, uniformly indicate that consultation of the dead was viewed as unnecessarily supplanting the activity of listening to God through the appointed prophets.[174]

5.2. *Graeco-Roman Texts on Messengers from the Afterlife*

5.2.1. *A Common Motif*

The intimation in Deut 18:9 that other nations had contact with the realm of afterlife is borne out by the Graeco-Roman context. Various modes of interaction between the living and the dead are described in the literature from numerous cultures in the Mediterranean region. A common motif is a return of the dead – either those who are temporarily dead, 'shades', or those permanently dead, 'ghosts' – to the realm of the living in order to communicate. Narratives of post-mortem visitations occur with regularity, in which the living are informed about features of the afterlife, or about the consequences of wicked conduct in life on earth.

An early example is in Plato's *Republic*, the story of Er the Pamphylian.[175] Some days after being killed in battle, Er returns and relates what he has seen as a disembodied spirit in the realm of the dead. Within the *Republic*, the story functions as a lesson in the importance of living nobly and with due attention for one's eternal destiny.[176] Later Greek writers also employ the motif of messengers speaking about their knowledge of the afterlife.[177]

---

174. Sponk, *Beatific Afterlife*, 257.

175. Plato, *Resp.* 10.614–21.

176. Bauckham, 'Rich Man and Lazarus', 238.

177. E.g. Plutarch, *De sera* 22–33; Pliny, *Ep.* 5.5; Herodotus, *Hist.* 5.92. A variation on returns from the dead is the large body of 'descent' literature, in which individuals visit the realm of the dead and report on what they witness. See, e.g.,

Satire   For instance, Lucian describes a post-mortem returnee who is asked, 'What are things like in Hades?' He provides the answer, 'Wait, and I will see that you get information directly from the place'.[178] The Egyptian story of Setme and his miraculous son Si-Osiris recounts how Si-Osiris is able to convey to his father a message about the fate of a rich man and a poor man.[179] There is also extant a Jewish legend in which a godless woman who is suffering in hell is able to relay a warning to her still-living husband, and he subsequently repents of his wickedness.[180]

In these accounts of post-mortem visitations of the dead to the realm of the living, sometimes those who are temporarily deceased revive and return by their own volition. Alternately, the deceased are summoned through activities such as necromancy, and after conveying a message they return to the state of being dead. For instance, in Lucan's *Pharsalia* one of Pompey's dead soldiers is recalled by a witch in order to describe what he has seen in Hades and to prophesy the future; after he does so, he is allowed to return and remain in the realm of the dead.[181] Not just the temporarily dead but those who are permanently deceased and unable to revive physically appear as ghosts in necromantic settings in a range of literature.[182] The *Story of Jannes and Jambres*, based on the legend of the two magicians who opposed Moses in Egypt, recounts how Jannes is killed for his wickedness and how Jambres subsequently summons his shade through necromancy.[183] Upon being summoned, Jannes describes for his brother a variety of the punishments in hell. As was true of the Jewish apocalyptic tradition, in these and other stories the temporarily and permanently dead return for a variety of purposes. Sometimes they visit the realm of the living in order to comfort bereaved family, to warn of imminent disaster, to prophesy, to inform on or threaten their murderers, and also to reveal post-mortem fates.[184]

Hauge, *Tour of Hell*, on the relation of Luke 16:19–31 to the descent of Odysseus into Hades in Homer's *Odyssey*.

178. Lucian, *Demon.* 43; Lucian also employs the motif in *Philops.* 27.

179. See F. L. Griffith, *Stories of the High Priests of Memphis: The Sethon of Herodotus and the Demotic Tales of Khamuas* (Oxford: Clarendon, 1900); Gressmann, *Vom reichen Mann*, 31–32, was the first to suggest an origin in the Egyptian folktale.

180. Bultmann, *Synoptic Tradition*, 196–97.

181. *Pharsalia* 6.569–830; for a similar account of necromancy, see Apuleius, *Metam.* 8.4; cf. Bauckham, 'Rich Man and Lazarus', 239.

182. Valerius Maximus 1.7.6; Cicero, *Rep.* 6.9–26; Philostratus, *Vit. Apoll.* 8.31; Ovid, *Metam.* 10.

183. Cf. Bauckham, 'Rich Man and Lazarus', 241–43; the story is extant in fragmentary form. See also the allusion to this legend in 2 Tim 3:8.

184. Bauckham, 'Rich Man and Lazarus', 240.

5.2.2. *Conclusions on Afterlife Messengers in Graeco-Roman Literature*

In Graeco-Roman literature, soliciting and receiving a messenger from the dead is not an exceptional motif. The dead are portrayed as returning to the realm of the living either temporarily or on a permanent basis. The dead appear of their own accord, or after having been summoned by someone with the privilege of access to the spiritual world. These messengers conveyed a variety of communications that were often specific to their knowledge of the post-mortem state.

It is not necessary to assume that Luke was familiar with each of these Graeco-Roman texts, but we may presume that he was acquainted with the wider cultural milieu of which this motif was part. As such, we surmise that his audience also broadly knew these traditions. To determine how Luke 16:19–31 represents an affirmation or transformation of these traditions, we will listen to an intertextual dialogue between the parable, Deuteronomy and related Jewish texts, and Graeco-Roman literature on the topic of messengers from the afterlife.

5.3. *Conversing Together About Messengers from the Afterlife*

5.3.1. *The Possibility of Messengers*

Our intertextual conversation partners provide markedly different perspectives on the legitimacy of Lazarus returning in order to communicate a warning. In Graeco-Roman literature it is not uncommon for someone to return from the dead with a report intended to impact the living. Within this cultural milieu, the Lukan audience probably envisions the rich man requesting that Lazarus speak to the five brothers out of his recently acquired knowledge of the post-mortem state, speaking both of his own beatitude at Abraham's side and also of the rich man's suffering in the flames. The parable's depiction of the immediate punishment of the wicked prior to the final judgment allows the possibility that reports of these grave consequences can reach the living.[185] If Lazarus can be sent – even briefly – to bring a warning witness, the brothers might amend

---

185. On the question of life after death in the extra-canonical writings, Luke-Acts, and early Christian literature, see, e.g., S. H. Hooke, 'Life After Death: VI. The Extra-Canonical Literature', *ExpTim* 76 (1965): 273–6; W. J. P. Boyd, 'Apocalyptic and Life after Death', in *Studia Evangelica 5*, ed. F. L. Cross, TUGAL 103 (Berlin: Akademie, 1968), 39–56. For the Lukan perspective on eschatology, see Conzelmann, *Theology*; Osei-Bonsu, 'Intermediate State', 115–30; Marshall, 'Future States', 7–23; Mattill, *Last Things*; Maddox, *Purpose*, 100–157; Wilson, 'Lukan Eschatology', 330–47; Carroll, *Response*; Ellis, *Eschatology*. Lehtipuu, *Afterlife Imagery*, 243–98, considers the parable in relation to Luke's eschatology and concludes that in Luke 16:19–31, as elsewhere, Luke's eschatological teaching always calls people to repentance (303).

their wicked conduct. The rich man's proposal to Abraham is broadly consonant with the purposes of post-mortem visitations in the Graeco-Roman milieu.

But the parable is startling in its divergence from this intertextual pattern. In answer to the request, Abraham states in v. 29 that it is not necessary because the brothers 'have Moses and the prophets'. If the brothers require a warning witness, Abraham says, 'Let them listen to them'. This answer is emphasized by its repetition in v. 31, where it is joined with the declaration that one 'risen from the dead' is insufficient to convince someone if 'Moses and the prophets' have been ignored. Even if a messenger is sent from the afterlife, Abraham asserts, his mission will be wholly ineffectual. This refusal is not at all the expected answer when we consider the long tradition of post-mortem messengers.[186] In the parable's conclusion the culturally expected pattern has been altered and radically subverted.[187]

Though it does not cohere with the Graeco-Roman tradition in this respect, the parable also does not offer a clear echo of the Deuteronomic voice. The reason that Abraham withholds permission is not the injunction of the Jewish Scriptures against communicating with the dead. His answer to the rich man is not to cite the prohibition of necromancy or consultation of familiar spirits, but rather it is to indicate the sufficiency of 'Moses and the prophets'. It is true that the parable does not contradict Deuteronomy's injunction, but neither does Abraham rely on the legal proscription in order to provide a definitive answer to the rich man's request. Because the notion of a post-mortem messenger is not rejected out of hand, an intertextual dialogue may yet assist in discerning the patriarch's rationale.

5.3.2. *The Necessity of Messengers*

The rich man's request is denied by Abraham on the grounds that the brothers have 'Moses and the prophets'.[188] His rejoinder underlines Luke's conception of the sufficiency of the Jewish Scripture as a guide for proper conduct.[189] This conclusion is supported through considering the literary context of Deuteronomy's proscription of necromantic practice. Though no explicit reference is made in the parable to Deut 18:10–12, the conceptual link is clear, evident in the rich man's proposal to solicit a message from the dead for the benefit of the living. Luke's audience –

186. Green, *Luke*, 609.

187. N. T. Wright, *Luke for Everyone* (London: SPCK, 2001), 200; cf. Bauckham, 'Visiting', 96.

188. Lehtipuu, *Afterlife Imagery*, 187: 'Abraham refuses the request on the grounds that it is unnecessary…not because it is impossible'.

189. See, e.g., Luke 10:25–28; 11:42; 16:17; 18:18–20.

well-acquainted as they were with Deuteronomy – can know that this extraordinary contact is forbidden. The dead were not to be contacted on behalf of the living.

Furthermore, the Lukan audience can take into account the wider setting of the Deut 18 injunction. Dodd argues about the New Testament pattern of employing extensive portions of prior Scriptures, 'These sections were understood as *wholes*, and particular verses or sentences were quoted from them rather as pointers to the whole context than as constituting testimonies in and for themselves'.[190] This is in contrast to the view that New Testament authors typically severed texts from Scripture, jettisoning their contexts and employing the words in radically new ways.[191] The Deut 18 interdiction of necromancy should therefore be heard in the wider context of God's provision of reliable revelation. As noted previously, the people's need for direction is met in the divine promise of a נָבִיא (v. 15). Yahweh's own words will be put into the prophet's mouth, and the prophet will tell Israel everything that God commands (v. 18). The prohibitions of necromancy, divination, sorcery, interpretation of omens, witchcraft, and the casting of spells ought to be understood against this background: 'The declaration that Yahweh will raise up a prophet like Moses... comes in direct contrast to the vivid picture of the practices of the other nations'.[192] Because God has promised to speak to the people, there is no need to solicit alternate messengers. The Deuteronomic perspective – one confirmed by other Jewish Scripture[193] – is that reliable revelation comes not through alternate means, but only through the God-sent prophets.

This intertextual voice concerning the sufficiency of authoritative revelation is emphatically affirmed by Abraham in his words to the rich man: Ἔχουσι Μωϋσέα καὶ τοὺς προφήτας· ἀκουσάτωσαν αὐτῶν (v. 29). Every necessary warning and instruction has already been given. For the five living brothers of the rich man, 'What is the ghost of the beggar from their brother's gate compared to Moses and the prophets?'[194] Those who

190. C. H. Dodd, *According to the Scriptures: The Sub-Structure of New Testament Theology* (London: Nisbet, 1952), 126 (emphasis original).

191. It is a long-debated topic in studies of the New Testament's use of the Old, whether in citing from the latter the authors show respect for the original context. For an introduction to these issues, see S. Moyise, 'Does the NT Quote the OT Out of Context?', *Anvil* 11 (1994): 133–43; and essays in G. K. Beale, ed., *The Right Doctrine from the Wrong Texts? Essays on the Use of the Old Testament in the New* (Grand Rapids: Baker, 1994).

192. McConville, *Deuteronomy*, 302.

193. See, e.g., Isa 8:19–20.

194. Bernstein, *Formation*, 241.

listen to the parable in an intertextual conversation with Deuteronomy will reach a similar conclusion: a visitor with a message from the realm of the afterlife is not needed because God has already given sufficient testimony in the Scriptures.

6. *Conclusions on Intertextuality in Luke 16:19–31*

We have held a suggestive intertextual conversation involving Deuteronomy and Graeco-Roman literature about two prominent themes in Luke 16:19–31, poverty and possessions, and messengers from the afterlife. Having listened to our conversation partners the following conclusions can be adduced.

6.1. *Poverty and Possessions*

The source of the rich man's wealth is not elucidated in the parable. If we regard the rich man through Seneca's or Plutarch's lens of the stereotypically wealthy, it might be suggested that he gained his wealth through the exploitation of the socially less-powerful, and maintained his wealth through avarice and tight-fistedness. Consequently, the rich man is suffering post-mortem torments for his financial misconduct and neighbourly neglect. Yet there is an intertextual dissonance, for Deuteronomy's voice insists that wealth is a divine blessing on those who keep the commandments. The audience's difficulty is that in the parable no explicit moral judgment is passed on the rich man for the manner in which he lived or for how his wealth was acquired. If the origin of the rich man's wealth is uncertain, the same must be said for the miserable condition of Lazarus. According to passages in Deuteronomy, his poverty, skin affliction, and (possible) lack of burial can be interpreted as emblematic of God's curse on his unrepentant wickedness. However, this explanation does not satisfy, for Lazarus is rewarded with a post-mortem position at Abraham's side in the feast of God's kingdom. Thus another intertextual tension needs resolution: the rationale for the poor man's eschatological reward.

An intertextual conversation concerning the rich man's portrayal leads to more unambiguously negative conclusions. He embodies some of the moral dangers confronting the wealthy. While Deuteronomy is largely positive concerning prosperity, some Graeco-Roman writers draw attention to the serious attendant hazards of possessing wealth. Riches can engender a spirit of greed, a lifestyle of decadence, and unkindness in conduct. Luke's portrait of the overindulged, richly costumed, and self-centred man accords with such a picture and affirms the cultural voice.

Similar to other poor persons in the ancient world, Lazarus is powerless, not simply physically but socially. His portrait elicits a sympathetic response from the audience, and even an identification with the beggar at the gate. This affirms the recurrent suggestion of Deuteronomy, that God's covenant people must identify with the poor and take action to mitigate their suffering. Here our intertextual conversation indicates that there were possibilities for his material goods that the rich man left un-utilized. He failed to employ the beneficent means promoted by Deuteronomy – or by the prophets and in other Jewish literature – to care for his impoverished neighbour. He could have shared his goods and income, contributed alms or extended hospitality, but he did nothing. The intertextual dissonance surrounding the rich man's prosperity as a possible indicator of divine favour is resolved: he is not obedient, and is therefore punished in the afterlife.

The account of the rich man's failure is amplified by listening to a second intertextual voice, for neither does he conform to Graeco-Roman cultural mores regarding wealth and generosity. To some extent prosperous persons were expected to be willing to share their material resources with the suffering poor, whether through the forgiving of debts, the distribution of property, or general liberality. The inexcusability of the rich man's failure to respond to the destitution of Lazarus is unmistakable within such a conversation – as is Luke's warning and encouragement to his listeners.

6.2. *Messengers from the Afterlife*

Our conversation partners provide decidedly different perspectives on whether there is a legitimate prospect for Lazarus to return from Abraham's company in order to convey a warning to the five brothers. In Graeco-Roman literature it is not uncommon for the dead to return with a report intended to influence outlook and behaviour. Within this cultural tradition, Luke's audience probably envisions the rich man as requesting Lazarus to speak to the brothers out of his knowledge of the post-mortem state and the appalling cost of misconduct. The rich man's proposal is consonant with other accounts of post-mortem visitations, but the parable immediately diverges from this pattern: the request is rejected as unnecessary because the five brothers 'have Moses and the prophets'. Even if a messenger is sent from the dead, Abraham predicts that his mission may be ineffectual. The culturally well-known and expected pattern has been disrupted.

Although the parable does not correspond with the Graeco-Roman tradition in this respect, neither does it offer a clear reverberation of the voice of the Hebrew Scriptures. The reason that Abraham withholds permission for Lazarus to return is not the Deut 18 injunction against seeking communications from the dead, but the emphatic sufficiency of 'Moses and the prophets'. The unnecessity of Lazarus's return is indicative of the sufficiency of the Scriptures – a sufficiency which simul-taneously emphasizes the rich man's culpability for not listening. This conclusion is borne out by the broader context of Deut 18, where God promises reliable revelation: the people's need for direction is met in the provision of a נָבִיא. Because God promises to speak, there is no need to solicit messengers from the dead. *No.*

7. *Continued Echoes of the Conversation in Acts*

We have examined Luke 16:19–31 in interaction with various traditions, a conversation that affirms the importance of generosity toward the poor, and that modifies the expectation for a messenger from the dead. Looking to the parable's fuller literary context in Luke's two-volume work, how does our conversation on these two themes engage with Luke-Acts as a whole? We will briefly reflect on this question with reference to both themes before revisiting it more substantially in the next chapter.

7.1. *Acts on Poverty and Possessions*

Though Deuteronomy expects poverty to be eliminated (15:4), it acknowl-edges that this ideal will not be attained, and that the poor will invariably be present (15:11). Luke 16:19–31 affirms this tradition by depicting the rich man's failure to be open-handed to his brother 'in the gate'. In contrast to this neglect, the believers in Acts put the words of Jesus into practice through activities of charity and generosity. From the daily distri-bution for the support of widows (6:1–6), to almsgiving and generosity (9:36; 10:2), hospitality (10:48; 18:1–3; 28:1–2), famine relief (11:27–30; 24:17), and Paul's provision for his ministry companions (20:33–35), Acts highlights works of practical mercy. The benevolence in Acts that is perhaps most intertextually resonant is the communion of goods (2:45–47; 4:32–37), when the believers voluntarily sell their houses and hold all things in common. Our survey also noted possible Graeco-Roman echoes in Luke's portrait of this communion.[195] Writers such as Plato and Seneca referenced a 'golden age' and vaunted the ideals of friendship and the holding of goods in common. With the accounts of Acts 2–4, Luke may have intended his audience to see that the beginning of the church

---

195. On the way in which Luke reimagines the Graeco-Roman friendship tradition in Acts, see Mitchell, 'Social Function', 255–72.

was a return to the idyllic state enjoyed by humanity at the beginning of time.[196] More perceptibly, Luke echoes Deut 15:4 in his portrait of the church's mutual care in 4:34: οὐδὲ γὰρ ἐνδεής τις ἦν ἐν αὐτοῖς.[197] A phrase that is probably a strong recommendation or imperative in the Hebrew of Deuteronomy,[198] that is rendered as a future tense or prediction in the LXX, is in Acts formulated as a statement of fact. Luke portrays the community as fulfilling the Mosaic law through their obedience to God's will concerning possessions, with the result that no one in their midst is impoverished.[199]

7.2. *Acts on Messengers from the Afterlife*

Abraham's refusal to send Lazarus as a messenger from the dead runs counter to the pattern of Graeco-Roman culture. The Third Gospel's perspective is that no afterlife envoy is needed because of the sufficiency of 'Moses and the prophets'. Yet in Acts the intertextual dialogue with Deut 18 continues, for it is made explicit that the expected ministry of a 'prophet like Moses' has occurred in the person Jesus.[200] In Acts 3:22–26 Peter links Jesus directly with the prophecy of Deut 18, asserting that Jesus has provided reliable revelation from God.[201] Jesus as the 'prophet like Moses' is the hermeneutical key to understanding Israel's Scriptures, which in Acts are described with variations on the parable's signature phrase, 'Moses and the prophets'.[202] Throughout Acts the believers use these Scriptures in order to validate the claim that Jesus is the promised Messiah.[203] Not only the death but also the resurrection of Jesus is

196. Capper, 'Reciprocity', 509; in contrast to the continuity that Capper highg lights, R. B. Hays, 'Liberation of Israel in Luke-Acts: Intertextual Narration', in *Reading the Bible Intertextually*, ed. R. B. Hays, S. Alkier, and L. Huizenga (Waco, TX: Baylor University Press, 2009), 101–17, speaks of Acts portraying the church as 'counter-cultural' within the Empire (116–17).

197. Walton, 'Primitive Communism', 104, discusses this as an echo of Deut 15:4 (LXX), οὐκ ἔσται ἐν σοὶ ἐνδεής; he judges that the echo in Acts 4:34 is made more certain by the presence of ἐνδεής, a NT *hapax legomenon*.

198. See earlier discussion in this chapter, §4.1.4.

199. Capper, 'Reciprocity', 502; cf. Dupont, 'Poor and Poverty', 33.

200. For Jesus as a prophet in the Third Gospel, see 4:24; 7:16, 39; 9:7–9, 19; 13:33.

201. On the citation of Deut 18 in Acts 3, see Dodd, *Scriptures*, 53–57.

202. See, e.g., Acts 13:27; 26:22; 28:23; cf. Luke 24:27, 44.

203. See, e.g., Acts 13:32–41; 17:2–3; 19:28; 28:23; cf. J. T. Carroll, 'The Uses of Scripture in Acts', in *Society of Biblical Literature 1990 Seminar Papers*, SBLSP 29 (Atlanta: Scholars Press, 1990), 512–28, citing 521.

inexplicable apart from the content of the law of Moses, the prophets and the Psalms.[204] This theme of authoritative revelation in relation to the risen Jesus – and the way in which this theme is anticipated in Luke 16:19–31 – will be studied more closely in our next chapter.

204. Brawley, *Text to Text*, 124. While Brawley cites only from Luke's Gospel in support (24:25–27, 37, 44–47), we note several instances in Acts when the event of Christ's resurrection is interpreted with explicit reference to the Jewish Scriptures (e.g. Acts 2:25–32; 13:32–37; 17:2–3).

Chapter 5

LUKE 16:19–31 WITHIN LUKE-ACTS

1. *Reading the Parable Intratextually*

Luke 16:19–31 is known by the conventional title, 'The Parable of the Rich Man and Lazarus'.[1] As with other Synoptic parables it is recognizable as a story or narrative, having a beginning, middle, and conclusion.[2] But perhaps more than any other New Testament literary form the parables have been read atomistically, resulting in a neglect of the contiguous material essential for their interpretation.[3] By considering not just its immediate context but the Gospel as an entirety, interpretive light is shed on a particular parable.[4] One way such an intratextual reading can be achieved is through examining the broader work's themes and motifs: Are there thematic lines that can be traced from the beginning of the work, and can these themes be discerned in a parable, variously echoed or modified? Furthermore, how does the presence of these themes in a parable relate to their function in the subsequent material?

In this chapter we will focus on Lukan themes that are present both in Luke 16:19–31 and in Luke-Acts as a whole. Themes that emerged in the foregoing chapters' narrative, rhetorical, and intertextual investigations will be traced from Luke 1, to their convergence in the parable, through to Luke 24, and finally to their development in Acts. Luke's claim to have written a carefully ordered narrative (1:1–4) necessitates that the Gospel and Acts be read or listened to sequentially, completely, and repeatedly in

---

1. This is a title found almost universally in the literature on this parable; Jeremias, *Parables*, 186, is one of the few to propose an alternative title: 'The Parable of the Six Brothers'.

2. Cf. Aristotle, *Poet.* 1450b26.

3. B. Gerhardsson, 'If We Do Not Cut the Parables Out of their Frames', *NTS* 37 (1991): 321–35, citing 322; cf. Snodgrass, 'Allegorizing', 266.

4. Powell, 'Narrative Criticism', 243, aptly notes, 'We cannot determine the expected effects of a passage from Luke's Gospel by considering the passage as an isolated pericope but only by considering the role that the passage plays in the narrative as a whole'; cf. Wright, *Voice of Jesus*, 30–32.

order to understand their component parts.[5] Reading the parable within the Luke-Acts context has been a neglected area in past studies, but in this chapter we will see how Luke utilizes it to anticipate and prepare for his second volume and to develop his theological emphases.[6] Finally, we will consider a number of interpretive outcomes of our investigation.

2. *Reading Luke and Acts Together*

2.1. *The Unity of Luke-Acts*

Before studying the parable's themes in relation to the Lukan corpus, we will reiterate our presuppositions about the delineation of this literary context. The parable's backdrop is wider than the twenty-four chapters of Luke's Gospel, for as assumed throughout this work, it should be read in close literary conjunction not only with the Third Gospel, but also with Acts.[7] Situating the parable within this united narrative we expect to see connective elements, linking it not just to the immediate context of Jesus's ministry but to what will ensue in the story of the early Christian community.[8] We will investigate the parable's various forms of interaction with key Lukan themes, as these themes are affirmed, expanded, and employed to anticipate what is yet to be recounted in Luke's narrative.[9] In the next section we will review suggestive patterns of association and correlation between Luke and Acts as prefatory to our investigation of the parable's coherence within the wider work.

2.2. *Narrative Foresight*

In writing his two-volume corpus Luke demonstrates literary and narrative foresight. As he states in his prologue, he committed to writing the events already interpreted by many others (1:1–2), offering Theophilus his own orderly account (1:3–4). Luke is therefore in a position to craft his διήγησις in such a way as indicates that the message and content of the two

---

5. Powell, 'Narrative Criticism', 244.

6. An exception is Hintzen's study of the parable in relation to Acts in *Verkündigung*, 368–74.

7. See the discussion of the unity of Luke-Acts in Chapter 1, §§3.1-2, §7.

8. Green, 'Reaffirmation', 118, notes that 'Jesus' followers are increasingly in focus as Acts begins'.

9. Barrett, 'Preface to Acts', 1451–66, questions whether the Gospel is primary and Acts serves as confirmation, or if the Acts is primary and the Gospel serves as introduction; he concludes that there is merit to both models of understanding, and that they are in fact complementary.

volumes are closely interrelated. Green describes this as the 'intertextual reverberations' of Luke-Acts, as events and motifs are echoed from the Gospel into Acts.[10] With this continual interplay of texts Luke anticipates later aspects of his narrative as it moves toward its conclusion in Acts 28, and he encourages their mutual interpretation. Understanding his Gospel as establishing the first part of the story and setting a programme for what follows, we may also expect that the implications of Luke 16:19–31 will be explicated more fully in Acts.[11]

2.3. *Narrative Anticipation*

There is a consistent pattern of the Third Gospel anticipating the events and motifs that will be prevalent in Acts.[12] Talbert has compiled a list of internal thematic parallels between the two books, and argues for a 'correspondence of content and sequence between persons and events in the Third Gospel and those of the book of Acts'.[13] With reference to persons, a widespread parallelism of character has also been identified, such as the linking of Jesus and Stephen, Jesus and Peter, and Jesus and Paul.[14] Echoes and resemblances from the events of one volume to the next may have become clear to Luke's audience only on a second, third, or fourth reading or hearing of text, a phenomenon that encouraged reflection on and engagement with Luke-Acts as a whole.[15] The Lukan patterns of foreshadowing and paralleling have the cumulative effect of establishing

---

10. Green, 'Internal Repetition', 290–97.

11. Marshall, 'Former Treatise', 181.

12. See, e.g., Trompf, *Historical Recurrence*, 116–79, who situates Luke's internal repetitions within the context of Hellenistic historiography; cf. Rothschild, *Rhetoric of History*, 99–141.

13. C. H. Talbert, *Literary Patterns, Theological Themes, and the Genre of Luke-Acts*, SBLMS 20 (Missoula, MT: Scholars Press, 1974), 15–50; cf. Green, 'Internal Repetition', 283–99.

14. See, e.g., Praeder, 'Parallelisms', 23–39; cf. Parsons, 'Narrative Closure', who observes a circularity in Luke's Gospel, namely, 'the recalling at the end of a story of characters, settings or situations which have not recurred since the beginning', which serves to brings closure to the plot of the Gospel (204).

15. See B. Gaventa, 'Toward a Theology of Acts: Reading and Rereading', *Int* 42 (1988): 146–57; cf. Tannehill, *Narrative Unity*, 1:6. A. Thompson, 'Parallel Composition and Rhetorical Effect in Luke 7 and 8', *JSNT* 38 (2015): 169–90, evaluates whether the verbal, narrative, and thematic parallels that scholars have identified in Luke-Acts are a result of Luke's deliberate composition, and employs eleven tests to evaluate the proposed parallels between two healing/resurrection stories in Luke's Gospel.

audience expectation. These patterns invite attention to how the themes in Luke 16:19–31 are a continuation of ideas already introduced, and how these will be developed in latter parts of the narrative.

2.4. *Narrative Incompletion*

While Luke asserts that he has crafted his narrative with care (1:3), aspects of his story are left incomplete, but by design, not neglect. This narrative incompletion is seen in individual episodes and characters of the Gospel,[16] where gaps invite Luke's readers to fill the narrative with an imagination that has been shaped by the preceding stories.[17] Besides its occurrence in individual passages, the pattern of incompletion is true of the Third Gospel as a whole, which in some respects remains open-ended or unfinished; for instance, by the close of ch. 24, the promised Spirit has not yet come (24:49) nor has Jesus become a light to the Gentiles (2:32).[18] Green observes: 'The Gospel of Luke is incomplete in itself, for it opens up possibilities in the narrative cycle that go unrealized in the Gospel but do materialize in the Acts of the Apostles'.[19] Some of the Gospel's narrative loose ends are tied up in the events of Acts,[20] yet Acts concludes before the fulfilment of predictions such as the capture of Jerusalem (Luke 19:43–44; 21:22–24), the destruction of the temple (Luke 13:35; 21:6), and the death of Paul (Acts 20:25).[21] This open-endedness engages the audience in constructing coherence from a retrospective vantage point,[22] for the hearers are pressed to finish the story in accordance with

---

16. See, e.g., Jesus's address to three potential followers in 9:57–62, and how their response to his challenging words is not recounted. Similarly, many characters appear only once in the Gospel, with the audience learning 'just a small amount about that person' (Maxwell, *Between the Lines*, 135).

17. Kurz, 'Narrative Approaches', 201; cf. R. C. Tannehill, 'Freedom and Responsibility in Scripture Interpretation, with Application to Luke', in *Literary Studies in Luke-Acts: Essays in Honor of Joseph B. Tyson*, ed. R. P. Thompson and T. E. Phillips (Macon, GA: Mercer University Press, 1998), 265–78, especially 268–70.

18. Kurz, *Reading Luke-Acts*, 30.

19. Green, *Luke*, 10.

20. E.g. the coming of the Holy Spirit in Acts 2, 'being witnesses' (Luke 24:48) in Acts 1:8, 22; cf. Parsons, 'Narrative Closure', 220.

21. Kurz, 'Open-Ended', 294; Maxwell, *Between the Lines*, 147–48.

22. Alexander, 'Back to Front', 445; cf. T. M. Troftgruben, *A Conclusion Unhindered: A Study of the Ending of Acts Within Its Literary Environment*, WUNT 2/280 (Tübingen: Mohr Siebeck, 2010), who counters Marguerat's contention that the reader of Acts is being encouraged to 'finish the story' or 'carry on Paul's legacy'

the plot.[23] This notion of narrative incompletion/completion shapes how individual stories are read, particularly those considered 'open-ended', such as Luke 16:19–31.[24] We will see that also this parable is brought to a sense of completion through the Acts narratives.

2.5. *Prophecy and Prediction*

As a variation on narrative incompletion scholars identify the role of prediction in the Lukan corpus, where promises, prophecies, or other forecasting messages are fulfilled in the context of the narrative.[25] In her study of Luke-Acts as an historiographical work, Rothschild draws attention to the rhetorical function of the technique of prophecy-fulfilment.[26] In Greek and Jewish historiography authors employ various forms of prognostication, such as oracles, omens, or prophecies as a means to sanction their version of events or to prepare the audience for the unlikely episodes in the subsequent narrative.[27] As Rothschild observes, 'Prediction offered audiences the opportunity to both recollect what they knew about an event before it was narrated, as well as anticipate this upcoming version of the events'.[28] Within Luke-Acts there are numerous instances of prophetic activity. Besides Luke's repeated notation of the fulfilment of the Jewish Scriptures, there are new predictions, both divine and human.[29] Patterns of prediction and fulfilment constitute evidence

(163–65). Troftgruben argues that the ending of Acts conveys both closure and openness, and that particularly the irresolution of the end prompts the reader to watch for the continuing activity of God in the movement of witness (175–78).

23. Marguerat, 'End of Acts', 81. As Alexander, 'Back to Front', 440, similarly posits about the reputedly unsatisfying ending of Acts, 'Even without knowing the details of the story, [readers] will read the beginning of the Gospel with the benefit of some kind of hindsight and may well therefore pick up some of Luke's hints at the outset'.

24. Maxwell, *Between the Lines*, 133–35; see the discussion in Chapter 3, §4.5.5.

25. See J. T. Squires, *The Plan of God in Luke-Acts*, SNTSMS 76 (Cambridge: Cambridge University Press, 1993); Schubert, 'Structure and Significance', 165–86; F. Bovon, 'The Effect of Realism and Prophetic Ambiguity in the Works of Luke', in Bovon, *New Testament Traditions and Apocryphal Narratives*, trans. J. Haapiseva-Hunter (Allison Park, OR: Pickwick, 1995), 97–104.

26. Rothschild, *Rhetoric of History*, 142–84.

27. See Homer, *Od.* 11.100–37; Herodotus, *Hist.* 1.9.2–20; Dionysius of Halicarnassus, *Ant. rom.* 1.23.4–5.

28. Rothschild, *Rhetoric of History*, 144.

29. Divine predictions are made by angels or heavenly messengers (e.g. Luke 1:13–17, 31–36) and the risen Jesus (e.g. Luke 24:48–49; Acts 1:8); human

for belief in a providential God controlling human history,[30] and sanction the author's version of the events.[31] This pattern is pertinent particularly when we consider how Abraham's words about the five brothers' inability or unwillingness to repent (v. 31) have a predictive function in relation to later events of the Lukan narrative.

2.6. *Narrative Tension*

A synoptic reading of Luke and Acts reveals the presence of narrative tension or discordance. Citing the internal tensions between Luke and Acts that Parsons and Pervo point out, Marguerat agrees that these should not be dismissed too readily.[32] There is a unity in Luke-Acts at the theological level, but this unity needs to be constructed at the level of a narrative strategy. Marguerat identifies three narrative means by which Luke encourages his reader to maintain continuity: by prolepsis, a projection toward the future of the story; by narrative chains, lines drawn between the two parts of the narrative which allow the reader to gauge the narrative's continuity and progression; and by modelling, the presentation of one character next to another for comparison.[33] An example of tension identified by Marguerat, and one relevant to Luke 16:19–31, is the place and function of the wealthy in Luke's theology. Despite the Third Gospel's denunciations of rich people (6:24–25; 12:13–21; 20:47) and its attention to wealth's transience and dangers (12:33–34; 18:18–30), comparable words are absent in Acts, replaced by a focus on sharing and a regular narrative inclusion of the privileged and persons of high rank.[34] Such internal tension 'leads the reader to reread the gospel with Acts in mind, to seek for the hermeneutical keys to the narrative'.[35] The Acts accounts serve to adjust and augment the audience's understanding of the parable.

predictions are made by living prophets (e.g. Luke 1:67–79), Jesus during his ministry on earth (e.g. Luke 9:22, 44), and others (e.g. Acts 11:27–28; 20:23); see Rothschild, *Rhetoric of History*, 175–82.

30. Talbert, 'Promise and Fulfillment', 96.

31. Rothschild, *Rhetoric of History*, 183: 'Foretelling of events in anticipation of their actually taking place in a historical narrative is a subtle form of persuasion'.

32. See, e.g., Parsons and Pervo, *Rethinking*, 45–83; and discussion in Marguerat, 'Task of Reading', 43–64.

33. Marguerat, 'Task of Reading', 49–59; cf. Parsons, 'Narrative Closure', 213, who describes internal and external proleptic references in Luke and Acts.

34. Marguerat, 'Task of Reading', 45; for the attention to the privileged he cites 8:27; 9:36; 16:14; 17:34; 18:7.

35. Marguerat, 'Task of Reading', 64.

2.7. Conclusion

As we read Luke-Acts in order to unfold the meaning and function of Luke 16:19–31 within the entirety of the Lukan corpus, we will give attention to these narrative patterns of anticipation, incompletion, prophecy or prediction, and tension, as they relate to the parable's salient themes.

3. Identifying the Parable's Themes

Previously we noted two principal themes characteristic of Luke's Gospel that are present in this parable.[36] Besides the themes of material possessions and the response to poverty, and the source and efficacy of authoritative revelation, we identify three secondary Lukan themes: first, the role of the patriarch Abraham (16:22);[37] secondly, the possibility of repentance and its result (16:30);[38] and thirdly, the response to one risen from the dead (16:31).[39] We will see how Luke-Acts confirms and transforms the principal themes, and we will note intersections with the

---

36. See the discussion in Chapter 4, §2.

37. See 1:55, 73; 3:8, 34; 13:16; see also Acts 3:13; 7:2–8; 13:26. Abraham is identified as a thematic focus in the parable by Siker, *Disinheriting*, 114–18; Brawley, 'Abrahamic Covenant', 121–23; Kim, 'From Israel to the Nations', 304–17.

38. In both the Third Gospel and Acts, the language associated with repentance occurs with regularity; μετάνοια occurs in Luke 3:3, 8; 5:32; 15:7; 24:47; Acts 5:31; 11:18; 13:24; 19:4; 20:21; 26:20; μετανοέω occurs nine times in Luke (10:13; 11:32; 13:3, 5; 15:7, 10; 16:30; 17:3, 4) and five times in Acts (2:38; 3:19; 8:22; 17:30; 26:20). As such, it is identified as another Lukan theme in scholarship; see, e.g., Roose, 'Umkehr und Ausgleich'; G. D. Nave, *The Role and Function of Repentance in Luke-Acts*, SBLAB 4 (Leiden: Brill, 2002), 185; Morlan, *Conversion*; F. Méndez-Moratalla, *The Paradigm of Conversion in Luke*, JSNTSup 252 (London: T&T Clark, 2004); R. C. Tannehill, 'Repentance in the Context of Lukan Soteriology', in Tannehill, *The Shape of Luke's Story: Essays on Luke-Acts* (Eugene, OR: Cascade, 2005), 84–101.

39. It is widely accepted that resurrection is one of the Third Gospel's key themes (e.g. 9:22; 18:33; 24:1–11, 12, 13–32, 35; 24:34, 36–49). See C. H. Talbert, 'The Place of the Resurrection in the Theology of Luke', in Talbert, *Reading Luke-Acts in its Mediterranean Milieu*, NovTSup 107 (Leiden: Brill, 2003), 121–33; Anderson, *God Raised*; A. J. Thompson, *The Acts of the Risen Lord Jesus: Luke's Account of God's Unfolding Plan*, New Studies in Biblical Theology 27 (Downers Grove, IL: InterVarsity, 2011); I. H. Marshall, 'The Resurrection of Jesus in Luke', *TynBul* 24 (1973): 55–98; N. T. Wright, *The Resurrection of the Son of God*, Christian Origins and the Question of God 3 (Minneapolis: Fortress, 2003), 436–37.

secondary themes. To the continuation, concretization, and amplification of the parable's teaching on possessions and the required response to poverty we now turn.

4. *Riches and Poverty in Luke-Acts and the Parable*

4.1. *A Thematic Disconnect?*

Reading the first of the parable's principal themes we are confronted by an ostensible disconnect between Luke's two volumes. It requires little argumentation to establish that matters of wealth and the treatment of the poor are a paramount concern in Luke's Gospel.[40] Similarly, it is generally agreed that the notion of the use of riches for the alleviation of poverty is basic to Luke 16:19–31. The disconnect arises shortly thereafter, as the narrative continues subsequent to Luke 16 and especially in Acts. Any discussion of the theme of possessions in Luke's Gospel must account for how its literary function is altered, to the point of almost disappearing after ch. 16.[41] A similarly striking feature is the absence of the words πλούσιος and πτωχός from Acts. After employing this terminology regularly in his first volume Luke shifts away from its use, a change too dramatic not to demand investigation and invite explanation.[42]

In what follows we will examine this apparent discrepancy, and find that it is not a disconnect at all. On the contrary, there is a strong and suggestive link between the two volumes on this theme; the continuity exists in an altered and, we will argue, intentional fashion. In order to appreciate how the theme of poverty and possessions is transformed from its function in the Gospel and the parable to its role Acts, we commence with a survey of this theme in Luke's Gospel, with special attention to how it is present in 16:19–31. We will then turn to its function in Acts and how this reprised theme corresponds to the parable.

---

40. The centrality of this motif is evidenced also in the vast amount of scholarly literature on poverty and possessions in Luke-Acts; see Phillips, 'Wealth and Poverty', 231–69; Donahue, 'Two Decades', 129–44; cf. summary in Chapter 1, §5.1.

41. Johnson, 'Luke-Acts', 405. Apart from Jesus's words to the rich man in Luke 18:18–30 and Jesus's interaction with Zacchaeus in 19:1–10, the theme is absent.

42. For πλούσιος, see Luke 6:24; 12:16; 14:12; 16:1, 19, 21, 22; 18:23, 25; 19:2; 21:1; for πτωχός, see Luke 4:18; 6:20; 7:22; 14:13, 21; 16:20, 22; 18:22; 19:8; 21:3. See the discussion in E. Scheffler, *Suffering in Luke's Gospel*, ATANT 81 (Zurich: TVZ, 1993), 60–63.

4.2. *Riches and Poverty in Luke*

4.2.1. *Good News to the Poor*

It has been said that 'Luke has written more on the topic of wealth than any other New Testament writer'.[43] While the other Synoptic Gospels include instructions and warnings about material possessions,[44] a redactional emphasis on riches and poverty is evident not only in the material that Luke has in common with Mark and Matthew, but also in the uniquely Lukan material.[45] From an early juncture, attention is given to the poor and their plight.[46] The Lukan infancy narratives evince a sympathy for those without wealth or power, and an attendant antagonism toward those who are rich and mighty. For instance, Mary's song in 1:52–53 speaks of God filling the hungry with good things, but sending away the rich empty.[47] Like Matthew and Mark, Luke gives an account of John the Baptist's preaching, but only he records the exhortation that one who has two coats or food should share with those who have none (3:10), an inclusion indicating concern for the indigent. As is well-known, Luke also offers a different form of the first beatitude in Matthew's Sermon on the Mount, 'Blessed are the poor in spirit' (Μακάριοι οἱ πτωχοὶ τῷ πνεύματι, Matt 5:3); the Lukan version in 6:20 pronounces, Μακάριοι οἱ πτωχοί. According to Jesus's teaching on the Plain, the materially poor and outcasts will experience a radical reversal in their earthly condition.

In terms of his ministry activities, Jesus brings a message to the poverty-stricken and suffering. His oration in the Nazareth synagogue, in which he quotes Isa 61 with reference to himself in 'announcing good news to the poor' (εὐαγγελίσασθαι πτωχοῖς, 4:18) is viewed as programmatic for the Third Gospel.[48] While the Matthean account also depicts Jesus 'preaching to the poor' (Matt 11:5), Luke affords this motif a prominent place at the commencement of Jesus's ministry, and represents Jesus associating frequently with the marginalized members of Palestinian society: women, people with physical disabilities, non-Jews and social pariahs.[49] Where the poor might be defined today strictly in terms of a

---

43. Bock, *Theology*, 328; he summarizes the Lukan theology of wealth on 328–30 and 352–57; cf. Fitzmyer, *Theologian*, 137; Esler, *Community and Gospel*, 169.

44. See, e.g., Mark 6:7–11; 8:36; 10:17–22, 23–27; 12:38–40, 41–44; Matt 6:1–4, 19–21; 19:16–24.

45. See Esler, *Community and Gospel*, 165–69.

46. See Johnson, *Literary Function*, 132–40.

47. See Schottroff and Stegemann, *Hope of the Poor*, 28–29.

48. Johnson, *Literary Function*, 132; cf. Esler, *Community and Gospel*, 280–83.

49. See, e.g., 4:38–39, 40; 5:12–14; 7:1–9, 11–15, 36–50; 8:1–3.

constrained economic condition, Jesus is concerned with a class of people characterized primarily by a sense of exclusion and dishonourable status.[50] The poor are those of low social standing and left out of circles of power and influence; to these persons Jesus particularly attends in teaching and ministering.

While the theme of poverty and riches is present from the early chapters, Luke's distinctive emphasis on this trope is especially evident in material unique to his Gospel, most of which has been collected in the travel narrative (9:51–19:44).[51] Notably, it is in this section that Luke records the parables of the Good Samaritan (10:25–37), the Rich Fool (12:16–21), the Prodigal Son (15:11–32), the Dishonest Steward (16:1–9), and the parable of Lazarus and the Rich Man (16:19–31), each of which has material or financial referents, and either direct or implied exhortations with respect to the use of money.[52] In this connection, Nolland aptly observes that a number of Lukan parables mention money, but are not about money as such; for instance, the parable of the Two Debtors (7:41–43) has a message not about debt reduction but personal forgiveness.[53] An interpreter should not conclude from a reference to pecuniary matters that a parable has an economic message. Notwithstanding this caveat, it is clear that several Lukan parables have this emphasis. Of note within the travel narrative is Luke 16, where attitudes toward possessions are especially prominent.[54]

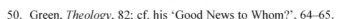

50. Green, *Theology*, 82; cf. his 'Good News to Whom?', 64–65.

51. See the discussion of the travel narrative in Chapter 2, §3.1. On the 'L' material, see Paffenroth, *Story*, 97–104; for a summary of this theme in Luke's collection, see Esler, *Community and Gospel*, 168–69.

52. See Parsons, 'Landmarks', 33–47; cf. Drury, *Parables*, 111–25.

53. Nolland, 'Role of Money and Possessions', 188–89: 'It is one thing to have money or possessions play an explicit or implicit role in the story; it is another thing to make the judgment that attitudes to wealth, or practices in the handling of wealth, have a central role in the purpose of the story'. See the interaction with Nolland's article by S. I. Wright, 'Reading Luke, Hearing Jesus, Understanding God: A Response to John Nolland's "The Role of Money and Possessions in the Parable of the Prodigal Son",' in Bartholomew, Green, and Thiselton, eds., *Reading Luke*, 210–28, especially 213–14.

54. Gillman, *Possessions*, 81. M. Matson, 'Luke's Rewriting on the Sermon on the Mount', *Society of Biblical Literature Seminar Papers 2000*, SBLSP 39 (Atlanta: SBL Press, 2000), 623–50, observes that in ch. 16 Luke creates a cluster of Sermon on the Mount material, a unit which deals with the relationship of possessions and the law (640–42).

4.2.2. *Warnings to the Rich*

While Jesus brings good news to the poor, he also directs words of censure to the rich and warns about the corrupting potential of wealth. Besides the upheaval of the rich and powerful in Mary's song (1:51–53), and the redactional emphasis in the Lukan beatitude of 6:20, it is striking that the blessing pronounced on the poor is followed by a 'woe' which is its 'exact antithesis'.[55] Luke alone includes Jesus's denunciation, 'Woe to you that are rich, for you have received your consolation' (v. 24), followed by a similarly sharp reproof of the well-fed and amused in v. 25. According to Jesus the rich must be under no illusions that they have a secure and irreversible position, nor that their enjoyment of good things will be uninterrupted.

The rich must also understand that acute spiritual dangers are associated with the possession of wealth. The parable of the Sower, present in all three Synoptic Gospels, reveals the Lukan perspective on the harmful influence of material prosperity.[56] In Luke's version the seed that falls among the thorns is not choked by the 'deceitfulness of riches' (ἡ ἀπάτη τοῦ πλούτου),[57] but simply by riches (πλούτου, 8:14). An abundance of material possessions is itself capable of hindering proper reception of the word of God.[58] While the narrative suggests that many wealthy persons will fail to use their resources rightly (e.g. Luke 18:22–25), prosperity does afford a rich person the opportunity to demonstrate faithfulness. Jesus insists in 16:11 – the immediate context of our parable – that fidelity in using earthly possessions, or 'unrighteous mammon' (τῷ ἀδίκῳ μαμωνᾷ), is indicative of an ability to handle true riches (τὸ ἀληθινόν).[59] Even so, it is impossible for two loyalties to co-exist in one heart: οὐ δύνασθε θεῷ δουλεύειν καὶ μαμωνᾷ (v. 13).[60] It is after this warning and in response to their disparagement of Jesus's words about the corrupting power of μαμωνᾶς (v. 14) that the Pharisees are characterized as 'lovers of money' (φιλάργυροι).[61] This uniquely Lukan characterization of the Pharisees is illustrative of his suspicious stance vis-à-vis wealthy persons. No.

---

55. Dupont, 'Poor and Poverty', 46.
56. Matt 13:1–9; Mark 4:1–12; Luke 8:4–8.
57. Matt 13:22; Mark 4:19.
58. Bock, *Theology*, 330.
59. See Johnson, *Literary Function*, 158.
60. Cf. Matt 6:24.
61. See the discussion of this term in Chapter 2, §3.2.

Another notable instance of Jesus cautioning the rich occurs in the parable of the Rich Fool in Luke 12:16–21.[62] According to its narrative context in 12:13–15, the parable is told as a warning against covetousness (πλεονεξία). The concluding verse describes an individual who lays up treasure for himself, but is not rich toward God (v. 21). Such a person is termed a fool (ἄφρων, v. 20) for his failure to recognize both the transience of earthly wealth and the alternative means to employ material blessing – an alternative described by Jesus in the narrative immediately following the parable in 12:33. To the recommended response to poor people we now turn.

4.2.3. *Treatment of Possessions and Response to Poverty*

More than castigating the rich and warning the wealthy, the Third Gospel delineates the proper use of possessions, both by way of exhortation and example. We already cited John the Baptist's explanation of the fruits of repentance in terms of generous sharing of clothing and food (3:11). Likewise, in a text unique to Luke, Jesus counsels lending without expectation of repayment (6:34–35). Later he advises the total renunciation of physical property, 'None of you can be my disciple if he does not forsake everything that he has' (14:33). This motif, too, is particular to Luke's Gospel: 'The members of the Lukan community who have possessions must be ready to forego them if they stand in the way of their fidelity to Jesus Christ'.[63] Consistent with the motif of renunciation is 18:22, 'Sell all and give to the poor'. While this saying is found also in Mark 10:21 and Matt 19:21, it is notable that only Luke in 18:28 records the disciples' assertion that they have actually given up their possessions to follow Jesus: ἡμεῖς ἀφέντες τὰ ἴδια.[64]

The twelve disciples are not Luke's only models of a proper treatment of possessions.[65] For instance, in 8:1–3 he acknowledges the women who support Jesus with their contributions. Generosity with possessions is likewise demonstrated in the parable of the Good Samaritan (10:25–37), for the Samaritan shows a pronounced diligence of care to the wounded

---

62. See Rindge, *Rich Fool*, 159–230.

63. Karris, 'Poor and Rich', 121.

64. Similarly, it is only Luke who includes the detail that Simon Peter, James, John, and Levi 'left everything' to follow Jesus (Luke 5:11, 28; cf. Mark 2:14; Matt 9:9).

65. Among commendable examples of financial conduct – though not unique to Luke (cf. Mark 12:42–43) – is the poor widow (Luke 21:1–4) who is said to have given more than anyone else.

stranger. Similarly, in reaction to Jesus's visit the tax collector Zacchaeus promises that he will not only make ample restitution to those he has defrauded, but he also dedicates half of his goods in support of the poor (19:8).

In connection with the parable of the Rich Fool in 12:16–21, Jesus offers an alternative to the πλεονεξία afflicting his hearers. Within the narrative context of v. 21 and its notion of 'being rich toward God' (εἰς θεὸν πλουτῶν), Jesus commands the selling of possessions and giving of alms: πωλήσατε τὰ ὑπάρχοντα ὑμῶν καὶ δότε ἐλεημοσύνην (12:33). This is a worthwhile alternative to the rich fool's focus on accumulation and consumption. It is only here and in 11:41 that Luke uses the terminology of giving alms (ἐλεημοσύνη). While the concept of almsgiving is not foreign to the other Gospels,[66] Luke's narrative presents this duty with special insistence, even as the primary recommendation for a person seeking a wise use of possessions.[67]

Besides the renunciation of possessions and giving of alms, the Third Gospel espouses another means of conduct in relation to material goods: the practice of hospitality.[68] First, Luke's narrative includes various instances of hospitality, including the hosting of Jesus by Levi (5:29), by Mary and Martha (10:38–42), and by Zacchaeus (19:1–10). Secondly, Jesus condemns a neglect of hospitality in 7:44–46 and 10:10–12, and encourages the reception of visitors even at personal inconvenience (11:5–8). Thirdly, in contrast to the practice of reserving places of honour at meals for high-ranking people and expecting reciprocal invitations from people of equal standing, Jesus says in 14:12–13 that friends and brothers and kinsmen should not be invited to feasts, but rather 'the poor, maimed, lame, and blind' (πτωχούς, ἀναπείρους, χωλούς, τυφλούς).[69]

---

66. See Kim, *Stewardship and Almsgiving*, 277–80, for the practice of almsgiving in the Jewish tradition. J. D. G. Dunn, *Beginning from Jerusalem*, Christianity in the Making 2 (Grand Rapids: Eerdmans, 2008), 459, states, 'Almsgiving was widely understood within Judaism as a central and crucial expression of covenant righteousness'; cf. Garrison, *Redemptive Almsgiving*, 46–59.

67. Rindge, *Rich Fool*, 190; cf. Luke Timothy Johnson, *Sharing Possessions: What Faith Demands*, 2nd ed. (Grand Rapids: Eerdmans, 2011), 16–19, who says that in Luke-Acts almsgiving is 'perhaps the dominant response called for' by those who would be followers of Jesus.

68. Heil, *Meal Scenes*, 142; cf. Smith, 'Table Fellowship', 613–38.

69. On the reciprocal nature of meal-invitations and hospitality in the first century, see J. H. Neyrey, 'Ceremonies in Luke-Acts: The Case of Meals and Table Fellowship', in Neyrey, ed., *The Social World of Luke-Acts*, 361–87.

Hospitality consistent with the tenor of this teaching is reflected in the parable of Great Supper (14:15–24) when the master invites the poor, maimed, blind, and lame to his banquet.

Finally, in connection with the giving and sharing that is both exhorted and modeled in Luke's Gospel, we highlight the saying, 'The poor you will always have with you'. It is significant that while present in various permutations in the other three canonical Gospels, Luke does not include it.[70] Instead, as discussed below, in Acts 4:34 the result of the community's thorough-going care for the needy is described: οὐδὲ γὰρ ἐνδεής τις ἦν ἐν αὐτοῖς. The absence of this broadly attested dominical saying from Luke, and a summary statement that indicates a starkly different reality among the believers in Acts, is suggestive of Luke's intent that his audience contemplate the desirability and effect of applying the teachings of Jesus about material goods in relation to the needy. We will consider this persuasion shortly, after examining the parable in relation to the motif of poverty and possessions in Luke's Gospel.

4.3. *The Parable and Possessions in Relation to Luke's Gospel*

4.3.1. *An Intensive Lesson*

In many respects our parable is congruous with the Lukan theme of poverty and possessions as developed in the Gospel.[71] To be sure, after sixteen chapters the parable 'addresses readers well educated on the topic',[72] but it does evince Luke's most intensive attention with respect to this theme.[73] The parable is a dramatic presentation of the dangers of wealth and the plight of poverty, and suggestive of how these two realities ought to intersect.

4.3.2. *The Parable and the Pharisees*

In examining the parable's function, its narrative setting and arrangement must again be emphasized, as these factors impact how Luke's audience reads or hears the account.[74] He signals in 16:1 that Jesus is addressing his disciples, while v. 14 identifies the presence of a secondary

---

70. See Mark 14:7, πάντοτε γὰρ τοὺς πτωχοὺς ἔχετε μεθ' ἑαυτῶν; cf. Matt 26:11 and John 12:8.

71. Cf. Borgman, *Hearing the Whole Story*, 156–70, for a discussion on possessions in the parables of Luke 12:13–34 and 16:1–31.

72. John T. Carroll, *Luke: A Commentary*, NTL (Louisville, KY: Westminster John Knox, 2012), 335.

73. Scheffler, *Suffering*, 62.

74. See the earlier discussion of the parable's immediate narrative context in Chapter 2, §3.2.

audience, the Pharisees.[75] They have listened to Jesus's words about faithfulness in handling possessions and his claim that one cannot serve God and Μαμωνᾶς. The 'greedy' Pharisees respond to Jesus's discourse on wealth by ridiculing him (ἐξεμυκτήριζον αὐτόν), likely because of their disquiet with the notions expressed.[76] Even if they are not the primary audience, it is certain that they are meant to hear the parable, and as such it functions partly as Jesus's response to his detractors.[77] They have already been warned not to neglect the poor (11:39–42),[78] and we note that Jesus's other encouragement in Luke to practise almsgiving (11:41) was also directed to the Pharisees. However, the Pharisees do not practise the mercy and hospitality enjoined by Jesus, for in 14:7–14 he criticizes the preferential treatment that they show at their banquets to the rich and honourable. The cumulative effect of this context suggests that the negative appellation 'lovers of money' applied to the Pharisees in v. 14 retains its rhetorical vigour when the rich man is introduced in v. 19. The Lukan audience has been prompted to identify the rich man with the lurking Pharisees.[79] *Maybe, but prob. not 1.2. Exaggeration*

4.3.3. *The Parable and Previous Warnings*

The thematic links from 16:19–31 to the rest of Luke's Gospel are further evident by reviewing the parable's details. When the rich man's attire is described in v. 19 (ἐνεδιδύσκετο πορφύραν καὶ βύσσον), the attentive reader recalls that in 7:25 Jesus spoke disparagingly about the luxurious clothing of the rich.[80] Within the Lukan perspective, the rich man's visible prosperity is suggestive of the spiritual danger he faces. Similarly evocative of the Lukan context is the rich man's daily entertaining. In v. 19 he feasts every day, εὐφραινόμενος καθ' ἡμέραν λαμπρῶς.[81]

---

75. Wright, 'Poverty and Riches', 220, contends that the narrative does not permit the assumption that the tax collectors and sinners (15:1) had departed.

76. Green, 'Narrative Criticism', 99; cf. Tannehill, *Narrative Unity*, 1:181. That the Pharisees are noted as a ridiculing audience is similar to the audience of the Luke 15 parables, which are told in response to their grumbling (διεγόγγυζον) that Jesus eats with tax collectors and sinners (15:2).

77. See Piper, 'Social Background', 1660–61; Minear, 'Jesus' Audiences'; Heil, *Meal Scenes*, 131, notes how the parable is part of a challenge to the Pharisees to repent.

78. Hintzen, *Verkündigung*, 366–68; cf. Tannehill, *Narrative Unity*, 1:181.

79. Roth, *Character Types*, 192.

80. Hays, 'Mint and Rue', 393; see the discussion of the rich man's clothing in Chapter 2, §6.1.2.

81. See the discussion of the rich man's feasting in Chapter 2, §6.1.2.

It is noteworthy that the rich man's activity is described with the same verb as in the rich fool's personal reflection in 12:19, ἀναπαύου, φάγε, πίε, εὐφραίνου.[82] The rich man's dissipation of wealth also parallels a motif in nearby Lukan parables, such as the son's 'squandering' in the parable of the Prodigal Son (15:13), and the steward's 'wastefulness' in the parable of the Dishonest Steward (16:1).[83] With this narrative preparation, Luke's audience understands that the rich man's selfish enjoyment of good things will not be without interruption or consequence.

While in the immediately previous parables the respective offences of the individuals are described negatively – with the verb ἁμαρτάνω in 15:21, and the adjective ἀδικία in 16:9 – in this parable such a 'judiciary description' is absent.[84] Instead, the rich man's actions have a markedly negative result in the afterlife. In vv. 22–23 the parable enacts reversals announced by Jesus, such as in the beatitudes and woes of 6:20–26. The woes are now memorably illustrated, for having received his consolation the rich man now thirsts and weeps in Hades,[85] while Lazarus receives the promised comfort (παρακαλεῖται) in the bosom of Abraham.[86] The expected Lukan pattern is maintained: the poor man is lifted up, and the rich man is brought low.[87] Through a comparison of Jesus's words of blessing and woe with the parable, the audience is persuaded to see the truth of his declarations about both poverty and wealth, and to respond appropriately.

4.3.4. *The Parable and the Alternatives*
Already within the parable, and also in Luke's Gospel as a whole, the audience recognizes worthy alternatives to the rich man's blame-worthy conduct. Habitually sitting outside the rich man's gate, Lazarus is described in v. 21 as longing to be filled (χορτασθῆναι) with food, even with discarded table scraps (ἀπὸ τῶν πιπτόντων ἀπὸ τῆς τραπέζης). This

82. Blomberg, 'Luke's Central Section', argues that Luke's Travel Narrative has a chiastic structure, in which are linked the parable of the Rich Fool and that of Lazarus and the Rich Man.

83. Ernst, *Lukas*, 472.

84. Kim, *Stewardship and Almsgiving*, 214.

85. Ibid., 190.

86. This image is suggestive of 'the warmest welcome and continuing care' (Tannehill, *Luke*, 252). Such a characterization is based on the description of Abraham's bosom in *T. Abr.* 20:14.

87. See York, *Reversal*, 70; he identifies the parable of Lazarus and the Rich Man as an example of this rhetoric of reversal, and a clear instance of 'bi-polar reversal' (62–71).

vivid image is indicative of the minimum level of assistance that the rich man might have given.[88] The use of the verb χορτασθῆναι is likely a Lukan allusion to what the poor and hungry are promised in the beatitude of 6:21, 'You shall be filled (χορτασθήσεσθε)'. The rich man, however, was not an agent for the relief of his needy neighbour as he ought to have been, and did not participate in this promise's fulfilment.

More than giving table scraps, Jesus calls rich persons to practise generous hospitality by inviting 'the poor, maimed, [and] lame' (πτωχούς, ἀναπείρους, χωλούς) to their feasts. This kindness will be rewarded at the resurrection of the just (14:12–14). However, the rich man did not participate in this activity either, despite the frequency with which he held banquets (καθ' ἡμέραν). Consequently, he may expect no eschatological reward (cf. 13:28–30).[89]

As a third worthy alternative to the rich man's neglect, the Lukan audience has heard repeated exhortations to give alms (11:41; 12:33). While the motif of almsgiving is not explicit in the parable, it is present by strong implication.[90] When the rich man asks Abraham in v. 24 to have mercy (ἐλέησον) by sending Lazarus to relieve his thirst, this is in striking contrast to his own failure to show mercy to Lazarus through giving alms (ἐλεημοσύνη).[91] The use of the cognate noun reveals the story's irony, for the unmerciful now requests mercy.[92]

Integral to the conversation between the rich man and Abraham is their filial relation, demonstrated in the rich man's repeated address to the patriarch as Πάτερ Ἀβραάμ (vv. 24, 27, 29) and Abraham's reference to him as τέκνον (v. 25). But because he did not share his clothing or food (as John the Baptist exhorted in Luke 3:11), the rich man is not entitled to the honorific of a 'child of Abraham'.[93] Within the Lukan narrative

---

88. Tannehill, *Narrative Unity*, 1:131.

89. Ibid., 1:186; on the connection of the parable to the Lukan motif of table fellowship, see Heil, *Meal Scenes*, 131–45; Neyrey, 'Ceremonies', 378–79. Smith, 'Table Fellowship', 625–26, contends that the theme of a luxurious banquet in 16:19–31 conveys both a negative and positive message: a critique of a dissolute earthly life, and an allusion to the blessings of heaven.

90. Dupont, 'Poor and Poverty', 30, notes the intriguing Vulgate addition to 16:21, 'et nemo illi dabat'. Cf. Matthews, 'Almsgiving and Repentance', 95, who suggests that Luke uses Abraham – the wealthy patriarch known as 'the great almsgiver of the Old Testament' (cf. Gen 14:20; 18:1–8) – as a foil to the rich man.

91. Tannehill, *Luke*, 253.

92. Johnson, *Luke*, 252.

93. Paffenroth, *Story*, 134; see the discussion in Chapter 2, §6.2.3.

the rich man is one of those who see 'Abraham, Isaac, and Jacob and all the prophets in the kingdom of God' (13:28), while they themselves are thrown out of the banquet (ἐκβαλλομένους ἔξω).[94]

That the rich man acknowledges his offence in not meeting the obligation of mercy is confirmed when he asks in v. 30 that a messenger be sent to his brothers so that 'they will repent' (μετανοήσουσιν). His acknowledgment of wrong is framed non-specifically, but he comprehends that there is a moral error to be redressed in his father's house. In answer Abraham insists on the sufficiency of the 'Moses and Prophets' for instilling a right view of the poor and their necessary support by the community.[95] The rich man's reluctance to accept the Scriptures' ability to persuade is indicative of his own lack of receptivity to 'Moses and the prophets'.

4.3.5. *The Parable and Two Contrasts*

The implication of the rich man's lack of mercy finds contextual confirmation in the parable of the Dishonest Steward in the 16:1–9.[96] While its meaning is contested, there is a general agreement that this parable concerns the advisability of using 'unrighteous mammon' for right purposes.[97] Besides reducing the amounts owed to his master, the steward may be presumed to have given alms to the poor.[98] Particularly when juxtaposed with someone who is commended for using worldly wealth to gain friends and to secure a welcome into eternal dwellings (16:9), the rich man is patently a negative example.[99] The Lukan motif of 'eschatological self-interest' – giving materially in the present to gain

94. On Abraham as an eschatological figure, see Kim, 'From Israel to the Nations'; cf. V. K. Robbins, *The Invention of Christian Discourse*, Rhetoric of Religious Antiquity 1 (Blandford Forum: Deo, 2009), 459, who identifies Abraham as an apocalyptic figure in Luke-Acts.

95. Hays, *Wealth Ethics*, 157; see the discussion of Deuteronomy and other Jewish texts on poverty and possessions in Chapter 4, §4.1.

96. Ernst, *Lukas*, 472, observes that 15:11–16:31 is a unit concerned with the theme of wealth.

97. See, e.g., the discussion in Fitzmyer, *Luke X–XXIV*, 1094–1104; Green, *Luke*, 588–94; Marshall, *Luke*, 614–22. For the relationship between the two parables of Luke 16, see Ball, 'Parables'; Feuillet, 'Mauvais Riche'; Story, 'Parables of Stewardship'; Piper, 'Social Background'; Hickling, 'Redaction'.

98. Karris, 'Poor and Rich', 122; cf. the discussion in Garrison, *Redemptive Almsgiving*, 64. Several scholars suggest that the prudent use of 'unrighteous mammon' in 16:9 is almsgiving: Fitzmyer, *Luke X–XXIV*, 1106–7; F. E. Williams, 'Is Almsgiving the Point of the "Unjust Steward?"', *JBL* 83 (1964): 293–97; Marshall, *Luke*, 621–22; W. Stegemann, *The Gospel and the Poor* (Philadelphia: Fortress, 1984), 62–63.

99. Bock, *Theology*, 356.

divine reward in the future – is to be inferred in our parable.[100] Though he had had the opportunity to do so, the rich man has not secured a place of post-mortem blessing by making Lazarus his friend, whether by giving alms or another way.[101]

Within Luke's Gospel a second figure who is likely contrasted deliberately with the rich man is the repentant tax collector Zacchaeus.[102] Earlier we observed his commitment to give half of his goods in support of the poor (19:8), which causes Jesus to pronounce emphatically in v. 9 that Zacchaeus is a son of Abraham (αὐτὸς υἱὸς Ἀβραάμ ἐστιν).[103] This is a narrative demonstration of John the Baptist's teaching that the reality of whether one aligns with Abraham is verified by the fruits of repentance (3:8–14).[104] Merciful and hospitable persons show themselves to be legitimate children of Abraham, who is the great host in God's kingdom (13:28). The exemplary conduct demonstrated by the repentant Zacchaeus is another narrative contrast to the rich man's failure.

4.3.6. *Conclusions*

The preceding section has demonstrated that Luke 16:19–31 is congruent with numerous aspects of the theme of poverty and possessions in Luke's Gospel, affirming and emphasizing this thematic concern. Consistent with the Gospel's message that its audience should demonstrate a 'complete commitment of their goods to the service of the Kingdom of God', the parable dramatically illustrates that the rich man should have acted differently with his wealth.[105] This alternative mode of conduct is elucidated in the remainder of the Third Gospel. But while the portrait of the rich man is consistent with Luke's characterization of the wealthy, and while the requisite response to Lazarus's poverty is evident from the Gospel's exhortations and exemplars of mercy, hospitality, and almsgiving, it is Luke's second volume that vividly illustrates a treatment of poor people that is consonant with Jesus's teaching. To Acts we now turn in our consideration.

---

100. Williams, 'Almsgiving', 294; he cites Luke 12:33 and 14:13–14 as instances of this motif.

101. Karris, 'Poor and Rich', 122; cf. Dupont, *Les Béatitudes*, 3:162–82.

102. Bock, *Theology*, 356; cf. the discussion in Chapter 4, §4.3.1, concerning whether Luke portrays Zacchaeus as needing to repent.

103. See also the crippled woman, whom Jesus calls a θυγατέρα Ἀβραάμ (Luke 13:16).

104. Méndez-Moratalla, *Paradigm of Conversion*, 219, observes that in the Lukan view, it is the attitude toward wealth that signals the presence of repentance or not (3:11–14; 5:28; 8:1–3; 15:12–14, 29–30; 19:2, 8).

105. Hays, *Wealth Ethics*, 261.

4.4. *Riches and Poverty in Acts*

4.4.1. *A Theme Transformed*

It is a well-rehearsed observation – though one requiring nuance – that the term 'poor' does not appear in Acts.[106] What might be called 'the silence of Acts' is rendered more striking by a consideration of the special place of the poor in its companion volume. Indeed, the terms πλούσιος and πτωχός are not found, and while ἐνδεής occurs in Acts 4:34, it is to emphasize the eradication of poverty among the believers. As mentioned, this disconnect between the Gospel and Acts must not be exaggerated.[107] This principal Lukan element is maintained in the second volume, yet transformed.[108] Luke now accentuates the community's actions in sharing material resources, giving alms, and providing relief to the needy. The Gospel's contrast between poor and rich is lacking in Acts because the impoverished and wealthy are now integrated and possessions have become a means of supplying the material needs of members.[109] We will now examine this altered portrait more closely.

4.4.2. *Negative Portrayal of the Rich*

As in Luke's Gospel, Acts includes occurrences of the misuse of wealth and examples of those who are wrongly fixated on material goods. The interest in this motif is evident already in Luke's version of the death of Judas Iscariot (Acts 1:18–20). In distinction from Matt 27:3–19, in which Judas simply returns the money to the chief priests, in Acts he buys a field with 'the wages of iniquity' (μισθοῦ τῆς ἀδικίας, 1:18), a possession that is ultimately left abandoned after he commits suicide. The corrupting potential of wealth is witnessed in the narrative of Simon the magician, who offers money to the apostles in exchange for the power to grant the Holy Spirit (8:9–24). Likewise, the owners of the slave girl who is freed from the spirit of divination seize Paul and Silas when they see they have lost their source of revenue (16:19). The riot in Ephesus is precipitated by anger over an anticipated loss of business for the silversmiths because of people being persuaded by Paul to abandon the gods (19:23–41). Finally, the Roman governor Felix's interaction with Paul (24:24–27)

106. See the observation in, e.g., Keck, 'Poor Among the Saints', 103.
107. See, e.g., J. A. Bergquist, 'Good News to the Poor: Why Does this Lucan Motif Appear to Run Dry in the Book of Acts?', *Bangalore Theological Forum* 18 (1986): 1–16.
108. For a summary of the presentation of rich and poor in Acts, see O'Toole, *Unity*, 129–35.
109. Kraybill and Sweetland, 'Possessions', 236.

demonstrates that some value money higher than the message about Jesus.[110] Felix wants to receive a bribe from Paul, even as he has opportunity to hear him speak about faith in Christ; ultimately, the governor loses interest. In these examples Luke represents the abuse of money and an attitude of greed in terms similar to those of his Gospel. As Gillman summarizes well: 'In both the Gospel and Acts resistance to the good news is marked by those who are "lovers of money"'.[111]

4.4.3. *Commendable Uses of Wealth*

Luke also represents believers responding generously to poverty and demonstrating models of proper financial conduct.[112] About this narrative trajectory from Luke's first volume to his second Tannehill observes, 'Jesus' preaching good news to the poor means that disciples must become involved in transforming greedy rich people into persons who will give their wealth to the poor'.[113] Several positive portraits of the rich can be highlighted, indicative of their potential to be receptive to the message about Jesus.[114] One example is the account of the Ethiopian eunuch, who is in charge of Candace's treasury (8:26–40). He wants to learn from the Scriptures about the Christ; being in a position of wealth and power has not blinded him to the message of Jesus.[115] Another Acts narrative implicitly commending a right attitude toward valuable possessions is when the believers at Ephesus burn scrolls on the magical arts. Luke notes that the scrolls were worth fifty thousand pieces of silver (19:19), but the illicit nature of these writings meant they could not be sold for re-use. This episode demonstrates the authenticity of the new believers' faith for they are willing to give up their highly valued possessions.[116]

---

110. O'Toole, *Unity*, 135.

111. Gillman, *Possessions*, 107.

112. For examples of wealthy people in Acts who are portrayed positively, see O'Toole, *Unity*, 133–34.

113. Tannehill, *Narrative Unity*, 1:132.

114. This evidence shows the overstatement of L. T. Johnson's comments in 'Narrative Perspectives', 211: 'Abraham's closing declaration [in Luke 16:31]... serves as a narrative anticipation of Luke's second volume, when the proclamation and demonstration of Jesus as the prophet whom God has raised will again gather the outcast but leave the wealthy and powerful unconvinced' (211). Instead, Luke demonstrates that the wealthy and powerful are among those persuaded by the preaching and teaching in Acts.

115. O'Toole, *Unity*, 133.

116. Gillman, *Possessions*, 106.

In the next four sections, we will review models of financial conduct and responses to poverty among the believers in Acts: a communion of goods, almsgiving and generosity, hospitality and famine relief.[117] Then we will investigate the ways in which this transformed theme corresponds with Luke 16:19–31, and with what effects.

4.4.3.1. *Communion of Goods.* An early and prominent example of the believers' handling of possessions is the communion of goods in 2:44–47 and 4:32–37.[118] Luke describes how everyone in the community had all things in common (εἶχον ἅπαντα κοινά, 2:44), for they sold their goods and divided the proceeds according to whoever had need (καθότι ἄν τις χρείαν εἶχεν, 2:45).[119] This is likely an intentional narrative reverberation of Jesus's injunction in Luke 18:22 to sell one's possessions and give to the poor.[120] As the believers continue to voluntarily sell their property and distribute the proceeds in Acts 4:34, Luke alludes to the words of Deut 15:4 (LXX), οὐδὲ γὰρ ἐνδεής τις ἦν ἐν αὐτοῖς.[121] The believers are portrayed as fulfilling the Mosaic law – and the teaching of Jesus – through their obedience to God's will concerning possessions.[122] A notable example of

117. D. P. Seccombe, 'Was There Organized Charity in Jerusalem before the Christians?', *JTS* N.S. 29 (1978): 140–43, contends that if there was already a system of charity in Jerusalem and Judea, there would have been little use for Christians to duplicate it, as Acts describes (141). But the evidence for such a system is lacking. Seccombe concludes that sharing and care for the poor would have been appropriate to the Christians from the beginning (143).

118. See the discussion of the communion of goods in F. J. Robertson Gregson, 'Everything in Common? The Theology and Practice of Sharing Possessions in Community in the New Testament with Particular Reference to Jesus and his Disciples, the Earliest Christians, and Paul' (PhD diss., Middlesex University, 2014), 53–71. Johnson, *Literary Function*, 183–210, focuses his study of possessions in Acts on 2:41–47 and 4:32–5:11.

119. Capper, 'Palestinian Context', traces the history of formal property-sharing in the Essene community, and its resemblance to Luke's account of the community of goods in Acts 2–4. He argues that this makes the account in Acts more historically plausible, for there is at least one other example of such a sharing of possessions at the same time in the same land.

120. Esler, *Community and Gospel*, 186; cf. Capper, 'Reciprocity', 502.

121. See the discussion in Chapter 4, §7.1.

122. As discussed in Chapter 4, §§4.2.4 and 7.1, some scholars hear Graeco-Roman echoes in Luke's depictions of the communion of goods. Particularly the broadly attested Greek proverb, 'Friends have goods in common' (κοινὰ τὰ τῶν φίλων), is considered as background to the practices in Acts 2–4. As noted, however, for Graeco-Roman writers this sharing of material goods takes place in the context of τῶν φίλων being a person's peers and social equals; see J. Dupont, 'La Communauté', in Dupont, *Études*, 518. This is in contrast with the manner of giving exhorted in Luke

this voluntary sale of personal assets is performed by Barnabas, who sells his field and presents the proceeds to the apostles (4:36–37). While this is the only specific instance Luke mentions, he notes that the result of such generous acts is that no one is impoverished.[123]

In relation to this communion of goods the cautionary story of Ananias and Sapphira in Acts 5:1–11 should be evaluated.[124] This husband and wife are dealt with severely by being struck dead because 'their action, if tolerated, would destroy the fellowship of the community'.[125] Despite the misconduct of some in the community, and though the communion of goods is not mentioned again subsequent to this episode, the theme of generosity and sharing of material goods continues in a variety of forms throughout the remainder of Acts.

4.4.3.2. *Almsgiving and Generosity.* A second motif pertaining to possessions is almsgiving and generosity. While there is no direct exhortation in Acts to give alms to the poor, there are repeated instances of ἐλεημοσύνη, and Luke portrays its practitioners positively.[126] For example, in 9:36 Dorcas is commended for her generosity, characterized as a woman who is 'full of good works and acts of charity' (πλήρης ἔργων ἀγαθῶν καὶ ἐλεημοσυνῶν).[127] Cornelius, a Roman centurion and God-fearer, is likewise known for his practice of giving alms (ποιῶν ἐλεημοσύνας πολλὰς τῷ λαῷ, 10:2).[128] Even as the audience recalls the Third Gospel's repeated

---

6:32–35 and 14:12–14, which is to be free of self-interest; see W. C. van Unnik, 'Die Motivierung der Feindesliebe in Lukas 6:32–35', *NovT* 8 (1966): 284–300, citing 293–300.

123. Some contend that Barnabas was exceptional in selling his field, and that Luke has generalized from this isolated instance; see, e.g., E. Haenchen, *The Acts of the Apostles* (Oxford: Blackwell, 1971), 233; H. Conzelmann, *Acts of the Apostles*, Hermeneia (Philadelphia: Fortress, 1987), 36. Capper, 'Palestinian Context', 341, counters this claim: 'Luke only had need, from a literary point of view, of one positive example to set against the negative example of Ananias and Sapphira. The presence of only one other example does not imply that Luke could not have named more.'

124. For a discussion of what was the actual offence of Ananias and Sapphira, see Walton, 'Primitive Communism', and Capper, 'Holy Community'.

125. O'Toole, *Unity*, 133.

126. Jervell, *People of God*, 140; as in the Gospel, in Acts almsgiving is 'a sign of true adherence to the law'.

127. Garrison, *Redemptive Almsgiving*, 67, suggests that 'Luke reports the story of Tabitha to indicate that she was raised from the dead *because* of her almsgiving' (emphasis original).

128. On the portrait of Cornelius, see C. W. Stenschke, *Luke's Portrait of Gentiles Prior to Their Coming to Faith*, WUNT 2/108 (Tübingen: Mohr Siebeck, 1999), 148–63.

censure of the wealthy and powerful, Cornelius's almsgiving demonstrates concretely that his position and possessions have not inhibited his care for the needy.[129] In both instances, the almsgiving of Dorcas and Cornelius are presented by Luke as acceptable models of conduct.

In addition to the recurring place of almsgiving, Luke's narrative illustrates how a spirit of generosity typifies the believers. For instance, he gives an account of the appointment of the seven men in Acts 6:1–6 who are entrusted with the daily distribution of food among the widows. Luke also includes the narrative of Peter and John healing the lame man who is begging for alms at the temple gate (Acts 3:1–10). It may be considered puzzling that Peter's response in v. 6 does not mention the money recently raised from the sale of the community's possessions (2:44–45), and that Peter insists he has no 'silver or gold' to give. Nevertheless, Luke likely does not intend that this encounter should dissuade the community from giving alms or providing material help for the poor. Peter responds to the man's request with much more than he expected to receive; he gives him the means to provide the necessities of life.[130] Healing the lame man is an act of lasting generosity.

This generosity likewise characterizes Paul's conduct. In his address to the Ephesian elders in Acts 20:33–35 he asserts that he is free from a desire for other people's wealth. Instead, he has worked with his own hands in order to provide for himself and for his companions.[131] He exhorts the elders in v. 35 to imitate his example by working hard, so that they too may 'support the weak' (ἀντιλαμβάνεσθαι τῶν ἀσθενούντων). Through pointing to his own example, Paul is a paradigm for believers seeking to live according to appropriate economic norms.[132] In v. 35 Paul explains that his actions are done in the spirit of a dominical saying, 'It is more blessed to give than to receive'.[133] Put into Paul's mouth, this

129. Gillman, *Possessions*, 102.

130. Ibid., 101.

131. On Paul's address to the Ephesian elders, see S. Walton, *Leadership and Lifestyle: The Portrait of Paul in the Miletus Speech and 1 Thessalonians*, SNTSMS 108 (Cambridge: Cambridge University Press, 2000); cf. his 'Paul, Patronage, and Pay: What Do We Know About the Apostle's Financial Support?', in *Paul as Missionary: Identity, Activity, Theology, and Practice*, ed. T. J. Burke and B. S. Rosner, LNTS 420 (London: T&T Clark, 2011), 221–33, citing 221: 'Paul's general missionary policy was that he maintained financial independence. He states in a number of places that he worked to support himself while proclaiming the gospel (notably 1 Thess 2:9; 1 Cor 4:12; 2 Cor 11:27; 12:14; cf. Acts 20:34).'

132. Phillips, 'Wealth and Poverty', 240.

133. Acts 20:35 is an example of an *agraphon*, a saying attributed to Jesus though it is not found in any Gospel manuscript. It also attested as a dominical saying in

dictum articulates a fundamental truth for the perspective on possessions in Luke's two-volume work.[134] As Pilgrim expresses well, the last saying of Jesus in Luke-Acts is 'a most fitting conclusion to Luke's presentation on the theme of wealth and poverty and the proclamation of the good news to the poor'.[135]

4.4.3.3. *Hospitality.* Our survey of Luke's Gospel noted several exhortations to and exemplars of hospitality. This motif is continued in Acts, particularly in connection with those individuals who are occupied with spreading the message of Jesus. Luke portrays the hospitality extended the 'emissaries of God' as indicative of a meaningful faith.[136] For instance, Simon the tanner gives Peter a place to stay in Joppa (9:43; 10:6), while Peter in turn welcomes Cornelius' messenger and then is hosted at Cornelius' home (10:48). Aquila and Priscilla offer lodging to Paul while he is ministering in Corinth (18:1–3). In Caesarea, Philip opens his house to Paul and his companions for an extended period of time (21:8–10). A remarkable demonstration of hospitality is recorded in 28:1–2 when the inhabitants of Malta give shelter to Paul and his fellow ship-wrecked travelers, showing what Luke terms an 'unusual kindness' (τυχοῦσαν φιλανθρωπίαν). Numerous instances demonstrate that the early believers view hospitality as a commendable use of personal resources.[137]

4.4.3.4. *Famine Relief.* A final illustration of the appropriate use of possessions is when the Antioch believers contribute financial help for the believers in Judea (11:28–30).[138] The prophet Agabus foretells that during the days of Emperor Claudius there will be a severe famine. This situation necessitates material relief for the Jerusalem church, which evidently was poorly positioned to endure a period of scarcity. In v. 29 Luke reports that the disciples in Antioch each gave as they were able (καθὼς εὐπορεῖτό τις ὥρισαν) for the relief (διακονίαν) of the Jerusalem church. Gregson aptly observes the significance of this church-level relief: 'It is an example

Apos. Con. 4.2; *Didasc.* 4.3; cf. Did. 1.5. In various permutations it is a maxim in Graeco-Roman literature. For discussion, see F. F. Bruce, *Jesus and Christian Origins Outside the New Testament* (Grand Rapids: Eerdmans, 1974), 82; cf. Robert E. Van Voorst, *Jesus Outside the New Testament: An Introduction to the Ancient Evidence* (Grand Rapids: Eerdmans, 2000), 180.

134. Gillman, *Possessions*, 111.

135. Pilgrim, *Good News*, 159.

136. Johnson, *Sharing Possessions*, 19.

137. Other examples of hospitality are, e.g., Lydia (16:15), the jailer of Philippi (16:34), Jason (17:6–7), Publius (28:7), and Paul (28:30).

138. On the historicity and significance of the famine relief in Acts 11, see the discussion in Gregson, 'Everything in Common?', 89–107.

where individuals contribute according to their ability, but it is also an example which shows corporate responsibility for the sharing'.[139] This giving is a demonstration of the believers' unity despite diverse locales and various ethnic compositions, and within Luke's two-volume narrative it is another application of Jesus's teachings on mercy and generosity.

4.5. *The Parable and Possessions in Relation to Acts*

4.5.1. *A Continuing Story*

Having surveyed the use of possessions in response to situations of need in Acts, we will now examine Luke 16:19–31 in relation to these accounts. The perspective on this motif is consistent throughout Luke-Acts, though not static. While Luke shifts away from the use of πλούσιος and πτωχός in Acts, the apparent disconnect with his Gospel is not without purpose. In Acts we discover a portrait of a community creatively engaged in employing material resources for the support of the poor, as Jesus's words are put into practice through activities of charity and generosity. In this altered manner Luke maintains his first volume's concentration on works of practical mercy. While the Gospels of Matthew and Mark also include instances of Jesus's teaching on possessions and poverty,[140] neither of these Gospels is conjoined with a second volume that affords the author an opportunity to demonstrate how this teaching is actualized. It is uniquely Luke who provides a narrative about the period after Jesus's ascension. In this connection, Alexander's comment is apropos: 'Luke conceived his work from the outset as a two-volume set in which the Gospel story would be balanced and continued with stories of the apostles'.[141] This continuing story is also heard when Luke 16:19–31 is read within its Luke-Acts context.

4.5.2. *The Parable and the Teaching of Jesus*

One aspect inviting our reflection is the manner in which an awareness of the early church's charity might have influenced the parable's audience. At the beginning of Acts Luke says that he intends to demonstrate the continuation of Jesus's actions and teachings (1:1). As a notable instance of close correlation between the two volumes, Acts provides an account of the application of Jesus's teaching on mercy and generosity. To be sure, the disappearance of parables as pedagogical vehicles in Acts has been

139. Gregson, 'Everything in Common?', 107.
140. See, e.g., Mark 6:7–13; 8:36; 10:17–22, 23–27; 12:38–40, 41–44; Matt 6:1–4, 19–21; 19:16–22.
141. Alexander, 'Back to Front', 438.

noted as an example of narrative incoherence in style between the two volumes.[142] Rather than indicating a literary disjunction, however, Jesus's parabolic encouragement of beneficence may be seen as fundamental to the charity enacted by the community in Acts.[143] Jesus's instructions are foundational for the believers, first witnessed in their selling of possessions in order to support the needy. Secondly, thematic continuity exists in the practice of almsgiving in both the Third Gospel and Acts; the earlier exhortations foreshadow later practices among the community of believers. Consequently, the reversal motif prevalent in Luke's Gospel is replaced by an application of the principles of generosity: 'There are no longer πλούσιοι and πτωχοί in the community, for now all share equally and everyone's needs are met'.[144] Through his narrative selections Luke shows that liberality, almsgiving, and mutual care are essential to a community devoted to Jesus.[145] Indeed, Hays observes that Luke 'continues the ethical paraenesis of his Gospel through his depiction of the practice of the community'.[146] This attention to beneficent activities stimulates the audience to an emulation of these activities and to a creative expression of their own commitment to the support of the needy.[147]

4.5.3. *The Parable and a Warning Contrast*

When we read Acts through the lens of the parable, the benevolent activity of the early community also stands in contrast to the rich man's neglect. First, he failed to relieve the suffering of hungry Lazarus with even his table scraps, but the church of Antioch responds to Jerusalem's anticipated need for food during famine with their generous contributions. Secondly, he failed to invite someone poor and lame to his daily feasts, but believers throughout Acts demonstrate hospitality to strangers, Jews, Gentiles, and other unlikely guests. Thirdly, the rich man failed to show mercy to the beggar at his gate through giving alms, but individuals such as Dorcas and Cornelius are commended and even rewarded as righteous for this act of kindness – a suggestive example for Luke's audience.

At the same time, Acts echoes the element of caution present in Luke 16:19–31.[148] Luke underlines the parable's warning by providing several

---

142. Parsons and Pervo, *Rethinking*, 50–51.
143. Spencer, 'Hermeneutical Hinge', 351–52.
144. York, *Reversal*, 172.
145. Karris, 'Poor and Rich', 117.
146. Hays, *Wealth Ethics*, 211.
147. Marguerat, 'Task of Reading', 45, notes how the warnings to the rich found repeatedly in Luke have been 'replaced by an ethic of sharing'.
148. Tannehill, *Luke*, 254.

examples of those who wrongly handle wealth or overvalue possessions, such as Judas Iscariot (Acts 1:18–20), Ananias and Sapphira (5:1–10), Simon the magician (8:9–24), the slave girl's owners (16:19), the Ephesian rioters (19:23–41), and the governor Felix (24:24–27). Additionally, for both Judas Iscariot and Ananias and Sapphira, Luke demonstrates their greed's grave consequences – a consequence that is similarly witnessed in the rich man's tormented afterlife. However, equally if not more prominent in Acts are those previously noted individuals and groups who treat possessions rightly, such as the apostle Paul (20:33–35) and the church of Antioch (11:28–30). Throughout his two-volume work Luke provides paradigms both of people who treat wealth wrongly and those who do so rightly in order to inculcate an imitation of the latter among his audience.[149]

4.5.4. *Conclusions*

Luke's portrait of the believers in Acts reveals his perspective that Jesus's words have the ability to form a community that cares for the poor to such an extent that poverty is eradicated among them.[150] Their attitude toward and handling of possessions is an ideal that is probably intended to stimulate the Lukan community.[151] Though economic or social conditions may change, the sharing of possessions remains a fundamental aspect of Luke's vision for his audience. Attention has been devoted to reconstructing this Lukan community, but it is impossible to be certain about its composition.[152] Nevertheless, it can be maintained that it likely comprised members on a spectrum from those loosely termed 'poor' to those termed 'rich'. As such, Luke 16:19–31 and the account of the early community would have resonance with broad segments of his audience. Having been warned by the parable, the Acts portrait of the believers' beneficent activities would enjoin the audience to emulate these activities as an expression of their own commitment to the needy. At the same time, the Acts portrayal would encourage those who were presently disadvantaged with the prospect of approaching aid.

149. Nickelsburg, 'Revisiting Poor and Rich', 567.

150. Tannehill, *Narrative Unity*, 1:132; cf. Marshall, *Luke*, 207, who notes how the 'renunciation' of wealth commanded in Luke is worked out in particular but not 'universally applicable' ways in Acts.

151. Dupont, 'Poor and Poverty', 31.

152. See, e.g., Esler, *Community and Gospel*, 24–33; Bauckham, ed., *All Christians*; Klink, ed., *Audience of the Gospels*.

5. *Authoritative Revelation in Luke-Acts and the Parable*

5.1. *A Scriptural Framework*

The parable's second principal theme is the source and efficacy of authoritative revelation. In contrast with the theme of possessions and poverty, this trope is not as explicitly present in the Third Gospel, for Jesus does not elaborate repeatedly on it. However, Luke presents revelation as having not an insignificant role and function, but one that is structural for Jesus's ministry and his followers. It is the Jewish Scriptures that provide a framework for understanding the events of Jesus's life, and that give shape to the belief and behavior of the community.

As discussed previously, the theme of authoritative revelation is prominent in the latter part of Luke 16:19–31, apparent in the repetition of the collocation Μωϋσέως καὶ τῶν προφητῶν (vv. 29, 31).[153] In response to the rich man's request to send Lazarus to warn his brothers, Abraham asserts that those who do not listen to 'Moses and the prophets' will neither be persuaded by one who is resurrected. While Abraham's words have a pessimistic tone, as a narrative conclusion they invite the audience to deliberate on the potential response of the rich man's five brothers: Will they listen to Scripture? Within Luke's broader narrative in which Jesus is resurrected and his message is disseminated, this first question is inseparable from another: Will people be convinced by someone who rises from the dead? Recalling our key interpretive assumption that the parable's audience listens with the hindsight afforded by a knowledge of later events, in this section we will investigate how this portrayal of authoritative revelation – and particularly revelation about someone risen from the dead – is transformed in subsequent episodes of the Lukan narrative.

In order to appreciate how the theme of authoritative revelation is both sustained and altered from its function in the Third Gospel and 16:19–31 to its role in Acts, we will survey this theme in both volumes. Then we will investigate the extent to which this reprised Lukan theme corresponds to the parable, and with what effects.

5.2. *Authoritative Revelation in Luke's Gospel*

5.2.1. *'Moses, the Prophets, and the Psalms'*
For Luke, the Jewish Scriptures are the *sine qua non* of authoritative revelation. These Scriptures are referenced on a regular basis throughout

---

153. See identification of themes in Chapter 4, §2.

Luke-Acts,[154] where citations and allusions to these writings are made both in general terms[155] and in connection with specific passages.[156] Luke describes the Jewish Scriptures in a variety of ways. As in our parable, they are spoken of most frequently as Μωϋσέως καὶ τῶν προφητῶν (16:16, 29, 31; 24:27).[157] In one instance Jesus refers to the content of the Scriptures as 'the Law, Prophets, and Psalms', τῷ νόμῳ Μωϋσέως καὶ προφήταις καὶ ψαλμοῖς (24:44). Other references mention the prophets alone, such as Jesus's description of 'all those things written through the prophets', πάντα τὰ γεγραμμένα διὰ τῶν προφητῶν (18:31).[158] The law is also referred to in isolation from other components of the Jewish Scriptures, when it is called the 'law of Moses' (τὸν νόμον Μωϋσέως) in 2:22,[159] the 'law of the Lord' (νόμῳ κυρίου) in 2:23, 24, 39,[160] and when Jesus uses 'Moses' as a shorthand designation for the law (5:14; 16:29; 31; 24:27).[161] In a few places ἐντολή, 'commandment', is employed as a summarizing reference to the law (1:6; 18:20; 23:56). We will consider these references to authoritative revelation in the Gospel, and observe that they have a range of connotations, both ethical and prophetic.

5.2.2. *Ethical Function of the Scriptures*

In the Third Gospel many of the references to Μωϋσέως, νόμος, and ἐντολή take place in contexts that are descriptive of individual ethical conduct, either actual or recommended.[162] For instance, Zacharias and Elizabeth in 1:6 are described as 'walking in all the commandments' (πορευόμενοι ἐν πάσαις ταῖς ἐντολαῖς). In 10:28 Jesus exhorts the legal expert 'to do this [i.e. the law] and live' (τοῦτο ποίει καὶ ζήσῃ). Later, he affirms the law's validity in conversation with the rich ruler, and acknowledges in 18:20, 'You know the commandments' (τὰς ἐντολὰς οἶδας). In addition to

---

154. See summary in O'Toole, *Unity*, 24–26; on Luke's use of Scripture, see studies of Evans and Sanders, *Luke and Scripture*; Barrett, 'Luke/Acts'; Fitzmyer, 'Use of Old Testament'; Ringgren, 'Luke's Use'; Hays, *Gospels*, 191–280.

155. See, e.g., Luke 16:16, 29, 31; 21:22; 24:27, 44.

156. See, e.g., the notations of fulfilment in Luke 4:21; 22:37.

157. See the slight variations of the collocation in Acts 13:15; 24:14; 26:22; 28:23.

158. Cf. Acts 26:27.

159. Cf. Acts 13:39; 15:5; 28:23.

160. Cf. the term 'law of the fathers' in Acts 22:3.

161. Cf. Acts 6:11; 15:1, 21; 21:21.

162. There is contention over Luke perspective on the law: Jervell, *People of God*, 133–51, describes Luke's view as 'fundamentally Mosaic', a view critiqued by Wilson, *Luke and the Law*, 103–17.

maintaining the Decalogue, Jesus affirms Mosaic purity legislation; even while he condemns the Pharisees for their punctilious tithing in 11:42, he upholds the need to perform all the commands of the law. Similarly, he instructs the healed leper in 5:14 to make an offering for purification, 'as prescribed by Moses' (καθὼς προσέταξεν Μωϋσῆς).[163]

Notably, what is perhaps the most explicit teaching in the Third Gospel about authoritative revelation occurs in 16:16–18, immediately before our parable. In v. 16 Jesus says, Ὁ νόμος καὶ οἱ προφῆται μέχρι Ἰωάννου· ἀπὸ τότε ἡ βασιλεία τοῦ θεοῦ εὐαγγελίζεται καὶ πᾶς εἰς αὐτὴν βιάζεται. While the precise meaning of this text is disputed, it is clear that the adjoining ministries of John and Jesus signal a significant change in the delivery of authoritative revelation.[164] The law and the prophets were formerly at the heart of God's revelation, but now the gospel of the kingdom is being preached by Jesus.[165] Together with Jesus's words in 7:28 – 'There is not a greater prophet than John the Baptist, but the least in the kingdom of God is greater than he' – 16:16 demonstrates that John the Baptist is regarded as the terminus of the old era of the law and prophets. Jesus belongs to a new age which is in continuity with the old, yet has superseded it.[166] As will be seen, the law and prophets are fulfilled in Jesus (24:27, 44). But even while v. 16 announces a transition from that former period, v. 17 insists that the law has not been abrogated. It is not the validity of the law and prophets that has ended, but the era which produced them.[167]

In this connection, scholars puzzle over the function of v. 18 in the midst of this discourse with the Pharisees. The interdiction against marrying a divorced woman is probably intended to show that Jesus was as rigorous as the Pharisees in maintaining the teaching of 'Moses and the prophets'.[168] For Jesus and his disciples, Scripture's ethical direction retains its authority. Thus in 16:29 Abraham can give this recommendation about living in such a way as to join him after death: listen to 'Moses and

163. Cf. Jesus's instruction to the ten healed of leprosy in 17:14.

164. See, e.g., discussion in Marshall, *Luke*, 626–32; Fitzmyer, *Luke X–XXIV*, 1114–24; Green, *Luke*, 602–4. Conzelmann, *Theology*, 87–127, used 16:16 as his starting point for a division of Lukan salvation history into three distinct periods: the law and prophets until John, the Satan-free ministry of Jesus on earth, and the time of the Spirit-led church.

165. D. Bock, 'Scripture and the Realisation of God's Promises', in *Witness to the Gospel: The Theology of Acts*, ed. I. H. Marshall and D. Peterson (Grand Rapids: Eerdmans, 1998), 41–62, citing 45.

166. Blomberg, 'Law in Luke-Acts', 60.

167. Marshall, *Luke*, 628.

168. Hickling, 'Redaction', 262.

the prophets'.[169] The patriarch insists that the Scriptures are sufficient for instilling a right view of the poor and their necessary support. In addition to this primary ethical import, within the Lukan context this reference to the Scriptures has a second dimension of meaning: speaking of the Messiah. In Luke's view, 'One could never claim fidelity to the Law apart from recognizing the figure to which the Law points'.[170] This brings us to consider the prophetic function of the Scriptures in Luke's Gospel.

5.2.3. *Prophecy and Fulfilment*

From his Gospel's opening words Luke highlights fulfilled prophecy. In 1:1 he characterizes his narrative as an account of 'the things which have been accomplished – or 'brought to fulfilment' – among us' (τῶν πεπληροφορημένων ἐν ἡμῖν πραγμάτων). He then accentuates how the divine plan and the Scriptures are fulfilled in the events associated with Jesus's life and ministry.[171] For instance, the law and the prophets foreshadow the ministry of John the Baptist (1:70; 3:4–6), and Jesus later explains his own ministry in terms of Isaianic prophecy (4:18–21). Through consistent literary framing, narrated events in the Third Gospel are grounded in God's purpose as demonstrated in Israel's Scriptures and history.[172] Consistent with this framing, Jesus in ch. 9 is seen conversing on the mountain with Moses and Elijah. This association at a critical juncture of Jesus's ministry is suggestive that his delivering work is to be understood as rooted in Israel's Scripture, both the law and the prophets.[173]

Subsequent to 16:19–31 variations of the term 'Moses and the prophets' continue to occur, often at key narrative moments. The first reference to Jesus's suffering, death, and resurrection as events that fulfill Scripture is in 18:31–33, where Jesus tells his disciples that 'all those things written by the prophets about the Son of Man shall be fulfilled' (τελεσθήσεται πάντα τὰ γεγραμμένα διὰ τῶν προφητῶν τῷ υἱῷ τοῦ ἀνθρώπου, v. 31). He does not offer an explicit scriptural citation to warrant his claim, but makes a general reference. As we will see, there is in the latter portions

169. Brawley, 'Abrahamic Covenant', 122.

170. Hays, *Wealth Ethics*, 158.

171. See, e.g., the quotations from the Scriptures in Luke 2:24; 3:4–6; 4:4, 8, 10–11, 12; 4:17–21. For a discussion of the promise–fulfilment schema in Luke-Acts, and a proposal to understand Luke's use of Scripture as a 'framing in discourse' to show a basic continuity between God's people in the past and the characters and events in Luke's narrative, see Litwak, *Echoes of Scripture*.

172. Green, *Theology*, 30.

173. R. W. L. Moberly, *The Bible, Theology and Faith: A Study of Abraham and Jesus* (Cambridge: Cambridge University Press, 2000), 52.

of the Third Gospel a pattern of generalized allusion to the Scriptures in connection with Jesus's suffering, death, and resurrection. At the Passover in 22:14–37, Jesus predicts his imminent distress and indicates that the Scriptures have prophesied the same. In this instance he refers to the fulfilling of Isaianic prophecy (53:12) in his being 'numbered with the transgressors'.[174]

The testimony of Scripture to Jesus's resurrection that is mentioned in 18:33 is then demonstrated particularly in the Gospel's final and climactic chapter, which is centred on the appearances of the risen Jesus to his disciples.[175] The phrase 'Moses and the prophets' occurs in 24:27 when the risen Jesus is speaking with the two disciples on the way to Emmaus.[176] As Jesus explains 'what was written in all the Scriptures about himself', he does so 'beginning from Moses and all the prophets' (ἀρξάμενος ἀπὸ Μωϋσέως καὶ ἀπὸ πάντων τῶν προφητῶν). After scolding them for their unbelief, Jesus takes on the role of an authoritative exegete.[177] He demonstrates how the law and prophets reach their apex in him in dying and 'entering his glory' (v. 26).[178] As in Luke's narrative previously, in ch. 24 the Scriptures have a prophetic function in pointing to Jesus; Luke does not elucidate the contents of this exposition, but the reference is again generalized. For a more specific account of the testimony of 'Moses and the prophets' to the crucified and risen Jesus, the reader must await Luke's second volume.[179]

Another variation of Μωϋσέως καὶ τῶν προφητῶν occurs in 24:44. The risen Jesus reminds his disciples of what he previously said about Scripture's testimony to himself, and also about the divine necessity of the Scripture being fulfilled: 'All things written about me in the law of

174. Kurz, 'Promise and Fulfillment', 147–48.

175. See P. Schubert, 'The Structure and Significance of Luke 24', in *Neutestamentliche Studien für Rudolf Bultmann zu seinem siebzigsten Geburtstag*, ed. W. Eltester, 2nd ed., BZNW 21 (Berlin: de Gruyter, 1957), 165–86, citing 176–77.

176. See Hays, *Reading Backwards*, 55–74, on the Lukan Christology that is reflected in 24:13–35, and evident throughout the Third Gospel.

177. For ch. 24 as a component of the Lukan portrait of Jesus as a literate teacher outside of the authoritative scribal elite class, see C. Keith, *Jesus Against the Scribal Elite: The Origins of the Conflict* (Grand Rapids: Baker Academic, 2014), 63.

178. See R. B. Hays, 'Reading Scripture in Light of the Resurrection', in *The Art of Reading Scripture*, ed. E. F. Davis and R. B. Hays (Grand Rapids: Eerdmans, 2003), 216–38.

179. Hays, *Gospels*, 272; or as he suggests in *Reading Backwards*, 56, the 'sketchy summary' of Luke 24 sends the reader 'back to the beginning of the Gospel to *reread* it, in hopes of discerning more clearly how the identity and mission of Jesus might be prefigured in Israel's Scripture' (emphasis original).

Moses and the prophets and the psalms must be fulfilled' (δεῖ πληρωθῆναι πάντα τὰ γεγραμμένα ἐν τῷ νόμῳ Μωϋσέως καὶ τοῖς προφήταις καὶ ψαλμοῖς περὶ ἐμοῦ). Here the reference to Moses is augmented with 'the law', and after citing 'the prophets', Jesus adds a reference to 'the psalms'.[180] This comprehensive denotation of the Jewish Scriptures reiterates Luke's emphatic statement in 24:27 about 'all the Scriptures' (πάσαις ταῖς γραφαῖς) reaching fulfilment in Jesus. In particular, Jesus in 24:46 draws his disciples' attention to what is written (γέγραπται), namely, that the Christ will suffer and rise from the dead (παθεῖν τὸν χριστὸν καὶ ἀναστῆναι ἐκ νεκρῶν). This reference, together with 24:26, accentuates the necessity of reading Scripture in light of Jesus's resurrection, for his resurrection is presented as the climactic event of the biblical story.[181]

It is remarkable that Luke 24 offers no polemic for the reality of Jesus's resurrection apart from the Scriptures' testimony about its necessity. Jesus adopts this approach in interacting with the Sadducees (20:37), as Paul does later in conversing with Herod Agrippa (Acts 26:8, 27). Anderson states about this Lukan perspective, 'Belief in the Scriptures is funda-mental, because those who refuse to listen to Moses and the prophets would not be convinced even if someone were raised from the dead... Both the general resurrection and Jesus's resurrection are to be believed, first and foremost, on the basis of the words of Scripture.'[182] As the thematic development of the 'Moses and the prophets' motif continues in Acts, we will observe its prominence in the believers' repeated use of the Scriptures to validate the claim that the risen Jesus is the Christ.[183]

5.3. *The Parable and Revelation in Relation to Luke's Gospel*

5.3.1. *'Things Fulfilled'*
We have argued that the parable's two references to 'Moses and the prophets' should not be viewed in isolation from their literary context in the Third Gospel, but must be seen on a narrative trajectory in Luke's account of 'the things fulfilled among us' (Luke 1:1), particularly as he develops the theme of authoritative revelation. The parable has

180. This is the only New Testament occurrence of the Psalms being named together with the law of Moses and the prophets. It is debated whether the ψαλμοί are referenced here because of their prominent place in the Lukan interpretation of Jesus's suffering (Green, *Luke*, 856), or mentioned as representative of all the 'Writings' of the Old Testament canon (Marshall, *Luke*, 905).

181. Hays, 'Reading Scripture', 216–20.

182. Anderson, *God Raised*, 282.

183. For references to the prophets and Moses (or the Scriptures) in relation to preaching the message about Jesus, see Acts 13:27; 19:28; 26:22–23; 28:23.

pronounced points of correspondence with Luke's Gospel as a whole, and particularly with the resurrection accounts in ch. 24. We will now investigate the parable's relation to the Gospel, focusing on the theme of revelation in relation to prophecy and resurrection.

5.3.2. *The Parable and Prophecy in the Gospel*

When Lazarus is requested to warn the rich man's brothers, Abraham twice recommends that they listen to 'Moses and the prophets'. In Chapter 4 we concluded that this response can first be understood with reference to the Jewish Scriptures' repeated imperatives to care for the needy.[184] We also observed that in the Graeco-Roman tradition it is not uncommon for someone deceased to return with a report intended to influence the outlook and behaviour of the living.[185] However, Abraham affirms that the Scriptures provide sufficient ethical direction, thereby eliminating the need to seek messengers from the dead. Besides reminding the Lukan audience of the scriptural mandate to respond mercifully to the destitute, 'Moses and the prophets' in vv. 29 and 31 have an anticipatory purpose in relation to Jesus. If the parable is read in isolation, this important implication might go unnoticed, but when re-read within the context of Luke's Gospel it becomes apparent. Particularly after Jesus opens Scripture to the Emmaus disciples in the Gospel's final chapter, a re-reading of Abraham's words in the parable have an increased rhetorical impact.

As we have seen, Luke 24 attributes the origin of a christological interpretation of the Jewish Scriptures to Jesus.[186] Together with Jesus's earlier assertion of the continuity between the era of the law and the prophets and himself (16:16), the Luke 24 narrative encourages the audience to reconsider all of Scripture in light of the Lukan story about him.[187] In the two instances where the risen Jesus explains the Scriptures in relation to his ministry (24:27, 44–47), he does not cite a specific passage to establish the necessity of his suffering, death, and resurrection.[188] Our survey of Acts will demonstrate, however, that 'Moses and the prophets' are emphatically prophetic of Christ in numerous and

---

184. See the discussion in Chapter 4, §§4.1.1–6.

185. See the discussion in Chapter 4, §5.2.1.

186. See also R. B. Hays, 'The Liberation of Israel in Luke-Acts: Intertextual Narration as Countercultural Practice', in Hays, Alkier and Huizenga, eds., *Reading the Bible*, 101–17, citing 111.

187. Hays, 'Liberation', 111; cf. R. Bauckham, 'The Restoration of Israel in Luke-Acts', in *Restoration: Old Testament, Jewish and Christian Perspectives*, ed. J. M. Scott, JSJSup 72 (Leiden: Brill, 2001), 435–87, citing 467.

188. Tiede, *Prophecy and History*, 100; see also Acts 3:18; 17:2–3; 26:22.

specific instances.[189] We may therefore conclude that, mindful of the two-volume arc of his narrative, Luke has framed Luke 16:19–31 to imply that the rich man's relatives can be saved from afterlife torments if they will listen to 'Moses and the prophets'. The brothers must not only heed the Scripture's repeated directives to care for the poor, but should be persuaded by the Scripture's testimony to Jesus. This implication of Abraham's closing words is demonstrated when we consider the parable in relation to Jesus's resurrection in the Third Gospel.

5.3.3. *The Parable and Resurrection in the Gospel*

We have seen that the Third Gospel accentuates what is written in the Scriptures not only in connection with Jesus's suffering and death, but also his resurrection (18:31–33; 24:25–27, 45–47). In addition to being foreshadowed by Jesus's own predictions (9:22; 11:29–32; 18:33), the resurrection is narrated in the stories of the empty tomb (24:1–12), and the stories of appearances of the risen Jesus (24:13–32, 34, 35; 24:36–49).[190] Furthermore, the resurrection of Jesus is a central motif in Luke-Acts, portrayed as a key component of God's salvific purpose and the impetus to the preaching of the apostles.[191]

Although the parable is placed in the narrative ~~ahead of~~ *before* Jesus's resurrection, Abraham speaks in v. 31 about 'one risen from the dead', τις ἐκ νεκρῶν ἀναστῇ. While the centrality of resurrection in Luke-Acts may not be in dispute, there is debate whether the parable's reference to one 'rising' from the dead is intended to anticipate the resurrection of Jesus in the closing chapters of the Third Gospel and Acts. That the parable is found textually and chronologically well before Luke's account of the death and resurrection of Jesus in chs. 22–24 leads some to dismiss the notion of any reference to Jesus in 16:31. As noted previously, the parable's resurrection-themed ending is considered a clear mark of a later Christian addition to Jesus's original parable.[192] Questions of the parable's

---

189. See survey below in §§5.4.2–3.

190. Talbert, *Reading Luke-Acts*, 121–22.

191. See Luke 9:22; Acts 2:24, 32; 3:15; 4:10; 5:30; 10:40; 13:32–33; 17:31; cf. Marshall, 'Resurrection', 55–98.

192. See, e.g., J. D. Crossan, 'Parable and Example in the Teaching of Jesus', *NTS* 18 (1972), 285–307, citing 298; cf. his *Parables*, 67. As textual connections which he deems altogether too coincidental to be originally authentic, Crossan cites the theme of disbelief in 16:31 and 24:11, 25 and 41; the double mention of Moses and prophets in 16:29, 31 and in 24:27, 44; the reference to one resurrected from the dead in 16:31 and 24:46; and the reference to being convinced or repenting in 16:30 and kerygmatic contexts throughout Acts (2:38; 3:19; 8:22; 17:30; 26:20).

provenance or its pre-Lukan version are not germane to our study.[193] More
to the point, a reference to Jesus's resurrection in v. 31 can be considered
coherent with the parable's Lukan context. In the first place, the verb
that is used (ἀνίστημι) is one of Luke's customary ways to describe the
resurrection of Jesus,[194] and may be judged a distinctively Lukan term.[195]
Secondly, in Luke's Gospel it is only here (v. 31) and in the resurrected
Jesus's discourse about himself with the Emmaus disciples (24:46) that
the verb ἀνίστημι is joined with the phrase ἐκ νεκρῶν.[196] Cognizant of
Luke's literary artistry in crafting an orderly narrative, this similarity of
usage is likely deliberate.[197] Thirdly, the reference to Lazarus's resurrection or return is combined with a repeated reference to 'Moses and
the prophets', already noted as a favourite Lukan term in the resurrection
narratives of Luke 24. Fourthly, as noted, Jesus repeatedly foretold his
death and resurrection in the Gospel of Luke; it is therefore probable that
on reflection the parable's audience would hear a secondary reference
to Jesus's resurrection in 16:31.[198] Based on these considerations, we
conclude that it is appropriate to see a close thematic correspondence
between the parable's conclusion and the later Lukan accounts of Jesus's
resurrection. As observed previously, in Luke's Gospel the right interpretation of Scripture is inseparable from the acceptance of one risen from

193. See the discussion in Chapter 1, §4.1.

194. A textual variant in v. 31 is the Freer manuscript's use of ἀπελθή ('go')
instead of ἀναστῇ. Tanghe, 'Abraham, son fils', 560–63, considers this reading more
original, as it is verbally parallel to the πορευθῇ of v. 30 and is not typical Christian
resurrection language (cf. Bauckham, 'Rich Man and Lazarus', 115). The manuscript
evidence for ἀπελθή is weak, however, and this variant unlikely.

195. See 18:33; 24:7, 46; Acts 2:24, 32; 3:26; 10:41; 13:33, 34; 17:3, 31; the
cognate noun ἀνάστσις does not occur in the Gospel, but is found repeatedly in Acts
(1:22; 2:31; 4:33; 26:23). On the term as characteristic of Luke, see A. Denaux and
R. Corstjens, *The Vocabulary of Luke*, BTS 10 (Leuven: Peeters, 2009), 137–38.
By contrast, the other evangelists use the verb less frequently to refer to Jesus's
resurrection: there are no instances in Matthew, five in Mark, and two in John.
Anderson, *God Raised*, 32–33, includes the use of ἀνίστημι in 16:31 as a reference
to Jesus's resurrection. While Anderson notes Abraham's 'provocative declaration' as
an allusion to the resurrection (n. 27), the parable does not feature prominently in his
study of resurrection in Luke-Acts.

196. Additionally, the cognate noun ἀνάστσις occurs with ἐκ νεκρῶν in Luke
20:35; cf. Acts 4:2; 10:41; 13:34; 17:3. However, the collocation is distinctively
Lukan.

197. See, e.g., Wright, *Resurrection*, 437; Ellis, *Luke*, 207; Johnson, *Literary
Function*, 143; Fitzmyer, *Luke X–XXIV*, 1128; Bock, *Luke*, 2:1377.

198. Forbes, *God of Old*, 195.

the dead.[199] Through his careful parable-framing Luke is preparing the audience to hear how all the Scriptures testify about the risen Jesus.

Despite the authority of the Scriptures, Abraham's words in v. 31 conclude the parable on a downbeat. The five brothers will not be convinced (πεισθήσονται) by one risen if they do not listen to 'Moses and the prophets'. In the parable's context Jesus has declared that it easier for heaven and earth to pass away than for one dot of the law to become void (v. 17), a point immediately illustrated by the parable in which 'Moses and the prophets' are sufficient witnesses to the resurrection.[200] Yet as Luke's narrative continues, individuals need to be persuaded of this same truth. For instance, in Luke 24:45 the disciples must have 'their minds opened' (διήνοιξεν αὐτῶν τὸν νοῦν) so that they can understand the Scriptures; Jesus's resurrection will remain a puzzle unless it is placed within the scriptural story.[201] As Hays says about the Emmaus disciples' puzzlement, 'Their incomprehension exemplifies the ironic dictum of Luke 16:31'.[202] The uncertainty of response intimated at the parable's conclusion is maintained in Luke's second volume, where it is evident that until the Jews understand their Scriptures, the fact of Jesus's resurrection will have no effect on them. This brings us to the motif of authoritative revelation in Acts.

5.4. *Authoritative Revelation in Acts*

5.4.1. *Lukan Attention to Scripture*
In his second volume Luke continues to draw attention to the functions of the Jewish Scriptures. In Acts the most frequent circumscription for the Scriptures is the same term repeated on two occasions in Luke 16, Μωϋσέως καὶ τῶν προφητῶν. This collocation occurs in various permutations in Acts 13:15; 24:14; 26:22; and 28:23. There are also other designations for the Scriptures in Acts, including Stephen's reference to the law as 'living words' (λόγια ζῶντα) in 7:38, and the description

---

199. Perry, *Resurrecting Interpretation*, 200, observes that the five brothers 'are denied a resurrected interpreter to assist them in their application of Moses and the prophets', while the disciples on the road to Emmaus benefit from the interpretation of the risen Jesus, retelling 'the story that the ex-disciples had until that point, failed to hear'. While this would appear to be an inconsistency within Luke's narrative, Perry does not take into account Jesus's expectation that the disciples would know this *without* his guidance.

200. Blomberg, 'Law in Luke-Acts', 55

201. Hays, 'Reading Scripture', 232.

202. Ibid., 232.

of Paul's and Apollos's explanations from 'Scripture' (τῶν γραφῶν) in 17:2–3 and 18:28. Similar to its function in Luke 18:31, τοῖς προφήταις in Peter's address to the crowd (Acts 3:18) and in Paul's conversation with Herod Agrippa (Acts 26:27) is a shorthand reference for all of the Jewish Scriptures. It encapsulates them, since Luke views both Moses (the author of the law) and David (the author of the Psalms) as prophets.[203]

With respect to the ethical function of the Scriptures, the believers in Acts are portrayed as living in accordance with the Mosaic legislation.[204] This is demonstrated, for instance, in almsgiving being regarded as a sign of true adherence to the law (9:36; 10:2). Similarly, Peter's rooftop vision does not abrogate purity regulations, but reveals that God can declare clean what was previously unclean, whether food (10:12–16) or Gentiles (10:28). Other Lukan instances of a high regard for the law in Acts are when Paul circumcises Timothy (16:1–3), takes vows (18:18), submits to a purification ritual (21:23–26), and insists that he has not violated the temple's purity (24:18).

While Luke continues to accentuate the ethical import of Scripture in his second volume, there is a shift in usage. As Green puts it, the primary significance of Scripture in Acts is now 'ecclesiological and hermeneutical, as the Christian community struggles with its own identity, not least over against those who also read the Scriptures but who refuse faith in Christ'.[205] This function is evinced in several quotations from Jewish Scripture in Acts.[206] As in our discussion of revelation in Luke's Gospel, we will concentrate on the motif of revelation in Acts as evidenced in the collocation 'Moses and the prophets' and its variations.

5.4.2. *'Moses and the Prophets'*

When we analyse the use of 'Moses and the prophets' in Acts there emerges a consistent pattern, akin to the Gospel usages in 18:31–33; 24:25–27; and 24:45–47. Luke frequently portrays the followers of Jesus using Scripture to validate the claim that he is the promised Messiah. In Acts, 'the whole of the Old Testament becomes fair territory for the

---

203. For Moses's identity as prophet, see Acts 3:22 and 7:37; for David's prophetic identity, see Acts 2:30.

204. Fitzmyer, *Theologian*, 185; he cites Acts 2:46 and 3:1. See also Jervell, *People of God*, 138.

205. Green, 'Acts', 18.

206. Bock, 'Realisation', 41–62, categorizes these quotations under five rubrics: covenant and promise (e.g. Acts 2:16–39), Christology (e.g. Acts 8:32–33), community mission (e.g. Acts 4:24–26), the commission to Gentiles (e.g. Acts 26:23), and challenge and warning to Israel (e.g. Acts 3:22–23).

discovery of proofs which show who Jesus really was'.[207] This herme-
neutic is witnessed in three of the four principal passages where variations
of this phrase occurs – 13:15; 24:14; 26:22–23; 28:23 – and it is also
suggested in several related instances of preaching and teaching about
Jesus.

The first occurrence to consider is 'the law and the prophets' (τοῦ
νόμου καὶ τῶν προφητῶν) in 13:15, an account of Paul's preaching in
the synagogue of Pisidian Antioch. Remarkably, this speech is the only
example of what Luke regularly reports as Paul's synagogue activity of
proclaiming Jesus from the Jewish Scriptures. It may therefore be said
that his discourse in 13:16–41 has structural significance, comprising not
only a survey of Israel's history (vv. 17–25), but also three quotations
from Scripture (vv. 33, 34, and 35), each of which is explained as being
realized in the person and ministry of Jesus.[208] The Third Gospel's generalized references to 'Moses and the prophets' in relation to Jesus's death
and resurrection have now been succeeded by specific citations of Jewish
Scripture. Essentially similar to Peter's approach in his Acts 2 sermon,
Paul in v. 33 quotes Ps 2:7 (LXX), in v. 34 quotes Isa 55:3 (LXX), and
in v. 35 cites Ps 16:10 (LXX) to confirm that Jesus's resurrection estab-
lishes his identity as the one who fulfills the promises made to the Jewish
ancestors.[209] Paul's statement in 13:27 summarizes his address, where
he speaks of Jesus's condemnation being in fulfilment of the prophets'
words, and being evidence of the people's inability to understand those
same prophets.

The second instance of a close variation of the phrase 'Moses and the
Prophets' is 24:14, during Paul's defense before governor Felix. Paul
affirms that he believes 'everything that is written in the Law and prophets'
(πᾶσι τοῖς κατὰ τὸν νόμον καὶ τοῖς ἐν τοῖς προφήταις γεγραμμένοις). The
phrase functions here not as a component of a christological explanation
of Jewish Scripture but as a validation of Paul's heritage. As such, it can
be eliminated from our consideration.

Thirdly, in his hearing before Herod Agrippa in Acts 26:22 Paul makes
a general appeal to 'the prophets and Moses'. Paul asserts that far from
being unduly innovative in his preaching, the Jewish Scriptures corrob-
orate what he has been saying about Jesus, that it is 'nothing other than

---

207. O'Toole, *Unity*, 24.

208. J. Jervell, 'The *Centre of Scripture* of Luke', in Jervell, *The Unknown Paul:
Essays on Luke-Acts and Early Christian History* (Minneapolis: Augsburg, 1984),
122–37, citing 128.

209. Carroll, 'Scripture in Acts', 521.

what the prophets and Moses said would happen' (οὐδὲν ἐκτὸς λέγων ὧν τε οἱ προφῆται ἐλάλησαν μελλόντων γίνεσθαι καὶ Μωϋσῆς). The message of his preaching is well within the parameters of previous authoritative revelation.

A final reference to 'Moses and the prophets' occurs in the final chapter of Acts. Here Luke gives an account of Paul's ministry in Rome, where he attempts to convince the Jews about Jesus using the testimony of τοῦ νόμου Μωϋσέως καὶ τῶν προφητῶν (28:23). It is evident that Paul is again adopting a christological reading of the Scriptures in his preaching.

As previously mentioned, a reference that is analogous to 'Moses and the prophets' is τοῖς προφήταις in 3:18 and 26:27. The term is used by both Peter and Paul as a shorthand reference for Scripture. Peter tells a largely Jewish crowd that the death of Jesus was foretold by 'the prophets', and Paul insists to Herod Agrippa that he is already acquainted with the events of Jesus's life through knowing 'the prophets'. Similarly, Moses has a prophetic function in Stephen's speech in 7:37, where 'Moses' is said to speak about the coming prophet Jesus.[210]

In summary, three of the four instances in Acts of the collocation 'Moses and the prophets' (or close variations), as well as three similar references to the same corpus of literature, represent the Jewish Scriptures as providing a necessary framework for understanding Jesus's life, death, and resurrection. Indeed, throughout Acts these Scriptures are used to elucidate important aspects of the identity and function of Christ.[211] The view of Scripture as a christological proof is also borne out in specific instances which emphasize the fulfilment of biblical promises and prophecies.[212] Just as can be observed in the Third Gospel, the opening chapters of Acts indicate that Scripture is being fulfilled through the events taking place in the community (1:16–20; 2:16–21), a phenomenon that continues in the subsequent narrative, when the words of the prophets are represented as illuminating events such as the harassment of the believers by the Sanhedrin (4:24–30) and the inclusion of the Gentiles in the community of believers (15:13–21). It is no exaggeration to say that 'Luke's history of Jesus and the church is driven by the fulfilment of prophecies'.[213] To the preaching about Jesus from the Scriptures we now return.

---

210. F. Bovon, 'Law in Luke-Acts', in Bovon, *Studies in Early Christianity*, WUNT 2/161 (Tübingen: Mohr Siebeck, 2003), 41–70, citing 61.

211. Carroll, 'Scripture in Acts', 520; he cites the fulfilment of Joel 2:1–2 (LXX); 3:1–5 (LXX), Pss 16:8–11 (LXX); 110:1 (LXX).

212. Carroll, 'Scripture in Acts', 520–21.

213. Squires, *Plan of God*, 153.

5.4.3. *Preaching in Acts*

Besides the already-noted specific references to 'Moses and the prophets' in Paul's speeches, there are several christological citations of Jewish Scripture in the addresses of other individuals. Peter in Acts 2:22–36 refers to Jesus being prophesied by Pss 16:8–11 and 110:1, and he explains Ps 118:22 with reference to Jesus in Acts 4:8–12. Similarly, Philip in 8:26–40 demonstrates to the Ethiopian eunuch the christological intent of Isa 53:7–8, the first among many passages that Philip explains to him (v. 35). Furthermore, Luke indicates repeatedly in Acts that Jesus is preached as the Christ on the basis of Jewish Scripture. For example, in 17:2 Paul spends three Sabbaths with the Jews in the synagogue of Thessalonica, 'reasoning with them from the Scriptures' (διελέξατο αὐτοῖς ἀπὸ τῶν γραφῶν). In 18:28 Apollos disputes with the Jews of Achaia, 'proving from the Scriptures that Jesus was the Christ'. To these examples can be added other instances of the apostles' 'teaching and preaching' (διδάσκοντες καὶ εὐαγγελιζόμενοι, 5:42), 'proving' (συμβιβάζων, 9:22), and 'testifying' (διαμαρτυρόμενος, 18:5) to audiences about Jesus's identity. In 17:11 the Bereans are commended for 'examining the Scriptures every day' (καθ' ἡμέραν ἀνακρίνοντες τὰς γραφάς) in order to scrutinize Paul's preaching about Christ. In some of these texts reference to the Scriptures is not made explicitly, yet it can be plausibly implied as consistent with the pattern of preaching to Jews and God-fearers in Acts, where instruction is required in order to understand how the Scriptures speak about the ministry of Jesus.

Taken together, the numerous accounts of preaching and testifying to Jews in Acts parallel the approach that is first implied in the story of the risen Jesus teaching the two Emmaus disciples (Luke 24:25–27), or conversing with the disciples in Jerusalem (Luke 24:44–47). The Acts accounts provide 'clear models for the reading strategy toward which Luke 24 gestures', one in which the crucified and resurrected Jesus is the hermeneutical key to Israel's Scripture.[214] In the Lukan perspective Jesus cannot be understood apart from these Scriptures.[215] We will now consider how Acts' portrayal of revelation, resurrection, and the responses to Jesus impacts an intratextual reading of Luke 16:19–31.

5.5. *The Parable and Revelation in Relation to Acts*

5.5.1. *Continued Misreading?*

The parable's conclusion fits the style and program of Luke-Acts conspicuously. Persisting at the parable's conclusion is the question whether

---

214. Hays, 'Liberation', 112.
215. Moberly, *Theology and Faith*, 51.

some will continue to misread 'Moses and the prophets', and consequently fail to comprehend the importance of Jesus's life, death, and resurrection.[216] Furthermore, within the broader Lukan narrative it becomes evident that there is one who will rise from the dead and bring a message that can save: the same one who tells this parable.[217]

5.5.2. *The Parable and Revelation in Acts*

In the parable, Abraham's references to revelation are occasioned by the request to send Lazarus from the dead to bring a warning. In the previous chapter we examined the law against necromancy in Deut 18:10–13 and its intertextual relevance for Luke 16:19–31.[218] Deuteronomy forbids the practice of seeking contact with the dead, and as such it provides a conceptual background to the rich man's request. We also argued that the wider setting of the Deut 18 injunction needs to be taken into account.[219] It is heard in the context of God's provision of reliable revelation; Israel's need for direction is met in the divine promise of a נָבִיא (Deut 18:15). Because God promises to speak there is no need to solicit alternate messengers. Deuteronomy's intertextual voice was soundly affirmed by Abraham in his words to the rich man in v. 29: 'They have Moses and the prophets. Let them listen to them' (Ἔχουσι Μωϋσέα καὶ τοὺς προφήτας· ἀκουσάτωσαν αὐτῶν. For the rich man's five brothers the testimony of 'Moses and the prophets' negates any need to hear from the dead Lazarus.

The parable audience will understand that a messenger from the realm of the dead is also not required because someone deceased – Jesus – has in fact returned. The risen Jesus teaches especially through his appeals to Israel's Scripture (Luke 24:27, 44).[220] This Jesus is one whom Peter in Acts 3:22–26 identifies expressly as the 'prophet like Moses', as promised in Deut 18.[221] Together, 'Moses and the prophets' and the new prophet

---

216. Green, *Theology*, 72. Cf. Trompf, *Historical Recurrence*, 144: 'The same people who would not listen to Moses in the past did not heed the proclamations of the church either… For Luke, then…disobedience was a recurring phenomenon in Jewish history.' Goulder, *New Paradigm*, 2:636, points out in this connection, 'The replies of Abraham to Dives are the *themes of Acts*' (emphasis original).

217. Hauge, *Tour of Hell*, 150, suggestively comments: 'A witness from the dead is sent, but it is another man who suffered τὰ κακά beyond measure (cf. 9:22; 18:33)'.

218. See the discussion in Chapter 4, §5.1.

219. See the discussion in Chapter 5, §5.3.2.

220. Moberly, *Theology and Faith*, 67.

221. See Acts 3:22–26; on the citation of Deut 8 in Acts 3, see Dodd, *Scriptures*, 53–57.

Jesus speak with a voice that demands a hearing; as Peter declares to the crowd at Pentecost in 3:22, 'You must listen to everything he tells you' (αὐτοῦ ἀκούσεσθε κατὰ πάντα ὅσα ἂν λαλήσῃ πρὸς ὑμᾶς).[222] In this connection Moberly states well, 'There is no knowledge available from a realm beyond this life which is more significant or helpful for understanding Jesus…than the moral and spiritual content already accessible in Israel's existing Scriptures'.[223] It is these Scriptures which are repeatedly opened in the preaching about Jesus in Acts and which confirm the truth of Abraham's words for the parable's audience.

5.5.3. *The Parable and Resurrection in Acts*

The theme of Jesus's resurrection, prominent in the Gospel and its climactic ch. 24, is maintained and expanded in Acts.[224] Throughout Acts the main task of the apostolic witnesses is to affirm the reality of his resurrection.[225] Jesus's resurrection is the focus of the preaching of the early community,[226] and it can be considered the core of the Lukan salvific message.[227] These contextual factors point up the legitimacy of hearing in the parable an intratextual allusion to the resurrection of Jesus, one of the parable's secondary themes that we previously identified. To be sure, the immediate significance of τις ἐκ νεκρῶν ἀναστῇ (v. 31) was not obvious in the parable's telling within the context of Jesus's ministry. However, on a re-reading this reference to Jesus would likely be clear. This is part of a Lukan narrative commentary through the use of double meanings.[228] With their knowledge of how the story of Luke-Acts culminates in Jesus's resurrection, the audience is prepared to detect in v. 31 an early allusion to the risen Jesus.[229]

222. Cf. the divine imperative in Luke 9:35 with reference to Jesus, 'Listen to him' (αὐτοῦ ἀκούετε).

223. Moberly, *Theology and Faith*, 51.

224. On the place of resurrection in the New Testament in general, see R. Bauckham, 'God Who Raises the Dead: The Resurrection of Jesus and Early Christian Faith in God', in *The Resurrection of Jesus Christ*, ed. P. Avis (London: Darton, Longman & Todd, 1993), 136–54.

225. Acts 2:32; 3:15; 4:33; 5:32; 10:41; 13:31; cf. Anderson, *God Raised*, 47.

226. See especially 2:24–32 and 13:30–37; cf. Thompson, *Risen Lord*, 76.

227. See, e.g., Anderson, *God Raised*, 13: 'The resurrection of Jesus in Luke-Acts constitutes the pivotal act of God in the salvation of Israel and the whole world, and it is consequently the focus of the Lukan message of salvation'.

228. Kurz, *Reading Luke-Acts*, 136.

229. E. Reinmuth, 'Ps-Philo, Liber antiquitatum biblicarum 33,1–5 und die Auslegung der Parabel Lk 16:19–31', *NovT* 31 (1989): 16–38, citing 37–38.

Previously we cited the Lukan pattern of predictions, both divine and human.[230] In this connection the secondary theme of Abraham in Luke-Acts and the parable also comes to the fore. Though he is not identified explicitly as a prophet as Zechariah (Luke 1:67), John the Baptist (Luke 1:76), or Anna (Luke 2:36) are identified, the patriarch has a role in the motif of prophecy in Luke-Acts.[231] Abraham predicts in Luke 16:31 that those who do not listen to the Scriptures will not be persuaded by 'one risen from the dead'. For the audience, says Carroll, 'this is a poignant anticipation of later narrative developments, when incapacity to read Scripture and resistance to the message about one raised from the dead will keep close company'.[232] Though it is read retrospectively, Abraham's prediction in Luke 16:31 sanctions Luke's version of events in Acts. Moreover, it draws attention to this prophecy's fulfilment in both the negative and positive responses to the risen Jesus in Acts.[233] *Not convincing.*

5.5.4. *The Parable and Responses in Acts* *How is it central if appears once?*

When Luke 16:19–31 is read intratextually, it anticipates another aspect of the subsequent narrative – and the last of the secondary themes of Luke-Acts identified above – namely, the potential for repentance among those who listen to 'Moses and the prophets'.[234] This anticipatory element is evidenced by three textual factors. First, when Lazarus is requested in v. 28 to warn or witness to the five brothers (διαμαρτύρομαι), the rich man employs a word that is uniquely Lukan. In Acts διαμαρτύρομαι is used repeatedly to describe the apostles' preaching about Jesus, which

---

230. Talbert, 'Promise and Fulfillment', 94, notes the numerous prophecies in Luke-Acts.

231. Dahl, 'Abraham in Luke-Acts', 153, points to the function of the promises to Abraham in the speeches of Stephen (Acts 7:2–8) and Paul (Acts 13:16–41), and observes, 'God's promise to Abraham [is] the first link in a series of prophecy and fulfillment'.

232. Carroll, *Luke*, 338; he cites Acts 3:17–26; 4:8–21; 13:26–41; 15:21. See also Goulder, *New Paradigm*, 2:636

233. Bovon, 'Effect of Realism', 104, observes that the ambiguous nature of prophecy emphasizes the divine role in accomplishing his purpose, and sets a choice before the reader of whether to understand or not. Cf. Alexander, 'Back to Front', 442: 'Luke, writing in full awareness of the tragic dimension of the story of Israel's rejection of the Gospel, invites the reader both to contemplate the tragedy for what it is and to read it as a warning of the possibility of having eyes, yet failing to "see"'.

234. Tannehill, *Luke's Story*, 85, notes the characteristic Lukan language of repentance present in 16:30 and subsequently in Acts.

in turn is often associated with the response of repentance.[235] Secondly, the rich man hopes that his brothers will repent (μετανοήσουσιν, v. 30), which in Luke-Acts is the appropriate response to the preaching about Jesus.[236] A final textual feature that anticipates the subsequent narrative is Abraham's use of the word 'convinced' (πεισθήσονται, 16:31). In Lukan usage, this verb is regularly joined with διαμαρτύρομαι in descriptions of the preaching in Acts,[237] and often implies conversion and resultant salvation.[238] This combination of distinctively Lukan terminology in vv. 28–31 heightens audience attention for the brothers' response.

We noted previously that whether the five brothers will be convinced by 'Moses and the prophets' is an open-ended aspect of the parable.[239] This narrative phenomenon stimulates interest and participation in the story, as the audience considers whether the parable will reach a satisfactory resolution in the Gospel or Acts.[240] In fact, many recognize in the parable's conclusion a thematic anticipation of the latter portions of Luke-Acts.[241] To Luke's audience, the allusion to future narrative events in v. 31 is clear: a believing acceptance of someone risen from the dead (Jesus) is inextricably linked to the right interpretation of 'Moses and the prophets'.[242] As such, Abraham's closing words afford a proleptic view into the events of the Acts narratives.

There is a range of perspectives, however, on the tenor of this expectancy as it concerns the Jewish people.[243] In Acts it is an open question

235. See, e.g., Acts 2:40; 8:25; 10:42; 18:5; 20:21, 23, 24; 23:11; 28:23.

236. Tannehill, *Luke's Story*, 84–101, discusses repentance as an integral theme in Luke; cf. Méndez-Moratalla, *Paradigm of Conversion*.

237. See, e.g., Paul's preaching in the Corinthian synagogue, described in 18:4 as 'persuading Jews and Greeks' (ἔπειθέν τε Ἰουδαίους καὶ Ἕλληνας) and in 18:5 as 'testifying to the Jews that Jesus was the Christ' (διαμαρτυρόμενος τοῖς Ἰουδαίοις εἶναι τὸν χριστὸν Ἰησοῦν).

238. See, e.g., Acts 17:4 and 28:24.

239. See the discussion in §2.4 of this chapter; cf. Kurz, *Reading Luke-Acts*, 17–37; Maxwell, *Between the Lines*, 133–35.

240. Nave, *Repentance*, 189; cf. Brawley, 'Abrahamic Covenant', 123: 'The siblings have Moses and the prophets, and the parable suspends on whether they will listen or not'.

241. See, e.g., Wright, *Resurrection*, 437; Ellis, *Luke*, 207; Johnson, *Literary Function*, 143; Fitzmyer, *Luke X–XXIV*, 1128; Lehtipuu, 'Characterization', 103; Bock, *Luke*, 2:1377.

242. See, e.g., Talbert, *Reading Luke-Acts*, 125.

243. On the presentation of the Jews in Luke-Acts, see, e.g., Sanders, *Jews in Luke-Acts*; Tyson, *Images*; Tyson, 'The Problem of Jewish Rejection in Acts',

whether the Jews will see the christological truth of 'Moses and the prophets' as explained by the believing community. Certainly there are instances of a divided response among Jewish audiences; some believe, but others reject the preaching about Christ.[244] As Sanders states baldly, 'There is a simple connection between the difficulty posed by Abraham at the end of the parable and the situation of the early church in attempting to convert Jews to Christianity: since the Jews cannot understand their own Scriptures, the fact of the resurrection of Jesus will likewise have no effect on them'.[245] Furthermore, when Paul in Acts 28:26–27 applies Isa 6:9–10 to his Jewish audience in Rome, this is understood by some to mean the discontinuation of the apostolic mission to the Jews.[246]

Luke's portrayal of the Jewish response to the message of Jesus cannot be said to be entirely negative, however.[247] Partial Jewish acceptance of Jesus is not eclipsed by a collective rejection, for Acts repeatedly accentuates that many Jews believe in the message.[248] Even in the final chapter of Acts, Paul's audience is divided between the Jewish people who believe and those who do not (28:24). Thus the Isaianic prophecy that is cited by Paul in Acts 28:26–27 need not be viewed 'as a wholesale repudiation of ethnic Israel but as an inducement for recalcitrant Jews to do an about-face'.[249] The ending of Acts itself appears to leave open the possibility that

in *Luke-Acts and the Jewish People: Eight Critical Perspectives*, ed. J. B. Tyson (Minneapolis: Augsburg, 1988), 124–37; Weatherly, 'Jews in Luke-Acts', 107–17; Verheyden, 'Unity', 28–29; D. Ravens, *Luke and the Restoration of Israel*, JSNTSup 119 (Sheffield: Sheffield Academic, 1995); Bauckham, 'Restoration of Israel', 435–87. Tannehill, *Narrative Unity*, 1:186, comments that the conclusion of the parable 'fits neatly with the actual resistance which the preaching of the risen Christ will encounter in Acts'; cf. Cadbury, *Making of Luke-Acts*, 279.

244. See, e.g., 13:45–51; 14:1–6; 17:12–14; 19:9; 28:24.

245. Sanders, *Jews in Luke-Acts*, 202; cf. his 'The Salvation of the Jews in Luke-Acts', in Talbert, ed., *New Perspectives*, 104–28. Grundman, *Lukas*, 330, proposes that 16:31 explains why the resurrection appearances of Jesus were restricted to his disciples. Hughes, 'Rich Man', 40, contends that the parable 'gives the readers of Luke-Acts [the] writer's reason why Christian evangelization of Jews fails so miserably in Acts'. Johnson, *Literary Function*, 110, calls the parable 'a grim foreshadowing' of the second rejection of Jesus in Acts.

246. Jervell, *People of God*, 41–74.

247. Weatherly, 'Jews in Luke-Acts', 107–17, contends that Sanders's analysis is flawed, having neglected positive elements of the Jews in Luke's portrayal.

248. See, e.g., Acts 13:43; 14:1; 17:4, 12; notable is 21:20, where 'thousands of Jews' (μυριάδες...ἐν τοῖς Ἰουδαίοις) are said to believe.

249. Anderson, *God Raised*, 271.

some Jews will accept Jesus as the promised Messiah, for Luke notes that Paul continues his preaching to *all* who came to see him (28:30).[250]

As observed previously, the conclusion of Acts lacks finality. While bringing certain aspects of his two-volume narrative to completion, Luke leaves a variety of questions unresolved. This is also true with respect to the mission among the Jewish people, for which no definitive answer is given.[251] The irresolution at the end of Acts serves to stimulate the Lukan audience to watch for and participate in the continuing activity of God through the preaching about Jesus. Kurz observes, 'By not closing out Paul's life but ending Acts on a note of bold, unhindered preaching, the story ends with an open thrust toward future evangelization up to and beyond the time of the intended audience'.[252] When Luke-Acts is re-read as a continuous narrative, the indeterminateness of this response is already apparent with Abraham's words to the rich man in 16:31. Although the rich man is suffering torments, perhaps his five brothers will yet listen to 'Moses and the prophets', be convinced by one risen from the dead, repent, and live.

6. *Summary and Interpretive Outcomes*

This chapter began with the aim of reading Luke 16:19–31 within its authorially signalled literary context, the Third Gospel and Acts. Luke's claim to have written a carefully ordered narrative has informed our reading, and we have seen how Luke employs this parable in order to presage the subsequent narrative.

With respect to the principal theme of poverty and possessions we saw the Lukan perspective that the rich man should have acted differently with his material wealth, an alternative mode of conduct that is elucidated in the rest of the Gospel. Luke then provides in Acts an account of the parable's implied teaching about mercy – and the Gospel's explicit teaching – being concretized. The blameworthy model of the rich man is contrasted with commendable patterns of care and generosity in Acts, as a community takes shape in which poverty is being eliminated. The portrait of the

---

250. R. C. Tannehill, 'Israel in Luke-Acts: A Tragic Story', *JBL* 104 (1985): 69–85; cf. his 'The Story of Israel within the Lukan Narrative', in Moessner, *Heritage of Israel*, 325–39.

251. Bauckham, 'Restoration', 485–86; cf. Kurz, 'Promise and Fulfillment', 169; V. Fusco, 'Luke-Acts and the Future of Israel', *NovT* 38 (1996): 1–17.

252. Kurz, *Reading Luke-Acts*, 35; cf. Troftgruben, *A Conclusion Unhindered*, 152, notes that Acts 28 'concludes little regarding a mission to Jews'.

believers' numerous beneficent activities enjoins the Lukan audience to emulate these activities as an expression of their own commitment to the needy. The portrayal also encourages those who are disadvantaged with the prospect of approaching aid.

Next considering the other principal theme of authoritative revelation, we observed Luke's narrative demonstration that only those who listen to 'Moses and the prophets' will be persuaded by one resurrected. Abraham's reference in the parable to 'one risen from the dead', while historically retrospective, is literarily prospective, and attests to Luke's persuasive design. Within his larger story, Jesus is the one who is risen and who can open minds to the christological thrust of all the Scriptures. The pattern of preaching in Acts likewise corroborates the Lukan perspective that 'Moses and the prophets' are read primarily as prophetic of Jesus in his suffering, death, and resurrection.

It is in this connection that the parable's secondary motifs figure. Situated within Luke's two-volume narrative arc, Abraham's closing words intimate the possibility that the rich man's relatives can be spared from post-mortem suffering through their repentance. At the same time, Abraham validates the repeated accounts in Acts where repentance is closely joined to a hearing of the Scriptures' testimony to Jesus. About him, 'Moses and the prophets' said that he would suffer, be killed, and rise on the third day – his resurrection being the climax of God's saving purpose.

Having investigated textual and thematic links from the parable to the rest of the Lukan corpus, it remains for us to consider the possible effects of these associations on his audience. An initial question concerns whether they could perceive and value these links, or if the proposed prolepses and parallels are not overly subtle and require an excessively advanced reading strategy. However, we have assumed that Luke's implied audience is competent to respond to the text in meaningful ways, and that it is Luke's expectation that his work will be understood in a manner congruent with its intricate design through successive readings or hearings.[253] Is Luke's choosing and arranging of his narrative material then merely a demonstration of literary artistry, or does it have a different purpose? While it is impossible to be certain about the author's motivation, we may propose three possible intentions behind Luke's placement of this parable within his broader work.

253. See Thompson, 'Parallel Composition', 184.

In the first place, the parable's interconnectedness with the wider Lukan narrative serves to establish the author's credibility. When the reader notices the repeated demonstrations of literary foresight, incompletion, prediction, and tension in the parable – and the way in which these relate to and are resolved in subsequent narratives in Luke-Acts – they are cumulatively suggestive of the reliability of Luke's work and the certainty of his message.[254]

Secondly, reading the parable with the retrospective vision afforded by Acts serves as a warning. With his repeated reference to 'Moses and the prophets' in resurrection contexts, Luke sounds a cautionary note about the possibility of knowing the Scriptures yet failing to respond to the risen one of whom they testify. This possibility, coupled with the accounts of both unbelief and faith in Acts, confronts the parable's hearers with whether they will listen to 'Moses and the prophets' and be convinced by someone risen from the dead. The parable's open-ended message simultaneously challenges and warns would-be adherents both within and outside the narrative.[255]

The parable's third effect when read within its Luke-Acts context is audience engagement. Noticing thematic associations and developments engages the hearers in the activity of making meaning from the text, and invites them to seek further developments in the story. The account of the early community creatively putting into practice Jesus's parabolic words about wealth and poverty would have a persuasive effect, as it presents a commendable prospect for Luke's audience. Likewise, the audience would be engaged by the open-endedness of the parable – and of the Luke-Acts narrative as a whole – with respect to responding to Scripture and to one risen from the dead. This open-endedness engages the Lukan audience's interest and promotes their participation in the continued dissemination of the message of the risen Jesus.

Eh, seems like a stretch.

254. Rothschild, *Rhetoric of History*, 139.
255. Green, 'Narrative Criticism', 112.

Chapter 6

CONCLUSIONS AND IMPLICATIONS

1. *Failure and Prospect*

We began with a neglected beggar, an indulgent rich man and his five oblivious brothers, and the patriarch Abraham. Their story is more than a story, and this parable more than an exceptional unit of text within the Third Gospel. We have seen that Luke 16:19–31 presents a portrait of failure, yet offers a prospect for alternative outcomes both in response to poor Lazarus and to one risen from the dead. Cognizant of the parable's multiple dimensions, we investigated it from three literary perspectives that have proved to be complementary – narrative criticism, rhetorical criticism, and intertextuality. Because reading this parable within its Luke-Acts context has been an undertreated aspect in past studies, we also examined how Luke uses this narrative in order to prepare his audience for the events and emphases of his second volume. We achieved this contextual consideration by reviewing principal themes of the Gospel, traced from their first occurrences in the work to their development in the following chapters and in Luke 16:19–31, and into the account of the early Christian community in Acts.

2. *Interpretive Outcomes and Conclusions*

2.1. *Luke 16:19–31 as Narrative*

In Chapter 2 we saw that the narrative texture of Luke 16:19–31 is rich with interrelated characters: Lazarus, the rich man, Abraham, and the rich man's five brothers. By vivid settings in life and after-life, as well as by colourful characterizations and the dynamics of interrelationships, the parable illustrates the helplessness and hope of the poor, the corruption of the wealthy, and the consequences of failing to listen to 'Moses and the prophets'. In this way the narrative engages and stimulates its audience to regard the warning message that is being communicated.

The beggar Lazarus is unquestionably wretched: he is ulcerated, unsheltered, unable to walk, malnourished, and even harassed by dogs (vv. 20–21). Portrayed in his condition of helpless suffering, he is paradigmatic of the needy in the Third Gospel who are promised God's favour and provision (1:52–53). Luke's use of the term πτωχός in the parable accords with the Gospel's signature message that God's mercy is shown not just to the economically disadvantaged, but to the sick, the blind, and the outcast (4:18–19). This truth is borne out by the beggar's surprising name, 'Lazarus', which is a subtle act of honouring him in the desolation of his earthly condition. Within the parable's story world it is expected that the rich man's name is known while the beggar is anonymous, yet Lazarus is dignified with a name and the rich man is not – a contrast consistent with the pervasive Lukan motif of reversal (e.g. 13:30). Though separated in life by barriers both physical and social, Lazarus and the rich man are in relationship as members of God's covenant people, making palpable the rich man's failure to share with the needy person at his gate.

While anonymous, the rich man is familiar to Luke's audience in a general way. They have heard Jesus routinely describe wealthy people in a warning and condemnatory way on account of their self-satisfaction (6:24–25), greed (12:16–21), and devotion to mammon (16:13). With this narrative preparation the audience is not surprised to see the rich man debased after death. Though he received good things, he did not employ them in acts of charity as instructed by 'Moses and the prophets' (v. 29). While the parable describes no outrightly wicked deed on his part, the rich man's 'sin of omission' is a failure to respond to the plight of Lazarus. To the audience this makes coherent his torment. From his position in Hades he assumes the privilege of calling Abraham 'father' (vv. 24, 27, 30), but the rich man is no 'child of Abraham'. Because he failed to share his clothing or food with one who lacked, the rich man is not entitled to such an honorific (Luke 3:8, 11).

The patriarch Abraham plays the role of heavenly host for Lazarus and post-mortem interlocutor for the rich man. Jesus announced in 13:28–29 that many will eat at the messianic banquet in God's kingdom with 'Abraham, Isaac, and Jacob and all the prophets'. While Lazarus enjoys this patriarchal fellowship in Abraham's bosom (v. 22), the rich man is among those who observe the festivity from a wretched position outside the banquet. Even so, he is permitted to converse with Abraham across the chasm (v. 26). In speaking with the rich man, Abraham reliably mediates God's judgment and legitimates what has been heard in the Gospel about the true nature of Abraham's children (3:8–9), the announcement of salvation for the poor (4:18–19), and the hazards of material wealth (12:16–21). Finally, the audience will hear Abraham's closing declaration about the sufficiency of 'Moses and the prophets' in relation to one risen from the dead (v. 31) substantiated in the Acts narratives about the preaching to the Jews about the risen Jesus.

While their role in the narrative is 'off-stage', the rich man's five brothers are referenced as possible recipients of a warning given by Lazarus risen from the dead (vv. 27–28). The rich man is concerned that they will come to share in his torturous fate, presumably because they are likewise dismissive of their responsibility to the destitute. Abraham's prediction of their response has a doubtful tone (v. 31), but whether the brothers are ever persuaded by 'Moses and the prophets' falls outside the bounds of the narrative. As a parable with an omitted ending, the story invites the audience to fill the narrative gap by considering potential responses among the rich man's family to the Scriptures' testimony. Being engaged in this contemplation simultaneously poses the question about the prospect of their own response to 'Moses and the prophets' in relation to someone who is risen from the dead.

2.2. *Luke 16:19–31 as Rhetoric*

Our investigation in Chapter 3 demonstrated a rhetorical potency in Luke 16:19–31. This is true whether it is evaluated in comparison with the Graeco-Roman rhetorical conventions for the progymnasmatic μυθός and παραβολή, or in relation to the Jewish usages of the מָשָׁל, two broad traditions for rhetorical comparison that have not been thoroughly explored in past studies of this parable.

With respect to the elementary writing exercises of the *progymnasmata*, the mixture of constructions encouraged in the rhetorical student's manipulation of fables is evident. This is seen in the shift from a description of the outward circumstances of Lazarus and the rich man (vv. 19–21) to an extended personal dialogue between the rich man and Abraham (vv. 24–31); rhetorically, this change heightens attention. The *progymnasmata* also suggest the incorporation of a μυθός into a narrative, and Luke 16:19–31 is in fact linked tightly with the immediate context as a companion piece to the parable of the Dishonest Steward (16:1–9), and as a rejoinder to the greedy Pharisees who sneered at Jesus for his views on money. A third feature formally consistent with the progymnasmatic μυθός is its conclusion with a gnomic statement, in which the audience is supplied with a concise statement of truth for reflection. Such a moral forms the parable's conclusion in v. 31, a statement about the significance of heeding the Scriptures that applies broadly to the Lukan audience and encourages their contemplation of this point. The currency of the literary genre of the παραβολή indicates the probability that Luke creatively employs this narrative in order to persuade his audience on subjects of importance. Because it is likely that Luke's audience was familiar with Graeco-Roman rhetorical structures and figures, they would be prepared to respond to the persuasion that is present in this discourse.

The parable has other persuasive features of classical rhetorical style and invention. The description of the beggar's physical state is laden with *pathos* and engenders pity for Lazarus (vv. 20–21), while the failure of the rich man to assist the beggar makes Lazarus the more piteous (v. 19). On the other hand, the picture of the rich man's torment is made evocative by its flames, thirst, and insurmountable chasm (vv. 23–24, 26). Nevertheless, the audience is not prompted to sympathize with the rich man but to conclude that this fate is deserved, on the basis of Abraham's words. Throughout, the patriarch grounds the parable's communication in a trustworthy and authoritative *ethos*. Already before he speaks, Abraham has credibility as the father of his people, the one first entrusted with God's salvific promises (Luke 1:55). He then demonstrates *logos* in his three negative responses to the rich man's requests. First, Abraham indicates the inherent legitimacy of the reversal of τὰ ἀγαθά of the rich man and τὰ κακά of Lazarus (v. 25). Next, he observes the sheer physical impassibility of the χάσμα μέγα as a reason that Lazarus cannot be sent on a relief mission (v. 26). Finally, Abraham insists on the adequacy of 'Moses and the prophets' to provide a warning to the living (v. 29). If what is simpler to do has not been done – listening to 'Moses and the prophets' – then the more difficult activity of sending a risen messenger will not elicit a different response. The logic of Abraham's argumentation, combined with his credibility as patriarch, accentuates the importance of listening to the Scriptures.

The parable's features are likewise paralleled in the various narrative מְשָׁלִים of the Jewish Scriptures. Like many of these narratives, Luke 16:19–31 is juridical or deliberative, eliciting a judgment on personal misconduct from those who hear it. The parabolic tradition in the Jewish Scriptures presented narrated events as ostensibly factual, as this parable does. The fictional narratives in the Jewish Scriptures are uttered by prophets, as Jesus, the prophet *par excellence* (Luke 7:16; 13:33), does here. The Jewish parabolic material is uniformly directed to kings or leaders, and while the addressees of Luke 16:19–31 include Jesus's disciples (16:1) the narrator also observes that Jesus is responding to the denigration of the listening Pharisees (16:14–15) who held a position of authority among the Jewish people. The parables in the Jewish tradition are bound to their literary context, and the Luke 16:19–31 audience is likewise given cues for understanding from the immediate and broader context. Collectively, these similarities suggest the likelihood that this parable was rhetorically effective among those among Luke's hearers who were familiar with the Jewish Scriptures. As the prophet Jesus tells this authentically detailed and ostensibly factual account in response to the leaders of the people, the audience is prompted to make a judgment about their misdemeanours. They are simultaneously invited to ponder the parable's message and their own response to it.

Considered rhetorically, Luke 16:19–31 is an apposite vehicle for Luke's persuasive purpose. Its realism prompts the listeners to lower their defenses, and to be more amenable to the parable's message. While disarming with realism, it also demonstrates the 'extraordinary within the ordinary' with elements of narrative extravagance. The excessive luxury and then the scorching afflictions of the rich man, the abject poverty and then the blissful state of Lazarus, were likely memorable in an oral culture and urged audience inquiry into causes and alternatives. The parable's rhetoric encourages reflection on how their own responses to possessions, poverty, and Scripture may need to be altered. This effect is intensified when the audience hears Luke 16:19–31 in the context of Acts, and anticipates how its lessons will be concretized by the early church.

2.3. *Intertextuality in Luke 16:19–31*

In Chapter 4 we held a suggestive intertextual conversation among Graeco-Roman and Jewish literature surrounding two prominent themes in the parable, possessions and poverty, and messengers from the afterlife.

2.3.1. *Possessions and Poverty*

The source of the rich man's wealth is not elucidated, but regarding him through Seneca's or Plutarch's lens of the stereotypically wealthy, it can be suggested that he gained his wealth through exploiting the socially powerless and that he maintained his wealth through avarice and tightfistedness.[1] Consequently, he is suffering post-mortem torments for his financial misconduct and neighbourly neglect. Yet there is an intertextual dissonance, for Deuteronomy's voice insists that wealth is a divine blessing on those who obey Yahweh's commandments.[2] The audience's difficulty is that no explicit moral judgment is passed for the manner in which the rich man lived or for how his wealth was acquired. If the origin of his wealth is uncertain, the same must be said for Lazarus's miserable

---

1. Seneca, *Ben.* 10.5–6; Plutarch, *Cupid. divit.* 525B-C.
2. Deut 6:1–3; 7:12–14; 8:6–9; 11:8–15; 28:4–5.

condition. According to Deuteronomy, his poverty, skin affliction, and (possible) lack of burial can be interpreted as emblematic of God's curse on his unrepentant wickedness.[3] However, this explanation does not cohere with the rest of the narrative, in which Lazarus is rewarded with a post-mortem position at Abraham's side in the feast of God's kingdom. Thus another intertextual tension is left to be resolved: the rationale for the poor man's reward.

An intertextual conversation concerning the rich man's portrayal leads to more unambiguously negative conclusions, for he embodies some of the moral dangers confronting the wealthy. While Deuteronomy is largely positive concerning prosperous people, Graeco-Roman writers draw attention to the serious attendant hazards of possessing wealth.[4] Riches can engender a spirit of greed, a lifestyle of decadence, and unkindness in conduct. Luke's portrait of the overindulged, richly costumed, and self-centred man accords with such a picture and affirms the cultural voice. As for Lazarus, similar to other poor persons in the ancient world, he is power-less both physically and socially. His portrait evokes audience sympathy and moves them to identify with the beggar at the gate. This affirms the recurrent suggestion of Deuteronomy that God's covenant people must identify with the poor and take action to mitigate their suffering.[5] Here our intertextual conversation indicates possibilities for his material goods that the rich man left un-utilized. He failed to employ any of the beneficent means promoted by Deuteronomy,[6] the prophets,[7] and in other Jewish literature[8] to care for his impoverished neighbour. In response to Lazarus he could have shared his goods and income, contributed alms, or offered hospitality, but in fact he did nothing. The intertextual dissonance surrounding the rich man's prosperity as a possible indicator of divine favour is resolved: he is not obedient, and is therefore punished in the afterlife.

The account of the rich man's failure is amplified by listening to a second intertextual voice, for neither does he conform to Graeco-Roman cultural mores regarding wealth and generosity. To an extent prosperous

---

3. Deut 28:18, 26–27, 47–48.

4. Plutarch, *Cupid. divit.* 525A-C; Seneca, *Ben.* 7.2.4.

5. Deut 10:19; 27:19.

6. See, e.g., Deut 14:28–29; 15:7–8; 23:24–25; 24:19–22; 26:12 (cf. Exod 22:21–22; 23:3, 6; Lev 19:10; 23:22).

7. See, e.g., Isa 3:13–15; Jer 5:26–29; Ezek 22:29; Amos 2:6–7; 4:1; 5:11–15; 6:4; 8:4–6; Mic 6:8.

8. See, e.g., Tob 1:3, 16–17; 4:7–11, 16; 1 En. 94:6–8; 96:4–8; Sir 4:1–10; 29:8–9.

persons were expected to be willing to share their material resources with the suffering poor, whether through the forgiving of debts, the distribution of property, or general liberality.[9] Heard within a conversation of Graeco-Roman and Jewish intertexts, the inexcusability of the rich man's failure to respond to the destitution of Lazarus is doubly pronounced – and thereby Luke's warning and encouragement, while implicit, is unmistakable. With the parable he challenges those gifted with material resources to share with the poor, a challenge that is taken up with enthusiasm and creativity in his second volume.

2.3.2. *Messages from the Afterlife*

Our conversation partners provide decidedly different perspectives on whether there is a legitimate prospect for Lazarus to return from Abraham's side in order to convey a warning message to the five brothers. In Graeco-Roman literature it is not uncommon for someone from the afterlife to bring a report intended to influence the outlook and behaviour of the living.[10] Within this cultural tradition, Luke's audience probably envisions Lazarus speaking to the brothers out of his recently acquired knowledge of the post-mortem state and the appalling cost of misconduct. The rich man's proposal is consonant with other accounts of post-mortem visitations, but the parable strikingly diverges from this pattern. Abraham states that contact with the dead is not necessary because the five brothers 'have Moses and the prophets' (v. 29). Even if a messenger is sent from the afterlife, Abraham predicts that his mission will be ineffectual (v. 31). The culturally well-known pattern has been subverted.

Although the parable does not correspond with Graeco-Roman tradition in this respect, neither does it offer a clear reverberation of the Deuteronomic voice. Abraham withholds permission for Lazarus to return not because of the injunctions against communicating with those in the realm of the dead, such as found in Deut 18:10–13,[11] but because of the emphatic sufficiency of 'Moses and the prophets'. The unnecessity of Lazarus's return is indicative of Luke's conception of the sufficiency of the Scriptures to direct proper conduct – a sufficiency which simultaneously emphasizes the rich man's culpability for not listening and obeying. This conclusion is borne out by the context of Deut 18, where there is

---

9. See, e.g., Seneca, *Vit. beat.* 24.4; Plutarch, *Cupid. divit.* 523F; Plato, *Leg.* 736D; Aristotle, *Pol.* 1320B 2–3, 7–9.

10. See, e.g., Plato, *Resp.* 10.614–21; Plutarch, *De sera* 22–33; Pliny, *Ep.* 5.5; Herodotus, *Hist.* 5.92; Lucian, *Demon.* 43.

11. See also Lev 19:31; 1 Sam 28:1–19; Isa 8:19–20.

not only a proscription of necromantic practice, but a promise of reliable revelation from God: the people's need for direction is met in the divine promise of a נָבִיא in Deut 18:15–18. Because God promises to speak, there is no need to solicit alternate messengers through necromancy and temporary visitors from the afterlife. This intertextual voice is soundly affirmed by Abraham. Words from the ghost of Lazarus could never match the truth and efficacy of 'Moses and the prophets'.

Hearing Luke 16:19–31 in the context of Luke's complete narrative the audience understands that a reanimated messenger is not required because another prophet has appeared with a divine message. Jesus is identified as the Deuteronomic 'prophet like Moses'; he is the prophet to whom everyone needs to listen (Acts 3:22). The Luke-Acts audience listens to 'Moses and the prophets' and Jesus speak about repentance and faith with a combined and congruous voice, just as Luke 9:35 demands a response from all those who hear Jesus's prophetic voice.

2.4. *Luke 16:19–31 within Luke-Acts*

Recognizing the literary design that links Luke and Acts as two volumes of the same work, in Chapter 5 we read this parable as a constituent part of the Lukan narrative. Reading within the Luke-Acts context develops our understanding of Luke's purpose, for he utilizes this parable to emphasize themes already introduced and to anticipate motifs that are more fully expressed later in his narrative. We considered patterns of anticipation, incompletion, prophecy or prediction, and tension in relation to the themes of possessions and poverty and authoritative revelation, while noting the parable's intersections with other Lukan themes of resurrection, the patriarch Abraham, and repentance. Listening for narrative connections engages the audience of Luke-Acts in the activity of making meaning from the text.

2.4.1. *Possessions and Poverty*
Considered within the broader Lukan perspective, the rich man's visible prosperity is suggestive of the potential danger he faces and the real possibility of his downfall (Luke 1:52–53; 6:24–25; 18:23–25). The audience consequently understands that his selfish enjoyment of good things will not be without cessation or consequence. The parable's events enact canons of reversal already announced (e.g. 6:20–26), as Lazarus receives promised comfort and satisfaction, while the rich man is left miserable and hungry. Through a comparison with Jesus's words of blessing and woe, the audience is persuaded to see the truth of his declarations.

The audience recognizes alternatives to the rich man's blameworthy conduct within both the parable and the rest of the Gospel. Habitually sitting outside the rich man's gate, Lazarus is described as longing to be filled with food, even with discarded table scraps (v. 21). Yet the rich man was not an agent for the relief of his needy neighbour. More than giving table scraps, Jesus calls the rich to practise a generous hospitality by inviting 'the poor' to their feasts and promises that this kindness will be rewarded at the resurrection of the just (14:12–14). Though involved in feasting on a daily basis, the rich man did not extend an invitation to someone who was hungry or unable to work for wages; therefore he will receive no eschatological reward. A third worthy alternative to the rich man's neglect is giving alms (11:41; 12:33), a motif that is present in the parable by strong implication. The inference of the rich man's lack of mercy finds confirmation through a juxtaposition with the parable of the Dishonest Steward in 16:1–9, in which the steward is commended by Jesus for using worldly wealth to gain friends and be welcomed into eternal dwellings (16:9).

Jesus's encouragement of beneficence is fundamental to the multi-pronged charitable activities of the believers in Acts. The believers sell their goods to care for the poor, and they hold their possessions in common (2:45–47; 4:32–37). Individuals are commended for their almsgiving (9:36; 10:2). Hospitality is shown frequently and widely (9:43; 10:48; 18:1–3; 28:1–2), and the church in Antioch provides famine relief for the believers in Judea (11:28–30). The cumulative effect of seeing Jesus's words about mercy and generosity applied concretely and diversely in Acts commends his instruction as practicable. The portrait of the early community's beneficent activities thus enjoins the Lukan audience to emulate these activities as an expression of their own commitment to the needy. The portrayal also encourages those who are disadvantaged with the prospect of approaching aid.

Using the parable as a window into Acts, we can regard the benevolent activity of the early church standing in contrast to the rich man's culpable neglect, and also presenting an alternative prospect for the conduct of Luke's audience. First, the rich man failed to relieve Lazarus with even his table scraps, while the church of Antioch, for instance, responds to Judaea's anticipated need for food during famine with their generous contributions (11:28–30). Secondly, the rich man failed to invite a poor and disadvantaged person to his daily feasts, but believers throughout Acts demonstrate hospitality to strangers, Jews, Gentiles, and other unlikely guests (9:43; 10:48; 18:1–3; 28:1–2). Thirdly, the rich man failed to show mercy through giving alms, but individuals such as Dorcas (9:36) and Cornelius (10:2) are commended as righteous for this act of kindness – another suggestive example for Luke's audience.

The parable's element of warning also retains its persuasive effect in Acts. While it is told as a response to the greedy Pharisees (16:14), the parable's caution is intended broadly for Luke's audience. In Acts he provides paradigms of those who handle wealth or possessions wrongly, such as Ananias and Sapphira (5:1–11), Simon the magician (8:9–24), the slave girl's owners (16:19), and the governor Felix (24:24–27). However, throughout Luke's second volume are also examples of those who treat possessions rightly, including Barnabas who sells his field and contributes the proceeds to the apostles (4:36–37), the Ephesian believers who destroy their valuable but illicit scrolls (19:19), and Paul who works manually to support the needy in the spirit of Jesus's words (20:33–35). This consistent narrative offers more than an idealized portrait of a community in which there were no poor (4:34), but serves as an encouragement to the Lukan audience. They can witness the parable's implicit message about mercy being concretized in the early community, and observe the rich man's neglect contrasted with commendable patterns. Luke provides paradigms of people who treat wealth both wrongly and rightly to encourage an imitation of the latter among his audience.

2.4.2. *Authoritative Revelation*

Abraham twice recommends that the five brothers listen to 'Moses and the prophets' (vv. 29, 31). While reminding the audience of the scriptural mandate to respond mercifully to destitute people, this reference also has a proleptic function within Luke-Acts. Abraham says the five brothers will not be convinced if they do not listen to 'Moses and the prophets', and the subsequent Lukan narrative demonstrates the need to be persuaded or to have one's faculties of perception opened to the Scriptures (24:45). It is only then that the Scriptures can be seen as essentially prophetic of Jesus (24:27, 44). The consistent pattern of preaching to the Jewish people in Acts corroborates the Lukan perspective that 'Moses and the prophets' should be read primarily as prophetic of Jesus in his suffering, death, and resurrection.[12] Analysed within the two-volume development of Luke's narrative, the parable is implying that the rich man's relatives can be kept from post-mortem suffering if they listen to 'Moses and the prophets'. Such listening is evidenced not only through heeding Scripture's directives to care for poor persons but also through being persuaded by its clear testimony to Jesus.

12. Acts 13:32–37; 26:22–23; 28:23.

Although the parable is situated in advance of the accounts of Jesus's resurrection, Abraham speaks about 'one risen from the dead' in v. 31. The immediate referent is Lazarus, but Luke's vocabulary strongly connotes the resurrection of Jesus. The reference to 'one risen from the dead', while historically retrospective, is literarily prospective, and it attests to Luke's persuasive design. Knowing in advance how the Luke-Acts narrative culminates in and centres on Jesus's resurrection, the audience is prepared to detect this early allusion to the risen Jesus. The right interpretation of 'Moses and the prophets' is inseparable from an acceptance of one arisen from the dead (Luke 24:27, 44–45; Acts 26:22–23). The audience is therefore impelled to see a correlation between the parable's conclusion and the later narratives about Jesus's resurrection. Likewise, Abraham's prediction in v. 31 sanctions Luke's portrayal of the believers' kerygmatic activity in Acts and the variable responses to it. The patriarch's words also draw attention to further outcomes of the preaching about the resurrected Jesus. Therefore, just as it warns about neglecting the beggar sitting at one's doorstep, the parable sounds a caution about the possibility of knowing 'Moses and the prophets' yet failing to respond to the one of whom they ultimately testify.

The thematic anticipation in the parable's conclusion is consistent with the open-endedness of Luke-Acts as a whole. Rather than being cause for reader uncertainty, the irresolution after Acts 28:31 – particularly with respect to the Jewish response to the message of Christ – stimulates the Lukan audience with the consideration of alternate prospects. The audience is prompted both to watch for and participate in the ongoing activity of preaching about the risen Jesus. When Luke-Acts is read as a continuous narrative, the indeterminate nature of this preaching enterprise is intimated in Abraham's words to the tormented rich man; his five brothers may yet listen to 'Moses and the prophets', be convinced by one risen from the dead, repent, and live.

3. *Implications from the Study*

Scholarly interest in the mythological backgrounds of its afterlife imagery may have led to a neglect of the parable's integral place within not only the Third Gospel, but also the Acts of the Apostles. We have employed a trio of literarily based methods to show that this parable illustrates, anticipates, and advances key aspects of the author's theological interests in Luke-Acts. These insights were seen primarily in relation to the themes of poverty and possessions and of authoritative revelation, and secondarily in relation to the patriarch Abraham, the possibility of repentance, and Jesus's resurrection. This intersection of numerous Lukan themes in a single unit of text is illustrative of the author's skill in crafting a carefully ordered and convincing narrative in this particular parable, and in Luke-Acts as whole. This general observation suggests two implications, both of which are premised on the assumption that what is true for Luke 16:19–31 particularly is true for the Lukan parables generally.

As a first implication we emphasize the desirability of employing a combination of methods in the study of the Lukan parables, rather than approaching them from a single interpretive perspective. The texture of these parables is thick with narrative, rhetorical and intertextual aspects, and we have demonstrated that a plurality of methodological perspectives can be merged in an investigation. This blending of methods provides a fulsome interpretation of the parable and can supply new insights to the reader.

A second implication from the foregoing study, and one with a bearing on Luke-Acts research in general, resides in our demonstration that Lukan parables can be studied for their meaningful resonances in the work's second volume. This has been an under-developed area in past scholarship, but to read an individual parable in the Third Gospel without consideration of its echoes in Acts is to disregard a significant portion of material intended to shape audience response. We have established that re-reading Luke-Acts through the lens of a parable discloses intriguing new prospects for understanding Luke's narrative and its persuasive purpose.

4. *Areas of Further Research*

At least two avenues for future research are suggested by this project. First, we investigated one of eleven parables in Luke's special collection[13] and observed how he utilizes it in order to prepare for the themes and interests of his second volume. Not only could each of the Lukan parables be investigated for its reverberations in Acts, but a corollary study could consider whether Luke's literary design is similarly evident in those parables that

13. The parables of the Two Debtors (7:41–43); the Good Samaritan (10:25–37); the Friend at Midnight (11:5–8); the Rich Fool (12:16–21); the Barren Fig Tree (13:6–9); the Prodigal Son (15:11–32); the Dishonest Steward (16:1–8); Lazarus and the Rich Man (16:19–31); the Dutiful Servant (17:7–10); the Unrighteous Judge (18:2–8); the Pharisee and Tax Collector (18:10–14).

are held in common with Mark and Matthew.[14] To what degree has Luke re-fashioned the parables from this shared collection in order to prepare his audience for engaging with and appropriating the message of Acts, and what does this indicate about his communicative purpose?

Secondly, we have noted the parable's vivid aspect of warning, where the rich man is portrayed as suffering post-mortem consequences for his failure to respond to the poverty of Lazarus. This invites attention to the place and function of warnings in Acts. While there are no parables in Acts that offer a similar narrative portrait of the eschatological costs of unbelief in the risen Jesus or disobedience to his words, it is intriguing whether this motif is present in an altered form in the apostles' preaching and teaching. Such an instance may be Acts 3:23, Peter's words of warning that anyone who does not listen to God's promised prophet 'shall be destroyed from among the people' (ἐξολεθρευθήσεται ἐκ τοῦ λαοῦ). One might investigate how this and other kerygmatic warnings compare with the portrait in Luke 16:19–31, and what the form of such warnings indicates about the composition of Luke's audience.

---

14. The parables of the Sower (Luke 8:4–15; cf. Mark 4:1–20; Matt 13:1–23); the Mustard Seed (Luke 13:18–19; cf. Mark 4:30–32; Matt 13:31–32); the Wicked Tenants (Luke 20:9–19; cf. Mark 12:1–12; Matt 21:33–46); the Waiting Servants (Luke 12:35–48; cf. Mark 13:34–47; Matt 24:45–51).

Bibliography

The abbreviations used in the present volume follow the *SBL Handbook of Style* (2nd ed.).

Primary Sources

Unless otherwise noted, cited works by ancient authors are from the Loeb Classical Library edition.

Aristotle. *On Rhetoric: A Theory of Civic Discourse*. Translated by G. A. Kennedy. New York: Oxford University Press, 1991.
Elliger, K., and W. Rudolph, eds. *Biblia Hebraica Stuttgartensia*. Editio funditus renovata. Stuttgart: Deutsche Bibelgesellschaft, 1984.
Nestle, Eberhard, Erwin Nestle, Barbara Aland, Kurt Aland, Iōan D. Karavidopoulos, Carlo Maria Martini, Bruce M. Metzger, and Holger Strutwolf, eds. *Novum Testamentum Graece*. 28th ed. Stuttgart: Deutsche Bibelgesellschaft, 2012.
Patillon, Michael. *Aelius Theon Progymnasmata: Texte etabli et traduit*. Paris: Société d'édition Les Belles Lettres, 1997.
Rahlfs, Alfred, ed. *Septuaginta*. Stuttgart: Deutsche Bibelgesellschaft, 1935, repr. 1979.

Secondary Sources

Aalen, S. 'St. Luke's Gospel and the Last Chapters of I Enoch'. *NTS* 13 (1966–67): 1–13.
Abasciano, Brian J. 'Diamonds in the Rough: A Reply to Christopher Stanley Concerning the Reader Competency of Paul's Original Audiences'. *NovT* 49 (2007): 153–83.
Abrahams, Israel. *Studies in Pharisaism and the Gospels*. New York: Ktav, 1967.
Aletti, Jean-Noël. *L'Art de Raconteur Jésus Christ: L'écriture narrative de l'évangile de Luc*. Parole de Dieu. Paris: Seuil, 1989.
Alexander, Loveday C. A. *The Preface to Luke's Gospel: Literary Convention and Social Context in Luke 1.1–4 and Acts 1.1*. SNTSMS 78. Cambridge: Cambridge University Press, 1993.
———. 'Reading Luke-Acts from Back to Front'. Pages 419–46 in *The Unity of Luke-Acts*. Edited by J. Verheyden. BETL 142. Leuven: Leuven University Press, 1999.
———. 'The Relevance of Greco-Roman Literature and Culture to New Testament Study'. Pages 85–101 in *Hearing the New Testament: Strategies for Interpretation*. Edited by Joel B. Green. 2nd ed. Grand Rapids: Eerdmans, 2010.
Allen, David M. 'Introduction: The Study of the Use of the Old Testament in the New'. *JSNT* 38 (2015): 3–16.

Alter, Robert. *The Art of Biblical Narrative*. London: Allen & Unwin, 1981.

Anderson, Garwood P. 'Seeking and Saving What Might Have Been Lost: Luke's Restoration of an Enigmatic Parable Tradition'. *CBQ* 70 (2008): 729–49.

Anderson, Kevin L. *'But God Raised Him from the Dead': The Theology of Jesus' Resurrection in Luke-Acts*. Paternoster Biblical Monographs. Bletchley, Milton Keynes: Paternoster, 2006.

Bailey, Kenneth E. *Jesus through Middle Eastern Eyes: Cultural Studies in the Gospels*. Downers Grove, IL: IVP Academic, 2008.

———. *Poet and Peasant: A Literary Cultural Approach to the Parables in Luke*. Grand Rapids: Eerdmans, 1976.

Baker, David L. *Tight Fists or Open Hands? Wealth and Poverty in Old Testament Law*. Grand Rapids: Eerdmans, 2009.

———. 'Rich and Poor, Proud and Humble in Luke-Acts'. Pages 214–33 in *The Social World of the First Christians*. Edited by L. M. White and O. L. Yarbrough. Minneapolis: Fortress, 1995.

Ball, Michael. 'The Parables of the Unjust Steward and the Rich Man and Lazarus'. *ExpTim* 106 (1995): 329–30.

Barrett, C. K. *The Acts of the Apostles*. 2 vols. ICC. Edinburgh: T. & T. Clark, 1994.

———. 'Luke/Acts'. Pages 231–44 in *It Is Written: Scripture Citing Scripture. Essays in Honour of Barnabas Lindars, SSF*. Edited by D. A. Carson and H. G. M. Williamson. Cambridge: Cambridge University Press, 1988.

———. 'The Third Gospel as a Preface to Acts? Some Reflections'. Pages 1451–66 in *The Four Gospels 1992: Festschrift Frans Neirynck*. Vol. 2. Edited by F. Van Segbroeck, C. M. Tuckett, G. Van Belle, and J. Verheyden. BETL 100. Leuven: Leuven University Press, 1992.

Bass, Kenneth. 'The Narrative and Rhetorical Use of Divine Necessity in Luke-Acts'. *Journal of Biblical and Pneumatological Research* 1 (2009): 48–68.

Bates, Matthew W. 'Cryptic Codes and a Violent King: A New Proposal for Matthew 11:12 and Luke 16:16–18'. *CBQ* 75 (2013): 74–93.

Bauckham, Richard. *The Fate of the Dead: Studies on the Jewish and Christian Apocalypses*. NovTSup 93. Leiden: Brill, 1998.

———. 'God Who Raises the Dead: The Resurrection of Jesus and Early Christian Faith in God'. Pages 136–54 in *The Resurrection of Jesus Christ*. Edited by Paul Avis. London: Darton, Longman & Todd, 1993.

———. *Jesus and the Eyewitnesses: The Gospels as Eyewitness Testimony*. Grand Rapids: Eerdmans, 2006.

———. 'The Relevance of Extracanonical Jewish Texts to New Testament Study'. Pages 65–84 in *Hearing the New Testament: Strategies for Interpretation*. Edited by Joel B. Green. 2nd ed. Grand Rapids: Eerdmans, 2010.

———. 'The Restoration of Israel in Luke-Acts'. Pages 435–87 in *Restoration: Old Testament, Jewish and Christian Perspectives*. Edited by James M. Scott. JSJSup 72. Leiden: Brill, 2001.

———. 'The Rich Man and Lazarus: The Parable and the Parallels'. *NTS* 37 (1991): 225–46.

———. 'Visiting the Places of the Dead in the Extra-Canonical Apocalypses'. *PIBA* 18 (1995): 78–93.

———, ed. *The Gospels for all Christians: Rethinking the Gospel Audiences*. Grand Rapids: Eerdmans, 1998.

Bauer, Walter, Frederick Danker, W. F. Arndt, and F. W. Gingrich. *A Greek–English Lexicon of the New Testament and Other Early Christian Literature*. 3rd ed. Revised and edited by Frederick Danker. Chicago: University of Chicago Press, 2000.

Beale, G. K., ed. *The Right Doctrine from the Wrong Texts? Essays on the Use of the Old Testament in the New.* Grand Rapids: Baker Books, 1994.

Beavis, Mary Ann. 'Parable and Fable: Synoptic Parables and Greco-Roman Fables Compared'. *CBQ* 52 (1990): 473–98.

Beck, David. R. 'The Narrative Function of Anonymity in Fourth Gospel Characterization'. *Semeia* 63 (1993): 143–58.

Bennema, Cornelis. 'A Theory of Character in the Fourth Gospel with Reference to Ancient and Modern Literature'. *BibInt* 17 (2009): 375–421.

Berger, Klaus. 'Hellenistiche Gattungen im Neuen Testament'. Pages 1031–1432 in *ANRW* 25.2. Edited by Wolfgang Haase. Berlin: de Gruyter, 1984.

Bergquist, J. A. 'Good News to the Poor: Why Does this Lucan Motif Appear to Run Dry in the Book of Acts?' *Bangalore Theological Forum* 18 (1986): 1–16.

Bernstein, Alan E. The *Formation of Hell: Death and Retribution in the Ancient and Early Christian Worlds.* Ithaca, NY: Cornell University Press, 1993.

Bird, Michael F. 'The Unity of Luke-Acts in Recent Discussion'. *JSNT* 29 (2007): 425–48.

Bishop, Eric F. F. 'A Yawning Chasm'. *EvQ* 45 (1973): 3–5.

Bitzer, Lloyd F. 'The Rhetorical Situation'. Pages 247–60 in *Rhetoric: A Tradition in Transition.* Edited by W. R. Fisher. East Lansing, MI: Michigan State University Press, 1974.

Black, C. Clifton. 'Kennedy and the Gospels'. Pages 63–80 in *Words Well Spoken: George Kennedy's Rhetoric of the New Testament.* Edited by C. C. Black and D. F. Watson. Waco, TX: Baylor University Press, 2008.

———. 'Rhetorical Criticism'. Pages 166–88 in *Hearing the New Testament: Strategies for Interpretation.* Edited by Joel B. Green. 2nd ed. Grand Rapids: Eerdmans, 2010.

———. 'Rhetorical Criticism and Biblical Interpretation'. *ExpTim* 100 (1988–89): 252–58.

———. *The Rhetoric of the Gospel: Theological Artistry in the Gospels and Acts.* St. Louis, MO: Chalice, 2001.

Bloch-Smith, Elizabeth. *Judahite Burial Practices and Beliefs about the Dead.* JSOTSup 123. Sheffield: Sheffield Academic, 1992.

Blomberg, Craig L. *The Historical Reliability of the Gospels.* 2nd ed. Downers Grove, IL: IVP Academic, 2007.

———. *Interpreting the Parables.* 2nd ed. Downers Grove, IL: IVP Academic, 2012.

———. 'The Law in Luke-Acts'. *JSNT* 22 (1984): 53–80.

———. 'Midrash, Chiasmus, and the Outline of Luke's Central Section'. Pages 217–59 in *Gospel Perspectives: Studies in Midrash and Historiography.* Edited by R. T. France and David Wenham. Eugene, OR: Wipf & Stock, 2003.

Bock, Darrell L. *Luke.* 2 vols. BECNT. Grand Rapids: Baker Books, 1994.

———. 'The Parable of the Rich Man and Lazarus and the Ethics of Jesus'. *SwJT* 40 (1997): 63–72.

———. *Proclamation from Prophecy and Pattern: Lucan Old Testament Christology.* JSNTSup 12. Sheffield: Sheffield Academic, 1987.

———. 'Scripture and the Realisation of God's Promises'. Pages 41–62 in *Witness to the Gospel: The Theology of Acts.* Edited by I. Howard Marshall and David Peterson. Grand Rapids: Eerdmans, 1998.

————. *A Theology of Luke and Acts: Biblical Theology of the New Testament*. Grand Rapids: Zondervan, 2012.

————. 'Understanding Luke's Task: Carefully Building on Precedent'. *CTR* 5 (1991): 183–202.

Borgman, Paul. *The Way According to Luke: Hearing the Whole Story of Luke-Acts*. Grand Rapids: Eerdmans, 2006.

Boring, M. Eugene, Klaus Berger, and Carsten Colpe. *Hellenistic Commentary to the New Testament*. Nashville, TN: Abingdon, 1995.

Boucher, Madeleine. *The Mysterious Parable: A Literary Study*. CBQMS 6. Washington, DC: Catholic Biblical Association of America, 1977.

Bovon, François. *Das Evangelium nach Lukas*. Vol. 3. EKKNT. Zurich: Benziger, 2001.

————. *Luke 2: A Commentary on the Gospel of Luke 9:51–19:27*. Translated by Donald S. Deer. Edited by Helmut Koester. Hermeneia. Minneapolis: Fortress, 2013.

————. *New Testament Traditions and Apocryphal Narratives*. Translated by Jane Haapiseva-Hunter. Allison Park, OR: Pickwick, 1995.

————. *Studies in Early Christianity*. WUNT 2/161. Tübingen: Mohr Siebeck, 2003.

Boyd, W. J. P. 'Apocalyptic and Life after Death'. Pages 39–56 in *Studia Evangelica Volume 5*. Edited by F. L. Cross. TUGAL 103. Berlin: Akademie, 1968.

Braun, Willi. *Feasting and Social Rhetoric in Luke 14*. SNTSMS 85. Cambridge: Cambridge University Press, 1995.

Brawley, Robert L. 'Abrahamic Covenant Traditions and the Characterization of God in Luke-Acts'. Pages 109–32 in *The Unity of Luke-Acts*. Edited by J. Verheyden. BETL 142. Leuven: Leuven University Press, 1999.

————. 'For Blessing All Families of the Earth'. *CurTM* 22 (1995): 18–26.

————. *Text to Text Pours Forth Speech: Voices of Scripture in Luke-Acts*. Bloomington, IN: Indiana University Press, 1995.

Breech, James. *Jesus and Postmodernism*. Minneapolis: Fortress, 1989.

Bretherton, Donald J. 'Lazarus of Bethany: Resurrection or Resuscitation?' *ExpTim* 104 (1993): 169–73.

Brodie, T. 'Greco-Roman Imitation of Texts as a Partial Guide to Luke's Use of Sources'. Pages 17–46 in *Luke-Acts: New Perspectives from the Society of Biblical Literature*. Edited by C. H. Talbert. New York: Crossroad, 1984.

————. 'The Unity of Proto-Luke'. Pages 627–38 in *The Unity of Luke-Acts*. Edited by J. Verheyden. BETL 142. Leuven: Leuven University Press, 1999.

Brookins, Timothy. 'Dispute with Stoicism in the Parable of the Rich Man and Lazarus'. *JGRChJ* 8 (2011): 34–50.

Brown, Colin, ed. *The New International Dictionary of New Testament Theology*. 4 vols. Grand Rapids: Zondervan, 1975–86.

Bruce, F. F. *Jesus and Christian Origins Outside the New Testament*. Grand Rapids: Eerdmans, 1974.

Bultmann, Rudolf. *History of the Synoptic Tradition*. Translated by John Marsh. 2nd ed. New York: Harper & Row, 1968.

Burnett, Fred W. 'Characterization and Reader Construction of Characters in the Gospels'. *Semeia* 63 (1993): 3–28.

Burridge, Richard A. 'The Gospels and Acts'. Pages 507–32 in *Handbook of Classical Rhetoric in the Hellenistic Period (330 B.C.–A.D.400)*. Edited by Stanley E. Porter. Leiden: Brill, 1997.

————. *What Are the Gospels? A Comparison with Graeco-Roman Biography*. Cambridge: Cambridge University Press, 1992.

Busse, Ulrich. 'Johannes and Lukas: Die Lazarusperikope, Frucht eines Kommunikations-prozesses'. Pages 281–306 in *John and the Synoptics*. Edited by A. Denaux. BETL 101. Leuven: Leuven University Press, 1992.

Cadbury, Henry J. *The Making of Luke-Acts*. 2nd ed. London: SPCK, 1958.

———. 'The Name for Dives'. *JBL* 84 (1965): 73.

———. 'A Proper Name for Dives'. *JBL* 81 (1962): 399–402.

Caird, G. B. *The Gospel of Luke*. Harmondsworth: Penguin, 1963.

Capon, Robert Farrar. *The Parables of Grace*. Grand Rapids: Eerdmans, 1988.

Capper, Brian. 'Holy Community of Life and Property amongst the Poor: A Response to Steve Walton'. *EQ* 80 (2008): 113–27.

———. 'The Palestinian Cultural Context of Earliest Christian Community of Goods'. Pages 323–56 in *The Book of Acts in its Palestinian Setting*. BAFCS 4. Edited by Richard Bauckham. Grand Rapids: Eerdmans, 1995.

———. 'Reciprocity and the Ethic of Acts'. Pages 499–518 in *Witness to the Gospel: The Theology of Acts*. Edited by I. Howard Marshall and David Peterson. Grand Rapids: Eerdmans, 1998.

Capron, F. '"Son" in the Parable of the Rich Man and Lazarus'. *ExpTim* 13 (1901–1902): 523.

Carroll, John T. *Luke: A Commentary*. NTL. Louisville, KY: Westminster John Knox, 2012.

———. *Response to the End of History: Eschatology and Situation in Luke-Acts*. SBLDS 92. Atlanta: Scholars Press, 1988.

———. 'The Uses of Scripture in Acts'. Pages 512–28 in *Society of Biblical Literature 1990 Seminar Papers*. SBLSP 29. Atlanta: Scholars Press, 1990.

Cassidy, Richard J. *Jesus, Politics, and Society: A Study of Luke's Gospel*. Maryknoll, NY: Orbis, 1978.

Cathcart, Kevin J. 'The Trees, the Beasts and the Birds: Fables, Parables and Allegories in the Old Testament'. Pages 212–21 in *Wisdom in Ancient Israel: Essays in Honour of J. A. Emerton*. Edited by John Day, Robert P. Gordon, and H. G. M. Williamson. Cambridge: Cambridge University Press, 1995.

Cave, C. H. 'Lazarus and the Lukan Deuteronomy'. *NTS* 15 (1969): 319–25.

Chatman, Seymour. *Story and Discourse: Narrative Structure in Fiction and Film*. Ithaca, NY: Cornell University Press, 1980.

Clark, Andrew C. *Parallel Lives: The Relation of Paul to the Apostles in the Lucan Perspective*. Paternoster Biblical Monographs. Carlisle: Paternoster, 2001.

Clarke, W. K. L. 'The Use of the Septuagint in Acts'. Pages 66–105 in *The Beginnings of Christianity*. Part 1, vol. 2. Edited by F. J. Foakes Jackson and Kirsopp Lake. London: Macmillan, 1922.

Classen, C. J. *Rhetorical Criticism of the New Testament*. Boston: Brill, 2002.

Clines, David J. A. *The Dictionary of Classical Hebrew*. 8 vols. Sheffield: Sheffield Academic/Sheffield Phoenix, 1993–2011.

Coats, G. W. 'Parable, Fable, and Anecdote'. *Int* 35 (1981): 368–82.

Coggins, Richard J. 'The Old Testament and the Poor'. *ExpTim* 99 (1987): 11–14.

Collins, John Joseph. *The Apocalyptic Imagination: An Introduction to Jewish Apocalyptic Literature*. 2nd ed. Grand Rapids: Eerdmans, 1998.

Comfort, Philip. 'Two Illustrations of Scribal Gap Filling in Luke 16:19'. Pages 111–13 in *Translating the New Testament: Text, Translation, Theology*. Edited by S. E. Porter and M. J. Boda. Grand Rapids: Eerdmans, 2009.

Conzelmann, Hans. *Acts of the Apostles*. Hermeneia. Philadelphia: Fortress, 1987.

———. *The Theology of St Luke*, ET of *Die Mitte der Zeit: Studien zur Theologie*. Translated by Geoffrey Buswell. London: Faber & Faber, 1960.

Craigie, Peter C. *The Book of Deuteronomy*. NICOT. Grand Rapids: Eerdmans, 1976.

Creed, John Martin. *The Gospel According to St. Luke*. London: Macmillan, 1960.

Crossan, John Dominic. *In Parables: The Challenge of the Historical Jesus.* New York: Harper & Row, 1973.

———. 'Parable'. Pages 146–52 in *Anchor Bible Dictionary*. Vol. 5. Edited by David Noel Freedman. New York: Doubleday, 1992.

———. 'Parable and Example in the Teaching of Jesus'. *NTS* 18 (1972): 285–307.

Crossley, James G. *Why Christianity Happened: A Sociohistorical Account of Christian Origins (26–50 CE)*. Louisville, KY: Westminster John Knox, 2006.

Culpepper, R. Alan. 'Story and History in the Gospels'. *RevExp* 81 (1984): 467–78.

Curkpatrick, Stephen. 'Between *Mashal* and Parable: "Likeness" as a Metonymic Enigma'. *HBT* 24 (2002): 58–71.

———. 'Parable Metonymy and Luke's Kerygmatic Framing'. *JSNT* 25 (2003): 289–307.

Dahl, Nils A. 'The Story of Abraham in Luke-Acts'. Pages 139–58 in *Studies in Luke-Acts: Essays Presented in Honor of Paul Schubert*. Edited by Leander E. Keck and J. Louis Martyn. Nashville, TN: Abingdon, 1966.

Danker, Frederick W. *Jesus and the New Age: A Commentary on St. Luke's Gospel*. Philadelphia: Fortress, 1988.

Darr, John A. *Herod the Fox: Audience Criticism and Lukan Characterization*. JSNTSup 163. Sheffield: Sheffield Academic, 1998.

———. *On Character Building: The Reader and the Rhetoric of Characterization in Luke-Acts*. Louisville, KY: Westminster John Knox, 1992.

———. 'Narrator as Character: Mapping a Reader-Oriented Approach to Narration in Luke-Acts'. *Semeia* 63 (1993): 43–60.

Dawsey, James M. *The Lukan Voice: Confusion and Irony in the Gospel of Luke*. Macon, GA: Mercer University Press, 1986.

Dean, Margaret E. 'The Grammar of Sound in Greek Texts: Toward a Method for Mapping the Echoes of Speech in Writing'. *Australian Biblical Review* 44 (1996): 53–70.

Degenhardt, Hans Joachim. *Lukas, Evangelist der Armen: Besitz und Besitzverzicht in den lukanischen Schriften.* Stuttgart: Katholisches Bibelwerk, 1965.

Denaux, Adelbert, and Rita Corstjens. *The Vocabulary of Luke*. BTS 10. Leuven: Peeters, 2009.

Derrett, J. *Law in the New Testament*. London: Darton, Longman & Todd, 1970.

Dicken, Frank. *Herod as a Composite Character in Luke-Acts.* WUNT 2/375. Tübingen: Mohr Siebeck. 2014.

Doble, Peter. 'The Psalms in Luke-Acts'. Pages 83–117 in *The Psalms in the New Testament*. Edited by Maarten J. J. Menken and Steve Moyise. New Testament and the Scriptures of Israel. London: T&T Clark, 2004.

Docherty, Thomas. *Reading (absent) Character: Towards a Theory of Characterization in Fiction*. Oxford: Clarendon, 1983.

Dodd, C. H. *According to the Scriptures: The Sub-Structure of New Testament Theology*. London: Nisbet, 1952.

———. *Historical Tradition in the Fourth Gospel*. Cambridge: Cambridge University Press, 1963.

Donahue, John R. 'Two Decades of Research on the Rich and Poor in Luke-Acts'. Pages 129–44 in *Justice and the Holy: Essays in Honour of Walter Harrelson.* Edited by Walter J. Harrelson, Douglas A. Knight, and Peter J. Paris. Atlanta: Scholars Press, 1989.

Downing, F. Gerald. 'Theophilus's First Reading of Luke-Acts'. Pages 91–109 in *Luke's Literary Achievement: Collected Essays.* Edited by C. M. Tuckett. JSNTSup 116. Sheffield: Sheffield Academic, 1995.

Drury, John. *The Parables in the Gospels: History and Allegory.* London: SPCK, 1985.

Dschulnigg, Peter. 'Rabbinische Gleichnisse und Gleichnisse Jesu'. *Jud* 47 (1991): 185–97.

Dunkerley, R. 'Lazarus'. *NTS* 5 (1959): 321–27.

Dunn, James D. G. *Beginning from Jerusalem.* Christianity in the Making 2. Grand Rapids: Eerdmans, 2008.

Dupont, Jacques. 'L'après-mort dans l'œuvre de Luc'. *RTL 3* (1972): 3–21.

———. *Les Béatitudes.* 3 vols. Paris: Gabalda, 1969–73.

———. *Études sur les Actes des Apôtres.* Paris: Cerf, 1967.

———. 'The Poor and Poverty in the Gospels and Acts'. Pages 25–52 in *Gospel Poverty: Essays in Biblical Theology.* Translated by Michael D. Guinan. Chicago: Franciscan Herald, 1977.

Ellis, E. Earle. *Eschatology in Luke.* Philadelphia: Fortress, 1972.

———, ed. *The Gospel of Luke.* New Century Bible. London: Nelson, 1966.

Ernst, J. *Das Evangelium nach Lukas.* Regensburger Neues Testament 3. Regensburg: Pstet, 1977.

Esler, Philip Francis. *Community and Gospel in Luke-Acts: The Social and Political Motivations of Lucan Theology.* SNTSMS 57. Cambridge: Cambridge University Press, 1987.

Evans, Craig A. *Jesus and his Contemporaries: Comparative Studies.* AGJU 25. Leiden: Brill, 1995.

———. 'Jesus' Rhetoric of Criticism: The Parables Against his Friends and Critics'. Pages 256–79 in *Rhetorical Criticism and the Bible.* Edited by Stanley E. Porter and Dennis L. Stamps. JSNTSup 195. Sheffield: Sheffield Academic, 2002.

———. *Luke.* NIBC. Peabody, MA: Hendrickson, 1990.

———. 'Luke's Use of the Elijah/Elisha Narratives and the Ethic of Election'. *JBL* 106 (1987): 75–83.

———. 'Parables in Early Judaism'. Pages 51–75 in *The Challenge of Jesus' Parables.* Edited by Richard N. Longenecker. Grand Rapids: Eerdmans, 2000.

Evans, Craig A., and James A. Sanders. *Luke and Scripture: The Function of Sacred Tradition in Luke-Acts.* Minneapolis: Fortress, 1993.

Evans, C. F. *Saint Luke.* London: SCM, 1990.

———. 'The Central Section of St. Luke's Gospel'. Pages 37–53 in *Studies in the Gospels: Essays in Memory of R. H. Lightfoot.* Edited by D. E. Nineham. Oxford: Blackwell, 1955.

Eve, Eric. *Behind the Gospels: Understanding the Oral Tradition.* Minneapolis: Fortress, 2014.

———. 'Memory, Orality and the Synoptic Problem'. *Early Christianity* 6 (2015): 311–33.

Farmer, William R. 'Notes on a Literary and Form-Critical Analysis of Some of the Synoptic Material Peculiar to Luke'. *NTS* 8 (1962): 301–16.

Feuillet, A. 'La parable du mauvais riche et du pauvre Lazare antithèse de la parabole de l'intendant astucieux'. *NRT* 101 (1979): 212–23.

Fitzmyer, Joseph A. *The Gospel according to Luke X–XXIV*. AB 28a. 2 vols. Garden City, NY: Doubleday, 1981–85.

———. *Luke the Theologian: Aspects of his Teaching*. London: Chapman, 1989.

———. 'The Use of the Old Testament in Luke-Acts'. Pages 524–38 in *Society of Biblical Literature 1992 Seminar Papers*. SBLSP 31. Atlanta: Scholars Press, 1992.

Flusser, David. *Jewish Sources in Early Christianity*. Tel-Aviv: MOD, 1989.

———. *Die rabbinische Gleichnisse und der Gleichniserzahler Jesus.* JudChr 4. Bern: Lang, 1981.

Forbes, Greg W. *The God of Old: The Role of the Lukan Parables in the Purpose of Luke's Gospel*. JSNTSup 198. Sheffield: Sheffield Academic, 2000.

Foster, Paul. 'Echoes without Resonance: Critiquing Certain Aspects of Recent Scholarly Trends in the Study of the Jewish Scriptures in the New Testament'. *JSNT* 38 (2015): 96–111.

Freedman, H., and Maurice Simon. *Midrash Rabbah*. Vol. 8. London: Soncino, 1983.

Friedman, Richard Elliott, and Shawna Dolansky Overton. 'Death and Afterlife: The Biblical Silence'. Pages 35–59 in *Judaism in Late Antiquity: Part 4. Death, Life-after-Death, Resurrection and the World-to-Come in the Judaisms of Antiquity.* Edited by Alan J. Avery-Peck and Jacob Neusner. HdO 1: Der Nahe und Mittlere Osten 49. Leiden: Brill, 2000.

Fuks, Alexander. 'Isokrates and the Social-Economic Situation in Greece'. *Ancient Society* 3 (1972): 17–44.

———. 'The Sharing of Property by the Rich with the Poor in Greek Theory and Practice'. *Scripta Classica Israelica* 5 (1979): 46–63.

Funk, Robert W. *Parables and Presence: Forms of the New Testament Tradition*. Philadelphia: Fortress, 1982.

Fusco, Vittorio. 'Luke-Acts and the Future of Israel'. *NovT* 38 (1996): 1–17.

Garland, David E. *Luke*. Zondervan Exegetical Commentary on the New Testament. Grand Rapids: Zondervan, 2012.

Garrison, Roman. *Redemptive Almsgiving in Early Christianity*. JSNTSup 77. Sheffield: JSOT, 1993.

Gaventa, Beverly R. 'Toward a Theology of Acts: Reading and Rereading'. *Int* 42 (1988): 146–57.

Gelin, Albert. *The Poor of Yahweh*. Translated by Kathryn Sullivan. Collegeville, MN: Liturgical, 1964.

Gempf, Conrad. 'Public Speaking and Published Accounts'. Pages 259–303 in *The Book of Acts in Its First Century Setting*. BAFCS 1. Edited by Bruce W. Winter and Andrew D. Clarke. Grand Rapids: Eerdmans, 1993.

Gerhardsson, Birger. 'If We Do Not Cut the Parables Out of their Frames'. *NTS* 37 (1991): 321–35.

———. 'The Narrative Meshalim in the Old Testament Books and in the Synoptic Gospels'. Pages 289–304 in *To Touch the Text: Biblical and Related Studies in Honor of Joseph A. Fitzmyer, S.J.* Edited by Maurya P. Horgan and Paul J. Kobelski. New York: Crossroad, 1989.

———. 'The Narrative Meshalim in the Synoptic Gospels'. *NTS* 34 (1988): 339–63.

Gillman, John. *Possessions and the Life of Faith: A Reading of Luke-Acts*. Collegeville, MN: Liturgical, 1991.

Gilmour, Michael J. 'Hints of Homer in Luke 16:19–31'. *Did* 10 (1999): 23–33.

Glombitza, Otto. 'Der reiche Mann und der arme Lazarus: Luk xvi 19–31, Zur Frage nach der Botschaft des Textes'. *NovT* 12 (1970): 166–80.

Goulder, M. D. *Luke: A New Paradigm*. 2 vols. JSNTSup 20. Sheffield: JSOT, 1989.

Gowan, Donald. 'Wealth and Poverty in the Old Testament'. *Int* 41 (1987): 341–53.

Gowler, David B. '"At His Gate Lay a Poor Man": A Dialogic Reading of Luke 16:19–31'. *PRSt* 32 (2005): 249–65.

———. 'Characterization in Luke: A Socio-Narratological Approach'. *BTB* 19 (1989): 54–62.

———. *Host, Guest, Enemy and Friend: Portraits of the Pharisees in Luke and Acts*. New York: Lang, 1991.

Green, Joel B. 'Acts of the Apostles'. Pages 7–24 in *Dictionary of the Later New Testament and Its Developments*. Edited by Ralph Martin and Peter Davids. Downers Grove, IL: InterVarsity, 1997.

———. 'Good News to Whom? Jesus and the "Poor" in the Gospel of Luke'. Pages 59–74 in *Jesus of Nazareth, Lord and Christ: Essays on the Historical Jesus and the New Testament*. Edited by Joel B. Green and Max Turner. Grand Rapids: Eerdmans, 1984.

———. *The Gospel of Luke*. NICNT. Grand Rapids: Eerdmans, 1997.

———. 'Internal Repetition in Luke-Acts: Contemporary Narratology and Lucan Historiography'. Pages 283–99 in *History, Literature and Society in the Book of Acts*. Edited by Ben Witherington III. Cambridge: Cambridge University Press, 1996.

———. 'Luke-Acts, or Luke and Acts? A Reaffirmation of Narrative Unity'. Pages 101–19 in *Reading Acts Today: Essays in Honour of Loveday C.A. Alexander*. Edited by Steve Walton, Thomas E. Phillips, Lloyd Keith Pietersen, and F. Scott Spencer. LNTS 427. New York: T&T Clark, 2011.

———. 'Narrative Criticism'. Pages 74–112 in *Methods for Luke*. Edited by J. B. Green. Cambridge: Cambridge University Press, 2010.

———. 'Narrative and New Testament Interpretation: Reflections on the State of the Art'. *LTQ* 39 (2004): 153–66.

———. *The Theology of the Gospel of Luke*. New Testament Theology. Cambridge: Cambridge University Press, 1995.

Gregory, Andrew. 'The Reception of Luke and Acts and the Unity of Luke-Acts'. *JSNT* 29 (2007): 459–72.

Gregson, Fiona J. Robertson. 'Everything in Common? The Theology and Practice of Sharing Possessions in Community in the New Testament with Particular Reference to Jesus and his Disciples, the Earliest Christians, and Paul'. PhD diss., Middlesex University, 2014.

Grensted, L. W. 'The Use of Enoch in St. Luke xvi. 19–31'. *ExpTim* 26 (1914): 333–34.

Gressmann, H. *Vom reichen Mann und armen Lazarus: eine literargeschichtliche Studie*. AKPAW: Phil.-hist. Kl. 7. Berlin: Königlich Akademie der Wissenschaften, 1918.

Griffith, F. L. *Stories of the High Priests of Memphis: The Sethon of Herodotus and the Demotic Tales of Khamuas*. Oxford: Clarendon, 1900.

Griffiths, John Gwyn. 'Cross-cultural Eschatology with Dives and Lazarus'. *ExpTim* 105 (1993): 7–12.

Grobel, K. '"…Whose Name Was Neves"'. *NTS* 10 (1964): 373–82.

Grundmann, Walter. *Das Evangelium nach Lukas*. THNT 3. Berlin: Evangelische Verlagsanstalt, 1961.

Haenchen, Ernst. *The Acts of the Apostles*. Oxford: Basil Blackwell, 1971.

Hands, A. R. *Charities and Social Aid in Greece and Rome*. London: Thames & Hudson, 1968.

Hatcher, Karen M. 'In Gold We Trust: The Parable of the Rich Man and Lazarus'. *RevExp* 109 (2012): 277–83.

Hatina, T. R. 'Intertextuality and Historical Criticism in New Testament Studies'. *BibInt* 7 (1999): 28–43

Hauge, Matthew Ryan. *The Biblical Tour of Hell*. LNTS 485. London: T&T Clark, 2013.

Hays, Christopher M. 'Beyond Mint and Rue: The Implications of Luke's Interpretive Controversies for Modern Consumerism'. *Political Theology* 11 (2010): 383–98.

———. *Luke's Wealth Ethics: A Study in their Coherence and Character*. WUNT 2/275. Tübingen: Mohr Siebeck, 2010.

Hays, Richard B. *Echoes of Scripture in the Gospels*. Waco, TX: Baylor University Press, 2016.

———. *Echoes of Scripture in the Letters of Paul*. New Haven, CT: Yale University Press, 1989.

———. 'The Liberation of Israel in Luke-Acts: Intertextual Narration as Countercultural Practice'. Pages 101–17 in *Reading the Bible Intertextually*. Edited by R. Hays, S. Alkier, and L. Huizenga. Waco, TX: Baylor University Press, 2009.

———. *Reading Backwards: Figural Christology and the Fourfold Gospel Witness*. Waco, TX: Baylor University Press, 2014.

———. 'Reading Scripture in Light of the Resurrection'. Pages 216–38 in *The Art of Reading Scripture*. Edited by Ellen F. Davis and Richard B. Hays. Grand Rapids: Eerdmans, 2003.

Hays, Richard B., and Joel B. Green. 'The Use of the Old Testament by New Testament Writers'. Pages 222–38 in *Hearing the New Testament: Strategies for Interpretation*. 2nd ed. Edited by Joel B. Green. Grand Rapids: Eerdmans, 2010.

Hedrick, Charles. *Parables as Poetic Fictions*. Peabody, MA: Hendrickson, 1994.

Heil, John Paul. *The Meal Scenes in Luke-Acts: An Audience-oriented Approach*. SBLMS 52. Atlanta: SBL Press, 1999.

Hemer, Colin. *The Book of Acts in the Setting of Hellenistic History*. Edited by Conrad Gempf. WUNT 1/49. Tübingen: Mohr, 1989.

Hendrickx, Herman. *The Parables of Jesus*. San Francisco: Harper & Row, 1986.

Hengel, Martin. *Acts and the History of Earliest Christianity*. London: SCM, 1979.

Herzog, William R. *Parables as Subversive Speech: Jesus as Pedagogue of the Oppressed*. Louisville, KY: Westminster John Knox, 1994.

Hickling, C. J. A. 'A Tract on Jesus and the Pharisees? Conjecture on the Redaction of Luke 15 and 16'. *HeyJ* 16 (1975): 253–65.

Himmelfarb, Martha. *Ascent to Heaven in Jewish and Christian Apocalypses*. New York: Oxford University Press, 1993.

———. *Tours of Hell: An Apocalyptic Form in Jewish and Christian Literature*. Philadelphia: University of Pennsylvania Press, 1983.

Hintzen, Jochen. *Verkündigung und wahrnehmung: Über das Verhältnis von Evangelium und Leser am Beispiel Lk 16, 19–31 im Rahmen des lukanischen Doppelwerkes*. Frankfurt: Hain, 1991.

Hochman, Baruch. *Character in Literature*. Ithaca, NY: Cornell University Press, 1985.

Hock, Ronald F. 'Lazarus and Micyllus: Greco-Roman Backgrounds to Luke 16:19–31'. *JBL* 106 (1987): 447–63.

Holladay, C. R., P. Gray, and G. R. O'Day, eds. *Scripture and Traditions: Essays on Early Judaism and Christianity in Honor of Carl R. Holladay*. NovTSup 129. Leiden: Brill, 2008.

Hooke, S. H. 'Life after Death: VI. The Extra-Canonical Literature'. *ExpTim* 76 (1965): 273–76.

Huffman, Norman A. 'Atypical Features in the Parables of Jesus'. *JBL* 97 (1978): 207–20.

Hughes, Frank W. 'The Parable of the Rich Man and Lazarus (Luke 16.19–31) and Graeco-Roman Rhetoric'. Pages 29–41 in *Rhetoric and the New Testament: Essays from the 1992 Heidelberg Conference*. Edited by Stanley E. Porter and Thomas H. Olbricht. JSNTSup 90. Sheffield: JSOT, 1993.

Hultgren, Arland J. *The Parables of Jesus: A Commentary* Grand Rapids: Eerdmans, 2000.

Ilan, Tal, and Thomas Ziem. *Lexicon of Jewish Names in Late Antiquity.* Part 1. TSAJ 1. Tübingen: Mohr Siebeck, 2002.

Instone-Brewer, David. *Traditions of the Rabbis from the Era of the New Testament*. Vol. 1. *Prayer and Agriculture*. Grand Rapids: Eerdmans, 2004.

Iser, Wolfgang. *The Act of Reading: A Theory of Aesthetic Response*. London: Routledge & Kegan Paul, 1974.

Iverson, Kelly R. 'Orality in the Gospels: A Survey of Recent Research'. *CurBR* 8 (2009): 71–106.

Jeremias, Joachim. *The Parables of Jesus.* Rev. ed. London: SCM, 1963.

Jervell, Jacob. *Luke and the People of God: A New Look at Luke-Acts*. Minneapolis: Augsburg, 1972.

———. *The Unknown Paul: Essays on Luke-Acts and Early Christian History.* Minneapolis: Augsburg, 1984.

Jewett, R. 'The Rhetorical Function of Numerical Sequences in Romans'. Pages 227–45 in *Persuasive Artistry: Studies in New Testament Rhetoric in Honor of George A. Kennedy*. Edited by Duane F. Watson. JSNTSup 50. Sheffield: JSOT, 1991.

Johnson, Luke Timothy. *The Gospel of Luke*. SP 3. Collegeville, MN: Liturgical, 1991.

———. *The Literary Function of Possessions in Luke-Acts*. SBLDS 39. Missoula, MT: Scholars Press, 1977.

———. 'Luke-Acts, Book of'. Pages 403–20 in *Anchor Bible Dictionary*. Vol. 4. Edited by David Noel Freedman. New York: Doubleday, 1992.

———. 'Narrative Perspectives on Luke 16:19–31'. Pages 207–211 in *Translating the New Testament: Text, Translation, Theology*. Edited by S. E. Porter and M. J. Boda. Grand Rapids: Eerdmans, 2009.

———. *Sharing Possessions: What Faith Demands*. 2nd ed. Grand Rapids: Eerdmans, 2011.

Jülicher, Adolf. *Die Gleichnisreden Jesu*. Darmstadt: Wissenschaftliche Buchgesellschaft, 1963.

Just, Arthur A., ed. *Luke*. ACCS 3. Downers Grove, IL: InterVarsity, 2003.

Karris, Robert J. 'Poor and Rich: The Lukan *Sitz im Leben*'. Pages 112–25 in *Perspectives on Luke-Acts*. Edited by Charles H. Talbert. Danville, VA: Association of Baptist Professors of Religion. Edinburgh: T. & T. Clark, 1978.

Keck, Leander E. 'The Poor Among the Saints in the New Testament'. *ZNW* 56 (1965): 100–129.

Keith, Chris. *Jesus Against the Scribal Elite: The Origins of the Conflict.* Grand Rapids: Baker Academic, 2014.

———. *Jesus' Literacy: Scribal Culture and the Teacher from Galilee*. LNTS 413. New York: T&T Clark, 2011.

Kennedy, George A. *Classical Rhetoric and Its Christian and Secular Tradition from Ancient to Modern Times*. London: Croom Helm, 1980.

————. *New Testament Interpretation through Rhetorical Criticism.* Chapel Hill: University of North Carolina Press, 1984.

————. *Progymnasmata: Greek Textbooks of Prose Composition and Rhetoric.* Leiden: Brill, 2003.

Kermode, Frank. *The Genesis of Secrecy: On the Interpretation of Narrative.* Cambridge, MA: Harvard University Press, 1979.

Kilgallen, John J. 'Luke 15 and 16: A Connection'. *Bib* 78 (1997): 367–74.

————. *Twenty Parables of Jesus in the Gospel of Luke.* Rome: Editrice Pontificio Istituto Biblico, 2008.

Kim, Hyochan Michael. '"From Israel to the Nations": A Critical Study of the Abraham Motif in Luke-Acts'. PhD diss., Trinity Evangelical Divinity School, 2007.

Kim, Kyoung-Jin. *Stewardship and Almsgiving in Luke's Theology.* JSNTSup 155. Sheffield: Sheffield Academic, 1998.

Kimball, Charles A. *Jesus' Exposition of the Old Testament in Luke's Gospel.* JSNTSup 94. Sheffield: Sheffield Academic, 1994.

Kingsbury, Jack Dean. *Conflict in Luke: Jesus, Authorities, Disciples.* Minneapolis: Fortress, 1991.

Kirkwood, William G. 'Storytelling and Self-Confrontation: Parables as Communication Strategies'. *Quarterly Journal of Speech* 69 (1983): 58–74.

Kittel, G., and G. Friedrich, eds. *Theological Dictionary of the New Testament.* 10 vols. Translated by G. W. Bromiley. Grand Rapids: Eerdmans, 1964–76.

Klink, Edward W., III., ed. *The Audience of the Gospels: The Origin and Function of the Gospels in Early Christianity.* LNTS 353. London: T&T Clark, 2010.

Knight, George W. 'Luke 16:19–31: The Rich Man and Lazarus'. *RevExp* 94 (1997): 277–83.

Koptak, Paul E. 'Intertextuality'. Pages 332–34 in *Dictionary for Theological Interpretation of the Bible.* Edited by K. Vanhoozer, C. Bartholomew, D. Treier, and N. T. Wright. Grand Rapids: Baker Academic, 2005.

Kraybill, Donald, and Dennis M. Sweetland. 'Possessions in Luke-Acts: A Sociological Perspective'. *PRSt* 10 (1983): 215–39

Kreitzer, Larry. 'Luke 16:19–31 and 1 Enoch 22'. *ExpTim* 103 (1992): 139–42.

Kremer, Jacob. 'Der arme Lazarus: Lazarus, der Freund Jesu: Beobachtungen zur Beziehung zwischen Lk 16:19–31 und Joh 11:1–46'. Pages 571–84 in *À cause de l'Évangile: Études sur les Synoptiques et les Actes offertes au P. Jacques Dupont.* Edited by F. Refoulé. Paris: Cerf, 1985.

Kurz, William S. 'Luke-Acts and Historiography in the Greek Bible'. Pages 283–300 in *Society of Biblical Literature 1980 Seminar Papers.* SBLSP 19. Missoula, MT: Scholars Press, 1980.

————. 'Narrative Approaches to Luke-Acts'. *Bib* 68 (1987): 195–220.

————. 'The Open-Ended Nature of Luke and Acts as Inviting Canonical Actualisation'. *Neot* 31 (1997): 289–308.

————. 'Promise and Fulfillment in Hellenistic Jewish Narratives and in Luke and Acts'. Pages 147–70 in *Jesus and the Heritage of Israel: Luke's Narrative Claim Upon Israel's Legacy.* Edited by David P. Moessner. Harrisburg, PA: Trinity, 1999.

————. *Reading Luke-Acts: Dynamics of Biblical Narrative.* Louisville, KY: Westminster, 1993.

Kvalbein, Hans. 'Jesus and the Poor: Two Texts and a Tentative Conclusion'. *Them* 12 (1987): 80–87.

Lefort, L. Th. 'Le nom du mauvais riche (Lc 16,19) et la tradition copte'. *ZNW* 37 (1938): 65–72.

Lehtipuu, Outi. *The Afterlife Imagery in Luke's Story of the Rich Man and Lazarus.* NovTSup 123. Leiden: Brill, 2007.

———. 'Characterization and Persuasion: The Rich Man and the Poor Man in Luke 16:19–31'. Pages 73–105 in *Characterization in the Gospels: Reconceiving Narrative Criticism.* Edited by David Rhoads and Kari Syreeni. JSNTSup 184. Sheffield: Sheffield Academic, 1999.

———. 'The Imagery of the Lukan Afterworld in the Light of Some Roman and Greek Parallels'. Pages 133–46 in *Zwischen den Reichen: Neues Testament und Römische Herrschaft.* TANZ 36. Edited by Michael Labahn. Tübingen: Francke, 2002.

Lenski, G. E. *Power and Privilege: A Theory of Social Stratification.* 2nd ed. Chapel Hill: University of North Carolina Press, 1984.

Levin, Christoph. 'The Poor in the Old Testament: Some Observations'. *R&T* 8 (2001): 253–73.

Lightfoot, John. *A Commentary on the New Testament from the Talmud and Hebraica, Matthew – I Corinthians.* Peabody, MA: Hendrickson, 1989.

Lim, Timothy H. 'Deuteronomy in the Judaism of the Second Temple Period'. Pages 6–26 in *Deuteronomy in the New Testament: The New Testament and the Scriptures of Israel.* Edited by Maarten J. J. Menken and Steve Moyise. LNTS 358. London: T&T Clark, 2007.

Litwak, Kenneth Duncan. *Echoes of Scripture in Luke-Acts: Telling the History of God's People Intertextually.* JSNTSup 282. London: T&T Clark, 2005.

———. 'The Use of the Old Testament in Luke-Acts: Luke's Scriptural Story of the "Things Accomplished among Us"'. Pages 147–70 in *Issues in Luke-Acts: Selected Essays.* Edited by Sean A. Adams and Michael Pahl. Gorgias Handbooks 26. Piscataway, NJ: Gorgias, 2012.

Loisy, Alfred. *L'évangile Selon Luc.* Frankfurt: Minerva, 1971.

Longenecker, Bruce W. *Remember the Poor: Paul, Poverty, and the Greco-Roman World.* Grand Rapids: Eerdmans, 2010.

Mack, Burton L. 'Teaching in Parables: Elaboration within a Chreia'. Pages 143–60 in *Patterns of Persuasion in the Gospels.* Edited by Burton L. Mack and Vernon K. Robbins. Sonoma, CA: Polebridge, 1989.

———. *Rhetoric and the New Testament.* Minneapolis: Fortress, 1990.

Maddox, Robert. *The Purpose of Luke-Acts.* Studies of the New Testament and its World. Edinburgh: T. & T. Clark, 1982.

Malina, Bruce J. 'Wealth and Poverty in the New Testament and Its World'. *Int* 41 (1987): 354–67.

Mallen, Peter. *The Reading and Transformation of Isaiah in Luke-Acts.* LNTS 367. London: T&T Clark, 2008.

Manson, Thomas W. *The Teaching of Jesus: Studies of Its Form and Content.* Cambridge: Cambridge University Press, 1948.

Marguerat, Daniel. 'The End of Acts and the Rhetoric of Silence'. Pages 74–89 in *Rhetoric and the New Testament: Essays from the 1992 Heidelberg Conference.* Edited by Stanley E. Porter and Thomas H. Olbricht. JSNTSup 90. Sheffield: JSOT, 1993.

———. *The First Christian Historian: Writing the 'Acts of the Apostles'.* Translated by Ken McKinney, Gregory J. Laughery and Richard Bauckham. SNTSMS 121. Cambridge: Cambridge University Press, 2002.

————. 'Luc-Actes: Une Unité à Construire'. Pages 57–81 in *The Unity of Luke-Acts*. Edited by J. Verheyden. BETL 142. Leuven: Leuven University Press, 1999.

Marguerat, Daniel, and Yvan Bourquoin. *How to Read Bible Stories: An Introduction to Narrative Criticism*. London: SCM, 1999.

Marshall, I. Howard. 'Acts and the "Former Treatise"'. Pages 163–82 in *The Book of Acts in its Ancient Literary Setting*. BAFCS 1. Edited by Bruce W. Winter and Andrew D. Clarke. Grand Rapids: Eerdmans, 1993.

————. *The Gospel of Luke: A Commentary on the Greek Text*. NIGTC. Exeter: Paternoster, 1978.

————. 'How Did the Early Christians Know Anything About Future States?' *JEBS* 9 (2009): 7–23.

————. *Luke: Historian and Theologian*. Exeter: Paternoster, 1970.

————. 'The Resurrection of Jesus in Luke'. *TynBul* 24 (1973): 55–98.

Mason, Steve. 'Chief Priests, Sadducees, Pharisees and Sanhedrin in Acts'. Pages 115–77 in *The Book of Acts in Its Palestinian Setting*. Edited by Richard Bauckham. BAFCS 4. Grand Rapids: Eerdmans, 1995.

Matera, Frank J. 'Jesus' Journey to Jerusalem (Luke 9.51–19.46): A Conflict with Israel'. *JSNT* 51 (1993): 57–77.

Matson, Mark. 'Luke's Rewriting on the Sermon on the Mount'. Pages 623–50 in *Society of Biblical Literature 2000 Seminar Papers*. SBLSPS 39. Atlanta: SBL Press, 2000.

Matthews, E. 'The Rich Man and Lazarus: Almsgiving and Repentance in Early Syriac Tradition'. *Diakonia* 22 (1988–89): 89–104.

Mattill, A. J., Jr. *Luke and the Last Things: A Perspective for the Understanding of Lukan Thought*. Dillsboro, NC: Western North Carolina, 1979.

Maxwell, Kathy Reiko. *Hearing Between the Lines: The Audience as Fellow-worker in Luke-Acts and Its Literary Milieu*. LNTS 425. London: T&T Clark, 2010.

McArthur, Harvey K., and Robert M. Johnston. *They Also Taught in Parables*. Grand Rapids: Academie, 1990.

McCall, Marsh H. *Ancient Rhetorical Theories of Simile and Comparison*. Cambridge, MA: Harvard University Press, 1969.

McConville, J. G. *Deuteronomy*. AOTC 6. Downers Grove, IL: InterVarsity, 2002.

McFague TeSelle, Sallie. *Speaking in Parables: A Study in Metaphor and Theology*. Philadelphia: Fortress, 1975.

Mealand, David L. *Poverty and Expectation in the Gospels*. London: SPCK, 1980.

Meier, John P. *A Marginal Jew*. Vol. 2. ABRL. New York: Doubleday, 1994.

Méndez-Moratalla, Fernando. *The Paradigm of Conversion in Luke*. JSNTSup 252. London: T&T Clark, 2004.

Merenlahti, Petri. *Poetics for the Gospels? Rethinking Narrative Criticism*. SNTW. London: T&T Clark, 2002.

Metzger, Bruce M. 'Names for the Nameless in the New Testament: A Study in the Growth of Christian Tradition'. Pages 79–99 in *Kyriakon: Festschrift Johannes Quasten*. Vol. 1. Edited by Patrick Granfield and Josef A. Jungmann. Münster: Aschendorff, 1970.

————. *A Textual Commentary on the Greek New Testament*. 2nd ed. Stuttgart: Deutsche Bibelgesellschaft/United Bible Societies, 1994.

Metzger, James A. *Consumption and Wealth in Luke's Travel Narrative*. BibInt 88. Leiden: Brill, 2007.

Minear, Paul. 'Jesus' Audiences, According to Luke'. *NovT* 16 (1974): 81–109.

Mitchell, Alan C. 'The Social Function of Friendship in Acts 2:44–47 and 4:32–37'. *JBL* 111 (1992): 255–72.

Moberly, R. W. L. *The Bible, Theology and Faith: A Study of Abraham and Jesus.* Cambridge: Cambridge University Press, 2000.

Moessner, David P. *Lord of the Banquet: The Literary and Theological Significance of the Lukan Travel Narrative.* Minneapolis: Fortress, 1989.

———. 'Luke 9:1–50: Luke's Preview of the Journey of the Prophet Like Moses of Deuteronomy'. *JBL* 102 (1983): 575–605.

Moloney, Francis J. 'Narrative Criticism of the Gospels'. *Pacifica* 4 (1991): 181–201.

Moore, A. L. *The Parousia in the New Testament.* NovTSup 13. Leiden: Brill, 1966.

Moore, S. D. 'Are the Gospels Unified Narratives?' Pages 443–58 in *Society of Biblical Literature 1987 Seminar Papers.* SBLSP 26. Atlanta: Scholars Press, 1987.

———. *Literary Criticism and the Gospels: The Theoretical Challenge.* New Haven, CT: Yale University Press, 1989.

———. 'Why There Are No Humans or Animals in the Gospel of Mark'. Pages 71–93 in *Mark as Story: Retrospect and Prospect.* Edited by Kelly R. Iverson and Christopher W. Skinner. SBLRBS 65. Leiden: Brill, 2011.

Morgenthaler, R. *Lukas und Quintilian: Rhetorik als Erzählkunst.* Zurich: Gotthelf, 1993.

Morlan, David S. *Conversion in Luke and Paul: An Exegetical and Theological Exploration.* LNTS 464. London: Bloomsbury T&T Clark, 2013.

Morris, Leon. *Luke: An Introduction and Commentary.* TNTC. Rev. ed. Leicester: Inter-Varsity, 1988.

Mosley, A. W. 'Jesus' Audiences in the Gospels of St Mark and St Luke'. *NTS* 10 (1963–64): 139–49.

Moxnes, Halvor. *The Economy of the Kingdom: Social Conflict and Economic Relations in Luke's Gospel.* Philadelphia: Fortress, 1988.

Moyise, S. 'Does the NT Quote the OT Out of Context?' *Anvil* 11 (1994): 133–43.

———. 'Intertextuality and Biblical Studies: A Review'. *Verbum and Ecclesia* 23 (2002): 418–31.

———. 'Intertextuality and the Study of the Old Testament in the New'. Pages 14–41 in *The Old Testament in the New Testament: Essays in Honour of J. L. North.* JSNTSup 189. Edited by Steve Moyise. Sheffield: Sheffield Academic, 2000.

———. 'Respect for Context Once More'. *IBS* 27 (2006): 24–31.

Nadella, Raj. *Dialogue Not Dogma: Many Voices in the Gospel of Luke.* LNTS 431. London: T&T Clark, 2011.

Nave, Guy D. *The Role and Function of Repentance in Luke-Acts.* SBLAB 4. Leiden: Brill, 2002.

Neusner, Jacob. *Genesis Rabbah: The Judaic Commentary to the Book of Genesis.* Vol. 2. Atlanta: Scholars Press, 1985.

———. *Rabbinic Literature and the New Testament: What We Cannot Show, We Do Not Know.* Valley Forge, PA: Trinity, 1994.

Neyrey, Jerome H. 'Ceremonies in Luke-Acts: The Case of Meals and Table Fellowship'. Pages 361–87 in *The Social World of Luke-Acts: Models for Interpretation.* Edited by Jerome H. Neyrey. Peabody, MA: Hendrickson, 1991.

Nickelsburg, George W. E. 'The Apocalyptic Message of *1 Enoch* 92–105'. *CBQ* 39 (1977): 309–28.

———. 'Revisiting the Rich and the Poor in 1 Enoch 92–105 and the Gospel According to Luke'. Pages 547–71 in *George W. E. Nickelsburg in Perspective.* Vol. 2, *An Ongoing Dialogue of Learning.* Edited by Jacob Neusner. JSJSup 80. Leiden: Brill, 2003.

———. 'Riches, the Rich and God's Judgment in 1 Enoch 92–105 and the Gospel According to Luke'. *NTS* 25 (1978–79): 324–44.

Nolland, John. *Luke*. 3 vols. WBC 35a–c. Dallas: Word, 1989–93.

———. 'The Role of Money and Possessions in the Parable of the Prodigal Son (Luke 15:11–32)'. Pages 178–209 in *Reading Luke: Interpretation, Reflection, Formation*. Edited by Craig G. Bartholomew, Joel B. Green, and Anthony C. Thiselton. Grand Rapids: Zondervan, 2005.

North, Wendy E. *The Lazarus Story within the Johannine Tradition*. JSNTSup 212. Sheffield: Sheffield Academic, 2011.

O'Day, G. R. 'Intertextuality'. Pages 546–48 in *Dictionary of Biblical Interpretation*. Vol. 1. Edited by J. H. Hayes. Nashville, TN: Abingdon, 1999.

Oesterley, W. O. E. *The Gospel Parables in the Light of their Jewish Background*. London: SPCK, 1936.

Osei-Bonsu, J. 'The Intermediate State in Luke-Acts'. *IBS* 9 (1987): 115–30.

O'Toole, Robert F. *The Unity of Luke's Theology*. Wilmington, DE: Glazier, 1984.

Paffenroth, Kim. *The Story of Jesus According to L*. JSNTSup 147. Sheffield: Sheffield Academic, 1997.

Pao, David W., and Eckhard J. Schnabel, 'Luke'. Pages 251–414 in *Commentary on the New Testament Use of the Old Testament*. Edited by G. K. Beale and D. A. Carson. Grand Rapids: Baker Books, 2007.

Parrott, Douglas M. 'The Dishonest Steward (Luke 16.1–8a) and Luke's Special Parable Collection'. *NTS* 37 (1991): 499–515.

Parsons, Mikeal C. 'Landmarks Along the Way: The Function of the "L" Parables in the Lukan Travel Narrative'. *SwJT* 40 (1997): 33–47.

———. 'Luke and the *Progymnasmata*: A Preliminary Investigation into the Preliminary Exercises'. Pages 43–63 in *Contextualizing Acts: Lukan Narrative and Greco-Roman Discourse*. Edited by Todd Penner and Caroline Vander Stichele. SBLSymS 20. Atlanta: Society of Biblical Literature, 2003.

———. 'Narrative Closure and Openness in the Plot of the Third Gospel: The Sense of an Ending in Luke 24:50–53'. Pages 201–23 in *Society of Biblical Literature 1986 Seminar Papers*. SBLSP 25. Missoula, MT: Scholars Press, 1986.

Parsons, Mikeal C., and Richard I. Pervo. *Rethinking the Unity of Luke and Acts*. Minneapolis: Fortress, 1993.

Paschal, R. W., Jr. 'Lazarus'. Pages 461–63 *Dictionary of Jesus and the Gospels*. Edited by J. B. Green, S. McKnight and I. H. Marshall. Downers Grove, IL: InterVarsity, 1992.

Patten, Priscilla. 'The Form and Function of Parables in Select Apocalyptic Literature and Their Significance for Parables in Mark'. *NTS* 29 (1983): 246–58.

Pautrel, R. 'Les canons du Mashal rabbinique'. *RSR* 26 (1936): 6–45.

Pax, E. 'Der Reiche und der arme Lazarus: Eine Milieustudie'. *SBFLA* 25 (1975): 254–68.

Pearce, K. 'The Lucan Origins of the Raising of Lazarus'. *ExpTim* 96 (1984–5): 359–61.

Penner, Todd. 'Madness in the Method? The Acts of the Apostles in Current Study'. *CurBR* 2 (2004): 223–93.

Penner, Todd. 'Reconfiguring the Rhetorical Study of Acts: Reflections on the Method in and Learning of a Progymnastic Poetics'. *PRSt* 30 (2003): 425–39.

Perrin, Norman. *Jesus and the Language of the Kingdom: Symbol and Metaphor in New Testament Interpretation*. Philadelphia: Fortress, 1976.

Perry, Simon. *Resurrecting Interpretation: Technology, Hermeneutics, and the Parable of the Rich Man and Lazarus*. Eugene, OR: Pickwick, 2012.

Phillips, Thomas E. *Reading Issues of Wealth and Poverty in Luke-Acts*. Studies in the Bible and Early Christianity 48. Lampeter: Mellen, 2001.

———. 'Reading Recent Readings of Issues of Wealth and Poverty in Luke and Acts'. *CurBR* 1 (2003): 231–69.

Pilgrim, Walter E. *Good News to the Poor: Wealth and Poverty in Luke-Acts*. Minneapolis: Augsburg, 1981.

Piper, Ronald A. 'Social Background and Thematic Structure in Luke 16'. Pages 1637–62 in *The Four Gospels 1992: Festschrift Frans Neirynck*. Vol. 2. Edited by F. Van Segbroeck, C. M. Tuckett, G. Van Belle, and J. Verheyden. BETL 100. Leuven: Leuven University Press, 1992.

Plett, Heinrich F. 'Intertextualities'. Pages 3–29 in *Intertextuality*. Edited by H. F. Plett. Research in Text Theory 15. Berlin: de Gruyter, 1991.

Plummer, Alfred. *A Critical and Exegetical Commentary on the Gospel According to S. Luke*. ICC. 5th ed. Edinburgh: T. & T. Clark, 1901.

Porter, Stanley E., and Mark J. Boda, eds. *Translating the New Testament: Text, Translation, Theology*. Grand Rapids: Eerdmans, 2009.

Porter, Stanley E., and Matthew B. O'Donnell. 'Comparative Discourse Analysis as a Tool in Assessing Translations, Using Luke 16:19–31 as a Test Case'. Pages 185–99 in *Translating the New Testament: Text, Translation, Theology*. Edited by S. E. Porter and M. J. Boda. Grand Rapids: Eerdmans, 2009.

Porter, Stanley E., and A. W. Pitts, eds. *Christian Origins and Hellenistic Judaism: Social and Literary Contexts for the New Testament*. TENTS 10. Leiden: Brill, 2013.

Powell, Mark Allan. 'Narrative Criticism'. Pages 240–58 in *Hearing the New Testament: Strategies for Interpretation*. Edited by Joel B. Green. 2nd ed. Grand Rapids: Eerdmans, 2010.

———. 'Narrative Criticism: The Emergence of a Prominent Reading Strategy'. Pages 19–43 in *Mark As Story: Retrospect and Prospect*. Edited by Kelly R. Iverson and Christopher W. Skinner. SBLRBS 65. Leiden: Brill, 2011.

———. 'The Religious Leaders in Luke: A Literary-Critical Study'. *JBL* 109 (1990): 93–101.

———. *What Is Narrative Criticism?* Minneapolis: Fortress, 1990.

Praeder, Susan Marie. 'Jesus–Paul, Peter–Paul, and Jesus–Peter Parallelisms in Luke-Acts: A History of Reader Response'. Pages 23–39 in *Society of Biblical Literature 1984 Seminar Papers*. SBLSP 23. Chico, CA: Scholars Press, 1984.

Rabinowitz, Louis I. 'Study of a Midrash'. *JQR* 58 (1967): 143–61.

Ravens, David. *Luke and the Restoration of Israel*. JSNTSup 119. Sheffield: Sheffield Academic, 1995.

Ray, Charles A., Jr. 'The Rich Man and Lazarus'. *TTE* 56 (1997): 77–84.

Regalado, Ferdinand O. 'The Jewish Background of the Parable of the Rich Man and Lazarus'. *AsJT* 16 (2002): 341–48.

Reinstorf, Dieter H. 'The Rich, the Poor, and the Law'. *HTS* 60 (2004): 329–48.

Rengstorf, Karl Heinrich. *Das Evangelium nach Lukas*. Göttingen: Vandenhoeck & Ruprecht, 1974.

Resseguie, James L. *Narrative Criticism of the New Testament: An Introduction*. Grand Rapids: Baker Academic, 2005.

———. 'Reader-Response Criticism and the Synoptic Gospels'. *JAAR* 52 (1984): 307–24.

Reich, Keith A. *Figuring Jesus: The Power of Rhetorical Figures of Speech in the Gospel of Luke*. BibInt 107. Leiden: Brill, 2011.

Reinmuth, Eckart. 'Ps-Philo, Liber antiquitatum biblicarum 33,1–5 und die Auslegung der Parabel Lk 16:19–31'. *NovT* 31 (1989): 16–38.

Rhoads, David. 'Narrative Criticism: Practices and Prospects'. Pages 264–85 in *Characterization in the Gospels: Reconceiving Narrative Criticism*. Edited by David Rhoads and Kari Syreeni. JSNTSup 184. Sheffield: Sheffield Academic, 1999.

Ricoeur, Paul. 'Biblical Hermeneutics'. *Semeia* 4 (1975): 29–149.

Rindge, Matthew S. *Jesus' Parable of the Rich Fool: Luke 12:13–34 Among Ancient Conversations on Death and Possessions*. SBLECL 6. Atlanta: SBL Press, 2011.

Ringgren, H. 'Luke's Use of the Old Testament'. *HTR* 79 (1986): 227–35.

Robb, Julie. 'The Prophet Like Moses: Its Jewish Context and Use in the Early Christian Tradition'. PhD diss., King's College London, 2003.

Robbins, Vernon K. *The Invention of Christian Discourse*. Rhetoric of Religious Antiquity 1. Blandford Forum, UK: Deo, 2009.

———. 'Narrative in Ancient Rhetoric and Rhetoric in Ancient Narrative'. Pages 368–84 in *Society of Biblical Literature 1996 Seminar Papers*. SBLSP 35. Atlanta: Scholars Press, 1996.

———. 'Progymnastic Rhetorical Composition and Pre-Gospel Tradition'. Pages 111–47 in *The Synoptic Gospels: Source Criticism and the New Literary Criticism*. Edited by Camille Focant. BETL 110. Leuven: Leuven University Press, 1993.

———. 'Writing as a Rhetorical Act in Plutarch and the Gospels'. Pages 142–68 in *Persuasive Artistry: Studies in New Testament Rhetoric in Honor of George A. Kennedy*. Edited by Duane F. Watson. JSNTSup 50. Sheffield: JSOT, 1991.

Rodd, Cyril S. *Glimpses of a Strange Land: Studies in Old Testament Ethics*. London: T&T Clark, 2001.

Rodríguez, Rafael. *Oral Tradition and the New Testament: A Guide for the Perplexed*. London: Bloomsbury T&T Clark, 2014.

———. 'Reading and Hearing in Ancient Contexts'. *JSNT* 32 (2009): 151–78.

Rohrbaugh, Richard L. 'The Pre-Industrial City in Luke-Acts: Urban Social Relations'. Pages 125–49 in *The Social World of Luke-Acts: Models for Interpretation*. Edited by J. H. Neyrey. Peabody, MA: Hendrickson, 1991.

Roose, Hanna. 'Umkehr und Ausgleich bei Lukas: die Gleichnisse vom verlorenen Sohn (Lk 15.11–32) und vom reichen Mann und armen Lazarus (Lk 16.19–31) als Schwestergeschichten'. *NTS* 56 (2010): 1–21.

Roth, Catharine P., trans. *St. John Chrysostom: On Wealth and Poverty*. Crestwood, NY: St. Vladimir's Seminary Press, 1984.

Roth, S. John. *The Blind, the Lame and the Poor: Character Types in Luke-Acts*. JSNTSup 144. Sheffield: Sheffield Academic, 1997.

Rothschild, Clare K. *Luke-Acts and the Rhetoric of History: An Investigation of Early Christian Historiography*. WUNT 2/175. Tübingen: Mohr Siebeck, 2004.

Rowe, C. Kavin. 'History, Hermeneutics and the Unity of Luke-Acts'. *JSNT* 28 (2005): 131–57.

———. 'Literary Unity and Reception History: Reading Luke-Acts as Luke and Acts'. *JSNT* 29 (2007): 449–57.

Rusam, Dietrich. 'Deuteronomy in Luke-Acts'. Pages 63–81 in *Deuteronomy in the New Testament: The New Testament and the Scriptures of Israel*. Edited by Maarten J. J. Menken and Steve Moyise. LNTS 358. London: T&T Clark, 2007.

Sanders, Jack T. *The Jews in Luke-Acts*. London: SCM, 1987.

———. 'The Salvation of the Jews in Luke-Acts'. Pages 104–28 in *Luke-Acts: New Perspectives from the Society of Biblical Literature*. Edited by C. H. Talbert. New York: Crossroad, 1984.

Sandmel, Samuel. 'Parallelomania'. *JBL* 81 (1962): 1–13.

Scheffler, Eben. *Suffering in Luke's Gospel*. ATANT 81. Zurich: TVZ, 1993.

Schmidt, Brian B. *Israel's Beneficent Dead: Ancestor Cult and Necromancy in Ancient Israelite Religion and Tradition*. FAT 11. Tübingen: Mohr Siebeck, 1994.

Schnackenburg, Rudolf. *The Gospel According to St John*. 2 vols. New York: Crossroad, 1982.

Schnider, F., and W. Stenger. 'Die offene Tür und die unüberschreitbare Kluft: struktur-analytische Überlegungen zum Gleichnis vom reichen Mann und armen Lazarus'. *NTS* 25 (1979): 273–83.

Schottroff, Luise. *The Parables of Jesus*. Translated by Linda M. Maloney. Minneapolis: Fortress, 2006.

Schottroff, Luise, and Wolfgang Stegemann. *Jesus and the Hope of the Poor*. Translated by Matthew J. O'Connell. Maryknoll, NY: Orbis, 1986.

Schubert, Paul. 'The Structure and Significance of Luke 24'. Pages 165–86 in *Neutestamentliche Studien für Rudolf Bultmann zu seinem siebzigsten Geburtstag*. Edited by W. Eltester. 2nd ed. BZNW 21. Berlin: de Gruyter, 1957.

Schwantes, Milton. *Des Recht der Armen*. BBET 4. Frankfurt: Lang, 1977.

Scott, Bernard Brandon. *Hear then the Parable: A Commentary on the Parables of Jesus*. Minneapolis: Fortress, 1989.

Seccombe, David P. 'Incongruity in the Gospel Parables'. *TynBul* 62 (2011): 161–72.

———. *Possessions and the Poor in Luke-Acts*. SNTU 6. Linz: Fuchs, 1982.

———. 'Was there Organized Charity in Jerusalem before the Christians?' *JTS* n.s. 29 (1978): 140–43.

Sellin, Gerhard. 'Lukas als Gleichniserzähler: die Erzählung vom barmherzigen Samariter (Lk 10,25–37)'. *ZNW* 65 (1974): 166–89; *ZNW* 66 (1975): 19–60.

Shellard, Barbara. *New Light on Luke: Its Purpose, Sources and Literary Context*. JSNTSup 215. Sheffield: Sheffield Academic, 2002.

Siker, Jeffrey S. *Disinheriting the Jews: Abraham in Early Christian Controversy*. Louisville, KY: Westminster John Knox, 1991.

Skinner, Christopher W. *John and Thomas—Gospels in Conflict? Johannine Characterization and the Thomas Question*. Princeton Theological Monograph Series 115. Eugene, OR: Wipf & Stock, 2009.

Smith, Dennis E. 'Table Fellowship as a Literary Motif in the Gospel of Luke'. *JBL* 106 (1987): 613–38.

Snodgrass, Klyne. 'From Allegorizing to Allegorizing: A History of the Interpretation of the Parables of Jesus'. Pages 248–68 in *The Historical Jesus in Recent Research*. Edited by J. D. G. Dunn and S. McKnight. Winona Lake, IN: Eisenbrauns, 2005.

———. *Stories with Intent: A Comprehensive Guide to the Parables of Jesus*. Grand Rapids: Eerdmans, 2008.

Spencer, F. Scott. 'Acts and Modern Literary Approaches'. Pages 381–414 in *The Book of Acts in Its Ancient Literary Setting*. BAFCS 1. Edited by Bruce W. Winter and Andrew D. Clarke. Grand Rapids: Eerdmans, 1993.

Spencer, Patrick E. 'The Unity of Luke-Acts: A Four-Bolted Hermeneutical Hinge'. *CurBR* 5 (2007): 341–66.

Spronk, Klaas. *Beatific Afterlife in Ancient Israel and in the Ancient Near East.* AOAT 219. Neukirchen-Vluyn: Neukirchener, 1986.

Squires, John T. *The Plan of God in Luke-Acts.* SNTSMS 76. Cambridge: Cambridge University Press, 1993.

Staley, Jeffrey Lloyd. *The Print's First Kiss: A Rhetorical Investigation of the Implied Reader in the Fourth Gospel.* SBLDS 82. Atlanta: Scholars Press, 1988.

Stanley, Christopher D. '"Pearls Before Swine": Did Paul's Audiences Understand His Biblical Quotations?' *NovT* 41 (1999): 124–44.

Stein, Robert H. 'The Genre of the Parables'. Pages 30–50 in *The Challenge of Jesus' Parables.* Edited by Richard N. Longenecker. Grand Rapids: Eerdmans, 2000.

Stegemann, Wolfgang. *The Gospel and the Poor.* Translated by Dietlinde Elliot. Fortress: Philadelphia, 1984.

Stemberger, Günter. 'Dating Rabbinic Traditions'. Pages 79–96 in *The New Testament and Rabbinic Literature.* Edited by R. Bieringer. JSJSup 136. Leiden: Brill, 2010.

Stenschke, Christoph W. *Luke's Portrait of Gentiles Prior to Their Coming to Faith.* WUNT 2/108. Tübingen: Mohr Siebeck, 1999.

Stern, David. *Parables in Midrash: Narrative and Exegesis in Rabbinic Literature.* Cambridge, MA: Harvard University Press, 1991.

Sternberg, Meir. *The Poetics of Biblical Narrative: Ideological Literature and the Drama of Reading.* Bloomington, IN: Indiana University Press, 1985.

Stigall, Joshua Jay. 'Reading the Parable of the Rich Man and Lazarus (Luke 16:19–31) as the Authorial Audience'. PhD diss., Baylor University, 2012.

————. 'The Progymnasmata and Characterization in Luke's Parables: The Parable of the Rich Fool as a Test Case'. *PRSt* 39 (2012): 349–60.

Strauss, M. L. *The Davidic Messiah in Luke-Acts: The Promise and Its Fulfillment in Lukan Christology.* JSNTSup 110. Sheffield: Sheffield Academic, 1995.

Story, J. Lyle. 'Twin Parables of Stewardship in Luke 16'. *American Theological Inquiry* 2 (2009): 105–20.

Syreeni, Kari. 'The Gospel in Paradigms: A Study in the Hermeneutical Space of Luke-Acts'. Pages 36–57 in *Luke-Acts: Scandinavian Perspectives.* Edited by Petri Luomanen. Publications of the Finnish Exegetical Society 54. Göttingen: Vandenhoeck & Ruprecht/ Helsinki: Finnish Exegetical Society, 1991.

Szukalski, J. A. *Tormented in Hades: The Rich Man and Lazarus (Luke 16:19–31) and Other Lucan Parables for Persuading the Rich to Repentance.* Eugene, OR: Pickwick, 2013.

Talbert, Charles H. *Literary Patterns, Theological Themes, and the Genre of Luke-Acts.* SBLMS 20. Missoula, MT: Scholars Press, 1974.

————. 'Promise and Fulfillment in Lucan Theology'. Pages 91–103 in *Luke-Acts: New Perspectives from the Society of Biblical Literature Seminar.* Edited by Charles H. Talbert. New York: Crossroad, 1984.

————. *Reading Luke-Acts in its Mediterranean Milieu.* NovTSup 107. Leiden: Brill, 2003.

————. *Reading Luke: A Literary and Theological Commentary.* New York: Crossroad, 1982.

Tanghe, Vincent. 'Abraham, son fils et son envoyé (Luc 16:19–31)'. *RB* 91 (1984): 557–77.

Tannehill, Robert C. 'Israel in Luke-Acts: A Tragic Story'. *JBL* 104 (1985): 69–85.
———. *Luke*. ANTC. Nashville, TN: Abingdon, 1996.
———. 'Freedom and Responsibility in Scripture Interpretation, with Application to Luke'. Pages 265–78. In *Literary Studies in Luke-Acts: Essays in Honor of Joseph B. Tyson*. Edited by Richard P. Thompson and Thomas E. Phillips. Macon, GA: Mercer University Press, 1998.
———. *The Narrative Unity of Luke-Acts: A Literary Interpretation.* 2 vols. Philadelphia: Fortress, 1986.
———. *The Shape of Luke's Story: Essays on Luke-Acts*. Eugene, OR: Cascade, 2005.
Taylor, Robert Oswald Patrick. *The Groundwork of the Gospels*. Oxford: Blackwell, 1946.
Thatcher, Tom. *Jesus the Riddler: The Power of Ambiguity in the Gospels*. Louisville, KY: Westminster John Knox, 2006.
Thoma, Clemens. 'Literary and Theological Aspects of the Rabbinic Parables'. Pages 26–40 in *Parable and Story in Judaism and Christianity*. Edited by C. Thoma and M. Wyschogrod. Studies in Judaism and Christianity. New York: Paulist, 1989.
Thompson, Alan J. *The Acts of the Risen Lord Jesus: Luke's Account of God's Unfolding Plan*. New Studies in Biblical Theology 27. Downers Grove, IL: InterVarsity, 2011.
Thompson, Andrew. 'Parallel Composition and Rhetorical Effect in Luke 7 and 8'. *JSNT* 38 (2015): 169–90.
Thurén, Lauri. *Parables Unplugged: Reading the Lukan Parables in their Rhetorical Context*. Minneapolis: Fortress, 2014.
Tiede, David L. *Prophecy and History in Luke-Acts*. Philadelphia: Fortress, 1980.
Tolbert, Mary Ann. *Perspectives on the Parables*. Philadelphia: Fortress, 1979.
Trench, Richard C. *Notes on the Parables of Our Lord.* 11th ed. New York: D. Appleton & Co., 1861.
Troftgruben, Troy M. *A Conclusion Unhindered: A Study of the Ending of Acts Within Its Literary Environment*. WUNT 2/280. Tübingen: Mohr Siebeck, 2010.
Trompf, G. W. *The Idea of Historical Recurrence in Western Thought: From Antiquity to the Reformation*. Berkeley, CA: University of California Press, 1979.
Tucker, Jeffrey T. *Example Stories: Perspectives on Four Parables in the Gospel of Luke*. JSNTSup 162. Sheffield: Sheffield Academic, 1998.
Tyson, Joseph B. *Images of Judaism in Luke-Acts*. Columbia, SC: University of South Carolina, 1992.
———. 'The Problem of Jewish Rejection in Acts'. Pages 124–37 in *Luke-Acts and the Jewish People: Eight Critical Perspectives*. Edited by J. B. Tyson. Minneapolis: Augsburg, 1988.
Van Bruggen, Jakob. *Christ on Earth: The Gospel Narratives as History*. Translated by Nancy Forest-Flier. Grand Rapids: Baker Books, 1998.
Van Der Horst, Pieter W. 'Abraham's Bosom, the Place Where He Belonged: A Short Note on ἀπενεχθῆναι in Luke 16.22'. *NTS* 52 (2006): 142–44.
Vanderploeg, J. 'Les pauvres d'Israël et leur piété'. *OtSt* 7 (1950): 236–70.
Van Gemeren, Willem A., ed. *New International Dictionary of Old Testament Theology & Exegesis*. 5 vols. Grand Rapids: Zondervan, 1997.
Van Unnik, W. C. 'The "Book of Acts" and the Confirmation of the Gospel'. *NovT* 4 (1960): 26–59.
———. 'Die Motivierung der Feindesliebe in Lukas 6:32–35'. *NovT* 8 (1966): 284–300.

Van Voorst, Robert E. *Jesus Outside the New Testament: An Introduction to the Ancient Evidence*. Grand Rapids: Eerdmans, 2000.

Verheyden, Joseph. 'The Unity of Luke-Acts: What Are We Up To?' Pages 3–56 in *The Unity of Luke-Acts*. Edited by J. Verheyden. BETL 142. Leuven: Leuven University Press, 1999.

Vogels, Walter. 'Having or Longing: A Semiotic Analysis of Luke 16:19–31'. *EgT* 20 (1989): 27–46.

Wailes, Stephen L. *Medieval Allegories of Jesus' Parables*. Berkeley, CA: University of California Press, 1987.

Wallace, Daniel B. *Greek Grammar Beyond the Basics: An Exegetical Syntax of the New Testament*. Grand Rapids: Zondervan, 1996.

Walters, Patricia. *The Assumed Authorial Unity of Luke and Acts: A Reassessment of the Evidence*. SNTSMS 145. Cambridge: Cambridge University Press, 2009.

Walton, Steve. *Leadership and Lifestyle: The Portrait of Paul in the Miletus Speech and 1 Thessalonians*. SNTSMS 108. Cambridge: Cambridge University Press, 2000.

———. 'Paul, Patronage and Pay: What do We Know About the Apostle's Financial Support?' Pages 220–33 in *Paul as Missionary: Identity, Activity, Theology and Practice*. Edited by Trevor J. Burke and Brian S. Rosner. LNTS 420. London: T&T Clark, 2011.

———. 'Primitive Communism in Acts? Does Acts Present the Community of Goods (2:44–45; 4:32–35) as Mistaken?' *EvQ* 80 (2008): 99–111.

———. 'Rhetorical Criticism: An Introduction'. *Them* 21 (1996): 4–9.

Warden, Duane. 'The Rich Man and Lazarus: Poverty, Wealth and Human Worth'. *SCJ* 6 (2003): 81–93.

Watson, Duane F. 'Paul's Speech to the Ephesian Elders (Acts 20.17–38): Epideictic Rhetoric of Farewell'. Pages 184–208 in *Persuasive Artistry: Studies in New Testament Rhetoric in Honor of George A. Kennedy*. Edited by Duane F. Watson. JSNTSup 50. Sheffield: JSOT, 1991.

Weatherly, Jon A. 'The Jews in Luke-Acts'. *TynBul* 40 (1989): 107–17.

Weima, Jeffrey. 'What Does Aristotle Have to Do with Paul? An Evaluation of Rhetorical Criticism'. *CTJ* 32 (1997): 458–68.

Westermann, Claus. *The Parables of Jesus in the Light of the Old Testament*. Translated and edited by Friedemann W. Golka and Alastair H. B. Logan. Minneapolis: Fortress, 1990.

Wilder, Amos. *Early Christian Rhetoric: The Language of the Gospel*. Cambridge, MA: Harvard University Press, 1971.

Williams, F. E. 'Is Almsgiving the Point of the "Unjust Steward?"'. *JBL* 83 (1964): 293–97.

Wilson, Stephen G. 'Lukan Eschatology'. *NTS* 16 (1969–70): 330–47.

———. *Luke and the Law*. SNTSMS 50. Cambridge: Cambridge University Press, 1983.

Witherington, Benjamin G., III. *The Acts of the Apostles: A Socio-Rhetorical Commentary*. Grand Rapids: Eerdmans, 1998.

———. *New Testament Rhetoric: An Introductory Guide to the Art of Persuasion in and of the New Testament*. Eugene, OR: Cascade, 2009.

———. 'The Discourse of Riches and Poverty in the Book of Ben Sira'. Pages 559–78 in *Society of Biblical Literature 1998 Seminar Papers*. Vol. 2. SBLSP 37. Atlanta: Scholars Press, 1998.

Wright, N. T. *Jesus and the Victory of God.* Christian Origins and the Question of God 2. Minneapolis: Fortress, 1996.

———. *Luke for Everyone* (London: SPCK, 2001).

———. *The Resurrection of the Son of God.* Christian Origins and the Question of God. Vol. 3. Minneapolis: Fortress, 2003.

Wright, Stephen I. *Jesus the Storyteller.* London: SPCK, 2014.

———. 'Parables on Poverty and Riches'. Pages 217–39 in *The Challenge of Jesus' Parables.* Edited by Richard N. Longenecker. Grand Rapids: Eerdmans, 2000.

———. 'Reading Luke, Hearing Jesus, Understanding God: A Response to John Nolland's "The Role of Money and Possessions in the Parable of the Prodigal Son"'. Pages 210–28 in *Reading Luke: Interpretation, Reflection, Formation.* Edited by Craig Bartholomew, Joel B. Green, and Anthony C. Thiselton. Grand Rapids: Zondervan, 2005.

———. *Tales Jesus Told: An Introduction to the Narrative Parables of Jesus.* Carlisle: Paternoster, 2003.

———. *The Voice of Jesus: Studies in the Interpretation of Six Gospel Parables.* Paternoster Biblical Monographs. Carlisle: Paternoster, 2000.

Wuellner, W. 'Where Is Rhetorical Criticism Taking Us?' *CBQ* 49 (1987): 448–63.

York, John O. *The Last Shall Be First: The Rhetoric of Reversal in Luke.* JSNTSup 46. Sheffield: JSOT, 1991.

Young, Brad H. *The Parables: Jewish Tradition and Christian Interpretation.* Peabody, MA: Hendrickson, 1998.

Zimmermann, Ruben. 'Jesus' Parables and Ancient Rhetoric: The Contributions of Aristotle and Quintilian to the Form Criticism of the Parables'. Pages 238–58 in *Hermeneutik der Gleichnisse Jesu: Methodische Neuansätze zum Verstehen urchristlicher Parabeltexte.* Edited by R. Zimmermann. WUNT 2/231. Tübingen: Mohr Siebeck, 2008.

Index of References

INDEX OF AUTHORS